# Cold War in the High Himalayas

The USA, China and South Asia in the 1950s

# Cold War in the High Himalayas

The USA, China and South Asia in the 1950s

*S. Mahmud Ali*

St. Martin's Press
New York

St. Martin's Press, Scholarly and Reference Division,
175 Fifth Avenue, New York, N.Y. 10010

First published in the United States of America in 1999
Printed in Great Britain

ISBN: 0–312–22693–4

*Library of Congress Cataloging in Publication Data*

Ali, S. Mahmud, 1952–
    Cold war in the high Himalayas : the USA, China, and South Asia in
the 1950s / S. Mahmud Ali.
        p.  cm.
    Includes bibliographical references and index.
    ISBN 0–312–22693–4 (cloth)
    1. Himalaya Mountain Region–Politics and government.   2. South
Asia–Foreign relations–United States.   3. United States–Foreign
relations–South Asia.   4. South Asia–Foreign relations–China.
5. China–Foreign relations–South Asia.   6. Cold War.   I. Title.
DS485.H6A62   1999
954.96–dc21
                                                               99-32300
                                                                    CIP

# Contents

# Foreword

One of the many benefits of the end of the cold war is the opportunities it has provided to make sense of its history. The opening up of the archives of the former Soviet Union has been the most obvious boost, and this has already had important consequences for our understanding of the origins of the cold war and the struggle for Europe that was at its heart. In addition historians have examined in detail its most important conflicts, such as Vietnam. Those areas of struggle between east and west that rarely made the headlines at the time are still, however, suffering from neglect.

One such area is South Asia. As the scene of the first great post-war decolonisation it was an area of great sensitivity in the competition between the first and second worlds to influence the politics of the emerging third world. The importance of this rivalry is given far too little attention in cold war historiography. More specifically, the study of US-Chinese relations is often discussed as part of a triangular diplomacy involving the Soviet Union, without any mention of India and Pakistan as critical players. Indian Prime Minister Pandit Nehru's personal authority in the international politics of the 1950s is now largely forgotten.

Moreover, the internal and external conflicts that developed within the region in the stormy years after partition have not been resolved. The position of Tibet, whose unhappy fate figures prominently in this book, is still an issue of enormous sensitivity for the People's Republic of China. India and Pakistan have yet to find a way to resolve the differences, and we now must rely on mutual nuclear deterrence to prevent yet another war.

Mahmud Ali knows South Asia well. He experienced first hand its conflicts before coming to Britain. He has now established himself as an able commentator on its affairs, with an unusually detached perspective. He has now provided a great service by throwing light on one of lesser known aspects of the cold war, the close co-operation between India and the United States against communist China, focusing on Tibetan resistance to China's occupation of their country. With impressive documentation he has opened up to scrutiny a fascinating though sad episode, demonstrating the complex interaction between American efforts to contain communism and the pursuit of more parochial concerns by regional leaders.

*Lawrence Freedman, London, 1999*

# Acknowledgements

This book is the end-product of a process which began at King's College, London, in 1986. The text, however, was not completed until the summer of 1998. Over these twelve-odd years, a very large number associates, colleagues and friends have helped in a variety of ways, often willingly, sometimes unwittingly, and occasionally, inadvertently. Some, because of their official positions, have been unable or unwilling to be identified by name but their contribution is no less significant for that. Among the many people whose assistance, advice and support made this project possible, a few must be mentioned. They are Anders H. Andersen, Jane Ardley, David Cowhig, Prof. Lawrence Freedman, Prof. A Tom Grunfeld, David L. Haight, Michael Adam Janson, David Kauffner, John Kauffner, Prof. David Kopf, Dr Peter Mangold, Chris Mullin, M.P., Dr David Page, June Payne, Kirsten J. Pedersen, Maura Porter, Wangdu Tsering Shakya, Daniel Smith and Elizabeth Wright. The book has also benefited considerably from the encouragement extended by Jonathan Price, Chief Editor at Curzon Press.

The patience, tolerance and forbearance shown by Selina, my wife, and Sunehra, my daughter, proved indispensable to the completion of this project. By taking care of most of my worldly needs during the period of protracted research and the writing itself, they made this a realistic enterprise and joined the legion of my collaborators. However, the end-product, warts and all, is essentially my own responsibility and I alone am liable for any damage that may have been caused.

*S. Mahmud Ali, London*

# List of Appendices

# List of Annexures

# Dramatis Personae

**Dean Acheson**  US Secretary of State in the early 1950s, Dean Acheson was the first US policymaker to deal with Tibetan plea for support. In June 1951, three months after the first US-India Mutual Defence Assistance Agreement was signed, he told the Tibetans that his government was sympathetic and willing to provide arms and ammunition to the resistance, but only if the Tibetans maintained a cohesive struggle against Beijing. This was the beginning of Washington's formal entry into Tibetan affairs and the evolution of Indo-US relationship into a strategic alliance against Communist China.

**Gompo Tashi Andrugtsang**  Tibetan merchant-prince and resistance leader. He enjoyed the Dalai Lama's tacit support and rose to command the formal structure of the Tibetan resistance, the *Chushi Gangdruk*. His fighters harried the PLA and took the war from the eastern provinces of Kham and Amdo to the central U Tsang and southern Lhoka regions in the late 1950s, and to Lhasa itself in 1959. However, he claims to have been uninvolved in the Lhasa revolt and the flight of the Dalai Lama in March 1959 when he was fighting the PLA away from the capital. This account strengthens the view that the Dalai Lama's flight was masterminded by US-armed guerrillas and the Dalai Lama's Chamberlain, Phala, co-ordinating closely with the CIA based in Dhaka, East Pakistan.

**Mohammad Ali**  Pakistani Prime Minister in the early 1950s who took his country into deepening military alliance with the US although Pakistan's primary motivation was fear of India rather than of Communism. His correspondence with his Indian counterpart, Nehru, brought them close to an agreement in late 1953 on holding a plebiscite in Jammu & Kashmir. However, Delhi's discovery of an imminent US-Pakistan security agreement led Nehru to renege on that accord. In the late 1950s, as Pakistan's Foreign Minister, Mohammad Ali initiated border talks with the Chinese which provided Pakistan with strategic leverage vis-a-vis India but angered both Washington and Delhi.

**Chester Bowles** US civil servant and diplomat who served as President Eisenhower's ambassador to India and Nepal in 1951–1953. This was a crucial period for the development of the US-Indian security relationship. The Chinese had just taken control of Tibet and India was seeking to establish 'a third way' away from Cold War entanglements. Bowles conducted the Delhi element of the delicate, protracted and secret negotiations which led to the consolidation of covert collaboration on the basis of the first Mutual Defence Assistance Agreement between Washington and Delhi. Bowles and Nehru, and other senior Indian officials, discussed close co-operation in the security and intelligence fields while agreeing to disagree on other issues. He returned to Delhi as US ambassador after the Sino-Indian war, serving from 1963 to 1969 and fashioning an alliance that had strong and parallel strategic and economic elements to it.

**McGeorge Bundy** A Harvard Professor and a political scientist of repute, Bundy was appointed Special Assistant to the President for National Security Affairs in 1961 and left that post to take up the presidency of the Ford Foundation in 1966. In the intervening period, he stamped his authority on the National Security Council and the process of security policy formulation. Bundy was formally responsible for preparing the agenda for NSC meetings and this shaped the priorities in terms of time allocation for presidential briefings and discussions during most of the Kennedy-Johnson administrations. Policies relating to China, South Asia and Tibet were no exception.

**Ellsworth Bunker** Trained as a lawyer, Ellsworth Bunker moved from industry and commerce to more academic pursuits and then, to diplomacy. He was ambassador to India from 1956 to 1961, spanning the transition between the Eisenhower and Kennedy presidencies. During this period, he played a critical role in maintaining the covert alliance between Washington and Delhi while overtly, India moved close to China and the Soviet Union. Bunker was instrumental in getting the 2nd US-India Murual Defence Assistance Agreement signed in 1958 following which the level and intensity of covert collaboration against the Chinese in Tibet rose considerably.

**Chiang Kai-shek** Leader of the Kuo Min-tang (nationalist) Chinese administration, Generalissimo Chiang was forced to flee to Taiwan after Mao Ze-dong's Red Army took control of Beijing, and then, of the whole of mainland China. Chiang continued to receive considerable military and economic assistance from the US and turned Taiwan into a base for anti-Communist operations. When the Tibetan resistance to China became a considerable force, Chiang's intelligence services extended covert assistance to it. In the late 1950s, when the CIA and Indian Intelligence Bureau became very active in aiding the Tibetan guerrillas, Taiwan's covert assistance declined in importance.

**Morarji Desai** Senior Congress politician and cabinet minister in the 1960s and 1970s. As Finance Minister during the 1962 war with China, Desai pushed for expanding ties with the US from the covert to the overt. In the late 1970s, as the Prime Minister in an anti-Congress coalition, he revealed the extent of US-Indian collaboration against China in the late 1960s, especially the activities of the CIA in India. His revelations stunned many knowledgeable Indians at the time. But even Desai chose not to speak about Indo-US co-operation in the period before the Sino-Indian war.

**'Wild Bill' Donovan** Commander of the wartime 'Office of Strategic Services', General Donovan established an activist culture for US intelligence organs and operatives. This was most visible when OSS officers carrying messages and gifts for the infant Dalai Lama from President Roosevelt visited Lhasa and established contact with the Tibetan Regency. Donovan appreciated Tibet's strategic importance in a period of fluidity. He pleaded for treating Tibet as an autonomous entity, supporting the Lamaist authorities with long-range radio transmitters without consulting the KMT government in Nanjing. Despite opposition from the Department of State, this course was adopted. In 1947, the OSS was merged with several other agencies into the CIA which then became a principal instrument of US policy in the region.

**John Foster Dulles** President Eisenhower's Secretary of State credited with fashioning the anti-Communist 'Containment' policy. Dulles was said to be fired with a missionary zeal to roll back Communist expansion in Europe and Asia and to this end he provided the intellectual stimulus to the erection of a *cordon sanitaire* of anti-communist alliances along the fringes of the Soviet Union and China. US relations with India and Pakistan were shaped by this drive. Dulles preferred overt alliances which he managed to secure with Turkey, Iran, Pakistan but not with India. But the degree of secret collaboration with Delhi against Beijing compensated for this lack of transparency. Dulles saw China as an appendage of the Soviet Union, and his refusal to endorse Vice President Nixon's suggestion to normalise relations with China effectively blocked any changes to US policy in the 1950s. His notorious refusal to shake Zhou En-lai's hand at a Geneva conference was reflective of the disdain in which he held Beijing, and the Nehru-Menon initiative to mediate between the US and China.

**Allen Dulles** US lawyer and diplomat, and brother of John Foster Dulles, Allen Dulles was appointed Deputy Director of the CIA in 1951. Promoted to Director of Central Intelligence 1953, he served in that capacity until 1961. Guiding the CIA through the formative years of the Cold War, Dulles turned the organisation into a large and much-feared instrument of covert diplomacy around the world. Under Dulles the CIA undertook many operations around and often within Communist states in what was called the 'humint' (human intelligence) area. One of its best-concealed clandestine operations was in Tibet where the CIA sponsored and aided Tibetan resistance in its bitter struggle against Communist Chinese forces from bases in India and to a lesser extent, Pakistan. The CIA was sometimes an activist alter ego to the somewhat more restrained Department of State. Taken together, the Dulles brothers could be described as key shapers and executors of the anti-Communist 'Containment' policy pursued by the Eisenhower administration and its successors into the 1980s.

**Subimal Dutt**  Indian Foreign Secretary and close confidante of Prime Minister Nehru, he signed one of the key US-India mutual defence assistance agreements. Dutt was identified by the Americans as one of the more pro-Western diplomats in Indian service and at least on one occasion his wife was cited as the source of diplomatic analyses of the limited significance of Delhi-Beijing warmth, frequent visits to Delhi by Zhou En-lai notwithstanding, in a US embassy telegram to the Department of State.

**J K Galbraith**  A political economist of considerable stature, Galbraith made his mark as a strategic thinker of ability while serving as the Director of US Strategic Bombing Survey in 1945. President Kennedy appointed Professor Galbraith US ambassador to India in 1961, at a time when tensions were already high along the Sino-Indian borders and rising. As the Administration sought to bring about a reconciliation between India and Pakistan by helping them resolve their dispute over Kashmir, Galbraith suggested that the 'plebiscite option' was diplomatically dead. Kennedy and his advisers forced Galbraith to recant but once war broke out between China and India, Washington was constrained to reverse itself and follow Galbraith instead. Galbraith played a crucial role in developing the US strategic response to that war, masterminding the strong US-Indian alliance against China which then resulted.

**Henry F Grady**  US diplomat who served as the US ambassador first to colonial, and then independent, India between 1947 and 1948. Grady had led a wartime US 'Technical Mission' to India in 1942, studying the suitability of the subcontinent as a base-area for major military operations then underway in China. His recommendations led to Washington seeking and obtaining extra-territorial facilities for US Army and Army Air Forces personnel and aircraft in India during the war. Grady returned to India as the US ambassador as the British were about to leave, and worked out with Nehru the juridical basis for stationing US combat aircraft and military personnel on Indian territory. Signed in early July 1947 by Nehru and Grady, this agreement was the first in a series of mutual defence co-operation agreements which allied India to the US in an anti-Chinese coalition throughout the 1950s and 1960s.

**Averell Harriman** Senior US diplomat with notable authority and political influence who served as ambassador to major countries (ie, the Soviet Union, the UK) and organisations (eg, NATO). Harriman was appointed Assistant Secretary of State for Far Eastern Affairs in 1961 in which capacity he served until 1963 when he became Under Secretary of State for Political Affairs. These posts gave him supervisory roles in shaping and managing US policies towards both India and China. In the early 1960s, especially just before, during and after the Sino-Indian war, Harriman was involved in negotiating with Indian and Pakistani leaders, seeking to realise Kennedy's hope of forging a South Asian front against China. Following the war, he and British Minister of Commonwealth Affairs, Duncan Sandys, worked together in Delhi and Rawalpindi shuttling between Nehru and Ayub Khan, to get ministerial discussions going between the two neighbours. Despite success in initiating such a process, the effort failed.

**Ngabo Ngwang Jigme** Tibetan nobleman serving as the governor of the eastern Kham province at the time of the Chinese invasion. Arrested, and then made the Vice Chairman of the Communist Chamdo Liberation Committee by the PLA, Ngabo led the Tibetan delegation sent to Beijing to negotiate with the Chinese. He and his team signed the '17-point agreement' which became the basis of Chinese claims to legitimacy in Tibet. Ngabo became a key player in the Chinese administration of Tibet after the Dalai Lama's flight, and remained so into the 1990s.

**Mohammad Ali Jinnah** Leader of the Muslim League and the acclaimed founder of Pakistan, Jinnah sought the incorporation of Kashmir into Pakistan. His failure to visit the state in late 1947 angered him, especially when Mountbatten, independent India's first Governor-General, had been able to visit the state. He is widely suspected to have instigated the tribal Pathan invasion of Kashmir in October 1947 although documentary evidence of such an initiative on his part has not been found.

**Carl Kaysen** Trained as an economist, Kaysen served with the OSS during the Second World War following which he returned to academe. President Kennedy appointed him Deputy Special Assistant for National Security Affairs under McGeorge Bundy. In this capacity Kaysen generated considerable analyses of what was in US security interest and what threats it faced during this period. Some of his work related to Kennedy's efforts to shift the focus of Indian and Pakistani leaders from their mutual antipathy to what in Washington's view was the common threat, the Communists to the north. Kaysen also played a role in turning Kennedy away from an even-handed approach to India and Pakistan to a greater emphasis on the strategic significance of India. After the assassination of the President, Kaysen returned to his academic career.

**Liaquat Ali Khan** Mohammad Ali Jinnah's deputy and Pakistan's first Prime Minister, Khan played a key role in masterminding the Pakistani response to Delhi's Kashmir policy. He reportedly met a group of Pakistani bureaucrats and military officers in September 1947, a month after Pakistan's independence, authorising the extension of modest support to Kashmiri 'freedom fighters'. This was the first known instance of proxy war in the subcontinent and it led to the first war between India and Pakistan. Khan was killed in an abortive coup in 1951.

**Mohammad Ayub Khan** Pakistan's military leader from 1958 to 1969, and a major shaper of Pakistan's early alliance with the US, and subsequent shift to China after Washington determined that India was 'the prize' in South Asia. Ayub Khan built up the Pakistani armed forces with US assistance in pursuit of a military balance with India and made the forces the key political actors in his new country. His emphasis on the military in the processes of state-building weakened Pakistan's democratic institutions and rendered that country vulnerable to authoritarian abuse, which is said to have led to its division in 1971.

**Nikita Khruschev** Soviet Communist Party leader who initiated close relations with India in the 1950s. Inviting Nehru to visit Moscow, and then visiting India for a month in November–December 1955, Khruschev laid the foundations of strong strategic and economic ties. These provided considerable diplomatic advantage to both countries, giving Moscow a major breach in the Containment wall being fashioned by the US and in 1971, led to a treaty of friendship and co-operation between India and the Soviet Union just before India's direct military intervention in the Bangladesh war.

**The Dalai Lama** Born Tenzin Gyatso to Amdoa parents, the 14th Dalai Lama was picked by a search-team of Lhasa clerics who negotiated with Muslim warlord Gen. Ma Bu-feng and brought the infant to Lhasa. He was crowned temporal and spiritual head of Tibet shortly after the Chinese invasion in 1950 but was escorted south to the Indian border. His representatives were forced to sign a treaty ceding suzerainty to Beijing and he was persuaded by a Chinese general to return to Lhasa. The Dalai Lama was asked by the US in secret correspondence to refute the 1951 agreement and leave Tibet to lead anti-Chinese resistance from exile. This he only did in March 1959 when a largely Khampa-Amdoa-Golok revolt turned into a general insurrection in Lhasa which the PLA violently crushed, killing many Tibetans. Since his flight, the Dalai Lama has led a peaceful campaign for the restoration of Tibet's autonomy, but with little success. His administration is based at Dharamsala in India's Himachal Pradesh.

**The Panchen Lama** Born Choekyi Gyaltsen, the 10th Panchen Lama was the second highest ranking religious leader in Tibet after the Dalai Lama. Based at the Tashilhunpo monastery in Shigatse, the Panchen Lama was treated by the Chinese as a counterpoise to the Dalai Lama and there was much rivalry between the two courts. The Panchen Lama remained loyal to Beijing and was appointed the chairman of the Preparatory Committee for the Autonomous Region of Tibet (PCART) after the Dalai Lama's flight. Although generally supportive of 'democratic reforms', the Panchen Lama was appalled by the practice and its consequences in Tibet and neighbouring provinces. In 1962, he wrote a severely critical 70,000-character secret report to Zhou. Mao would describe this as a 'poisoned arrow'. In 1964, the Panchen Lama was stripped of all powers and imprisoned, to be only released in 1978. He remained a vocal defender of Tibet until his sudden, and somewhat mysterious, death in January 1989.

**Harold Macmillan** British Prime Minister who shared some of the tribulations of the Cold War with President Kennedy. Macmillan corresponded frequently with the US President, always addressing him 'Dear friend'. While Kennedy tended to shift from one set of preferences, eg, first in favour of plebiscite in Kashmir, then against; first in favour of providing Pakistan with all the assurances Ayub Khan wanted, and then describing India as 'the key' – Macmillan appeared to offer a more steady appraisal of Asian affairs. Their Nassau summit in late 1962 highlighted their special relationship.

**Mao Ze-dong** Chinese Communist Party chairman who led the communist revolution to bloody success in October 1949. Mao announced plans to 'liberate' Taiwan, Hainan and Tibet shortly after the Red Army occupied Beijing. Massive US presence and aid to the Kuo Min-tang prevented Taiwan's capture, but the PLA occupied Tibet in 1950–51. Mao was persuaded by the degree of Tibetan resistance to delay 'democratic reforms' on the plateau until after 1962. However, US, Indian and Taiwanese aid to the Tibetan National Volunteer Defence Army (NVDA) was deemed unacceptable and once the three motorways girding Tibet were completed, Mao ordered major military operations. The flight of the Dalai Lama led to repression of the Tibetan people which in turn triggered a secret petition from the Panchen Lama in 1962. Describing the petition as 'a poisoned arrow', Mao appears to have ordered even stronger measures to assimilate Tibet. This led to considerable Red Guard violence during the Cultural Revolution.

**John McCone** Engineer and businessman who joined US government service as a senior technical adviser in 1947. After stints as Under Secretary for the Air Force and Chairman, Atomic Energy Commission, McCone was appointed Director, Central Intelligence in 1961 and served in that capacity until 1965. McCone's detailed knowledge of the lands and the peoples of Asia was somewhat sketchy and his understanding of the political complexities of the region limited, but his technical skills made the CIA an innovative exploiter of developments in the scientific field. The development of miniaturised nuclear-powered sensors and surveillance devices, like the one lost in the Himalayas by CIA and Indian intelligence operatives, took place during his tenure. This scientific bent would be McCone's legacy to the CIA.

**Walter P McConaughy**  US diplomat who saw Beijing occupied by the Red Army in 1949. McConaughy went on to serve as US ambassador to various countries until he was assigned to Pakistan in 1962 just as India and China were drifting to war and US military assistance to India was raising the temperature in Pakistan. McConaughy enjoyed President Ayub Khan's confidence and despite a distinct cooling of US-Pak relations following the Sino-Indian war, he was able to carry unpleasant messages to the Pakistani leader and be assured of a courteous response. McConaughy's tenure saw the brief Indo-Pak conflict in Kutch in 1964, Pakistan's clandestine Operation Gibralter in Kashmir in early 1965, and eventually, the second Indo-Pak war in September 1965 during which Washington formally terminated military aid to both India and Pakistan although security collaboration with India against China was to continue for some time.

**K P S Menon**  Indian Foreign Secretary and subsequently Indian ambassador to China, Menon represented India's first Minister of External Affairs and Commonwealth Relations, Pandit Jawaharlal Nehru, in the late 1940s. He corresponded with US envoys and played an important role in implementing Nehru's desire to build a covert security alliance with Washington.

**V K Krishna Menon**  Confidante and friend of Prime Minister Jawaharlal Nehru, Menon led the Indian delegation to the UN General Assembly during the 1950s, and sought to act as a conduit between Washington and Beijing. He failed in this and came to earn much loathing from both the Eisenhower and Kennedy administrations. His rise as India's Defence Minister was seen as India's weakness and the failure of the Indian forces in 1962 was blamed largely on his incompetence. US officials refused to transfer sensitive information or major tranches of hardware as long as Menon was a key player in Delhi. His removal from the scene in the aftermath of the war saw a dramatic rise in the level of security collaboration between the US and India.

**George R Merrell**  US *Charge d'Affaires* in Delhi in the late 1940s who first identified Tibet's strategic importance to possible US interests in the region. Merrell suggested that as Asia became increasingly turbulent in the post-War era, Tibet would remain an island of conservative stability. He also recommended that in the age of missile warfare Tibet's geopolitically pivotal position be taken into account. Merrell's colleagues in the

Department of State showed limited interest in the plateau, however, and the newly-formed CIA was the first to take a serious initiative to cultivate the Lhasa authorities.

**Lord Louis Mountbatten**   The last British Viceroy in India, Mountbatten became the first Governor-General of independent India. As the ceremonial head of Pandit Nehru's government, Mountbatten visited Jammu & Kashmir and was likely to have been aware of the chain of action initiated by Deputy Prime Minister Sardar Patel, the Indian official responsible for States affairs, V P Menon, Defence Minsiter Sardar Baldev Singh, and Prime Minister Nehru himself. Mountbatten insisted, however, that Kashmir's *Maharaja* sign an instrument of accession before India take any military action in the state, and that once military operations had ceased, a reference be made to the people for determining the ultimate political arrangement for their state. From available documents, it appears that his first injunction was honoured only by manipulating facts, and the second was not honoured at all.

**B N Mullik**   The first Indian officer appointed to the sensitive post of Director, Intelligence Bureau, Mullik was a confidante of Nehru, especially on delicate security matters, for many years. He was privy to Nehru's thinking on the nature of Sino-Indian rivalry, and the perceived need to prop Tibet up as an effective buffer between the two. Nehru ordered Mullik to extend 'all possible help' to the Tibetan resistance early in the 1950s even when officially, China and India had signed agreements and become friends. Mullik secured US assistance under Nehru's authorisation and built up a major covert operation with the CIA's assistance in support of the Tibetan guerrillas. In the late 1950s, his men occupied forward positions on Himalayan slopes hitherto unoccupied by either side, thereby triggering substantial Chinese reaction which, by 1959, was building up into a confrontation between the two border forces. Mullik's activist stance, ordered by Nehru and assisted by the CIA, contributed to this confrontation exploding into the 1962 Sino-Indian war. The publication of his memoirs in 1971 scandalised the Indian establishment but underscored India's 'real' policy in the period.

**Pandit Jawaharlal Nehru**   Leader of the Indian National Congress and independent India's first Prime Minister and Foreign Minister (until his death in 1964), Nehru left his imprint on India's domestic and foreign policy. He negotiated with US officials in early 1947, and signed the first defence agreement granting US combat aircraft and crew the same rights as their Indian counterparts five weeks before India's independence. Following the Chinese invasion of Tibet and the cooling of Sino-Indian relations, Nehru initiated talks with the US leading to another secret defence agreement. This is when covert collaboration began against the Chinese in

Tibet. Nehru also reached an accord with his Pakistani counterpart to hold a plebiscite in Jammu & Kashmir. However, when the impending US-Pakistan defence treaty became known, Nehru reneged on the plebiscite deal, and signed away India's rights in Tibet, choosing instead to cultivate Beijing. He then sought to act as a mediator between the US and China. Thwarted in this endeavour, he visited Moscow, inviting Khruschev and Bulganin to visit India and lay the foundation of a relationship which would culminate in the 1971 Treaty of Friendship and Co-operation. However, Nehru retained close relations with Washington, especially the Eisenhower administration. His relationship with Kennedy was cool initially, but as tension increased along the Himalayas and Kennedy identified India 'as the key' in the region, things improved. Clandestine collaboration reached the peak during the war with China when Nehru urged Kennedy to deploy the US Air Force to India and sign up to a long-term strategic alliance. The war ended before Kennedy could respond but Indo-US co-operation against China had expanded dramatically by the time of his death.

**Richard M Nixon**   Vice President in the Eisenhower administration, Nixon visited the Far East in December 1953 and on his return briefed the National Security Council. He felt Communist China was 'here to stay' and that the US should normalise relations with it and bring it into the fold of the international community. Although Eisenhower made generally positive comments, Nixon's view was not supported and was not taken up by the administration. It would be nearly two decades before Nixon, as President, would be able to partly realise his goal of establishing near-normal contacts with China.

**Thubten Norbu/Taktser Rinpoche**   The Dalai Lama's elder brother and an incarnate Lama, Norbu supported the Tibetan resistance,crossing over to India to contact Indian and US officials bearing messages from the Dalai Lama soon after Chinese occupation. Norbu was flown to the US by a CIA-front organisation to pursue higher studies and serve as a major figure in the international campaign supporting Tibetan independence. He was brought to Delhi in 1956 when the Dalai Lama was allowed by Beijing to visit India to celebrate the 2500th anniversary of the birth of Goutam Buddha. Norbu and the pontiff's other activist brother, Gyalo Thondup, encouraged the Dalai Lama to seek asylum in India. However, Nehru and Zhou En-lai persuaded the pontiff to return to Lhasa. Norbu remained active in the Tibetan nationalist movement into the late 1990s.

**Vijaya Lakshmi Pandit**   Pandit Jawaharlal Nehru's sister and senior Indian diplomat, Mrs Pandit was India's ambassador in Washington when she was asked to initiate secret negotiations regarding a strategic alliance between Washington and Delhi. These talks led to the first agreement being signed in March 1951. Mrs Pandit played an important role in India's efforts to act as a conduit between China and the US in the early 1950s. When she led a cultural delegation to Beijing, she was briefed by US diplomats and given a message from the Secretary of State for the Chinese leadership. On her return she was debriefed by US officials. When she was the Indian High Commissioner in London, she regularly briefed not just British, but US leaders, on China generally and on Sino-Indian developments in particular.

**K M Pannikar** Indian ambassador to Communist China, Pannikar helped Delhi forge a close and friendly relationship shortly after the fall of the KMT. However, he was not able to predict either the Chinese occupation of Tibet or the adverse consequences of that move for Sino-Indian relations. Pannikar's efforts appeared aimed at smoothing the diplomatic feathers ruffled by Delhi's heated correspondence following the PLA's march into Tibet. In this he was eminently successful and the 1954 *Panchshil* agreement owed a great deal to his efforts. However, since Delhi ceded virtually all rights it had enjoyed in Tibet, success was not too difficult to attain. Despite Pannikar's efforts, Sino-Indian fraternity proved shortlived, but the only Indian leader who accused him of failure was Nehru's deputy, Sardar Patel.

**Sardar Vallabhai Patel** Congress leader, deputy Prime Minister and the first Home Minister of independent India, Sardar Patel played a crucial role in the assimilation of the hundreds of princely states, including Jammu & Kashmir, into India. As recently published documents suggest, although his methods may not always have been entirely above board, they were almost always successful. Sardar Patel's actions solidified India's integration and state-building processes although the nature of his policies created grounds for dispute. Patel was the first senior Indian to question Nehru's China policy. His unusually lengthy critique of Nehru's Tibet policy pointed out that the undelineated nature of the Himalayan borders, the existence of populations affiliated to the Tibetan leadership on both sides of it, and the emergence of an activist Chinese state created a situation threatening to Indian interests. Although events proved his concerns right, Nehru refused to take any overt steps to counter this 'Chinese threat'.

**Lukhangwa Tsewang Rapten** With Lobsang Tashi, appointed a co-prime minister of Tibet in December 1950 as the Dalai Lama prepared to flee to the Indian border following the Chinese invasion. Both prime ministers were vocally pro-independence and were seen by the Chinese as unacceptably supportive of the *Mimang Tsongdu*, the coalescing popular resistance. When the Dalai Lama and his *Kashag* (cabinet) were forced to fire the co-prime ministers, Lukhangwa secretly crossed the Himalays to Kalimpong and became a key sponsor of the *Chushi Gangdruk*, the resistance army.

**Dean Rusk** President Kennedy's Secretary of State, Rusk was deeply involved in setting out policy parameters vis-a-vis China, India and

Pakistan. Rusk's original inclinations appeared to be supportive of Pakistan's demands that a UN-sponsored plebiscite be held to decide the fate of Kashmir. As the Chinese threat to India increased both Rusk and Kennedy decided that protecting India, and therefore the subcontinent, from Communist invasion would have to take precedence. Rusk reinforced Kennedy's own view that India was the key state in the region and India's security was crucial to US interests in the region. Rusk's efforts to get India and Pakistan to hold their dispute over Kashmir in abeyance and forge an anti-Communist front eventually collapsed.

**Maharaja Hari Singh**   The last monarch of Jammu & Kashmir who sought to retain the state's independence after Britain's departure from the subcontinent. Hari Singh's appointment of Colonel Kashmir Singh Katoch, an Indian army officer, as the Commander of his State forces, and Justice Meher Chand Mahajan, an Indian judge, as the State's Chief Minister, indicated his general preference for association with India to any affiliation with Pakistan. When tribal Pathan militias from Pakistan's North-West Frontiers joined *Sudhan* Pathan rebels fighting for freedom, Hari Singh fled to Jammu and reportedly signed a letter of accession to India. Indian troops were flown in and secured the Vale, but Hari Singh was eased out of power which was transferred to Sheikh Mohammad Abdullah and his secularist National Conference party.

**Tan Kuan-sen**   Chinese general in charge of the military administration in Lhasa in early 1959 who invited the Dalai Lama to a military stage performance at which the pontiff was not allowed his usual military escort. Popular resentment and resistance burst into an insurrection in March and tensions rose to an explosive peak. The general wrote to the Dalai Lama and received replies in which the Dalai Lama sought to calm him down. When General Tan ordered the summer palace at Norbulingka where the Dalai Lama was staying to be shelled, the Dalai Lama decided to leave. Once his flight was detected, Gen. Tan mounted a violent operation to restore the PLA's control of Lhasa.

**Lobsang Tashi**   Senior Tibetan cleric appointed co-prime minister with Lukhangwa Rapten by the Dalai Lama when the latter prepared to flee to Dromo following the Chinese invasion of Tibet. Lobsang Tashi was equally anti-Han domination and was seen by the PLA as a major source of obstruction to Beijing's control over the plateau. When the Dalai Lama and the Kashag were forced by the Chinese to fire the two co-prime ministers, Lobsang Tashi returnd to his clerical duties.

**Gyalo Thondup**   Brother of the Dalai Lama who had family links in Taiwan which he made full use of in his campaign to seek help for the Tibetan resistance. Gyalo Thondup eventually became an emissary carrying messages from the Dalai Lama to US officials in India and in Washington.

He was one of the first Tibetans to meet Chinese leaders including Deng Xiao-ping to negotiate the restoration of Tibet's autonomy and the possible return of the Dalai Lama to Lhasa.

**The Pangda Tsang brothers**  Rapgya, Topgyay and Yempel Pangda Tsang were merchant princes of the eastern Kham province who became prominent in 1933 when they mounted an abortive separatist campaign to free Kham from the authority of both Lhasa and Beijing. Joint operations of Chinese and Tibetan forces defeated the Khampa rebels but the brothers were so influential that they were pardoned and allowed to retain their position and wealth. Rapgya Pangda Tsang, the baron of Po Dzong and governor of the Markham district, was the political leader. Topgyay and Yempel concentrated on trading across the Himalayas. Their establishments in Kalimpong and Markham became centres of Khampa recruitment and training. Their large mule trains carried 'war surplus' ordnance from Kalimpong to Kham, returning with payments in Chinese silver dollars. The first such train was reportedly sent to Kham after the PLA's probing attack in eastern Tibet in April 1950, but before the main invasion in October.

**George K C Yeh**  KMT ambassador in Washington in the early 1960s who liaised with US diplomats in co-ordinating a common position regarding Tibet. Dr Yeh was supportive of US asistance to the Tibetan national resistance, but he also upheld the Taiwanese refusal to endorse Tibetan independence. It is possible, indeed likely, that Dr Yeh also met the Dalai Lama's brothers, especially Gyalo Thondup, to discuss what Taiwan could do to bolster the Tibetan resistance, but US archival documentation does not offer records of such meetings.

**Yuan Zhongxian**  Chinese ambassador to Delhi in the 1950s, Yuan negotiated with the Tibetan emissary Tsipon Shakabpa and conveyed in clear terms Beijing's view that Lhasa could only expect regional autonomy but not independence. The ambassador kept a close watch on US and Taiwanese activities in support of the Tibetan resistance from Kalimpong, and his reports to Beijing formed the basis of the Chinese complaints of Indian complicity in the 'imperialist designs' against Chinese authority in Tibet. Yuan saw Sino-Indian relations pass from warmth to chill and then to normalcy again.

**Zhang/Chang Jingwu**  Military commander of the PLA's south-western forces which occupied parts of Kham and Amdo in 1950, general Zhang was a member of the Chinese delegation which negotiated the 17-point agreement with the Dalai Lama's emissaries in Beijing in 1951. Following that agreement, General Zhang arrived in Dromo on the Tibetan side of the Indo-Tibetan border where he persuaded the young Dalai Lama that the PLA's intentions were benign and that the Dalai Lama should return to Lhasa. This the latter did, but he soon discovered that Gen Zhang, as the head of Lhasa's Military administration, was taking over almost absolute control. Zhang eventually forced the Dalai Lama to fire the co-prime ministers, Lobsang Tashi and Lukhangwa Rapten.

**Zhou/Chou En-lai** Mao Ze-dong's deputy, Communist China's first Premier and Foreign Minister, Zhou was Beijing's sophisticated face to the world throughout the 1950s and 1960s. A veteran traveller to countries straddling the polarities of the Cold War, Zhou built diplomatic bridges with both India and Pakistan. Following the Korean armistice, he also negotiated with the Americans in Geneva. It was during one of these encounters that Secretary of State Dulles pointedly refused to shake Zhou's hand. A frequent visitor to Delhi, Zhou persuaded the Dalai Lama in 1956 to return to Lhasa, promising him that Chinese treatment of Tibet would be civilised. But Zhou could also be stern; in the late 1950s as Indian support for Tibetan guerrillas made things difficult for the PLA his letters to Nehru became correct and then cold. His dealings with the Pakistanis, on the other hand, became effusive and warm, establishing the beginnings of a long-term strategic relationship, which was to be sustained over several decades.

# Chronology of Key Events

**1904**  Lord Curzon despatches Colonel Younghusband and a military mission to Tibet; the Dalai Lama flees the capital and the remaining officials are forced to sign an agreement extending extra-territoriality and other trade privileges to British-India. China's position as the suzerain power is effectively undermined and British-India emerges as the key patron to the Tibetan state.

**1911**  Republican revolution sweeps China and removes the Ch'ing from power. Civil war rages in much of the mainland, and by March 1912, fighting breaks out among Chinese factions and between the Han and the Tibetans in Lhasa, Shigatse and Gyantse. The 13th Dalai Lama is living in Darjeeling.

**1912**  Chinese President Yuan Shih-k'ai's military column sent to Lhasa in July gets bogged down in heavy fighting in the eastern Kham province. The two Chinese *Ambans* in Lhasa are interned; the Nepali Resident in Tibet negotiates their deportation and they leave with their escorts via India. In July, the Dalai Lama returns to Tibet.

**1913**  By April, all Han soldiers and officials have left Lhasa and Tibet is effectively free. The Dalai Lama declares independence for Tibet. In the autumn British, Chinese and Tibetan envoys negotiate a border agreement aimed at defining the precise frontiers between Tibet and British-India, held at Shimla and hence named the Shimla Convention. The three envoys are the Indian Foreign Secretary, Sir Henry McMahon, Chinese Pleni-potentiary, Chen Yifan (Ivan Chen), and Tibetan plenipotentiary, Lonchen Shatra.

**1914**  Delimited on the watershed principle and drawn along the Himalayan crestline, the new border is named the McMahon Line by the British after Sir Henry. Based on the latter's recommendations, this alignment is agreed on by the British and the Tibetans but not the Chinese. All three envoys initial on the final agreement in April, but only the British and Tibetan officials sign it in July. The Tibetan cede considerable territory, effectively transferring suzerainty from the Chinese to the British. The

Chinese government declares its envoy had no authority to even initial the agreement, and reject the validity of the treaty and the resulting border. The Chinese maintain that the border lies along the much older Chien Lung Line which extends far south of the Himalayas. They describe the Shimla Convention an 'unequal treaty' but fail to do anything about it.

**1933**   The 13th Dalai Lama dies. Khampa merchant-princes, the Pangda Tsang brothers, led by Rapgya Pangda Tsang, baron of Po Dzong and governor of Kham's Markham district, mount a campaign to free Kham from the control of both Lhasa and China. Khampa raids on local Tibetan garrisons briefly succeed, but combined operations by Tibetan and Chinese forces ultimately defeat the brothers who receive pardons. Power in Lhasa passes on to two clerical regents who work out a rotating system without telling anyone else.

**1935**   The future 14th Dalai Lama is born to an Amdoa peasant family of moderate means near Taktser in Amdo. His eldest brother, Thubten Jigme Norbu, is already considered a high incarnated Lama at the Kumbum monastery and is destined to become the *Taktser Rinpoche*, but then to leave his clerical calling for joining an active campaign for the independence of Tibet. The future Dalai Lama's second older brother, Gyalo Thondup, too would become a prominent figure in the Tibetan struggle against Chinese control.

**1938**   The 'discovery' of the 14th Dalai Lama becomes public. The Chinese seek to assert control over the final selection – out of three likley infants – but these efforts are thwarted. The infant is first moved to Kumbum monastery, and then, after an arduous and long journey over mountainous territory, to Lhasa where he is enthroned.

**1940**   The Indian Muslim League, under Mohammad Ali Jinnah's leadership, passes the 'Pakistan resolution' demanding separate homelands for South Asia's Muslims in the north-east and north-west of the subcontinent. The Muslim League's Kashmiri affiliate, Kashmir Muslim Conference, endorses the resolution, but a secular faction, the National Conference, rejects confessional politics.

**1942**   The Tibetan authorities, ie, the Regent and the *Kashag*, the cabinet, establish the Bureau of Foreign Affairs to deal with all other countries. This is the first practical step taken by Lhasa to assert its independence in so far as diplomacy is concerned.

**1943**   OSS officers Capt. Ilia Tolstoy and Lt. Brooke Dolan arrive in Tibet bearing gifts and messages for the Dalai Lama from President Roosevelt. Their ostensible purpose is to study the possibility of opening a land-route for supplying Gen. Stilwell's forces and Chinese nationalists from bases in India. They receive warm hospitality for several months but the Tibetans reject Chinese demands that Han inspectors be placed along the route in Tibet; the project collapses. However, the Tibetans request the US for delivery of long-range shortwave radio transmitters and generators to power these. Delivery is made in November.

**1945** Massive transfer of military *materiel* by the US to Chiang Kai-shek's KMT regime begins; the aim is now to deafeat Mao's Red Army.

**1946** After considerable internal debate in Washington over whether to work via Chiang Kai-shek's KMT regime or to deal with Lhasa directly, the OSS succeeds in pushing the latter line, and hands over diesel-fired generators to power the transmitters.

**1947** As Britain prepares to leave South Asia, the US seeks to ensure its strategic interests do not suffer under the new dispensation. In January, US *Charge' d'Affaires* in Delhi, George Merrell, urges Washington to pay particular attention to the strategic importance of Tibet. In the spring, US diplomats negotiate with Jawaharlal Nehru, the pre-eminent Indian leader, and the Member for Foreign Affairs in the Viceroy's Executive Council. In early July, Nehru and US Ambassador Henry Grady exchange documents making up the first security arrangement between the US and post-colonial India. India grants the US right to operate military aircraft on combat missions from Indian airbases, and have them maintained, repaired and serviced there. This formalises a tacit Indo-US alliance against Chinese Communist forces. In Washington, the OSS and several other intelligence organs are merged to form the CIA. In August, Britain's South Asian empire is partitioned and India and Pakistan emerge as independent states. In October, India and Pakistan go to war for the first time over Jammu & Kashmir.

**1948** The first Indo-Pak war over Kashmir intensifies. The US encourages UN mediation and Nehru takes the dispute to the Security Council. In China, the Communists push the KMT eastward and take control over the bulk of the mainland. US hardware transfers to the KMT continues.

**1949** UN-sponsored ceasefire comes into effect in Jammu & Kashmir. The disputed state is effectivly divided along the ceasefire line (CFL), with the north-western third becoming *Azad* (free) *Kashmir*, a Pakistani protectorate, and the remaining two-thirds becoming India's Jammu & Kashmir state. Indo-Pakistani negotiations fail to break the diplomatic stalemate as an uneasy peace ensues. In China, the Communists take Beijing, proclaiming the People's Republic of China (PRC) with themselves as the Central People's Government (CPG). Chiang and the KMT flee to Taiwan, also occupying coastal islands in the Matsu chain. Mao announces intention to 'liberate' Taiwan, Hainan and Tibet. The Tibetan Regency writes to Mao seeking assurances of non-intervention by the People's Liberation Army (PLA), but receives none.

**1950** Lhasa authorities appeal over the radio for help against a possible Chinese invasion. They receive no support. However, in Washington, the Administration adopts NSC-68, a policy-paper which aims not only at containment of further advances by Communist powers, but also to transform the domestic dynamics of these states so that they do not pose threats to the 'free world'. This forms the basis of overt and covert containment campaigns around the world. In June the opening of the Korean War sees a more active US response to Tibetan appeals. Kalimpong and Delhi become points of clandestine contact between Tibetan, Indian and US emissaries. Large mule convoys carrying 'war-surplus' US ordnance begin crossing the Himalayas into south-eastern Tibet. In October, the PLA crosses the Yangtse and occupies Kham, threatening further moves into Tibet unless Lhasa acknowledges Chinese suzerainty. This the Regency does not, and the Dalai Lama is given supreme authority to adminster Tibet. Later, he is taken south to Dromo on the Indian border to await uncertain developments. Lukhangwa Tsewang Rapten and Lobsang Tashi are appointed co-prime ministers of Tibet and take a hard, pro-independence line. In its pursuit of Containment clients and allies, the US signs a Mutual Defence Agreement with Pakistan whose motives, however, are shaped mainly by fear of India. The Indian security establishment discovers Delhi has no viable military option to defend Indian interests in Tibet; Delhi and Beijing begin an exchange of tough diplomatic notes. Secret talks between Washington and Delhi on security collaboration against China begin.

**1951** Delhi sends out teams of civil administrators to take charge of remote townships in north-eastern India south of the McMahon Line, until now administered by Tibetan lamas. Beijing protests this 'occupation' of 'Chinese territory'. Delhi rejects these out of hand and in March the first Mutual Defence Assistance Agreement between India and the US is signed. Secret collaboration between the CIA and IB begins along the Sino-Indian borders. The IB opens a 'Tibetan Office' at Kalimpong where a large expatriate Tibetan community is already engaged in recruiting Khampa fighters and procuring arms and ammunition for the growing anti-Chinese resistance in Kham and Amdo. Reinforced by the agreement with the US, and possibly unaware of a similar US-Pak accord, Delhi makes military moves along the Pakistan border but calm is restored. The Dalai Lama's brothers, Thubten Norbu and Gyalo Thondup, cross the Himalayas into India where they contact US and Taiwanese officials and secure assistance for the Tibetan resistance, which, however, remains patchy, fragmented, and ineffective. The Dalai Lama is persuaded to send a delegation to Beijing under Ngwang Ngabo Jigme, the former Governor of Kham, recently in PLA custody at Chamdo, but now the Vice-Chairman of the 'Chamdo

Liberation Committee'. After a month of difficult talks, the Tibetan delegation signs a '17-point agreement' acknowledging Chinese sovereignty over Tibet. PLA General Zhang Jingwu arrives in Dromo via India, convinces the Dalai Lama of Beijing's peacable intent and persuades him to return to Lhasa. Dean Acheson agrees to offer aid to the Tibetan resistance. US diplomats send secret letters to the Dalai Lama asking him to refute the 17-point agreement and to lead the resistance from India. Warfare by Khampa, Amdoa and Golok guerrillas against the PLA intensifies. Indo-Pak tensions over Kashmir spill over across their international borders; troop-deployments do not, however, lead to war.

**1952** Thubten Norbu, the Dalai Lama's eldest brother and confidante, is flown to the US where he meets Department of State officials and becomes a conduit for messages between Lhasa and Washington. Tensions along Indo-Pak borders as troops are moved about by both sides,but calm prevails. Indian Prime Minister Nehru tells army officers that China is a source of grave threats to India, and instructs his Intelligence Bureau to extend 'all possible help' to the Tibetan resistance, albeit covertly.

**1953** Prime Ministers Nehru and Mohammad Ali write a number of letters which lead to a broad agreement on holding a UN-sponsored plebiscite in Jammu & Kashmir and the appointment of a plebiscite-administrator. However, disagreement remains on whether the result should treat Kashmir as a unitary state or if regional results should decide the fate of major divisions within Kashmir. When these technicalities are being discussed, Nehru learns of Pakistan's forthcoming alliance with the US and reneges on the plebiscite. In Geneva, US and Chinese delegates meet for the first time to discuss disputes. US Vice President Richard Nixon tours East Asia and reports to the NSC his impression of the apparent permanence of the Chinese Communists. He recommends normalisation of US-PRC relations but this view is not supported by anyone else.

**1954** Eisenhower writes to Nehru to reassure him of the anti-Communist nature of the US-Pakistan alliance. Nehru's response shows he is not reassured. As the US-Pakistan agreement is signed, Nehru moves to negotiate the *Panchshil* Treaty with China, accepting Chinese sovereignty over Tibet, losing extra-territorial rights on the plateau, and transferring all communications facilities to Beijing. Sino-Indian friendship becomes a part of Indian non-alignment. Pakistan and the US sign a Mutual Defence Assistance Agreement. Secretary of State John Foster Dulles refuses to shake Zhou En-lai's hand at a Geneva meeting, deepening US-PRC cleavages. Crisis begins over the Quemoy and Matsu islands off Chinese coasts where the PLA lobs shells at KMT units and Washington threatens reprisals. The Dalai Lama and Panchen Lama travel to Beijing to attend the National People's Congress, and to meet Chinese leaders. The US National

Security Council recommends continuation of covert operations against China. Despite differences over Pakistan, India and the US reach an agreement to transfer $350-million in military hardware to India over three years. Delhi takes the initiative to mediate between China and the US. The US signs a defence assistance agreement with Taiwan. The Tibetan resistance begins gelling into a cohesive structure.

**1955** US-Pakistan Defence Support Agreement is signed, freeing up Pakistani resources for military modernisation. Bandung conference of Afro-Asian states is held and engenders the non-aligned movement. Both India and Pakistan offer to mediate with China on US's behalf. Nehru confidante Krishna Menon's efforts are sustained for much longer than Pakistani ones but in July, UK-mediation leads to US-PRC talks. Rebuffed, Nehru visits Moscow and invites Khruschev to visit India. In September, Pakistan signs up to the Baghdad Pact (later CENTO). In November, Khruschev and Bulganin arrive in India to spend a month travelling from Calcutta to Kashmir. Indo-Soviet strategic alliance, extending Delhi's leverage in its relations with the US, China and the Soviet Union itself, is initiated. This strand becomes increasingly important. In Tibet, the Kanting rebellion triggers massive fighting between the PLA and Tibetan guerrillas. Taiwanese assistance begins arriving to supplement the modest CIA aid. The US delivers cargo aircraft and communications equipment to reinforce Indian defence preparedness along the Himalayan borders. Large-scale economic aid too is given.

**1956** Secretary of State Dulles assures Nehru that if Pakistan uses US hardware against India, US would aid India directly. To reinforce that message, the US signs an agreement enabling it to control disposal of US equipment given to Pakistan. Vice President Nixon visits South Asia to shore up the anti-Communist alliance. Beijing announces the demise of 'reactionaries and serf-owners and imperial agents' in Tibet but with a network of supply bases in Taiwan, Thailand, India, and Pakistan, the Tibetan resistance makes even greater strides against the PLA. The Hungary and Suez crises shake Nehru's faith in his Soviet and British allies and he is forced to explore his US links once again. The Dalai Lama arrives in India to celebrate the 2500th anniversary of the birth of Goutam Buddha and asks for asylum. Nehru is adamant that he go back to Tibet and asks Zhou En-lai to visit Delhi which he does. The Dalai Lama is persuaded to return by Zhou who assures him that things will improve in Tibet. In December, Nehru visits Washington and is lionised as an honoured guest. In discussions with Eisenhower, he restores the primacy of the US-Indian alliance in dealing with China.

**1957** The CIA and the Indian IB significantly expand covert collaboration in support of the Tibetan resistance. Despite completion of major motorways girding Tibet and linking remote stretches of it with Xinjiang and Lhasa, the PLA is forced out of large areas liberated by the *Chushi Gangdruk*. In February, Mao admits that Tibetans are not yet 'ready for democratic reforms' and announces that reforms would not be implemented before 1962. Induction of the long-range C-130 Hercules transport aircraft allows the CIA to move large batches of Tibetan guerrillas to Guam, Saipan and even to Colorado for specialist training and then return them to form the nucleus of a special band of fighters prepared to carry out complicated missions on order from the CIA's regional headquarters in Dhaka. While US-Indian covert operations achieve tactical success, the year ends with a recommendation from Robert McClintock of the Department of State to sign a 'Pacific Pact' with China which would unify and neutralise Korea and Vietnam, and admit both China and Tibet to the UN. As with Nixon's suggestions four years earlier, this recommendation sinks without a trace.

**1958** India, responding to increased Chinese activities along the frontiers, particularly Chinese occupation of Ladakh's Aksai Chin plateau through which runs the new Tibet-Xinjiang motorway, asks for greater US assistance. The 1951 Indo-US Mutual Defence Assistance Agreement is renewed. Bitter exchanges between Delhi and Beijing follow. Washington gets Pakistan, Iran and Turkey to sign up the London Declaration and form the CENTO. While the NVDA engages the PLA in eastern and southern Tibet, along the eastern and western reaches of the Himalayas, Indian and Chinese border guards begin 'eyeball-to-eyeball confrontations'. Clashes reach a crescendo at year-end.

**1959** PLA operations against the NVDA force the population of large stretches of eastern Tibet to seek shelter in Lhasa. Guerrillas are ordered to move in with the refugees and await orders. In March, shortly after the Dalai Lama's final theological and theosophical examinations, the local PLA commander invites him to a military stage performance over which disputes begin. There is a popular uprising against the Dalai Lama's feared arrest and in the end the PLA begins shelling the summer palace. The Dalai Lama, his immediate family and retinue, flee Lhasa in disguise. As the PLA begins a violent destruction of the resistance, the Dalai Lama proclaims a new government, declares independence and crosses the border into India. US-aided resistance units escort him. The Chinese openly identify India as a source of trouble and begin a major operation against the NVDA. By the end of the year, the Tibetan resistance is virtually decimated outside small pockets. The CIA is determined to identify and support residual resistance in Tibet, but this proves difficult. The US signs two agreements with Pakistan, one assuring the latter of certain security guarantees, and the other giving the US rights to establish base facilities near Peshawar. U-2 sorties over the Soviet Union begin from Peshawar and Soviet telecommunications are monitored and analysed at a facility in Badaber. Clashes increase between Chinese and Indian border guards as Delhi tries to secure hitherto unmanned forward positions.

**1960** Washington copes with the Dalai Lama's pleas for supporting Tibetan claim to independence. The Dalai Lama's brothers, Thubten Norbu and Gyalo Thondup, carry messages back and forth. The US is supportive of Tibet but does not wish to weaken consensus in the United Nations and urges acceptance of the violation of Tibetan human rights as the most effective complaint against China. India's Border Roads Organisation recruits former Tibetan guerrillas to build high-altitude roads along the borders. Defence Minister Krishna Menon orders forward movement of Indian military presence. Delhi is still extremely reluctant to openly endorse alliance with US and warns Washington not to operate clandestine sorties in support of the Tibetan resistance over Indian airspace. Aircraft from the US and the Soviet Union reinforce Indian air force. Pakistan begins secret negotiations with China over Kashmir-Xinjiang borders. PLA units penetrate deep inside Delhi-claimed territory but this is not disclosed to the Indian public.

**1961** Under Secretary of State Chester Bowles meets Nehru in Delhi and is told that at some points, PLA units are 150 miles inside India. Pakistani President Ayub Khan visits the US and reviews delivery of US hardware to Pakistani forces. Krishna Menon meets Kennedy but is received with less tolerance than he was by Eisenhower and Dulles. US-Indian relations plunge as Delhi takes over the Portuguese enclaves of Goa, Daman and Dieu. Kennedy sends off an unusually stiff protest note to Nehru.

**1962** Correspondence between Kennedy and Nehru on the one hand and Kennedy and Ayub Khan on the other shows changes in Kennedy's views regarding the importance of India and Pakistan to US interests. Kennedy supports Pakistan's demand for a plebiscite in Kashmir and is tough on Delhi until Pakistan and China sign an 'interim agreement' on their border. As things hot up along Sino-Indian borders, he accepts the view that plebiscite is 'dead', and that 'India is the key'. As clashes mount, India makes increasing demands on US deliveries of *materiel* and Kennedy orders compliance. He also asks his diplomats to get India and Pakistan to negotiate on Kashmir and if possible, form a tacit coalition against China. Despite US aid, Indian forces are routed by the Chinese in a sudden thrust across the Himalayas starting on 20 October. In desperation, Nehru writes to Kennedy asking for massive and immediate air support, and the forging of an overt strategic alliance. By the time Kennedy has read these two letters, the Chinese announce a unilateral ceasefire and withdraw.

# Preface

History is often as much about what is known to historians or what they can surmise from what they know as it is about what actually happened and which events shaped, coloured or otherwise influenced which other events. History has traditionally dealt with politics, ie, acts of commission or omission by those exercising power, or by those seeking it, and historians have had to find and collate records of what monarchs, princes, cardinals and, more recently, presidents and prime ministers, have had to say about what they have been doing. Often, statements by such leaders have been backed up with documents – transcripts of speeches, treaty documentation, even diary entries. But few government leaders do precisely what they say in public they are doing; nor do they consistently abide by their declared commitments. Statements are often made to reassure an anxious populace or a concerned neighbour, to calm an angry great power, or to convey messages and send signals which may differ significanly from the overt commentary. There are subtle codes which recipients need to grasp to be able to correctly interpret the intended meaning and import of the missive, and historians are often not privy to these. Sometimes the recipients misinterpret the message and great tensions may then arise which flabbergast the originator who is then confounded into taking steps that further intensify misunderstanding. If this spiral is not arrested, originally avoidable confusion can lead to warfare. History is replete with instances of unwanted bloodshed and destruction. One explanation of such misunderstanding is the pervasive secrecy in which governments tend to operate. This secrecy is the product of the tradition in which the modern state and statecraft have evolved. In short, in politics and diplomacy, appearances can be and often are deceptive. This is why the apparent certitudes of history are problematic. And the history of the recently-concluded Cold War, including that of its Asian version, is no different.

Historians also tend to focus on the most powerful actors. Modern history has, to that extent, been largely about the policies of the greatest of the great powers – the so called super powers – the United States and the now-defunct Soviet Union. This trend may have been assisted by the nature of the Cold War itself. It was, after all, a clash of titans and a conflict between two states capable of wreaking the most widespread havoc on earth. Chroniclers of the Cold War understandably concentrated on what they saw as evidence of the perennial and potentially cataclysmic conflict between the super powers.

This was more often the case in the earlier phases of the not-so-Cold War. Czechoslovakia, Berlin, Korea, Hungary and Cuba were seen as major mileposts in the evolving historiography of the period. But the struggle between capitalism and communism was a many-splendoured and variegated drama, a veritable smorgasbord of subplots and sideshows as intriguing, and for the people whose lives were turned upside down if not threatened or destroyed by them, just as important as the main plot unfolding on the centre stage of world politics.

The subplot which was played out across the high Himalayas from India and Pakistan into the Tibetan plateau in the 1950s and the 1960s was one such sideshow. It involved a superpower, an emerging power seeking to establish itself as a major player and at the same time restore its ancient pride, and two post-colonial successor states with asymmetric power-potential and interests but both mainly intent on their mutual rivalry.

There was also a residual rump state far away from the scene of action, but owing to its super power connections, able actively to participate in the gory histrionics. But for the thousands of Tibetans, mainly from the eastern mountains of Kham and Amdo, and later on also from the central U-Tsang region around Lhasa, who fought and often died in the belief that theirs was a realistic goal, this Himalayan drama was the only show in town. In the end, the liberation of Tibet from Han-Chinese occupation and control was not achieved because the Tibetan freedom fighters were only being manipulated as pawns in someone else's war whose objectives were very different to those being pursued by the guerrillas themselves. The war which lasted from 1950 to around 1974, consumed over a hundred thousand Tibetan lives in combat and perhaps several hundred thousand more indirectly. Proportional to the overall Tibetan population, this was one of the world's most expensive failures, but that failure itself was merely an instrument of the strategy being pursued jointly by the United States and the newly-independent India to 'bleed' Communist China and thereby neutralise its effectiveness.

Conventional wisdom has until now maintained that beginning in the post-War period, the staunchly anti-Communist US and Nehruvian India have been at loggerheads in their diplomatic worldviews. Nehru himself may have encouraged this assumption by repeatedly adhering to a line hewing to the concept of non-alignment and equidistance between the two super powers and their rival military blocs. In his many letters to the Chief Ministers of various Indian states, in the speeches he made at home and abroad, and in defining and defending his government's foreign and security policies in the Indian parliament, Nehru consistently spoke of his administration's principle of non-alignment. In one such address in the *Loksabha*[1] in June 1952, he said:

> *So far as policy is concerned, in spite of the fact that we deal largely with the UK and the US – **we buy our things from them and we have accepted help from them** – we have not swerved at all from our policy of non-alignment with any group. We stuck to our policy even though we had to deny ourselves the offered help. That is why other countries realize that we cannot be bought by (sic) money. It was then that help came to us and we gladly accepted it; we shall continue to accept help provided there are no strings attached to it and provided our policy is perfectly clear and above board and is not affected by the help we accept. I realize – I frankly accept – that there are always certain risks involved. There may be no apparent risk but our sense of obligation might affect our policy without our knowing it. All I can say is that we should remain wide awake and try to pursue our policy consistently and honestly. There have been times when one word from us would have brought us many of the good things of life. We preferred not to give that word. If at any time help from abroad depends upon a variation, howsoever slight, in our policy, we shall relinquish that help completely and prefer starvation and privation to taking such help.[2]*

Given the strength of anti-colonialist sentiments sweeping India at the time and the pressures on its leadership to assert India's new-found independence, Nehru may not have had any choice to cultivating an image of noble detachment. His rhetoric largely went down well at home where his personal popularity in the Indian heartland remained strong. Abroad, his statements came to be associated with the Afro-Asian solidarity movement against what were frequently described as Western imperialist-colonialist powers. That association, reinforced by repetation, eventually was accepted at face value as the honest appraisal of India's foreign and security policy in a polarised world. It became the principal motif in all historical appreciation of South Asian diplomacy in the 1950s and 1960s. The result was a belief that while Pakistan was 'the most allied ally' of the US, India was most non-aligned of the neutrals. This view is well-distilled in a recent work which is being quoted at some length to demonstrate the strength and widespread acceptance of the belief.

> *It has always been something of a mystery that the United States of America should, virtually without exception, find itself on more intimate terms with Pakistan than with democratically-elected Indian leaders. Why should this be? . . . Another irritant to American policy towards New Delhi has been India's habit of moralising and*

*pontificating about western responsibilities and obligations to the post-colonial world, and her inclination to take an independent stance on global issues, such as her refusal to join the American policy of containment aimed at the Soviet Union. It is this latter point, expressed through the language of non-alignment, that has caused the greatest amount of consternation for Washington. Non-alignment has been invariably too clever by half for the Americans, who have perceived it as a piece of muddled logic, or worse an act of calculated duplicity, allowing India to condemn 'power bloc' rivalries and military alliances, while closely associating herself with the Soviet Union . . . For Foster Dulles and his generation of American strategic thinkers, this refusal to uphold the principle of a 'free world', in favour of seeking reconciliation through negotiation, was simply so much hot air. The talk of Afro-Asian solidarity and 'global peace' was even pernicious since it detracted attention away from the real threat to global security and lead to 'fraternisation' with rebel states such as the Soviet Union and China.*[3]

As the most prominent shaper and proponent of India's foreign and security policies for the first seventeen years of independence, Nehru's own statements have generally been accepted as the expression of the direction and thematic explanation of those policies. Analysts have to that extent observed the visible. But documentation collected from various archives suggests that they may have been mistaken. It now appears that India has, in fact, been closely allied to and involved in the US policy of containment from the very inception of that policy. Covert collaboration between the US and India against the Chinese Communists began before India became independent and continued for several decades afterwards. As Britain gave way to the US as the major Western power in Asia, the leader of emergent India determined the development of a strategic linkage between India and the US to be in India's short-to-medium term security interest. A military alliance against the Chinese Communists was forged in the form of a modest treaty which authorised the US Army Air Forces to operate major combat missions into China in support of Generalissimo Chiang Kai-shek's Kuomintang administration from Indian airbases *after* India became independent. The architect of that visionary alliance has not been identified, but the Indian leader who in early July 1947, six weeks before India emerged as the world's first truely post-colonial successor state, took Delhi into this relationship was Pandit Jawaharlal Nehru, then the Member for External Affairs and Commonwealth Relations on the Viceroy's Executive Council. For the next seventeen years Nehru, as India's first Prime Minister and Minister for External Affairs, charted a course that strengthened the Indo-US military and security alliance against Beijing. His government signed a series of treaties enabling progressively closer military and intelligence co-operation between the two allies. The last of these was signed in November 1962, at the height of the border war with China. This account is essentially an appraisal of the documentation linking South Asia to American efforts at containing China in the 1950s and the necessary reappraisal of the security linkages between that super power patron and its subcontinental client-states.

The entity which suffered the most while the US, China, India and Pakistan pursued their interests was not considered a state and this may have been the main reason why it suffered so much. Tibet, a primarily theocratic polity occupying the Tibetan plateau north of the Himalayan mountain range, tasted true freedom in the recent past only in 1912. The Lhasa authorities threw out the two Chinese *Ambans* representing the Ch'ing empire and their military escorts following Sun Yat-sen's republican revolution in 1911 which led to near-anarchic situation in China. In 1912–1950, Tibet acted like an independent state, issuing passports to its official delegations visiting various countries, and receiving similar missions in return. The closest ties were with British-India and then, since 1947, with independent India. These linkages had been formalised in 1904 when Curzon's military expedition to Tibet under Colonel Younghusband forced the Lhasa authorities to sign agreements opening the plateau up to trans-Himalayan trade and giving British-India extra-territorial rights at three trade-marts outside the capital. British-Indian influences were reinforced through the Shimla agreement of 1913–4 which displaced China as the pre-eminent regional power with British-India while retaining Beijing's *de jure* suzerainty over the plateau. The agreement laid down Tibet's southern frontiers which would become a bone of future contention since the Chinese never accepted it as a valid treaty. The British interest appears to have been to create a buffer state separating their Indian empire from the Chinese giant to the north and north-east while the Tibetans found the Chinese more onerous than the British. But the latter did not go so far as to acknowledge Tibetan independence; nor did they provide Tibet with sufficient assistance enabling Lhasa effectively to defend itself when the crunch came. As with many other instances in Britain's colonial history, this was empire-building on the cheap aimed at securing difficult frontiers and acquiring benefits without paying an inordinate cost for either. Tibet's perceived interests were highlighted in the process, but they were not the key element in the calculus and received only modest attention.

The Tibetan state itself suffered from a number of weaknesses. A theocratic-feudal polity based on a remote, rugged and 12–18,000 foot plateau with little technology, no infrastructure and a small population, it was not organised sufficiently to protect its interests in the face of a determined foe. The basis of its cohesion was mass devotion to the Dalai Lama, the head of the pre-eminent Gelugpa sect of Tantric Buddhism. Its lay officialdom had not been exposed to the intricacies of 20th-century diplomacy or the devastation of modern warfare. Like its clerical counterpart, it had no preparation for functioning effectively in a competitive environment shaped by power-political drives of much better organised actors. While many Tibetans valued independence, and large numbers would eventually die for it, their understanding of the meaning of independence, and their ability to give practical shape to that meaning, were extremely limited. And in a resurgent China, they had an adversary they could not match. The Chinese, despite violent upheaval rending the post-Ch'ing mainland, maintained their claim on the plateau in both the 1931 and 1946 constitutions. This was not challenged by any of Tibet's external friends. During World War II, Delhi, London and Washington showed considerable interest in securing Tibet's assistance in providing a land-route to send supplies to the US and KMT forces fighting the Japanese in China, but none of them treated Tibet as anything other than having a peripheral interest to the main drama. This would not change after the World War gave way to the Cold War.

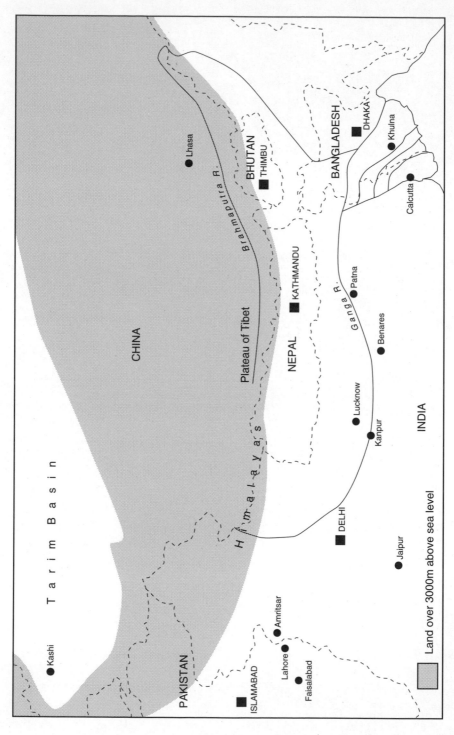

The western Himalayan theatre

# Introduction

For most of the 1950s, the World's attention was focused on dramatic instances of confrontation and even conflict between what came to be called the West, effectively a political-military-economic alliance of Western European states led by the US, on the one hand, and the Communist bloc, a generic term applied somewhat loosely to a coalition of Marxist states led by the Soviet Union, on the other. The emergence of the two nuclear-armed superpowers, and the formation of the NATO and Warsaw Pact alliances pitted the more industrially developed countries of the global 'north' in a struggle between polarities. Crises over even relatively peripheral issues, such as the fate of Formosa, Tibet, and the Korean peninsula came to assume systemic import. Much blood was spilt and much treasure squandered by both sides in attempts to defeat 'the enemy'. Some of these events shaped, certainly coloured, policy-formulation in world capitals for several decades afterwards. To that extent, the Cold War drama in Asia was a significant aspect of the history of the post-1945 world. Understanding what actually happened can only help us to grasp the character of the processes which made the world such a dangerous place for so many over such a long period of time. And yet, not even today are all the pieces of the historical jigsaw in place.

The role of the US in these crises and confrontations is relatively well-documented; that of its allies and client-states, far less so. In fact, contemporary historiography appears to have been built upon an easy acceptance of the validity and accuracy of rhetorical flourishes, declaratory exhortations, nationalistic propaganda and sometimes, outright deception. Much of what is considered the history of the Cold War in Asia in the 1950s, is contrafactual. This account is the result of an attempt to correct some of the more glaring discrepancies. That discrepancies do exist became clear on April 17, 1978, when the Prime Minister of India, Morarji Desai, reported to the *Loksabha*, the lower house of the Indian parliament, that in the 1960s, the Governments of the United States and India had collaborated 'at the highest political level' in covert operations aimed at challenging the authority and integrity of the People's Republic of China. Desai's report was

1

said to have 'stunned' the House. This, after all, was the Prime Minister of a country whose leaders had for decades vociferously criticised the US, and especially the Central Intelligence Agency (CIA), for a variety of sins, now revealing that his predecessors in office themselves had, in fact, been closely involved in such activities for years.

Desai's revelations were triggered by press reports that radiation from a secret piece of Plutonium-239 powered equipment lost in the Himalayan snows in the mid-1960s by the CIA was threatening millions of Indians bathing in, or using the water of, the river Ganges.[1] Desai told his parliamentary colleagues that successive Indian Prime Ministers starting from Jawaharlal Nehru through Lal Bahadur Shastri to Indira Gandhi had taken the decision to covertly collaborate with the CIA's activities based in India. One such CIA mission had been to install a plutonium-powered device at 25,000 feet on the Nanda Devi mountain in the Himalayas in 1965. Desai explained that the device was intended to 'obtain information about missile developments'. Although the Prime Minister did not say so, it was widely assumed that the device contained sensors designed to monitor both missile launches and nuclear explosions conducted by the Chinese. He said that in early 1964,

> *In the light of the international situation prevailing at the time, the Indian and the American Governments at the highest level decided that a remote control sensing device with a nuclear powerpack should be installed near the highest point of the Nanda Devi range of the Himalayas. (In 1965) An expedition of Indian mountaineers went up the Nanda Devi followed by a joint Indo-American expedition scientifically equipped and carrying the device. The aim was to install it at a height of 25,000 feet. When the expedition was approaching the summit, it was overtaken by a blizzard which made further ascent impossible and the expedition was obliged to retreat to a lower camp at 23,000 feet. In the precipitate descent under very trying and exacting conditions, they had to leave the powerpack securely cached.[2]*

The pack, which weighed 33lbs and was powered by between 2 and 3lbs of plutonium, could not be recovered that winter. Search for it resumed in May 1966 and continued until 1968, but without success. Water samples from the Ganges were taken and tested for radiation until 1970. It was assumed that an avalanche had carried the powerpack, and its capsules of plutonium-239, deep down into the mountainside, and presumably, from there to the headwaters of the Ganges. Meanwhile, in 1967, Indian intelligence and CIA operatives were able to install a new monitoring device on a neighbouring peak. Mr Desai informed the House that after it had worked for a year, this second device was removed in 1968 and returned to the US. American intelligence satellites took on these monitoring tasks in

1969. Desai also assured the legislators that the 'project' had not been a CIA initiative, but was, rather, a scheme originated by 'scientific departments of this country'. In addition to nuclear-powered sensors, Washington and Delhi had agreed, also in 1964, to build an early-warning radar network along the Himalayan borders between India and China. Its purpose would have been to detect Chinese troop movements[3] near the disputed boundary. In the end, the radar network was not built, but taken together, the two projects underscored the nature of the clandestine military and security alliance forged between the US and India and the mutuality of their hostility to and insecurity vis-a-vis Communist China.

A month after Desai's revelations to his parliamentary colleagues, reports suggesting that the US-Indian alliance went much deeper than these disclosures hinted at began appearing. These said, among other things, that shortly after the border war between China and India in October–November 1962, the Indian Government at its highest level decided to provide base facilities to US U-2 high-altitude photo-reconnaissance aircraft at a military airfield in the eastern state of Orissa. Between 1963 and 1965, the U-2s operating out of India flew over Tibet and neighbouring Chinese provinces, monitoring the People's Liberation Army's [PLA] deployments, dispositions and movements in areas close to the Indian borders. A newly established 'Aviation Research Wing' of the Cabinet Secretariat, ie, the Prime Minister's office in New Delhi, co-ordinated US-Indian cooperation in clandestine airborne activities.[4] And this happened at a time when senior Indian officials and political leaders were condemning Pakistan for having offered base facilities near Peshawar for US U-2 operations over the Soviet Union.

That both India and the United States would be interested in obtaining information about Chinese nuclear tests and its ballistic missile development project was easy to understand; that they were working together in secret in such potentially hazardous manner at a time when the authorities in Delhi determinedly declared their non-aligned policy at every opportunity was less so. Was this pragmatism at its best on India's part? Was Nehru's non-aligned rhetoric grand deception at the strategic level? Was this US-Indian collaboration against China a well-thought out stratagem that made sense in the period following India's rather humiliating defeat in the 1962 war, and the first Chinese nuclear test in 1964? What were the justifications of that secret collaboration against China *before* Beijing became such an acknowledged source of threats to India? Was the Indian leadership forced into the difficult position of a major client of the greatest military-economic power on earth by its own insecurities vis-a-vis a China perceived to be inimical to its interests? These questions have not been asked, far less answered, in contemporary historiography of the early years of the Cold War in Asia. This narrative seeks to address some of them, using largely official documentation extracted with some difficulty from various archives on three continents.

Classified documents in US archives show that both India and Pakistan became closely aligned to the United States shortly after they emerged as independent states. The ruling elites in both successor states pursued similar policies where alliances were concerned. Both engaged in secret negotiations with the US, and occasionally, with other powers, in pursuit of a framework of security relationships which apparently offered a measure of protection and predictability in a hostile and uncertain world. The insecurity afflicting South Asian elites seeking to build the world's first truly post-colonial states[5] dovetailed with the adversarial bipolarity dividing the geopolitical centre of the world, creating a resonance between the centre and the periphery which deepened regional fissures and made local cleavages even sharper and more intractable than they already were. This outcome was virually inevitable given, firstly, the asymmetry in power relations between the central power, the patron,and the peripheral clients, and secondly, the fundamental incompatibility between the founding-principles of the two successor-states which dogged, and continues to dog, their bilateral relations. Since their inception as independent states, India and Pakistan had identified each other as the principal source of threats to respective national security whereas their patron, the US, has persistently sought to bring these two neighbours together into a team of partners in Washington's Cold War struggle against the 'Communist threat'.

This US anxiety about monolithic 'Communist expansionism' was deepened by the Marxist takeover of Czechoslovakia, rising tension over Berlin, and the 'loss' of China to Mao's Red Army in 1949. It saw the formulation by Washington of NSC-68 in April 1950 which set the tone for the US 'Containment' policy against Communists every-where.[6] Despite what Nehru said about India's non-aligned foreign policy around this time, what he, as India's Foreign Minister did, underscored his pragmatic approach to *Realpolitik*. What Nehru did not share with his American allies was the sense of loss which the latter felt over the defeat of the Kuomintang authorities by the Chinese Communists. Certainly for those with any knowledge of US support for Chiang Kai-shek's KMT administration in the late 1940s, Communist victory was a shock. The US had funded a very substantial build up of the KMT's military strength especially once the war in Europe wound down and Marxism rather than fascism appeared to have become the 'enemy'. Under the Sino-American Cooperative Organization Agreement, Washington shipped *materiel* worth $17,666,927.70 to the KMT[7] between V-J Day and 2 March 1946. In addition, the US transferred 131 naval vessels of various types worth $141,315,000 under Public Law 512 which enabled the US Government to give property away in grants.[8] Between 1 January 1948 and 31 March 1949, Washington gave away to the KMT ordnance worth $60,608,497.58, and sold *materiel*[9] worth another $5,306,164.03. The 80th Congress passed the 'China Aid Act' as Public Law 472 which instructed that a sum of $338 million was 'to remain available for obligation for the period of one year following the date of the enactment of this Act.' Another $125 million was to be offered 'for additional aid to China through grants.'[10] On top of this, the US supplied the KMT ordnance, military hardware and other war*materiel* worth over $781 million between V-J day and 30 June 1948 via Lend-Lease transfers.[11] Despite that level of assistance, the KMT was forced to flee to Taiwan in October 1949 and most of the resources provided by the US to it was lost. But more than the material loss the loss of face and of pride and confidence had to be lived down. The centre of the nearly unipolar post-war order was not able or willing to accept the defeat of its ally, and of its own interests in that region, easily. Communist China, seen in Washington as an activist cat's paw working at Moscow's behest, became a source of considerable unhappiness in US establishment circles. Much of the Containment policy was fashioned to prevent Communist China from 'breaking out'. What happened in Tibet in the 1950s, for instance, needs to be seen in this context.

During World War II, Tibet's importance to the Allied powers rose in direct proportion to the difficulties faced by General 'Vinegar Joe' Stilwell's forces in their struggle against the Japanese. After the fall of Burma and the loss of both land and air-bridges from India to China across northern Burmese territory, supplies and provisions had to be delivered over the 'hump' of south-eastern Tibet by air. The Tibetans maintained strict neutrality throughout the war, but were gracious in their treatment of downed US airmen whose aircraft were forced to crash-land on Tibetan territory. The OSS decided to explore the possibility of persuading the infant Dalai Lama's regents to grant right of passage to US military traffic from India to China via Tibet and sent out two junior officers carrying a letter and gifts from President Roosevelt to the Dalai Lama. Although these officers were treated with warmth by the Lhasa authorities, complications arose over what stores would be considered warlike and what role the Chinese would play in escorting the mule trains and convoys. The discussions became protracted and before they could be successfully concluded, the Japanese surrendered. Nonetheless, the US administration, pushed by General 'Wild Bill' Donovan of the OSS, gradually came to see the Tibetan plateau as a strategically significant territory. As we shall see, this view was not shared with equal enthusiasm by the Department of State and it was the OSS and its progeny,the CIA, which took the principal role of shaping US-Tibetan relations.

Post-War events in and around Tibet did not occur in isolation. The links between the sequences could not be detected at the time: the PLA's march into the province of Kham, Tibetan resistance, covert operation by the US and its Indian allies with assistance from Pakistan, Indo-Pakistani rivalry and conflict and their dissatisfaction with Washington's inability to respect each client-state's zero-sum concerns, India's move to achieve reconciliation with China, US anxiety to secure Pakistani assistance in protecting the Middle-Eastern oilfields from possible Soviet threats, India's reaction to that effort leading to Soviet entry into the South Asian security scene, subsequent reconciliation between Washington and Delhi as China's response to US-Indian covert operations became more vociferous, and Pakistan's efforts to expand its own range of security options – all these strands were linked to each other in a complex web. As the actors chose to operate under the veneer of benign innocence, concealing their real policy and action beneath a shroud of disinformative rhetoric and downright deception, the picture has largely been unclear until now as to what actually happened. But it has been possible to piece together a generally credible version which challenges much of what has until now passed as conventional wisdom, and even history.

The main narrative begins in October 1950 when the People's Liberation Army [PLA] crossed the Dri Chu/Yangtse river and marched into Tibet, thereby triggering major insecurity not only in Lhasa, but in Delhi and distant Washington as well. It ends in October 1962 when the PLA crossed the Himalayas, marching into the Ladakh Division of Jammu & Kashmir and the North East Frontier Agency, thereby triggering a major flurry of activity in world capitals. It seeks to discover the nature of the time-event continuum connecting these two terminal acts and disentangle the complex of linkages between elite-perceptions, policy formulation and misjudgement among the actors involved in this drama. The tension between the motivations driving security policy-making in the two rival regional protagonists on the one hand, and the focus of security concerns of their patron-power on the other, led to very different approaches they took in responding to their security needs. Pakistan made all that it could by flaunting its treaty relations with the US while India not only kept its alliance-building efforts a secret, but took up a declaratory stance castigating such efforts in vitreolic rhetoric until the desperation of defeat forced Delhi to execute a *volte face* in late 1962. The account necessarily has several sometimes parallel, often discrete, but always interconnected, strands. It is as though history evolved in a vertical and circuitous concertina of events.

At the top was the US-led campaign to 'contain' Communism; this layer of the 'event-concertina' saw alliance-building efforts by the superpowers, primarily the US, in South Asia. The next layer involved the efforts by the client states, India and Pakistan, to exploit the advantages of their relationship with their patron-power, often designed to deter or counter perceived threats from each other rather than from the supposed Communist adversary. Continuous jockeying by all the actors, as each pursued its own objectives, rendered the region's security environment very fluid. This fluidity itself contributed to the unpredictability marking South Asian diplomacy and conflict-management. Both of these layers were connected to the Chinese Communist efforts to secure control over Tibet and to the Tibetan resistance to Beijing's military occupation.

Both India and Pakistan collaborated with the US in the latter's relatively modest aid to the Tibetan resistance. Pakistan eventually ceased such activities when it found building up a strategic relationship with Beijing better suited its purposes; India, on the other hand, began its own covert operations against Beijing's authority on the plateau. By the 1960s, covert coercion had become an essential tool in the diplomatic/security repertory of both. The development of this secret policy by Delhi with US support encouraged the Tibetan resistance without providing it with the wherewithal to defeat the Chinese.

As a bleeding sore, this operation raised the cost for Beijing to maintain its hold on Tibet without imposing excessive penalties on India. But it violated both the letter and the spirit of the Sino-Indian treaty of 1954, and when Delhi's operations threatened Beijing's control over the plateau in the early 1960s, the Chinese leadership responded with overwhelming conventional force, a response which appears to have taken the Indian political, intelligence, and military leadership by surprise. On another level of misunderstanding, the US's failure to discern or identify the elemental difference dividing its South Asian clients meant Washington's efforts to forge a subcontinental bulwark against what the American authorities saw as 'the Communist threat' were never very effective. And, in fact, by aborting the one visible attempt by both India and Pakistan to resolve the Kashmir dispute by peaceful and democratic means, American Containment policies deepened regional cleavages, giving them a permanence beyond the means of the local players to overcome it. This was then the legacy of the early years of the Cold War's Asian variety for the South Asian subcontinent.

# CHAPTER 1

# The Early Treaties

The closing stages of the Second World War in the Asian theatre saw a rapid rise in the deployment of US forces in South and South-East Asia. The primary objectives of these deployments were to reinforce British forces in the campaign against Japan, and to strengthen the hands of Generalissimo Chiang Kai-shek's KMT administration in Chongqing which was fighting both the Japanese regular forces and the Communist Red Army under Mao Tse-tung. Having to provide operational support to two major campaigns demanded a substantial buildup of combat and logistic capability. The Indian heartland became a principal staging area for significant US operations in the Asian theatre. As the threat from Japan receded, the growing strength of Mao's revolutionary armies became the focus of US strategic concern. India's location lent it a geo-strategic significance that was not lost on Washington. As the British began to wrestle with the consequences of the depletion of reserves brought on by the war, and the increasingly difficult demands generated by imperial overstretch, the US administration prepared itself for dealing with the likely successors so as to maintain its strategic interests in the region after the departure of the colonial power. The subcontinent itself was not of key significance to US interests, but it could play an important role in Washington's post-war power-political activities. The ability to project air power across Asia was an essential component of the capacities of what the US called its 'National Military Establishment', and it was in this area that Washington first sought Pandit Jawaharlal Nehru's assistance, shortly before he became Prime Minister of independent India.

There were several good reasons why Washington could expect a friendly response to its overtures. Perhaps the most effective one was the one least acknowledged. For much of the duration of the wartime alliance between the US and Britain, Washington had urged London to give serious consideration to the demands being made by the Indian nationalists for the grant of autonomy if not outright independence. Churchill was reluctant to preside over the dissolution of the empire, and Washington would not push him too hard while the war demanded synergy, but once the war ended and

Churchill was out of office, the calculations changed. The Indian Congress leadership was aware of the gentle persuasive pressures Washington had brought to bear on London during the war, and was happy to deal with the emergent centre of global power in the post-war world. As Mountbatten began to draw imperium to a close, negotiations began between the American ambassador in Delhi and the principal architect of Indian foreign and security policy in the period just preceding the Partition, ie, Nehru. Initially, the US pursued the modest objective of retaining its rights to use India's airspace and ground facilities for continued combat operations by its military aviation after India became independent. The agreement the US ambassador, Henry F Grady, was instructed to reach with Pandit Nehru would ensure that US armed forces and security services could continue to operate with the wartime freedom which they had enjoyed under imperial dispensation. Exchanges between Henry Grady and Pandit Nehru took place in the spring of 1947 as the colonial authorities wrapped up their operations. The first agreement on security co-operation between the United States and India was reached in early July, nearly six weeks before India became independent.[1]

Fairly detailed negotiations in the spring and early summer of 1947 culminated in a formal note on 1 July from Ambassador Grady to Pandit Nehru, 'the Indian Member[2] for External Affairs and Commonwealth Relations'. The ambassador asked that after its independence India continue to permit 'temporary' stationing of US service personnel on Indian soil for servicing US military aircraft, that facilities be made available at the airfields in Maripur [Karachi],[3] Agra, Barrackpore and/or Kharagpore, and that night-landing permits be granted at Palam until the latter became a civil-aviation aerodrome when another airfield would be designated for the purpose. The Americans offered normally to provide 48-hours notice for any such incoming flights; aircraft entering India from the west would land at Maripur and those from the east would land at either Barrackpore or Kharagpore. Agra would serve as the intermediate staging facility and in an emergency, US military aircraft would have the right to land at any Indian airfield. The Americans asked that in terms of services, maintenance, accommodation, messing and transportation facilities, their military personnel and aircraft be afforded the same treatment as afforded the personnel and aircraft of the Indian Air Force. Where Customs, health and passport issues were concerned, the US ambassador sought the same facilities and privileges for US aircrews and aircraft as those enjoyed by the personnel and aircraft of the Royal Air Force at the time. In his reply to Ambassador Grady on 5 July 1947, Pandit Nehru agreed to the terms proposed by the US envoy but demanded that the US pay for all POL (petroleum, oil and lubricants), maintenance, servicing, spares and repairs carried out by Indian staff, and that the accounts of these transactions be maintained by the US Air Attache posted at the US Embassy in Delhi.[4]

The amendments proposed by Pandit Nehru were accepted by Ambassador Grady and the former's response on 5 July, which contained a verbatim copy of Grady's note dated 1 July, made up the substance of the treaty which became immediately effective until 24 October 1947. It was thereafter to be extended for two years in the first instance. Either side was empowered to give six months notice prior to termination. This first agreement on security co-operation between the US and India met Washington's strategic needs of being able to maintain the airbridges connecting the KMT's forces in China with supplies of *materiel* and logistical backstops. However, it also established a precedent for Delhi and Washington working closely together on sensitive matters and reaching an agreement which provided a framework for continued collaboration without public discussion or debate. The US authorities achieved this by identifying the moving spirit and the principal shaper of Indian foreign and security policy even before India's independence, and dealing with him directly. This pattern was to be maintained for much of the following decade in strengthening the covert collaboration between the two allies despite their differences over the degree of threat posed by the Chinese Communists to their respective national security interests.

The US Ambassador wrote to Nehru on 24 September 1947, seeking extension of the agreement for two years. By this time, however, Pandit Nehru was not only the Minister for External Affairs and Commonwealth Relations, he was also the Prime Minister of independent India. Post-Partition South Asia was a turbulent place as rioting mobs tore the cities asunder and rival republican establishments in Delhi and Karachi struggled to emerge from the ashes of a dying empire. Hundreds of thousands of civilians were being killed or maimed and millions sought shelter across what had overnight become international boundaries between two rival neighbouring states. The demise of the colonial authority left much of the region in a state of flux and often chaotic disorder reigned across large stretches for weeks before the new rulers established some form of control. Nehru was not able to concentrate on matters of diplomacy or of external security alliances for several months, although he ensured that the US military continued to enjoy the privileges granted in the original agreement. He replied to the US amabassdor on 22 April 1948.

In this note, Nehru pointed out that the Partition of Britain's South Asian empire and the creation of Pakistan, and independent India, had altered the regional scene which needed to be reflected in the text of the agreement. Flights landing in or departing from Karachi could no longer be discussed in an agreement between the US and India; also, for aircraft flying into India from the east, Nehru replaced Barrackpore and Kharagpore with Dum Dum near Calcutta. He also suggested that the US military authorities work with Pan-American Airways for logistic support at Dum Dum and Barrackpore where such facilities would not be available even for Indian forces. A more interesting point made by the Indian Prime Minister in this note was that his government had withdrawn the privilege granted in the original agreement to the US National Military Establishment to carry fare-paying passengers in US military aircraft into, across and out of India. The Indian leader wrote, 'It is considered that fare-paying passengers, if requiring international air transport, should be carried by civil airlines and not on State aircraft.'[5] On the face of it, Nehru's point was a legitimate and reasonable one. However, the only fare-paying passengers the US National Military Establishment carried on its aircraft were staff of the OSS[6] and other important agencies and departments of the US government engaged in sensitive security and intelligence-related duties and who for budgetary and audit purposes had to pay their way on Department of Defence aircraft. It seems unlikely that the Prime Minister of India was not aware of this. What can only be surmised from this particular comment in his note is that he was seeking to assert a degree of control over what Washington did on Indian territory and in Indian airspace.

That this was no minor matter became clear in the reply sent by the US *Charge' d'Affaires ad interim* who, following the end of Grady's tenure, headed the US embassy in Delhi until the arrival of a new ambassdor. The *Charge'* wrote on 3 May 1948 to acknowledge that the US Government found the points made by the Indian Prime Minister 'satisfactory'. However, he also wrote:

> *The United States Government agrees, as a matter of general principle, that fare-paying international passengers should be carried by civilian air services, where available, rather than state aircraft. Regulations of the United States National Military Establishment permit the carriage of passengers by United States Military aircraft under exceptional circumstances, and when such travel is deemed to be in the national interest. However, it is anticipated that any such traffic into or through India would be either nil or negligible. If desired by the Government of India, the Embassy will be pleased to discuss this matter further.*[7]

Nehru appears to have recognised that he had made his point and that the US had taken on board his concerns. He did not feel it either appropriate or necessary to push this line of argument any further, and the agreement was extended. Shortly after this, Loy W. Henderson was appointed the US Ambassador to India, and under his authority, US diplomats initiated secret talks with Indian officials early in the summer of 1949 to renew the agreement. The mutuality of security interests as perceived in both Washington and Delhi meant that by the end of June a basic framework had been agreed. On 2 July, Ambassador Henderson wrote to Prime Minister Nehru[8] formalising the stationing of US service personnel at 'specified airfields' 'on special occasions', and on a temporary basis, 'for the

11

purpose of servicing American military aircraft transiting India in groups or units'.[9] It became clear from that sentence that the US Army Air Forces (soon to become US Air Force) were undertaking significant operations which required the transit of groups and units of military aircraft across India. These operations, in support of Chiang Kai-shek's KMT forces facing Mao's Red Army onslaughts, had become so substantial that Henderson sought persmission to station four liaison officers in India 'for purposes of expediting flights of United States Military aircraft.'[10] The general principle was that US authorities would give 48-hours notice to the Indian Air Headquarters of all projected arrivals. However, military contingencies being what they were, Henderson noted that 'If in a special case it should be impossible or impracticable to give such notice, information regarding flight plans and other pertinent data should be furnished at the earliest possible moment'.[11]

Building on the provisions of the July 1947 agreement, this latest draft provided for US aircrew and military aircraft to be accorded the same treatment as that extended to the airmen and aircraft of the Indian Air Force. India would not charge any landing or housing fees and would provide radio, meteorological information and other flying aids free. Non-specialist servicing equipment would be provided on loan where such loans did not conflict with the needs of the Indian Air Force. Parking would be provided on aprons and refuelling facilities too would be made available. Washington undertook to install its own specialist equipment for carrying out major repairs to presumably combat-damaged aircraft and also to pay for all supplies of POL, spares and repair-work done by Indian personnel. Hanger-space would be provided by Indian authorities for repair and maintenance only in emergencies. American aircrews would be charged for accommodation and messing. Accounts would be maintained by the US Air Attache at the embassy in New Delhi, and US officers of appropriate rank would maintain contact with their Indian counterparts to ensure that the agreement was implemented without any difficulties on either side. The agreement only covered US military aircraft carrying proper insignias, and US service personnel in uniform. This was to allay Delhi's concern that Indian facilities might be utilised for covert operations by US intelligence services without Indian officials being able to monitor or control these. In addition, Washington offered reciprocal facilities to Indian military aircraft and aircrews on continental United States airbases. However, given that by the end of the World War the US had acquired a global military operational agenda, especially in and around China, and that the much more modestly organised Indian Air Force was restricted to operations in the subcontinent, that reciprocity was little more than a formality.

Underscoring the urgency which the situation in China was assuming for Washington, Henderson asked that the agreement become effective on 5 July 1949 for an indefinite period with each side able to terminate collaboration giving the other six months notice. This draft envisaged a significant enhancement of the extent and nature of military co-operation between the US and India. It must have led to considerable discussions at the highest levels of the Indian security establishment. In the end, Nehru and his colleagues in that establishment may have decided that working with Washington against the Chinese Communists might prove to be in India's long-term interest. With no public fanfare to mark this dramatic and defining shift in Indian foreign and security policy, on 4 July 1949, one day before the deadline proposed by Ambassador Henderson, India's Foreign Secretary,[12] K P S Menon, wrote to Henderson conveying the wishes of the Government of India to implement the proposed agreement from the following day. From 5 July 1949, Delhi thus became an ally of Washington in the latter's struggle against the Chinese Communists, and India was turned into a veritable strategic airbase for the US Air Forces operating in China. This relationship, and the consequent tensions it created between the two allies, were to inform much of the course of South Asia's security and diplomatic future over the next several decades. At this stage, the 'loss' of China to the Communists and the KMT's flight to Taiwan transformed the strategic scene in Asia and imposed new pressures on the US-Indian alliance.

In terms of declaratory politics, Nehru consistently stressed the need for what he called the Afro-Asian world, ie, post-colonial successor states such as India, to find a third option away from alliances with either power-bloc. These ideas were, in the decade following the independence of India, to become the building-blocks of the Non-Aligned Movement (NAM). Addressing gatherings at home and abroad, Nehru would highlight the nobility of neutrality in the growing disputation and adversarial interaction between the US-led Western coalition on the one hand, and the Soviet-led Communist grouping on the other. He proposed to maintain equidistance between the two antagonists and in addition, offered a hand of friendship to all. However, idealistic professions of peace and friendship notwithstanding, Nehru was more likely to have been a realist driven by the gaps between perceptions of India's national interest and its capacity to pursue those interests directly. His efforts to establish India as a major actor on the global stage may have been thwarted by the recognition of the lack of material wherewithal which was essential in a world shaped by the exercise of power by the principal actors. The fact that this was the period in which Washington was launching an activist policy to contain the spread of Communism threw up opportunities which Nehru would not pass up.

The US establishment, to be represented by the Dulles brothers[13] for almost a decade, sought to protect 'the free world' from Communist encroachment. To this end, they shaped Washington's overt diplomacy and covert operations in support of the former. The aim was to build up a network of alliances which could pool their political, economic and military resources in the joint endeavour against what in Washington was seen as monolithic Communist expansionism. In Asia, this exercise was aimed at protecting the KMT and destroying the Chinese Communist revolution without having to initiate a war if this proved possible. The Indian leader, on the other hand, sought the cushion of time to build India up to face a hostile world without having to rely on outsiders. Their interests appeared to converge in China, especially when the Chinese Communists threatened Tibet, which for the past forty years had effectively been a British-Indian protectorate and a buffer between the subcontinent and the Chinese giant. This convergence was sufficient for the forging of a secret alliance binding Washington and New Delhi, but not enough for the latter to acknowledge it. As long as the alliance worked, Washington respected Delhi's sensitivities, although not with any pleasure. Also, given the asymmetry in objectives and power-relationships, the alliance left differing imprints on the two partners and the tensions were as significant as the coherence with which collaboration was pursued. The impact of this secret alliance was fundamental enough to shape the region's strategic architecture and form its future history. And this work is an attempt at a clearer understanding of that history.

### Tibet: A Bone of Himalayan Contention

US-Indian military collaboration had found sharper focus as the Asian drama unfolded in the final phases of the Second World War. Notwithstanding the 1978 revelations by Morarji Desai, the covert alliance between the US and India had a long history which is better understood when events on the Tibetan plateau in the 1940s and 1950s are seen as links in the chain of regional evolution. Tibet had been converted into a virtual British-Indian protectorate by the Younghusband expedition sent into the plateau by Curzon and Kitchener in 1904. The Dalai Lama fled from Lhasa, but Col. Younghusband forced the remaining members of the Tibetan leadership to sign an agreement giving Britain major trading concessions on the plateau, in effect transferring suzerainty to Curzon's court in Calcutta. The British maintained that ultimate authority still vested in the Chinese empire, but this authority was subject to British and Tibetan agreement. It was this position which was formalised in the Shimla Convention in 1914 which the Chinese Plenipotentiary initialled but did not sign, and which the Chinese authorities have never accepted as anything other than an 'unequal treaty'. However, following the 1911 Republican revolution, China was in ferment and its central authorities had been unable to prevent the two Chinese *Ambans* and their military escorts in Lhasa from being deported from Tibet. Since then the theocratic establishment in Lhasa, with tacit and modest support from the British in India, enjoyed virtual independence.

This picture of relatively tranquil obscurity only changed in the 1940s. Shortly after the US entered the Second World War, it emerged as the principal Western power in Asia. Britain's preoccupations in Europe and North Africa had drained its ability to shape events in the east. It was in this context that the military picture on the Chinese mainland activated US concerns. The KMT's position in China had become precarious in the face of a Japanese pincer – with one prong bursting out of Manchuria, and the other slicing through South East Asia – on the one hand, and Communist moves on the other. How to help the KMT materially was the drive behind Washington's first move into Tibet. In 1942, following General 'Vinegar Joe' Stillwell's forces being put into serious difficulties by the Japanese in Burma, and the consequent closure of the Burma Road linking China with allied bases in India, the US felt it had to find alternative land routes for resupplying its own and allied KMT forces in China. Shortly afterwards, Capt Ilia Tolstoy and Lt Brooke Dolan of the OSS arrived in Lhasa via India bearing gifts and a letter for the infant Dalai Lama from President Roosevelt. They were there ostensibly to study the feasibility of supplying US-KMT forces from India overland via Tibet.[14] Washington had arranged their trip with the authorities in Delhi without London or Chongqing being informed, and the British were concerned about possible US encroachment[15] on what had been a British sphere of influence since 1904. But apparently, there was little London could do. The two OSS officers spent a month at Gyantse conferring with British personnel stationed there. They then spent the next three months in Lhasa exchanging views with Tibetan nobles and British officials.

Formally, Washington accepted the British view that China exercised suzerainty over Tibet. After all, the acknowledged authority on the mainland at this time was in the hands of the friendly KMT. However, the OSS was prepared to pursue an independent line and when Tibetan officials asked Tolstoy for long-range radio transmitters and electricity-generators 'for broadcasting within Tibet', the OSS prevailed over the Department of State which argued that the KMT ought to be asked first. In the end, the OSS delivered the equipment to Lhasa in November 1943 without the KMT's views being solicited. As it happened, petrol-fired generators proved unsuited to the rarefied Tibetan air, and it was not until December 1946 that OSS officers presented diesel-powered ones to Tibetan envoys at Kalimpong in North-Eastern India.[16] OSS Director 'Wild Bill' Donovan defended his decision by claiming the equipment would only cost $4,500 but 'would open all Tibet regions 1,200 miles east and west for Allied influence and further modernisation of territory which (would) be strategically valuable in the future.'[17] These and subsequent events established the OSS, and then the CIA, as the principal instrument of US policy towards Tibet, suggesting that Washington sympathised with the Tibetan claims to independence, and made North-Eastern India, especially Kalimpong, the base of covert activities by the US-Indian alliance on the plateau.

However, the Department of State did not share the OSS's enthusiasm regarding Tibet. It was not moved even by the plea made by its own *Charge' d'Affaires* in Delhi, George R. Merrell. In January 1947, Merrell asked Washington for deeper involvement in Tibetan affairs in the US's long-term, strategic, interests in eastern Asia. He wrote, 'Tibet is in a position of inestimable strategic importance both ideologically and geographically.'[18] Merrell claimed that should hostile governments come to power in India, China, Burma or Indochina, in the face of possible anarchy in East Asia, Tibet offered 'a bulwark against the spread of Communism throughout Asia, an island of conservatism in a sea of political turmoil.'[19] The *Charge's* analysis was delivered in a long cable to Washington. In conclusion, he observed that 'in an age of rocket warfare (Tibet) might prove to be the most important territory in all Asia.'[20] This view did not find any resonance in the Department of State although a decision was taken to maintain communications with Lhasa. The US saw the KMT's struggle to retain control over the Chinese mainland in the face of rising Communist pressures a far more significant source of concern, and Tibet's efforts to establish itself as a truly independent state in the post-War world became marginalised against the backdrop of that bigger drama.[21]

Shortly after taking control in Beijing in October 1949, the People's Republic of China (PRC) authorities announced plans to 'liberate' Tibet, Formosa (Taiwan) and Hainan. On 31 January 1950, responding to this threat, Tibetan leaders in Lhasa used the OSS-supplied radio transmitters to broadcast an appeal for help against any Communist invasion.[22] Despite its earlier reluctance to get involved in Tibet, Washington now relented. What changed the administration's stance may not have anything to do with Tibet itself. The 'loss of China' to Mao Ze-dong and his Red Army had hardened Washington's position. In April 1950, the US National Security Council formulated and adopted NSC-68, a policy-paper designed not just to prevent further Communist expansion, but to transform the domestic dynamics of communist states so that they no longer posed a threat to the 'free world'.[23] Fears of a co-ordinated global assault by the Communists were reinforced in June when North Korean forces moved across the 38th Parallel to invade the South. That, a vocal China lobby in the US Congress which accused the administration of 'abandoning' China, and a genuine concern that unless threats were addressed early on, the situation could dramatically deteriorate, contributed to the creation of the context in which a vigorously anti-Communist worldview became the core of an activist US policy. Tibet became a cog in that very much larger wheel of global confrontation. In June 1950, around the time of the North Korean invasion of the South, US officials in Delhi met Tibetan representatives who hinted they might make a formal request for arms. The response they received was generally friendly.

However, the Chinese forces proved too quick in their westward march into Tibet for external assistance to make any impact. The PLA crossed the

Drichu into the mountainous Kham province, home to the redoubtable Khampa highlanders, on 7 October 1950 and proceeded to take control of the eastern stretches of what had traditionally been considered territory under Lhasa's control. According to Chinese claims, altogether, 21 large and small-scale engagements were fought, 'a total of 5,738 enemy troops had been liquidated' and 180 Chinese troops were killed or wounded.[24] In Beijing, Mao's deputy and Chinese Premier Zhou En-lai told Radio Beijing's listeners 'The PLA is determined to march westward to liberate the Tibetan people and defend the frontiers of China. We are willing to undertake peaceful negotiations to bring about this step which is necessary for the security of our motherland. The patriots in Tibet have welcomed this and we hope that the local authorities in Tibet will not hesitate to bring about a peaceful solution to this question.'[25] By early December the magnitude of the PLA's victory in the east became clear to Lhasa, and on 16 December, the Dalai Lama's advisers escorted the young god-king south to Yatung or Dromo, close to the Indian border, to await an uncertain future. There he was persuaded to despatch two delegations to China to try to negotiate a peace treaty with the Communists so that violence could end and the devastating effects on Tibet of China's overwhelming military superiority was at least partly mitigated.

## South Asia on the Containment Bandwagon

The US administration was determined to avoid getting involved in a military conflict which could burgeon into another World War, but it was equally determined to deter the Communist powers from reaching a position of apparent invincibility. Efforts were made to shore up existing alliances and develop new ones. In the subcontinent, this effort initially received a mixed response. Nehru was keen to avoid having his country marked as an American stooge so soon after discarding its colonial shackles. An open alliance with the US would contradict his frequent commentary on the nobility of non-alignment and given the strength of leftist tendencies in many parts of India, could weaken his domestic authority. Pakistan, on the other hand, suffered from grave insecurities, especially following its failure to wrest the disputed state of Jammu & Kashmir, in a war that had been brought to an end via UN mediation encouraged by Washington. It is not clear that the Pakistani leadership feared any Marxist threat to its existence; nonetheless, Karachi accepted Washington's overtures and asked for military assistance from the US shortly after the outbreak of the Korean War. This coincided with the opening rounds of the PLA's war against Tibetan forces in Kham and Amdo.

Negotiations between Washington and Karachi took up most of the autumn of 1950. In November, the Pakistani ambassador to the US, M A H

Ispahani, was instructed by his superiors to formally seek American military assistance so as to raise the level of Pakistan's defensive capability in the face of an apparently growing Communist threat. The ambassador received a reply from Assistant Secretary of State George C. McGhee on 29 November. McGhee asked for *pro forma* assurances before completing the transfer of military hardware[26] under the Mutual Defence Assistance Act of 1949. The US sought assurances that the military *materiel* would be used 'to foster international peace and security within the framework of the Charter of the United Nations through measures which will further the ability of nations dedicated to the principles and purposes of the Charter to participate effectively in arrangements for individual and collective self-defence in support of those purposes and principles'[27] Pakistan could employ this assistance to ensure 'its internal security, its legitimate self-defence or permit it to participate in the defence of the area of which it is a part.'[28] At the same time, Pakistan was also asked to assure its prospective patron-state that the former 'will not undertake any act of aggression against any other state.'[29] McGhee's letter made it clear that Washington reserved all rights to the equipment, services, supplies and information transferred under the proposed agreement and should it find Pakistan in breach of these understandings, the agreement would be annulled. Pakistan was asked to give prior assent to future terms and conditionalities relating to the transactions to be subsequently announced by the US. An affirmative reply from the Government of Pakistan would, together with this letter, constitute an agreement between the US and Pakistan. In short, if Pakistan agreed, it would become a client-state of the US.

The authorities in Karachi took two weeks to consider the ramifications of this offer. On 15 December, the Pakistani Ambassador replied to George McGhee, simply saying that the assurances 'required by the Government of the United States . . . are agreed to by my Government. The Government of Pakistan is prepared to accept terms and conditions of payment for the items transferred, to be agreed upon between the Government of Pakistan and the Government of the United States . . .'[30] A modest supply of military *materiel* soon began reaching the Karachi port aboard US vessels. The number of US military personnel stationed in Pakistan on the staff of the US embassy in Karachi rose significantly. They were to advise the Pakistani military leadership in the integration of the new equipment into the Pakistani order of battle and begin the process of transforming the army into the principal conduit as well as the main beneficiary of US assistance to the country. This process would help develop the Pakistani armed forces, especially the army, into the most effective institutional body in Pakistan, thereby imposing structural direction upon the development of this new country's polity. But the consequences of that imposition were neither intended nor foreseen at the time by either party. For the moment, Washington was pleased to have found a new ally in its struggle to build up a bulwark south of the Communist-controlled landmass in the Eurasian heartland. For its part, Karachi was happy to have established a military-political linkage with the world's greatest power at a time when Pakistan's own future was less than certain. Although the agreement was designed to bolster defences against Communist expansionism, for the Pakistani leadership, the accord had a more fundamental purpose nearer to home. This asymmetry in purpose and interests would threaten US-Pakistani convergence in future.

Despite its success in corralling Pakistan into the alliance-building exercise, Washington still saw India as the great prize in the post-colonial world. The agreement allowing US combat aircraft operating in China to be repaired, serviced and maintained in Indian airbases was running out and given the pressures indicated by the Korean War on the one hand, and the PLA's march into Tibet on the other, Washington felt an urgent need to engage Delhi in a much closer military-security alliance than Nehru was apparently prepared to accept. However, a pragmatic politician of the realist school, the Indian leader saw the danger to India's security posed by Chinese Communist expansion and moved to prepare his domestic constituency for taking unpopular and yet what he considered necessary steps to protect India's strategic interests. The pressures built on all sides around the 7th of October 1950 when US forces crossed the 38th Parallel and the PLA crossed the Drichu river into eastern Tibet. For Nehru the challenge was to strike a balance between the upsurge of anti-imperialist and anti-colonialist sentiments brought to the fore by a successful struggle against the British on the one hand and the need to develop medium-to-long-term security arrangements on the other which would protect India from diverse threats in a hostile environment until India was capable of protecting itself. The Chinese Communists were seen by many Indians as the liberators of a tormented land and people not unlike their own. Also, the danger of subversion and sabotage by large pockets of Indian communist organisations strewn across the country had to be taken into account. Pragmatic realism notwithstanding, Nehru's administration walked a tightrope both at home and abroad.

One aspect of Delhi's China policy was to try to maintain cordial relations with Beijing. Supporting the PRC Government's claim to the Chinese seat in the United Nations, Nehru cultivated warm relations with the Communist leadership, often serving as an intermediary between Beijing and the outside world. But the difficulties of this posture were underscored by China's Tibet policy. Inheriting its imperial legacy of considerable influence with the Tibetan regency, Delhi treated Tibet as a buffer between India and China. Delhi's mission in Lhasa and trading posts at Gyantse and Yatung enjoyed extra-territorial privileges as did the dozen-plus Indian guest-houses in Tibet. Small Indian garrisons guarded these facilities, operating Tibet's only telecommunications network. In effect,

India was the 'regional big power' in Tibet until Beijing's assertion of control. That Nehru was concerned by the Communists' success in China became clear in his address to Indian army officers in Sri Nagar shortly after the KMT's flight from the mainland. He said, 'The Chinese revolution has upset the balance of power and the centre of gravity has shifted from Europe to Asia, thereby directly affecting India.'[31] The Indian leader may have overemphasised the consequences of Mao's assumption of authority in Beijing, but Delhi was clearly troubled by the emergence north of the Himalayas a potential great power with an uncertain agenda which threatened India's hitherto peaceful northern frontiers. As PLA forces defeated the Tibetan military detachment and local militias in Tibet's eastern provinces, messages exchanged by Delhi and Beijing took on an increasingly caustic tone. India sent two stern protest notes on 21 October and 28 October.[32] One of these said:

> *Now that the invasion of Tibet has been ordered by the Chinese government, peaceful negotiations can hardly be synchronised with it and there naturally will be fear on the part of Tibetans that negotiations will be under duress. In the present context of world events the invasion by Chinese troops of Tibet cannot but be regarded as deplorable and in the considered judgment of the Government of India not in the interest of China or of peace. . . . India can only express its deep regrets that inspite of the friendly and disinterested advice repeatedly tendered by it, the Chinese Government should have decided to seek a solution of the problems of its relations with Tibet by force instead of by the slower and more enduring method of peaceful approach.[33]*

Nehru also hinted that India's support for Beijing's claim to represent China at the UN Security Council could no longer be assured. China's response, equally curt, rejected Delhi's right to offer advice. It also challenged the legitimacy of the Indian mission in Lhasa and of the Indian trading agencies at Yatung and Gyantse and their military escorts. Beijing described them as a violation of Chinese sovereignty.[34]

> *The Central People's Government of the People's Republic of China would like to make it clear that Tibet is an integral part of Chinese territory and the problem of Tibet is entirely a domestic problem of China. The Chinese People's Liberation Army must enter Tibet to liberate the Tibetan people and defend the frontiers of China. This is the resolved policy of the Central People's Government.[35]*

Beijing did not say what it was liberating the Tibetan people from, but it rejected any linkage between its occupation of the plateau and its 'participation in the United Nations'. The Chinese also accused Delhi of allowing foreign anti-communist forces to shape India's foreign policy:

20

*No foreign interference shall be tolerated [in Tibet] . . . With regard to the viewpoint of the Government of India on what it regards as deplorable, the Central People's Republic of China cannot but consider it as having been affected by foreign influences hostile to China in Tibet, and hence expresses its deep regret.*[36]

There is no evidence to suggest that India was already involved in anti-Chinese covert operations in Tibet at this stage. US combat air missions in support of the KMT flown with substantial logistical support in India had largely come to an end with the eviction of the KMT from the Chinese mainland. But the material infrastructure and the juridical basis of US-Indian collaboration were still in place. India may not have been directly involved in such covert operations, but its north-eastern territory was being used by US operatives to send out large caravans of mules carrying World War II 'surplus' ordnance via Sikkim over the Nathu La pass into Tibet, presumably for Khampa and Amdoa resistance groups. These deliveries appear to have begun in June 1950 when the Tibetan delegation met US diplomats in Delhi, a month after China's probing attack at Dengko in eastern Tibet, but four months before the PLA's main invasion.[37] Indian control over the north-eastern submontane region remained patchy until late in 1950, but US covert activities in the region are unlikely to have been possible without Delhi's connivance or, at least, acquiescence. Nehru admitted that China's fears of Anglo-American 'intrigues in Tibet' intended to bring the latter 'into the anti-Communist bloc' were very real. Nonetheless, he considered these unjustified and claimed he had tried to allay such concerns, 'but I don't know with what success.'[38] In fact, Nehru's senior colleague, Deputy Prime Minister Sardar Ballavbhai Patel believed Nehru had failed to persuade China's Communist leaders that India was a benign and friendly neighbour. Challenging the management of India's China policy, Patel also pointed out to India's Minister for External Affairs that the Tibetans had elected to accept Delhi's guidance in foreign policy matters while India failed to protect or help its protege when help was most needed. In a very critical note to Nehru early in December 1950, Patel wrote:

*. . . I have carefully gone through the correspondence between the External Affairs Ministry and our Ambassador (K. M. Pannikar) in Peking and through him the Chinese Government. I have tried to peruse this correspondence as favourably as posible, but I regret to say that neither of them comes out well as a result of this study.*

*The Chinese Government have tried to delude us by professions of peaceful intentions. My own feeling is that at a crucial period they managed to instil into our Ambassador a false sense of confidence in their so-called desire to settle the Tibetan problem by peaceful means.*

> *There can be no doubt that, during the period covered by this correspondence, the Chinese must have been concentrating for an onslaught on Tibet. The final action of the Chinese, in my judgement, is little short of perfidy.*
>
> *The tragedy of it is that the Tibetans put faith in us; they chose to be guided by us; and we have been unable to get them out of the meshes of Chinese diplomacy or Chinese malevolence . . . .*
>
> *Our Ambassador has been at great pains to find an explanation or justification for Chinese policy and actions. As the External Affairs Ministry remarked in one of their telegrams, there was a lack of firmness and unnecessary apology in one or two of our representations that he made to the Chinese Government on our behalf. It is impossible to imagine any sensible person believing in the so-called threat to China from Anglo-American machinations in Tibet. Therefore, if the Chinese put faith in this they must have distrusted us so completely as to have taken us as tools or stooges of Anglo-American diplomacy or strategy. This feeling, if genuinely entertained by the Chinese in spite of your direct approaches to them, indicates that, even though we regard ourselves as the friends of China, the Chinese do not regard us as their friends . . . China is no longer divided or weak. The [Tibetan] border is no longer safe . . . The undefined state of the frontier and the existence on our side of a population with its affinities to Tibetans or Chinese have all the elements of potential trouble between China and ourselves.*[39]

On this point the Prime Minister fully agreed with his deputy. He ordered immediate steps to secure the Indo-Tibetan borders. However, this was more easily said than done. It was discovered that in the remote, sparsely populated mountainous North-Eastern Frontier Agency (NEFA), executive as well as moral, authority was being exercised by Tibetan Lamas. To obviate possible Chinese claims to sovereignty south of the Himalayas, Delhi rushed Indian civil servants to establish some measure of administrative control. A high level North and North-Eastern Border Defence Committee was established with senior officials from intelligence and security agencies and from the armed forces as well as from the ministries of Defence and External Affairs. It was asked to study major security problems threatening the region following China's move into the trans-Himalayan highlands and report back in 1951. The Indian Intelligence Bureau, aware of intense 'international espionage and subversive activities of the Communists and other foreign agents' in the region, opened its own offices at Kalimpong, Darjeeling and Gangtok.[40] This was the beginning of Delhi's activist policy aimed at neutralising the possibly adverse consequences for Indian security of the Chinese occupation of Tibet.

In fact, India was unable to act directly against China. Shortly after the PLA's march into Tibet, a high-level meeting was convened to consider Delhi's options and advise the Prime Minister. The meeting was attended by the Foreign Secretary, Chief of Army Staff General Cariappa, Indian ambassador to Beijing K. M. Pannikar and the Director of the Intelligence Bureau. All the participants other than the Chief of the Army Staff were in favour of an immediate military operation against the PLA. Cariappa said given the current operational needs in Jammu & Kashmir and elsewhere, the army would only be able to deploy one infantry battalion in addition to the company stationed at Gyantse to Tibet if it were ordered to move. After further discussions, Cariappa offered to deploy two battalions but no more.[41] A military option was clearly out of the question for the moment. It appears that in recognition of its military weaknesses vis-a-vis Beijing, Delhi opted to adopt the twin-track policy of bluster on the one hand and covert operations on the other. Talking of 'legitimate Tibetan autonomy within the framework of Chinese suzerainty', India refuted China's suggestion of foreign influences in Delhi's policy-making processes, at the same time darkly hinting at potential costs to China if it continued its military activities on the Tibetan plateau.

> *The Government of India has read with amazement the statement . . . that the Government of India's representation to it [China] was affected by foreign influences hostile to China and categorically repudiates it. At no time has any foreign influence been brought to bear upon India in regard to Tibet . . . There is no justification whatever for any military operations against [Tibet]. Such a step involving an attempt to impose a decision by force could not possibly be reconciled with a peaceful settlement . . . Every step that the Government of India has taken in recent months has been to check the drift to war all over the world . . . It cannot help thinking that the military operations by the Chinese Government against Tibet have greatly added to the tensions of the world and to the drift towards general war which it is sure the Government of China also wishes to avoid.[42]*

Delhi assured Beijing it had no political or territorial ambitions in Tibet, claiming the Indian presence on the plateau to be mutually beneficial, and one that did not challenge China's suzerainty. India also informed China that it would not change the status of its diplomatic, commercial and military missions in Tibet. With both sides standing firm, the question of face took on increasing significance. As the PLA poured in more men and *materiel* onto the plateau and India refused to either withdraw its missions or alter their extra-territorial status, relations plunged. India now embarked on a difficult mission to pry Beijing's grip on Tibet loose without any visible action. Once it was clear that Delhi had no military options to counter the increasingly vocal assertions of the Chinese Communist authorities in Beijing, Nehru appears to have been persuaded that India had no alternative to deepening, and formalising, its security links to the US. He asked his sister Vijaya Lakshmi Pandit, at the time the Indian ambassador in Washington, to begin secret negotiations with the US government aimed at covert collaboration against the Chinese in Tibet in particular, and a wider security relationship between India and the US in general. The Indian leader obliquely noted this shift in a speech in the *Loksabha* during a two-day debate on India's Tibet policy in December 1950.

> *In matters of foreign policy especially, one has to decide almost every hour what has to be done. We had this debate in the House because new situations have arisen and new dangers threaten the world . . . Idealism alone will not do. What exactly is idealism? Surely it is not something so insubstantial as to elude one's grasp. Idealism is the realism of tomorrow.*[43]

Three months later, in March 1951, India and the US signed their first, secret, security agreement. As with Pakistan, the US's first major security treaty with India was in the form of a couple of notes exchanged between the Department of State and the Indian ambassador in Washington. On being instructed by Prime Minister Nehru, ambassador Vijaya Lakshmi Pandit had sought military assistance from Washington around the turn of the year. On 7th March 1951, Acting Secretary of State James E. Webb replied to her asking for statutory assurances that the military hardware, services and information to be transferred by Washington to Delhi would be used 'to foster international peace and security within the framework of the Charter of the United Nations through measures which will further the ability of nations dedicated to the principles and purposes of the Charter to participate effectively in arrangements for individual and collective self-defence in support of those purposes and principles; and, moreover, that the items to be provided by the Government of the United States of America are required by the Government of India to maintain its internal security, its legitimate self-defense or permit it to participate in the defense of the area of which it is a part, and that it will not undertake any act of aggression against any other state.'[44] As with Pakistan, here too the US required that 'the Government of India will obtain the consent of the Government of the United States of America prior to the transfer of title to or possession of any equipment, materials, information, or services furnished, will take appropriate measures to protect the security of any article, service, or information furnished, and agrees to the Government of the United States of America's retaining the privilege of diverting items of equipment or of not completing services undertaken if such action is dictated by considera-tion of United States national interest.'[45] Webb also asked Mrs Pandit to confirm that the Government of India would accept terms and conditions for payment to be subsequently stipulated by Washington. A confirmatory note to these effects would constitute a formal Mutual Defense Assistance Agreement.

Ambassador Pandit replied to the Secretary of State on 16th March. Her note referred to Webb's note of the 7th, which was repeated verbatim, and simply said 'The terms, conditions and assurances affecting such a transfer as quoted above have been carefully considered and I have the honour to inform you that the Government of India are in agreement with the terms, conditions and assurances proposed.'[46] This reply effectively sealed the agreement between India and the US, providing a legal foundation to their secret collaboration against China. Soon, large numbers of US military and intelligence personnel arrived in India to expand covert operations in Tibet with their Indian allies. The agreement, similar to the one signed a few months earlier with Pakistan, provided for the transfer of military hardware, shoring up India's communications and air-defence networks, and sharing intelligence. The strategic linkage it created between India's attempts to defend itself from perceived threats from the north, and Washington's efforts to erect a *cordon sanitaire* around the Communist bloc, was more significant. The treaty allowed the CIA to develop close links to India's security and intelligence establishment, train its senior staff and equip its field offices. The Indian Intelligence Bureau, thus reinforced, established a 'Tibetan Office' at Kalimpong to facilitate contact between the Tibetan resistance and world capitals.[47] The heart of the US-Indian joint venture against the Chinese occupation of Tibet, it provided a focus for the fashioning of a unified Tibetan guerrilla force, the National Voluntary Defence Army – NVDA – to engage the PLA in combat. It was also the point of contact for the brothers of the Dalai Lama – Thubten Norbu, also known as the Taktser Rinpoche, and Gyalo Thondup, who trekked across the Himalayas into India bearing messages for US, Indian and Taiwanese officials. Despite denials from Delhi, Karachi and Washington, the US and the two South Asian successor states now embarked on an elaborate operation to support the Tibetan resistance against the Chinese forces on the plateau. The tide of these exertions would rise and fall over the next two decades, but it was clear to the US that it had finally succeeded in establishing a patron-client relationship tying the whole of the subcontinent to Washington's Containment strategy.

# CHAPTER 2

# Histrionics in the High Himalayas

The Tibetan drama took a new turn shortly after Communist victory in Beijing. The Chinese radio made repeated proclamations of the intent to 'liberate' Tibet, Hainan, and Taiwan. Deeply concerned, the Tibetan Foreign Bureau in Lhasa wrote to Mao in late 1949:

> Tibet is a peculiar country where the Buddhist religion is widely flourishing and which is predestined to be ruled by the Living Buddha of Mercy, Chenresig (i.e., the Dalai Lama). As such, Tibet has from the earliest times up to now, been an independent Country whose political administration had never been taken over by any Foreign Country; and Tibet also defended her own territories from Foreign invasions and always remained a religious nation.
>
> In view of the fact that Chinghai and Sinkiang etc. are situated on the borders of Tibet, we would like to have an assurance that no Chinese troops would cross the Tibetan frontier from the Sino-Tibetan border, or any such Military action (sic). Therefore please issue strict orders to those Civil and Military Officers stationed on the Sino-Tibetan border in accordance with the above request, and kindly have an early reply so that we can be assured.
>
> As regards those Tibetan territories annexed as part of Chinese territories some years back, the Government of Tibet would desire to open negotiations after the settlement of the Chinese Civil War.[1]

Mao did not respond. Nor did the governments of Britain, India and the US who had been sent copies. Disheartened, Lhasa officials decided to seek Moscow's help. There even were plans to send a delegation to Hong Kong to open negotiations with the Chinese. This was when the US ambassador in Delhi was instructed to advise the Tibetans that Washington's reluctance to engage in active support did not indicate a lack of interest in Tibet or sympathy with the Tibetans. However, in the absence of any visible evidence of material support, the Lhasa leadership in December 1949 appointed Tsipon Shakabpa the leader of a delegation set up to negotiate with the Chinese. Shakabpa arrived in India soon afterwards with a view to travelling on to either Hong Kong or Singapore to meet and negotiate with Chinese representatives, but his delegation was not granted visas by the British authorities. Shakabpa was thus forced to spend almost a year holding secret talks with the Chinese Ambassador in Delhi instead. The US was not particularly enthusiastic about these attempts at Sino-Tibetan conciliation, but Washington did not feel able to intervene strongly. The outbreak of war in Korea on 23 June 1950 swung the Truman administration into a more activist posture than hitherto. In the months that followed, correspondence between the US embassy in Delhi and the Department of State in Washington became increasingly preoccupied with the question of how to respond to the growing threat of what was described as Chinese expansionism in Tibet on the one hand and Tibetan request for military assistance and diplomatic support on the other.[2] While US officials debated these issues among themselves, and occasionally with their Indian counterparts, the Chinese envoy to Delhi progressively toughened the demands which he made on Shakabpa's Tibetan delegation.

On 16 September 1950, Ambassador Yuan Zhongxian made a three-point proposal:

(i)   Tibet must be regarded as a part of China;
(ii)  China will be responsible for Tibet's defence;
(iii) All trade and international relations with foreign countries will be handled by the People's Republic of China.[3]

Shakabpa conveyed the Chinese demands to Lhasa but received no reply. On 7 October 1950, Gen. MacArthur's forces crossed the 38th Parallel into North Korean territory and Beijing declared its support for Pyongyang, deploying Chinese troops to the latter's defence. At about the same time, PLA Gen. Zhang Guohua's forces in the South-West Military Region of China, numbering about 40,000 men, crossed the Drichu river into eastern Kham. The Tibetan forces in the province, a combination of regulars and local militias, added up to about 8,000 all ranks. Fighting lasted two weeks during which the Tibetans lost about half of their men in action.[4] On 19 October, the PLA captured the provincial capital, Chamdo, along with the Governor, Kalon Ngabo Ngawang Jigme.

The outcome of this unequal encounter could not have been in doubt, but it caused a shock to the Tibetans themselves, to the Indians, and even the US. The timing of the PLA's advance was significant; its precision in matching the deployment of Chinese forces to the defence of North Korea is unlikely to have been coincidental. The occupation of Kham appears to have been a component of a strategic decision by Beijing to make a bold stand in defence of what in Communist Chinese eyes were significant national interests. However, at the time, there was a congruence in Tibetan and Chinese circles as to the immediate reason behind the attack. In an interview with the Reuters news agency in Calcutta, Shakabpa was reported to have said 'The Chinese forces had entered Tibet. This was because his delegation had been delayed in India due to visa difficulties'.[5]

The Chinese explanation, offered in the form of an editorial about a month after the fall of Chamdo, played on the same theme.

> *The British Government deliberately delayed issuing transit visas for Hong Kong to the Lhasa delegation, making it impossible for them to come to Peking. According to reports from various sources, when the Lhasa delegation were loitering in India, the British High Commissioner Nye and other foreign imperialist elements used every effort to persuade the delegation not to come to any agreement with the Chinese People's Government. Then on the 12th August, when the Indian Government saw that the operations of Chinese Government's forces to enter Tibet were about to begin, they informed the Chinese Government that the British Government had withdrawn its refusal to issue visas to the Tibetan delegation and that facilities for the departure of the delegation for Peking were available. But more than two months have passed and still 'the stairs have been created but no one has come down'. It is obvious that the delay of the Lhasa delegation in coming to Peking to carry on peaceful talks is the result of instigation and obstruction from foreign states who must bear the responsibility for obstructing and sabotaging the peaceful talks. It is only necessary for the local Tibetan authorities to strive to correct their former errors and abandon the erroneous position of relying on foreign influences to resist the entry of the People's Liberation Army and the Tibetan question can be settled peacefully.[6]*

Given the mutually exclusive positions of the Chinese government and the Lhasa authorities on the question of Tibet's sovereignty, it is not clear that 'peaceful talks' between the two sides would resolve the dispute preventing the application of force. Also, the advance of the US-led United Nations forces in Korea is likely to have made a major impact on the Chinese strategic calculations. However, British tardiness on the visa question did provide a useful pretext to Beijing which it sought fully to exploit. These pressures proved too much for the regency and Lhasa's elite-structure. The Tibetan National Assembly requested the Dalai Lama, still only a minor at fifteen, to take over nearly absolute religious and secular authority from the regent. The Dalai Lama was anxious to qualify in his major theological and theosophical tests before taking on formal responsibilities of state, but eventually he agreed. On 17 November 1950, the 14th Dalai Lama ascended the throne. The Chinese appear to have been only slightly impressed by these events. They made a full play of having the Governor of Chamdo, Kalon Ngabo, in their hands. Ngabo was asked to send emissaries to the *Kashag* (the Tibetan equivalent of the cabinet) with a list of demands from the PLA commanders. These demands, delivered on 7 December by two Tibetan envoys, contained eight points which were an elaboration of the demands made by the Chinese ambassador in Delhi a few months earlier. With a part of Tibet under PLA control, the Lhasa authorities felt they had to act.

The Tibetan National Assembly met on 12 December. It appears that two decisions were taken – the first was that it was unsafe for the Dalai Lama to stay in Lhasa and that he should take shelter elsewhere, although perhaps not outside Tibet; and the second was to begin negotiating with the Chinese, although there was no suggestion that Tibet's sovereignty could be compromised in the process. There is some indication that the *Mimang* (Tibetan National Assembly) advised the Dalai Lama to establish temporary headquarters at Dromo near the Indian borders.[7] Soon after this, the Dalai Lama appointed Lukhangwa Tsewang Rapten and Lobsang Tashi joint caretaker prime ministers. He also sent a couple of emissaries to Chamdo to assist Ngwang in his dealings with his Chinese interlocutors. They carried a five-point response to Ngabo's message. This the Chinese subsequently refuted. However, meanwhile, on the night of 16 December, in what was to become his first flight from Lhasa, the Dalai Lama left the capital incognito in the company of his immediate retinue. While the young god-king and his entourage made their way southwards across snowclad mountains, the Lhasa authorities despatched their first appeal to the Secretary General of the United Nations. But the UN was at this time absorbed in the violence on the Korean peninsula and efforts to come to grips with that conflict took precedence over everything else. A great deal depended on the US, but Washington appeared to be suffering from a dilemma that was difficult to understand from the Tibetan point of view. On the one hand, the US had repeatedly expressed its support to the Tibetans; and yet, when the question of substantive diplomatic or military assistance arose, it seemed unable to take any visible step to back up its own position. As the year drew to a close, the Department of State finally made its position on Tibet clear in a memorandum to the British government which, until now, had taken the lead in international diplomacy regarding events on the plateau. The US memo said:

> The United States, which was one of the early supporters of the principle of self-determination of peoples, believes that the Tibetan people has (sic) the same inherent right as any other to have the determining voice in its political destiny. It is believed further that, should developments warrant, consideration could be given to recognition of Tibet as an independent State. The Department of State would not at this time desire to formulate a definitive legal position to be taken by the United States Government relative to Tibet. It would appear adequate for present purposes to state that the United States Government recognizes the de facto autonomy that

*Tibet has exercised since the fall of the Manchu Dynasty, and particularly since the Simla Conference. It is believed that, should the Tibetan case be introduced into the United Nations, there would be an ample basis for international concern regarding Chinese Communist intentions toward Tibet, to justify under the United Nations Charter a hearing of Tibet's case in either the U.N. Security Council or the U.N. General Assembly.[8]*

The British may have appreciated Washington's point of view; however, Whitehall itself had been deferring to the ambiguous stance adopted vis-a-vis Tibet by Delhi, and when the Indian envoy to the UN, Sir Benegal N. Rau, pointed out that discussion of the Tibet issue would force Delhi to express criticism of China which, in turn, would in all probability adversely affect India's ability to mediate in the Korean conflict, neither the US nor Britain challenged the logic of that argument. Tibet's hope of its fate receiving global attention, and moral if not material support from major powers, faded.

## The 17-Point Agreement and its Fallout

Against this backdrop of virtually total helplessness, the Tibetans began taking greater interest in the possibility of negotiations. The PLA in Kham had, in the meanwhile, not only released Ngabo from imprisonment, but had appointed him Vice-Chairman of 'the Chamdo Liberation Committee'. This was a group of Chinese and Tibetan officials and army commanders brought together at Beijing's behest to advise Kham's Chinese administrators and prepare the province for eventual 'democratic reforms'. The Chamdo Liberation Committee was also to provide a model for similar committees set up elsewhere in Tibet subsequently in the wake of the PLA's westward march. In January 1951, Ngabo initiated a series of talks with the PLA commanders in Chamdo while the co-prime ministers in Lhasa sent Surkhang Dzasa and Chomphel Thubten to Delhi to exchange views with the Chinese ambassador there. The outcome of all these discussions was the Dalai Lama's decision in February 1951 to send a 15-man delegation to Beijing for negotiations with the Chinese. Ngabo, appointed leader of the delegation, was instructed to travel overland from Chamdo with several members of the team; the other group, led by Dzasa Khemey Sonam Wangdi, travelled via India and Hong Kong. The delegations met up in Beijing and talks began on 29 April. The Chinese were represented by Plenipotentiaries Li Weihan, General Zhang Jingwu, Zhang Guohua, and Sun Zhiyuan.[9] The Chinese presented the Tibetans with a draft treaty which declared that Tibet was an integral part of China and that the PLA had the right and the responsibility to 'defend' that part of the 'motherland' as much as it had any other. The Tibetan delegation rejected the draft and its subsequent versions for many days. Negotiations broke down several times as the mutual exclusivity of the two positions became apparent. Stalemate dragged on. In the end, the Chinese presented the Tibetans with a stark choice – either sign the treaty as drafted by Beijing's representatives or face the consequences of the resumption of the PLA's westward march. The Tibetans capitulated. The full text of the 'Agreement of the Central People's Government and the Local Government of Tibet on Measures for the Peaceful Liberation of Tibet', otherwise known as 'the 17-point agreement', was broadcast by Radio Beijing on 27 May and caused consternation in Dromo and Lhasa. The Preamble to the agreement proclaimed:

> *The Tibetan nationality is one of the nationalities with a long history within the boundaries of China, and like many other nationalities, it has done its glorious duty in the course of the creation of and development of the great Motherland. In order that the influences of aggressive imperialist forces in Tibet might be successfully eliminated, the unification of the territory and sovereignty of the CPR (Chinese People's Republic) accomplished, and national defense safeguarded; in order that the Tibetan nationality and people might be freed and return to the big family of the CPR to enjoy the same rights of national economic, cultural and educational work, the CPG (Central People's Government), when it ordered the People's Liberation Army (PLA) to march into Tibet, notified the local government of Tibet to send delegates to the central authorities to conduct talks for the conclusion of an agreement on measures for the peaceful liberation of Tibet. In the latter part of April 1951 the delegates with full powers of the local government of Tibet arrived in Peking. The CPG appointed representatives with full powers to conduct talks on a friendly basis with the delegates with full powers of the local government of Tibet. As a result of the talks both parties agreed to establish this agreement and ensure that it be carried into effect.*[10]

The 17 clauses following the Preamble authorized the entry into Tibet of Chinese forces and empowered the Beijing government to handle Tibet's defence and external affairs. China agreed not to alter Tibet's existing political system, and not to interfere with the powers and status of the Dalai Lama and the Panchen Lama. Tibet was to enjoy regional autonomy and the people's religious beliefs and customs were to be respected. Internal reforms were to be effected after consultation with leading Tibetans and there would be no compulsion. A committee including 'patriotic Tibetans' would be established to ensure that the agreement was implemented. In short, Tibet was juridically integrated into the Chinese 'motherland'. The Dalai Lama was subsequently said to have been shocked by the stipulations, but he wanted to wait for a briefing by the delegates before repudiating the 'agreement'. He was also advised to await

31

a visit by General Zhang Jingwu, who was leading a military contingent to Dromo enroute to Lhasa. Following the PLA general's arrival at Dromo, and his meeting with the Dalai Lama, the latter agreed to accept the Chinese assurances of peaceful intent and return to Lhasa, there to resume his office of state. The Tibetan leadership was now at least apparently reconciled to the reality of the Chinese military occupation and sought to soften the blow, as it were, on the Tibetan people and the plateau's political and socio-economic structure. Seen from the outside, Tibet was now integrated into the People's Republic of China. These events suggested to the makers of US security policy relating to Asia that traditional diplomacy might not be effective in securing US strategic interests in the region and a more activist stance with the help of India and Pakistan was, instead, the right posture to adopt against the Chinese in so far as Tibet was concerned.

In the early stages of the anti-Communist alliance between the US, India and Pakistan, Washington found it easier to operate bilaterally with each of its clients. There was no direct link, for instance, between the Intelligence Bureau of India and Pakistan's Military Intelligence Directorate although each of these organisations worked closely with the Pentagon's intelligence officers and the CIA's local operatives. Covert operations at this stage were preparatory and reactive to the extent that the partners, especially the IB and the CIA, were engaged in monitoring Chinese deployments on the southern reaches of the Tibetan plateau, providing the Khampa and Amdoa resistance with ordnance and medical supplies, and setting up an effective communications network linking Lhasa with Washington using the US consular facilities in Calcutta.[11] If the capital of India's West Bengal state was to play a crucial role in the development of secret diplomatic linkages between the Tibetan administration and its friends in the US, Dhaka, the capital of Pakistan's eastern wing, came to be the control centre of the CIA's covert operations intended to provide external assistance to the Tibetan resistance. The Tibetan administration was represented by the Minister, Tsipon Shakabpa, who, following the Chinese invasion, had stayed on in India; the young Dalai Lama himself was often represented in discussions with US and Indian officials by his elder brother Thubten Norbu. Both these men repeatedly met US diplomats and Indian intelligence staff in Kalimpong, Calcutta and Delhi. The framework of collaboration was a product of these confidential exchanges.

US policy appears to have developed two distinct strands from the very beginning: on the one hand, the Department of State pursued the formal line of circumspection and moderation; the CIA, on the other, translating policy into action, showed greater enthusiasm and vigour in supporting the resistance. Only when the two strands clashed did trouble begin. In 1951, there was no evidence of such conflict although documentation suggests an undercurrent of subtle divergences in terms of priorities and emphasis.

Using the secret channel to Lhasa, US officials in India sent a letter to the Dalai Lama early in May explaining what in Washington's views were 'clear dangers' of the PLA's occupation of Tibet for the Tibetan people, seeking a detailed exposition of what the Dalai Lama's, and his government's, views were with regard to the Chinese invasion and what he expected his well-wishers abroad to do. Lhasa did not reply.

At the beginning of June 1951, Secretary of State Dean Acheson replied to a note from the US mission in Delhi asking for advice on Shakabpa's plea for help made in the spring. Acheson said the US would be prepared to supply a limited quantity of light arms and ammunition but this would depend on the military situation on the plateau and the level of co-operation extended by the Indian government. His telegraph read, 'US unwilling commit itself to support any such undertaking from outside, but if resistance is maintained in Tibet from beginning the US would contribute in so far as attitude of Government of India makes it possible . . . US is sympathetic to Tibetan position and will assist in so far is practicable but can help only if Tibetans themselves make real effort and take firm stand.'[12] The US officials directly connected to the Tibetan operations were waiting for this green signal. They needed to know that should the Tibetans take a stand and fight the Chinese as indeed many Khampa and Amdoa groups were already doing in the mountains of eastern Tibet, Washington would stand by them. Thubten Norbu and Shakabpa met US diplomats on several occasions in June 1951. Not everything went according to plan, however. The first letter addressed to the Dalai Lama in May was either not received by him or was not replied to. The archives do not make clear what happened to the missive. At the beginning of July, the Americans sent out a second letter to the Dalai Lama, trying to persuade the god-king to leave his occupied land and lead the resistance from abroad.[13]

In the event, the Tibetan leader decided to stay on in Lhasa and try to work out a *modus vivendi* with the Chinese authorities, at the same time maintaining covert links with the US via CIA contacts operating through the Tibetan military/security high command. In so far as Acheson's condition that the Tibetan resistance take 'a firm stand' against the Chinese, Shakabpa and Thubten Norbu could point out that long before any US involvement on the plateau, Khampa highlanders from Gyalthang in south-eastern Tibet, subsequently annexed to the bordering province of Yunnan, had engaged the PLA in combat as early as in 1949, inflicting defeats until the Chinese were able to muster significantly superior forces to beat the Khampas and their Nakhi (Naxi) allies back. The highlanders on both sides of the Sino-Tibetan borders had traditionally opposed Han-Chinese domination, and the post-1949 Communist takeover was no exception.[14]

An even earlier conflict between Tibetans and the Han Chinese saw much of the latter 1940s bloody the townships and hamlets of Nangra and

Hormukha in the Amdo highlands in north-eastern Tibet. Here, the KMT had been represented by General Ma Pufang, a semi-independent Muslim warlord. General Ma fought the Red Army for several years with the help of Amdoa and Mongol tribesmen. When Communist victory seemed assured, General Ma fled with his wives and treasure on two US-built aircraft, and the PLA units advanced on Nangra and Hormukha. In December 1949, the two chiefs of the Nangra highlanders, Pon Wangchen and Pon Choje, led their militias into battle with the Red Army, several times their own strength in men and weaponry. Two months later, the citizens of Hormukha joined the Nangra bands. However, in the face of the PLA's overwhelmingly superior organisation and firepower, the Amdoa militias were nearly decimated. Having been dispersed in frontal combat, the residual elements of the resistance took to the mountains from where they mounted rather more successful hit-and-run raids and ambushes against the Chinese forces.[15] Amdoa resistance continued for several years until in 1952, a truce was arranged after mediation by lamas of the influential Dechen monastery. The truce lasted several months, but in 1953, the Chinese resumed the practices of 'denunciations, struggles, arrests and executions' on the Amdoa populace and fighting broke out afresh. However, the PLA had built up its strength significantly during the truce, and Amdoas were killed in their thousands, a 'peace of the graveyard' being imposed on the region in the mid-1950s. By then, resistance had picked up elsewhere in Tibet.

The Tibetan drama was made more complex than it already was because of a convergence in the interests of nationalist elements in Tibetan society and external powers such as India and the US. However, the picture on the plateau was already convoluted. For one thing, it would be difficult to employ a uniform sense of national identity to define 'nationalist' Tibetans. The people of Tibet were not united, except perhaps on questions of the sanctity and the inviolability of the person and the office of the Dalai Lama. But the once fraternal ties between the Dalai Lama and the Panchen Lama, and between their retainers in Lhasa and Shigatse, had already reached a breaking point. Tensions between the Lhasa sophisticates and the Khampa highlanders, for instance, were legendary. The Khampas, the Goloks and the Amdoas were themselves rarely united – concerned as they were primarily with the maintenance and enhancement of their rather narrowly defined tribal and clan-based honour and interests. The Chinese Communists sought to integrate Tibet and its population into the People's Republic, taking effective control over the region – Beijing's claim was that this 'integral part of the motherland' had been penetrated by 'aggressive imperialist forces', ie, Britain and the US. Beijing also wanted to 'liberate' the Tibetans, but its commentary never explicitly stated its aim of social transformation of a religio-feudal system. Different groups of Tibetans reacted differently to the Chinese operations, but over time, an overwhelming rejection of the ruthless social-engineering and brutal atheism imposed by the PLA on Tibet eventually united a large majority of Tibetans.

Khampa and Amdoa highlanders joined more urbane denizens of Lhasa and U-Tsang to spearhead a militant resistance to the Chinese occupation. The rejection of Han-Chinese domination became entwined with a rejection of Communist godlessness. The violent refusal to accept changes to the production and distribution structures went hand in hand with the resistance to Chinese threats to the Lamaist form of Buddhism and the place of monastic ritual and authority in it. The loss of property, threatened or actual, provided the backdrop of resentment which, when touched with the tinder of sudden shortages of essential goods in a largely barter-based subsistence system, led to an explosion of anger which found expression in a traditional outlet, violent militancy. Religion, politics, economy and culture combined to form a complex rationale behind the Tibetan reaction and resistance. This transformation of a disparate and informal refutation of Chinese attempts to secure and assert control in pockets of the Tibetan plateau into a well-organised and co-ordinated, albeit outgunned and outnumbered, challenge to the occupiers took place largely as a symbiosis between domestic reaction and external assistance. But because of an asymmetry in the perception of respective interests and objectives, this assistance was of secondary significance to both the benefactors and beneficiaries. It did play a catalytic role in strengthening certain elements in the resistance to the detriment of others, and thereby brought specific strands to the fore and shaped the anti-Chinese struggle in a particular fashion, but the external assistance worked because the resistance pre-existed it and was not its creation.

For the US, the Tibetan resistance was a part, albeit a useful one, of its overall security schema relating to the Containment policy vis-a-vis Communist China. The relative insignificance of the struggle bleeding both the Tibetans and the Chinese was hinted at in official reviews of policy by analysts in Washington. In this period, US officials considered the recently concluded Mutual Defence Assistance Agreements signed with Pakistan and India as crucial foundations of a strategic alliance-structure directed against Communist Chinese expansionism in the region. In that context, the Khampa and Amdoa guerrillas fighting the PLA in eastern Tibet were a peripheral factor. On 17 May 1951, National Security Council staff studying US objectives, policies and courses of action in Asia came up with a set of recommendations for the NSC. The section of the study dealing with 'Security and Stability of South Asia'[16] stated

*United States objectives with respect to South Asia are to improve the security position of the United States by contributing to the stability of the independent and non-Communist governments now in*

*authority, and by influencing these governments to provide active support for the United Nations campaign in Korea and for United States policies regarding Communist China. Furthermore, the United States should influence these governments in the direction of benevolent neutrality or active support of the non-Communist powers in the event of a global war.*[17]

To realise these objectives, the NSC study recommended a series of specific steps to be taken by the Administration. These highlighted Washington's interest in helping to develop a South Asian, regional, as opposed to national or bilateral, platform for addressing substantial security concerns. The NSC betrayed its belief that all Communist activism was masterminded and perhaps controlled by the Soviet Union, and this fundamental error in its premise threatened the ultimate effectiveness of US policy; but it would be decades before Washington would learn the truth about the absence of a Communist monolith on the world political stage. The study sought to take a holistic approach to security, considering economic development and political stability of the local, non-Communist, states, and their mutual co-operation as integral to Washington's long-term security interests. This approach to regional security issues may have been a function of the inheritance of the British imperial experience. As will be seen, Washington's regionalist angle did not strike a resonant chord in either Delhi or Karachi, but successive US governments consistently pursued the line established by the Truman administration. This NSC study was thus fundamental to the structure of US policymaking vis-a-vis the region which both explained what the US was trying to achieve and shaped the nature and content of Washington's support for the Tibetan resistance. The key recommendations[18] were:

a. Encourage more intimate consultation with South Asian Governments – particularly those of India and Pakistan,
b. Support participation of South Asian countries in United Nations organisations,
c. Adopt a sympathetic attitude toward any developments which might lead to the formation of a regional association of non-Communist countries in South Asia,
d. Expand information and educational exchange programs,
e. Continue to encourage creation of an atmosphere favourable to economic development and expansion of trade consistent with United States security interests,
f. Provide such economic assistance as will contribute to the stability of the area, strengthen the Western orientation of the region, and facilitate transfer to the United States of materials related to national security,
g. Provide so far as practicable within the framework of other demands related to national security, military supplies, equipment, and services

required for internal security, self-defence, or participation in defence of the area,

h. Depending on the political atmosphere and global military developments, seek to obtain such military rights in South Asia as the United States may determine to be essential,

i. Take all possible action consistent with United States security interests to prevent the USSR or its satellites from obtaining from South Asia strategic materials currently being denied to the Soviet Bloc by the United States,

j. Continue efforts to improve Indo-Pakistani and Afghan-Pakistani relations.

This remarkable combination of honest assertion of national self-interest and a measure of benign innocence was to provide the *raison d'etre* of Washington's security policy vis-a-vis the region for the next two decades. The study formalised the framework in which the US-Pakistan and US-Indian Mutual Defence Assistance Agreements of 1950 and 1951 respectively made sense. But the evidence often raises more questions about the nature of Indo-US relationship than they answer. One intriguing incident occurred at the end of May 1951 when Counsellor Steer from the US embassy in Delhi met the Indian Foreign Secretary, G S Bajpai, and asked him for the Indian Government's reaction to Beijing's announcement of the 17-Point Agreement. Bajpai told him, 'It was inevitable that the present Chinese Government should gain control of Tibet, and there was nothing that the Government of India could do about it.'[19]

This comment suggests that either Bajpai was not aware of the March 1951 Indo-US agreement or felt that Steer did not know about it and did not wish to let on. Had both men known about the agreement and known that the other knew, they would in all likelihood discuss the possibilities of collaboration against the Chinese in Tibet on the basis of that secret agreement. Since they did not, the probability that both countries engaged a 'back channel' to conduct the more sensitive aspects of security co-operation takes on significance. On one level, then, the official Indian position was that the Chinese occupation of Tibet was the reality and Delhi was pretty much reconciled to it; documentaion shows that on another, India and the US were working to develop a structure of resistance linking the Dalai Lama and his entourage with points of militancy spread across the plateau. This became clear towards the end of 1951 when, following the Tibetan National Assembly's recommendation to the Dalai Lama to ratify the 17-Point Agreement, the CIA organised the flight of Taktser Rinpoche, the Dalai Lama's elder brother, from India to the US, ostensibly for higher education. Taktser had met US officials, possibly for the first time, in Delhi, in July 1951. In mid-February 1952, he was taken to Washington to meet officials from the Department of State, the Special Operations Executive and other federal departments at a gathering chaired by Assistant Secretary of State John Allison. Taktser said he had received an unsigned letter from the Dalai Lama in which Tibet's god-king said that since the Chinese had given no open indication that they wanted to change matters, 'it is best to treat them that way'. The Americans said that Washington sympathised and understood that the Dalai Lama must adjust 'temporarily' to superior force.[20] Allison asked Taktser what the US could do to help Tibet under the circumstances. Taktser said it was 'important that the Dalai Lama and the Tibetan people can continue to hope that "something" could be done "afterwards".' Allison was clearly eager to help; Taktser, on the other hand, sought 'low-profile treatment' of Tibet by Washington, at least for the time being.[21]

While the Department of State pursued its relatively understated policy vis-a-vis Tibet, the armed forces and the intelligence services took an altogether different line. Early in March 1952, General Hoyt S. Vandenberg, Chief of Staff of the United States Air Force (USAF), writing on behalf of the Joint Chiefs of Staff, and representing the views not only of the Pentagon, but also of the Director Central Intelligence, wrote to Secretary of Defence Lovett, 'The JCS considers that the United States' current programs for covert operations in the Far East should be continued and, if practicable, be accelerated . . . Consideration should be given to accelerating covert unconventional operations in the Far East (including South-East Asia), directed toward increasing the solidarity of indigenous peoples and their support of United States objectives.'[22] Given the Cold War environment of the period, these recommendations were likely to have been followed up. In the Far East, the only indigenous people engaged in combat against the Chinese with some links to the US National Military Establishment at this time were the Tibetans, and the support of the JCS and the DCI was of crucial import to what they were doing, virtually as important as the conduit being provided by Delhi.

However, Tibet was not the only area of collaboration between the US and India. Delhi was also keen to play a mediating role between Beijing and the West, and Nehru sought to utilise the opportunity presented by his sister, Pandit Vijaya Lakshmi Pandit's visit to China, to strengthen this aspect of Indo-US relations. Mrs Pandit, who as Indian envoy in Washington in March 1951 had signed the first Indo-US Mutual Defence Assistance Agreement, was leading an Indian cultural delegation to China in the spring of 1952. When US Ambassador Chester Bowles asked the Secrtary-General of India's Ministry of External Affairs, G S Bajpai, about the possibility of using Indian good offices to communicate to Beijing US 'desire for peace and broader understanding in Asia', Bajpai recommended unofficial contacts through Mrs Pandit. Chester Bowles sought to 'associate the Government of India with US confidentially and emotionally in our efforts to secure peace and stability in Asia.' Bowles wanted Mrs Pandit to convey to Beijing 'dangers in their becoming spearhead for Soviet ambitions in Asia' and also 'our deepseated desire for peace and broader under-standing in Asia' and the fact that 'We have no desire to attack China or fight with China anyway.'[23] He briefed Pandit in Delhi before she left for Beijing. Indian officials appeared to relish their position as intermediaries between Washington and Beijing when nobody else was able to play this role. The Chinese sent messages to the Indian ambassador, K.M. Panikkar, who passed them on to Bajpai, who passed these on to Chester Bowles. Much of Sino-US communications on Korea was conducted via this channel. That Washington valued this route was shown in Dean Acheson's telegraph to Chester Bowles which carried a message to be carried by Mrs Pandit to the Chinese leaders. Acheson wanted to assure Beijing that the US was a peaceful country with no territorial designs and no ambition to impose its values; it only used force 'when others do'. Acheson's message said, in part, 'The United States has no desire to dominate the internal arrangements of any other nation. At the same time, this Government feels compelled to interpose, by force if necessary, in situations where nations use force in derogation of the rights and independence of other nations. The resort to aggression as the arbiter of differences between nations is to us intolerable. But when that policy of aggression has been abandoned, we have no desire to continue the strife or to harbour grudges.'[24]

Mrs Pandit did try to plead with Mao and Zhou on the US's 'peaceful intent'. Her efforts were subsequently discussed by the US *Charge'* in Delhi after US Counsellor Everett Drumright debriefed her on her return from China. According to the *Charge*'s report to the Department of State, Mrs Pandit had told Zhou 'India recognises Chinese suzerainty over Tibet, but had been distressed and concerned when China sent troops to Tibet and assumed full administrative control. Zhou replied China had merely asserted her legitimate rights in Tibet and had no aggressive designs whatever against India or any other country. Mrs Pandit had stressed to Zhou India earnestly desired to follow policy of neutrality, but would find it difficult to do so if China resorted to policy of territorial expansion.'[25] Mrs Pandit had extensive discussions of US attitudes with Zhou En-lai, handing to the Chinese Premier a copy of Secretary of State Acheson's telegram of 25 April 1952. Mrs Pandit also briefed the British Minister of Defence, Lord Alexander, when the latter briefly stopped over in Delhi. Early in July, Mrs Pandit had lunch with the Bowles when she described some of her impressions to the ambassador himself. She mentioned that she had told Premier Zhou En-lai how concerned the US was about Russian policy, especially in Korea, and that Washington was genuinely anxious to end fighting on the peninsula. She suggested that if China adopted policies 'wholly independent' from Russia, 'world peace might be brought closer.' This latter remark apparently caused Zhou to flush and to reply 'with considerable emphasis' that 'Russia was not running China and never would.'[26] There is no evidence that Washington took Zhou's claims seriously, certainly not for the next decade and a half, thereby missing an opportunity to reshape the global centre to its advantage until the Nixon-Kissinger strategic coup in the early 1970s.

While high-level diplomacy went on around them, the Tibetans themselves were beginning to try to wrest control from the Chinese. As early as the beginning of 1951, Lhasa was rife with rumours of a clandestine, anti-Chinese, popular organisation spreading its tentacles into the capital's influential classes. In March, as Lhasa prepared for the annual *Monlam* festival, two such bodies, *Mimang Tsongdu* (people's representatives/assembly) and *Magstog Ruchen* (people's organisation) emerged out of the shadows. Running parallel to the National Assembly and the *Kashag*, these two groups began attracting considerable support outside the traditional power-structure. But the joint-Prime Ministers, Lukhangwa and Lobsang Tashi, appeared either unable or unwilling to challenge these embryonic, and popular, centres of power. The former was made up of what could perhaps rather broadly be described as the lower middle classes of the citizenry, and the latter, largely of former soldiers.[27] On 31 March 1951, traditional festivities culminated in mass demonstrations aimed at the Chinese, with a group of leaders submitting a letter protesting Chinese military occupation to General Zhang Guohua, head of the Chinese military administration. The General was outraged by this act of clearly political activism on what was a religious/cultural pretext. He brought enormous pressures to bear on the prime ministers to take severe action against the *Mimang Tsongdu* and its leaders. Nearly a month passed as the two sides bickered incessantly, with General Zhang demanding tough action of everyone including the Dalai Lama, and the co-prime ministers refusing to act. In the end, the Dalai Lama relented and towards the end of April, the *Kashag* announced the resignation of the two prime ministers. Lukhangwa left Tibet to assume a leading role in the coalescing resistance from the Himalayan hill station of Kalimpong south of the mountains; Lobsang Tashi returned to his religious duties. The *Kashag* also announced the disbandment of the *Mimang Tsongdu*, briefly detaining its leaders. Although General Zhang's coercive tactics won out, he did not make many friends amongst the Tibetans. In fact, this set of events may have marked the end of the Chinese honeymoon in Lhasa as angry Tibetans began serious efforts to subvert the PLA's authority on the plateau. And now, at last, they appeared to have a few friends abroad willing to act.

At a review of the Tibetan situation in Washington in mid-May 1952, Department of State, CIA and G-2 (military intelligence) officials discussed reports on the Tibetan situation collected by Taktser. They concluded that Tibetan hostility to the PLA was increasing, there were armed clashes between Tibetans and Chinese soldiers in Lhasa, food shortages had become acute, and that the Tibetans had moved from passive acceptance of the Chinese occupation to public demonstrations and covert mobilisation. While the Dalai Lama and his entourage openly accepted the PLA's presence, 'there seems to be in operation a cleverly conceived covert plan to encourage hostility towards the Chinese forces and toward those lay ministers who appear to be collaborating most closely with the Chinese.' Also, 'from the stand-point of United States interests, developments in Tibet are moving in the right direction and are producing a desirable effect upon the Government of India.'[28] The meeting perceived 'incipient Tibetan resistance', and recommended 'avoidance of any public comment or communication with those thought to be organizing resistance.'[29] By this time, the clandestine communications network established by the CIA linking Lhasa with US diplomats in Calcutta and Delhi was fully functional. At the beginning of July 1952, the US Consul-General in Calcutta forwarded to the Department of State a message from the Dalai Lama brought in by an intermediary.[30] Two months later, the Consul visited Darjeeling where he met Gyalo Thondup, another brother of the Dalai Lama. The two men discussed recent reports of the god-king reducing taxes imposed on the Tibetan masses, and redistributing land from the estates of landlords among the poorer sections.[31] While the Dalai Lama sought to steal the Communist's reforming thunder by enacting and implementing his own reforms, outside Lhasa, the resistance gradually built up its strength with not inconsiderable help from beyond the mountains.

Around this time, the Tibetan story began to become a part of several other sideshows to the Cold War drama in Asia. To a large extent through the efforts of Gyalo Thondup, who had family connections in Taipei, the Tibetan resistance was by now beginning to receive a modest supply of provisions from the KMT government in Taiwan. The KMT had large bands of stragglers stuck in northern Burma[32] some of which units could have joined up with the Tibetan resistance in their common struggle against the PLA. However, Taipei was persuaded to bring these stragglers out of Burma into Taiwan. Also, once the CIA began playing a bigger role in aiding the Tibetan resistance, the KMT's profile began to suffer. This development coincided with a completely unrelated US decision to secure greater control over Taiwanese operations in Communist Chinese-controlled territory, which occasionally threatened to provoke a major response and escalate out of hand. Given the pressures generated by the events on the Korean peninsula, US caution was perhaps understandable. The Chief of the US Military Assistance Advisory Group (MAAG) in Taiwan, Major-General W.C.Chase, asked the Taiwanese Chief of General Staff, General Chow Chih-jou, 'that you make no significant attacks on Communist-held territory without first consulting me. This is in no way intended to limit your scheme of operations, but is merely to keep me informed, so that MAAG may be able to advise and assist in every possible way.'³³ General Chase did, however, ask that offensive action against Communist China by sea and air be increased! Nonetheless, when the US began directly providing assistance to the Tibetans, General Chiang Kai-shek's KMT government was extremely unhappy. Chiang clearly felt all anti-PRC operations were his prerogative and that the US should be providing all its assistance to that endeavour via Taiwan. US *Charge' d'Affaires* in Taipei, H P Jones, wrote to the Department of State that the Generalissimo objected to 'US policy behind the continuing support being granted Chinese "Third Force" elements through training, subsidies and other encouragement. This was contrary to evidence that the United States wished further to strengthen the Government of the Republic of China.'³⁴ Washington's response was that such support as it provided to 'Third Force' elements was 'modest, mainly limited to intelligence activities.'³⁵ Taiwan may or may not have been reassured, but the exchange highlighted the complexities of the wider, international, linkages that both aided and constrained the Tibetan resistance.

Meanwhile, Indo-US co-operation in another area related to Sino-US conflict cemented ties between Washington and Delhi. In 1951 and 1952, the CIA dropped a number of ethnic-Chinese and non-Han paratroopers into China on intelligence-gathering, sabotage and subversive missions. A few managed to evade capture for sometime and provide a measure of 'humint' on Communist-Chinese activities and effectiveness in the hinterland. However, a number were lost in combat and most of the others were arrested and brought to Beijing. A large number of these agents were put on humiliating public displays and repeatedly threatened with trial on charges of espionage for a hostile power. Indian ambassador K.M. Panikkar was asked to find out as much information about these 'detenus' as possible. In the summer of 1952, Panikkar visited Delhi where US Counsellor Everett Drumright debriefed him on the US agents in Chinese custody.³⁶ Over the next few years, as Beijing's rhetoric on the subject of these prisoners grew shrill, Indian officials played progressively more significant roles in attempting to defuse the crisis threatening to build between China and the US. In November, for instance, acting Secretary of State, David Bruce, sent a telegram to the US mission in Delhi requesting the Government of India to ask Delhi's envoy in Beijing, Raghavan, to 'present humanitarian appeal' to the Chinese Communist authorities on behalf of the American and other foreign detainees in Chinese custody.³⁷

## A Matter of Policy

Several strands to Washington's Asia policy appeared to be coming together in late 1953: the USAF had increased its strategic reconnaissance activities over mainland China and there was now better photographic intelligence available of Chinese military deployments and of its industrial and agricultural developments; however, at least one, and possibly several, strategic reconnaissance aircraft had been downed by the PLA, and the surviving crew-members had swelled the ranks of Western detainees being used by Beijing as pawns in a blackmail-and-propaganda campaign. There were attempts by Washington's Indian emissaries not only to secure the release of detained US and other allied 'detenus', but also to reassure Communist leaders that US intents were peaceable. Both India and Pakistan, but especially India, had become a trusted ally in the struggle against Communist China, and its residual reservations, if any, regarding this alliance were becoming weaker by the day. US policy in Asia appeared, finally, to be 'coming togeher'. The evidence for this perception in Washington is given by two Top Secret documents, both filed on 6 November 1953. One was a 'Statement of Policy by the National Security Council (NSC)' which associated US policy vis-a-vis China with the NSC's strategic evaluation of India's role in that scheme.[38] The NSC described the thrust of US policy toward Asia as 'Continue to exert political and economic pressures against Communist China including unconventional and covert pressures, at least until settlements satisfactory to the United States can be achieved in the areas around Communist China.'[39] The NSC's appreciation of the role Nehru's India could play in aiding Washington was matter-of-fact:

> *India, by reason of its size and population, its potential for economic and military growth, and the political leadership and prestige of Nehru in the other countries of South East Asia, also (in addition to Japan) offers a potentially important counterpoise to Communist China. But India's domestic and external problems make it unlikely that in the near future there will be rapid development of India's capabilities vis-a-vis Communist China. Barring Nehru's death or disability, the Congress Party over the next few years may be expected to retain control of the government, or to dominate a coalition if its majority should be cut. The Communist Party will probably not soon become a serious threat to the internal security of the nation or to the position of the government. Continuing economic and social backwardness, however, will be difficult to remedy. India can be expected to maintain its policy of non-alignment with either East or West, to continue to play an active role, in concert with other members of the Arab-Asian group where possible, in efforts to reduce tensions and to settle specific problems among the great powers and to take measures in defense of its own territory if necessary. Indian contribution to the security of the non-Communist area against Communist China will be heavily contingent upon the status of the still unresolved dispute over Kashmir, a problem which currently pins down the major portion of both Indian and Pakistani armed power.[40]*

Despite the establishment of the Mutual Defence Assistance Agreement of March 1951which raised the status of US-Indian security co-operation to the level of US-Pakistan collaboration following their 1950 agreement, the NSC did not seem to consider India a fully aligned ally. There was a difference between Washington's and Delhi's approach to Beijing: 'India, under Nehru's leadership, continues to believe that the best approach to the problem (relating to China) is to attempt to wean Mao's regime away from Russia by extensive use of non-Communist contacts with Communist China; Indian fears of Communist China, and Indian desires for a strong, third force, Asian bloc add emotional intensity to this belief.'[41]

The other policy document issued by the NSC on the same date related to the KMT regime in Taiwan.[42] It recommended certain courses of action which echoed the points made in the sister statement: The US should 'Encourage and covertly assist the Chinese National Government to develop and extend logistical support of anti-Communist guerrillas on the mainland of China, for purposes of resistance and intelligence.'[43] The document showed how NSC staffers sought to cushion increasing costs of escalating unconventional warfare and covert operations against Communist China using the KMT regime as a major US agency, most probably for concealing the nature of increased costs from the Congress. 'A policy of encouraging raids on the mainland could well increase the "operations" item of the budget. The total budget for "operations" was $13.3 million during 1952, when raiding activity was conducted on a limited scale. A policy of increasing logistical support of guerrillas could well increase the budget items of "food", for example, as well as "administration" and "ship repair". This would at the same time result in the loss of earnings from rice exports.'[44] There is no evidence that the Administration objected to any of these recommendations, either in terms of their strategic content, or in terms of the legitimacy of the operational details. The discordant note was to come from Vice President Richard M Nixon, who spent much of November and December 1953 touring the Far East. Having visited a number of countries bordering China, and accepted the hospitality of Generalissimo Chiang Kai-shek in Taiwan, Nixon reported back to the President and other members of the NSC just before Christmas. The essence of Nixon's impression was that Communist China was 'here to stay.' His recommendation was, therefore, to seek ways and means of normalising relations with that country and integrating it into the international system.[45] In his remarkably pragmatic, even visionary, report, the Vice President said he was convinced that the KMT would never recapture the mainland and that the Communist government was already too-well established to be ousted in anything short of a general war, which was not considered to be an option. The record does not register a great deal of reaction from the President himself, although a couple of his brief comments could be construed as generally supportive of his deputy.

However, the other members of the NSC did not display any enthusiasm for Nixon's view and while endorsing his broad thrust towards peace and security in Asia, asked that combat preparedness and the contemporary policy of sustained and significant covert activities aimed at weakening the Beijing leadership's authority be continued until there was 'clear evidence' that Communist China posed no threats to the 'free world'. Eisenhower may have decided that his Vice President was way ahead of his time and that he, the President, needed the support of the rest of the team much more than the benefits he would gain by challenging the hawkish majority. Without an overt endorsement from the President, the Vice President could not put into effect his vision of such a major restructuring of the complex system of alliances. And for the moment, at least, Eisenhower was unwilling to voice such an endorsement. Domestic political opinion, especially aroused over events in central and eastern Europe, and on the Korean peninsula, made the initiation of conciliatory overtures to Beijing particularly fraught. There was as yet no powerful evidence that the Chinese leadership was independent of Moscow and the deepening of the Cold War militated against pushing for normalisation with Communist China at this stage. After all, China was still an enemy in the Far East. Nixon was thus thwarted in his radical vision of a new global framework of strategic relationships. The realisation of this particular goal would take him nearly two decades.

Thus an opportunity of making a dramatic shift in the world's political-military architecture was missed. The elements which made up the ruling elite in Washington at this time appeared to be in the main dominated by those who saw the planet in relatively simple and starkly bipolar terms. All Communists were considered as either instruments of the Soviet Russian leadership in Moscow, or unthinking supporters of it. That the Chinese Communists could be an autonomous elite was not accepted by this dominant faction of the US establishment despite evidence to the contrary. The adoption of the starkest bipolarity as the essence of strategic perception and policy, and consequently, of resource allocation, meant that most foreign policy activities vis-a-vis Beijing were fundamentally confrontational. However, while Nixon may have been in a minority, he was not alone. Indeed, in the mid-1950s, there were other 'Asia hands' in Washington who would echo his recommendations. But the consequences of domestic developments such as the coalescence of an influential, rabidly right-wing, bloc within and without the Congress forced these voices of moderation to the margins and made it practically impossible for any policy-maker or politician to voice views that were different to the rightwingers'. Because of the asymmetry in power relations between the global centre, dominated as it was in the post-war period by the US, and the periphery, many relatively minor shifts in Washington made a relatively large impact elsewhere. The consistent pursuit of hostility with Beijing, very often covertly and with help from secret allies such as India and not-so-secret ones such as Pakistan, imposed an aura of adversarial violence on Asia from which the region is yet to emerge. In South Asia, Perhaps the most significant legacy of this era is to be found in the Kashmir dispute that continues to divide India and Pakistan into two most virulently rival camps to this day.

# CHAPTER 3

# The Kashmir Fallout

The dispute between India and Pakistan over the state of Jammu & Kashmir (hereinafter Kashmir) has been an unusually complex, and often bloody, problem since partition. More recently, since 1990, the dispute has been marked by an insurrection by separatist Kashmiris of diverse political and ideological hues.[1] It is widely claimed that between 1990 and 1997, more than 20,000 people were killed in separatist violence, and in the reprisals carried out by Indian armed forces, throughout the state. Despite meetings at the highest levels including several between the prime ministers of India and Pakistan, the dispute appeared nowhere near resolution in late 1998. Fifty-one years earlier, when the dispute arose, it was defined along relatively clear lines. One of around 565 princely states within imperial India, Kashmir was a feudal monarchy ruled by a hereditary *Maharaja (great king)*, a Hindu prince, descended from Ghulab Singh who had bought the state from the British East India Company for Rs.7.5 million in 1846. Ruled by Dogra Rajputs, Kashmiris were largely Muslim although Jammu in the south-west had a Hindu majority, and Ladakh in the north-east was predominantly Tibetan-Lamaist Buddhist.

The dissolution of Britain's Indian empire gave the princes two choices – to join either of the two new dominions, India or Pakistan. Independence was tacitly if not formally ruled out and the rulers were advised to consider the reality of physical contiguity and the general wishes of the people. For hitherto near-absolute rulers, this latter was a novelty. Against the backdrop of growing communal violence accompanying the partition, many Kashmiris, led by the Muslim Conference (allied to Jinnah's Muslim League), sought accession to Pakistan. The secularist National Conference (allied to Gandhi's Indian National Congress) led by Sheikh Muhammad Abdullah, sought a secular republican future that mirrored Nehru's India. Meanwhile, deeply troubled by the prospects for himself and his dynasty under either an Indian or a Pakistani dispensation, Maharaja Hari Singh appeared to be seeking independence so as to secure his own position.[2]

Neither the Congress nor the Muslim League found this acceptable. Both considered the accession of Kashmir to their respective new state fundamental to the latter's *raison d'etre*. For the putative Pakistan, Kashmir provided the letter 'K' to the acronym PAKISTAN.[3] More crucially, physically contiguous to West Punjab and the North-West Frontier Province, if Muslim-majority Kashmir did not join Pakistan, then the logic behind East Bengal joining in from a thousand miles away would be nullified and Pakistan's claim to being the homeland of the subcontinent's Muslim community would be contradicted. To the rulers of Pakistan, the failure to secure Kashmir's accession was a failure of the Pakistani ideal which left the country incomplete. If they accepted the state's accession to India, then it seemed to many in Pakistan that the Congress's claim that the 'two-nation theory' was wrong would be proved to be correct; that would be seen to negate the very premise of the Islamic state. Kashmir's accession was thus fundamental to the legitimacy of Pakistan's creation. The absolute nature of Pakistan's claim on Kashmir was reinforced by the strategic significance of a land through which the rivers giving Punjab, Pakistan's political heartland its name, flowed.

For India too, Kashmir was important. Manifesting a rejection of the Muslim League's 'two-nation theory' which underpinned the Partition and led to the creation of Pakistan, India claimed to be the secular, national, repository of the subcontinent's political identity. If Muslim-majority Kashmir joined Pakistan simply because of its confessional features, then the secular strands of the Indian Union would be torn apart, possibly damaging the dominion irreparably. At least, that perception appeared to drive policy-making in Delhi in the closing days of the empire. In short, Kashmir both reflected and reinforced the zero-sum philosophical 'duel to the death' into which India and Pakistan were born. Given the mutually exclusive nature of the two new neighbours' founding principles, neither felt capable of giving up its claim. The dispute was thus fundamental to the very process which led to the creation of India and Pakistan and the two new states were to engage in their first war over Kashmir in less than ten weeks of gaining independence. In the half-century since then, not much appears to have changed. The two armies still stand 'eyeball to eyeball' along the 'Line of Actual Control' (LAC) dividing Kashmir into Pakistan's 'Azad Kashmir' province, and the Jammu & Kashmir state of India. Shooting across the Siachen glacier on the northern fringes of the LAC near the Karakoram pass has become something of an annual event as each side tries to secure a better position during the brief summer. The dispute is clearly far from over.[4]

Accounts vary widely. What is clear is that while Indian leaders encouraged Maharaja Hari Singh to accede to India, Pakistan allowed Frontier Pathan tribal *lascar* militias to cross Pakistani territory at the end of the third week in October 1947 and enter Kashmir to join combat on the side of the *Azad Kashmir* (free Kashmir) forces. The latter were largely manned and led by the *Sudhan Pathans* of Kashmir's Sudhanuti *tehsil* who were engaged in a civil war with armed elements of the right-wing Hindu organisation *Rastriya Sayam-sevak Sangh* (RSS), and in a rebellion against the Maharaja's state military forces. When the *lascars* threatened to sack Sri Nagar, Kashmir's summer capital, Maharaja Hari Singh fled to Jammu and pleaded for Indian assistance. Lord Mountbatten, British-India's last Viceroy and independent India's first Governor-General, insisted that military assistance could only be given after Kashmir had acceded to India, if only provisionally. This was done, and even before the ink was dry on the accession document, Indian paratroopers had secured Sri Nagar airfield and flown in both artillery and armour to the mountains. The tribal 'raiders' or 'freedom-fighters', depending on one's viewpoint, were driven out of the Vale of Kashmir. However, this success of the Indian forces triggered Pakistan's direct involvement as regular units of the latter's army joined combat. By early 1948, the first Indo-Pak war proper had begun. A year of UN mediation encouraged by the US eventually led to a ceasefire coming into effect on 1 January 1949. The ceasefire line (CFL) became a de facto boundary between Pakistan's Azad Kashmir province and the Indian state of Jammu & Kashmir. The CFL was modified after the wars in 1965 and 1971 when it was renamed the LAC. However, its essential function as the intra-Kashmir boundary remained unchanged.

Following the ceasefire, protracted mediation by special representatives nominated by the United Nations Security Council managed to move the two sides to a basic agreement: that a plebiscite would be held to ascertain the opinion of the people of Jammu & Kashmir as to their preferred option of accession to either dominion. But this was to be conducted only after Pakistan vacated 'Azad Kashmir' and India withdrew the 'bulk' of its forces from the two-thirds of the state under Delhi's control. Disagreement on what 'the bulk' actually meant stalled discussions and further movement. India demanded that Pakistan withdraw fully from 'Azad Kashmir' as, in Delhi's view, Karachi was the aggressor; Pakistan claimed India had twisted the Maharaja's arm in securing the accession, the Maharaja did not have the right to impose a decision on the people of Kashmir and that a plebiscite must first be held before it would consider making any concessions. In short, a stalemate froze all movement. It was only after the US had signed up both Karachi and Delhi as allies in Washington's struggle to contain Communist activities that some flexibility was visible in the two capitals. To reinforce the perception that the US was keen to help the two states develop their economies, and perhaps also to shift the focus from their interminable political and military disputes to more constructive, collaborative endeavours, Washington sponsored and signed a number of comparable agreements with both the clients. There were agreements on helping with education and technical training, as well as co-operation in the fields of agricultural development, export-credit and trading concessions. There were, for instance, an agreement with India on funding educational exchanges in February 1950, and a very similar agreement with Pakistan in September 1950. There was a 'Point Four' general agreement between the US and India on technical co-operation signed in December 1950, and one between the US and Pakistan along similar lines[5] signed in February 1951. While Washington's concern with the need for reducing tensions between India and Pakistan should not be underestimated, Washington was also being driven by dramatic economic pressures at home which US allies had to take into account. The evidence of this came in early 1952.

As the Indian ambassador in Washington, B.R. Sen, reported to the Indian Finance Minister, Chintaman Deshmukh, President Truman himself explained to his fellow Americans the kind of pressures the US was under because of its massive economic expansion during the war years and thereafter. Truman said, 'we are now in the second year of a three-year programme which will double our output in aluminium, increase our electric power supply by 40 per cent, and increase our steelmaking capacity by 15 per cent. We can then produce 120 million tons of steel a year – as much as the rest of the world put together.'[6] That India was indirectly touched by the impact of this growth in the output of the US economy was made clear in a visit by Congressman Jacob K. Javits, a leading member of the House of Representatives Foreign Affairs Committee and one who had played an influential role in forging close relations between the US and India. Javits came to dine with Ambassador Sen, and suggested that this expansion in the US economy was largely driven by the possibility of a general war between the 'free world' led by the US and the Communists led by Moscow. The US did not wish to take the risks of slowing down, as it had in the 1920s and the 1930s, only to discover in the 1940s that it had to force the economy rapidly to expand so as to cope with the demands of war. The Korean War only served to deepen these anxieties.

That the Washington establishment was convinced of the possibility of general war breaking out was clear – that they were groping with possible courses of action if a general war did not break out became evident when Javits made his pitch during dinner. He said that 'if war did not come by the end of 1953, United States would have developed a basic productive capacity which she could maintain only by taking a larger interest in foreign markets than now. In other words, United States would then face a recession or even a real depression unless she could find an outlet for her high production.'[7] For his own part, Ambassador Sen wrote to the Finance Minister, 'I am sure you will agree that there is a real point in this argument. Javits emphasised the need on our side to realise this possibility and plan from now on that basis. As you will see, he makes several suggestion . . .'[8] The ambassador's suggestions were fleshed out in an appendix written by Counsellor W.R. Natu who recommended, among other steps, 'The first thing that India should do immediately is to announce boldly and calmly her willingness to go ahead with the Five-Year Plan as a whole, including that part of it which depends on foreign assistance.'[9] How much influence this correspondence had in Mr Deshmukh's subsequent economic management is not made clear by the documentation; however, that the Five-Year Plan got a full go ahead quite soon afterwards is known. Given this level of collaboration between Washington and Delhi, it is not surprising that India and Pakistan would have to take seriously US efforts to bring the two parties together in an attempt to resolve what in US view was potentially the most damaging distraction from globally significant objectives.

Washington's persuasive skills were put to severe test by the asymmetry of internal political developments in India and Pakistan. In India, the Congress, led by Nehru, established itself as the principal national political organisation which, either by itself, or in local coalition with regional parties or factions, could mount a successful bid for power. In Pakistan, the Muslim League, led as it was by immigrants from northern, south-western and eastern India who lacked roots, or constituencies, in the provinces that became part of the new country, was unable to establish itself as anything other than an instrument of the dominant elite faction. In the absence of national figures following the death of Jinnah in 1948 and the assassination of Prime Minister Liaquat Ali Khan in an abortive coup in 1951, the most cohesive elements of the state, ie, a tacit coalition of the civil and military bureaucracies, emerged as the wielders of the levers of state power. Politicians squabbled in their factional feuds which did nothing for stability or for the popularity of party-political structures, institutions and traditions. It was not easy for American or Indian leaders to know who to negotiate with in Karachi. Nonetheless, in the early 1950s, Washington was able to push its two recalcitrant South Asian allies to try and approach the Kashmir dispute in a rational and peaceful manner.

Following major military manoeuvres along their common borders by both neighbours during much of 1950 and 1951 and part of 1952, Prime Ministers Nehru and Mohammad Ali corresponded with each other for much of 1953 on ways of breaking the deadlock over Kashmir. Towards the end of the year, a broad consensus appeared to be emerging on the unavoidability of holding a plebiscite throughout Jammu & Kashmir. Some differences remained on such technical details as to whether the absolute result of the outcome would determine the fate of the whole of Jammu & Kashmir, or if results in particular regions could be seen as the determinant of what happened to those regions. The final sticking point appeared to be that while Ali demanded that the state was indivisible and either the whole state joined Pakistan or it joined India, Nehru seemed to suggest that regions such as Hindu-majority Jammu and Buddhist-majority Ladakh should not be forced to join Pakistan even if the overall Muslim majority of Kashmir chose to do so.[10] The fact that Nehru had agreed to the holding of a plebiscite without the prior withdrawal of Pakistani forces from 'Azad Kashmir' was a breakthrough. The differences were now of detail which, now that the basic principle had been established and agreed on, could gradually be addressed. The most painful dispute between Washington's two important clients in Asia was about to be negotiated, and hopefully, resolved, clearing the way for more significant, in US view, challenges facing the region. The timing of this development was crucial; Washington had just come to an agreement with Turkey, Iran and Pakistan to collaborate in securing the oil fields of the Middle East in the event of an attack by the Soviet Union. Resolution of the Kashmir dispute could only strengthen that policy.

Ironically, these two developments were seen in very different lights in Washington, Delhi and Karachi. As news of the approaching security coalition linking the US, Iran, Turkey and Pakistan reached India, something happened in Delhi. Nehru was no longer able to pursue discussions about the planned plebiscite, or indeed any peaceful attempts at resolving the Kashmir dispute. It is possible that the prospect of closer security links between Washington and Karachi threw up too disturbing a vision for the Indian elites for them to be able to continue negotiating over Kashmir; but since Pakistan and the US had already signed a Mutual Defence Agreement in 1950, and the imminent treaty relationship was aimed at building up the West's security strengths in the Middle-East rather than at any objective in South Asia *per se*, Nehru's decision to renege on his earlier commitments regarding Kashmir raises questions about his motive. It seems likely that having made the commitment to hold a plebiscite simply because Nehru had himself taken the Kashmir dispute to the United Nations and holding a plebiscite was the outcome of UN mediation, Nehru was now under intense pressure from within the Indian establishment to pull out, and the impending US-Pakistan agreement merely provided a convenient pretext enabling him to do so without either losing face or appearing casually to break his word. Nonetheless, it was an important pretext which proved crucial to the future history of the dispute and hence, to that of South Asia itself.

A month after writing to Ali about how the regional breakdown of the proposed plebiscite should shape the future of the respective parts of Jammu & Kashmir, Nehru wrote to Ali again. This time around, his letter was far more pessimistic in tone and content. Nehru wrote, ' On the 10th November, . . . I referred to various matters . . . In particular I referred to the news of a military pact between Pakistan and the United States of America . . . I pointed out that any such pact between Pakistan and the United States of America meant the alignment of Pakistan, both in regard to its foreign and defence policy, with a particular bloc of nations. So far as India is concerned, it has been our consistent policy to avoid any such alignment . . . I mention this because, in view of the developments that appear to be taking place, Pakistan's foreign and defence policy will become diametrically opposed to the policies we have so consistently and earnestly pursued. I can only express my regret that the area of disagreement between India and Pakistan should be extended over a wider field now ... Inevitably, it will affect the major question that we are considering and, more especially, the Kashmir issue ... The whole issue will change its face completely if heavy and rapid militarization of Pakistan itself is to take place.' [11] Nehru made no mention of US-Indian agreements.

Ali followed up with several letters to Nehru. In each of these, the Pakistani Prime Minister expressed surprise that a quadrilateral security arrangement linking the US, Turkey, Iran and Pakistan to the defence of Middle-Eastern oilfields from possible Soviet aggression might be construed to constrain India's ability to conduct negotiations with Pakistan on Kashmir. Nehru's view appeared to be somewhat illogical to the leaders of Pakistan although there is no evidence that they were aware of India's own security linkages with the US, a point which did not appear even once in any of the correspondence between the two prime ministers. Against this backdrop, Nehru's insistence is quite intriguing. It is possible he could not accept that the US should develop security linkages with Pakistan as well as with India, thus placing Pakistan at par with India in Washington's regional security calculus. Nehru might have been piqued by what he probably saw as Washington's inconsideration in proceeding to sign Pakistan up in a regional security alliance without consulting Delhi which suggested that the US wished to pursue an independent policy in South Asia without worrying too much about what India felt about such measures. It is also possible that Nehru was seeking to put pressure on both the US and Pakistan with a view to securing some undefined concessions from either Washington or Karachi or both. Alternately, Nehru may have genuinely been concerned that the proposed agreement would enhance Pakistan's military capability beyond India's ability to overwhelm it and thereby alter the balance of power in the region to the detriment of Delhi's freedom of action. Another possibility is that the Indian leadership was keen to get out of Nehru's commitment to hold a plebiscite in Kashmir because they suspected it would go against India, and saw this as an opportunity to pull out of that pledge. A combination of factors could have been the drive pushing the Indian foreign policy elite generally and Nehru in particular.

Whatever the motive, Nehru wrote to Ali on 18 January 1954, 'I am sorry that you do not appreciate the vital difference that this (the planned US-Pakistan agreement) has made to our approach to many problems. I do not and cannot challenge your Government's right to take any step it chooses. But, when that step is, according to our thinking, of vital significance to the peace and security of Asia and affects India directly, we can not ignore it and we have to think of other problems in relation to this new and, what we consider, dangerous development.'[12] The next letter from the Pakistani Prime Minister was sent on 24 February 1954. It was an expression of outrage at the new Chief Minister of Jammu & Kashmir, Bakhshi Ghulam Mohammad's proposal that the 'Constituent Assembly' of the Indian controlled state endorse Jammu & Kashmir's accession to India and the fact that the Assembly, actually, did so. Karachi saw this as evidence of Indian duplicity as while Nehru continued negotiations, his administration was securing legitimation of Kashmir's accession to India by indirect means. There is no record of an Indian response to this protest.

It appears that Delhi's anxieties were communicated to Washington and the Eisenhower administration treated this development with concern. Fearing a further deterioration of Indo-Pakistani relations and the loss of the opportunity to resolve the Kashmir dispute, President Eisenhower himself wrote to Nehru to dispel whatever anxieties the latter might have, the letter being handed over by the US Ambassador in Delhi to Nehru on 24 February. Eisenhower assured Nehru, 'I want you to know directly from me that this step does not in any way affect the friendship we feel for India. Quite the contrary . . . Having studied long and carefully the problem of opposing possible aggression in the Middle East, I believe the consultation between Pakistan and Turkey about security problems will serve the interests not only of Pakistan and Turkey, but also of the whole Free World . . . What we are proposing to do, and what Pakistan is agreeing to, is not directed in any way against India and I am confirming publicly that if our aid to any country, including Pakistan, is misused and directed against another in aggression, I will undertake immediately . . . to thwart such aggression.'[13] To ensure that India did not have any ground to feel marginalised, the US President added for good measure the offer, 'If your Government should conclude that circumstances require military aid of a type contemplated by our mutual security legislation, please be assured that your request would receive my most sympathetic consideration.'[14] Eisenhower felt he was doing all he could to allay Nehru's concerns.

The following day, 25 February 1954, President Eisenhower issued a public statement which essentially formalised the text of his letter to Nehru. The statement explained the context in which the security arrangements in the Middle-East had been worked out and the nature and objective of US military assistance to the participating countries. Eisenhower said, 'Let me make it clear that we shall be guided by the stated purposes and requirements of the mutual security legislation. These include specifically the provision that equipment, materials, or services provided will be used solely to maintain the recipient country's internal security and for its legitimate self-defence, or to permit it to participate in the defense of the area of which it is a part. Any recipient country also must undertake that it will not engage in any act of aggression against any other nation . . . I can say that if our aid to any country, including Pakistan, is misused and directed against another in aggression, I will undertake immediately, in accordance with my constitutional authority, appropriate action both within and without the United Nations to thwart such aggression.'[15]

A few days later, Prime Minister Nehru sent a rather terse reply to Eisenhower in which he simply wrote,

*Dear Mr President,*

*I thank you for your personal message which your Ambassador in Delhi handed to me on February 24th. With this message was a copy of your statement in regard to the military aid being given by the United States to Pakistan. I appreciate the assurances you have given. You are, however, aware of the views of my Government and our people in regard to this matter. Those views and the policy which we have pursued, after the most careful thought, are based on our desire to help in the furtherance of peace and freedom. We shall continue to pursue that policy.*[16]

Having rejected Eisenhower's assurances, Nehru now spoke at length in support of his own argument against the new security linkages between the US and Pakistan. During a long speech delivered in the *Lok Sabha* on 1 March 1954, Nehru said, 'This grant of military aid by the United States to Pakistan creates a grave situation for us in India and for Asia. It adds to our tensions. It makes it much more difficult to solve the problems which have confronted India and Pakistan.'[17]

Meanwhile, the Pakistani Prime Minister, Mohammad Ali, had kept up his protestations of innocence, repeating as he did some of the assurances contained in Eisenhower's notes. Nehru did not feel reassured. On 5 March 1954, he wrote to Ali, 'In your last letter, and in some of your previous letters, you have expressed your surprise at my connecting the US-Pakistan talks concerning military equipment with the Kashmir dispute. I have tried to point out to you the intimate connection between the two. I can only repeat that the decision to give this aid has changed the whole context of the Kashmir issue, and the long talks we have had about this matter have little relation to the new facts which flow from this aid.'[18] This insistent truculence notwithstanding, the Indian Prime Minister did not feel it necessary to explain his objections to the links between the US and Pakistan, especially given the existing security relationship between Washington and Delhi. Only in a speech given in New Delhi two years later did Nehru offer an explanation of sorts: 'I agree that it is not the intention of the US that United States military aid to Pakistan should be used against India. But the fact is that this aid increases the strength of Pakistan to attack India. We said very clearly that this aid had changed the entire face of the Kashmir problem because even if the Pakistani armies left the soil of Kashmir and entrenched themselves twenty or thirty miles away from the border, their increased strength would give them greater striking power to attack even from there. We had therefore to think and solve this problem in a different way as it had been made very complicated by this military aid and the military pacts.'[19] By then, of course, at least two dramatic changes had transformed the situation. The Jammu & Kashmir Constituent Assembly had ratified the State's accession to India, and the Indian constitution itself had been used to 'finalise' that ratification – the question of resolving the dispute via the plebiscite route was no longer accepted as an option by Delhi, and India had radically changed its policy vis-a-vis China in so far as Tibet was concerned. It appears that Nehru was now convinced that his China policy, or rather, India's Tibet policy, had been mistaken, that Delhi could not count on Washington's partnership in the covert collaboration against the PLA on the plateau, and now had to adapt itself to the new realities of trans-Himalayan power.

### The *Panchshil* Agreement

In early 1954, Nehru's emissaries began the delicate task of negotiating with Chinese officials a new arrangement of relationship between India and Tibet in particular and on Sino-Indian relations generally. It was delicate because Nehru appeared to believe he was playing a weak hand, having, in his view, lost the confidence and support of Washington. At the same time, he could not allow the Chinese to make his discomfiture too obvious. The question of keeping 'face' was perhaps as important as the need to make a dignified withdrawal from the legacy of imperial overstretch. Delhi could no longer maintain its post-Younghusband status in Tibet now that Beijing was driving the argument with force. India was for the moment at least unable to match Chinese power with its own strength. The two sides used the questions of trade transactions between sub-Himalayan Indian states and Tibet on the one hand, and Hindu pilgrims travelling to *Mt Kailash* and Lake *Manosarowar* in Tibet, and Tibetan Buddhists travelling to Bodhgaya and other Buddhist holy sites in India on the other, as the focus of negotiations. These issues provided the vehicle for what turned out to be the biggest shift in Delhi's Tibet policy since the Younghusband mission. The talks also re-established China's suzerainty over Tibet, giving the PLA's occupation a degree of legitimacy, and reduced India to a neighbouring state with limited interests and virtually no influence in Tibet. This radical reversal was institutionalised through the instrument of a treaty signed in Beijing in April 1954. It was called the 'Agreement between the Government of India and the Central People's Government of China on Trade and Cultural Relations between India and the Tibet Region of China'.

The title both reflected and confirmed the two basic issues in question: that Tibet was a part of China, and that transactions between that part of

China and India were limited to commercial and cultural exchanges. The agreement was summarised in a preamble which established the five principles of Sino-Indian relations. These were,

  (i) Mutual respect for each other's territorial integrity and sovereignty;
 (ii) Mutual non-aggression;
(iii) Mutual non-interference in each other's internal affairs;
 (iv) Equality and Mutual benefit; and
  (v) Peaceful co-existence.[20]

These five principles were informally called *Panchshil*, or the five stones, and the agreement eventually came to be referred to as the *Panchshil* treaty. It was to gain prominence when at an Afro-Asian summit at Bandung in Indonesia, the five principles would be taken up as the basis on which a new, non-aligned, movement was to be launched to bring the newly-independent post-colonial countries together. Under the terms of the *Panchshil* treaty, India agreed to withdraw the military escorts from its trade missions at Yatung and Gyantse in southern Tibet, and handover to China the postal, telephone, and telegraph services linking all the Indian trade and military encampments and installations in Tibet for which the Chinese agreed to pay 'reasonable' compensation. India also agreed to handover the twelve rest houses built by the British around their missions and marts and maintained by India since August 1947. China would pay some compensation. However, India was allowed to retain possession of the commercial missions and their premises, although title to all the land in the vicinity would revert to China. Trade concessions were now to become reciprocal, ie, parallel to the Indian trade agencies at Gyantse, Yatung and Gartok, China would open similar agencies in Delhi, Kalimpong and Calcutta, with each country providing 'every possible assistance' to the agencies of the other on its soil.

The Chinese government agreed to establish rest houses for Indian pilgrims visiting Mt Kailash and Lake Manasarowar. The key point of agreement was that discussions of specific measures aimed at implementing these steps would no longer involve the Tibetans in Lhasa or anywhere else, but be conducted between the Indian embassy in Beijing and the Chinese Foreign Ministry[21], thus ensuring Indian acceptance of the legitimacy of Tibetan subservience to Chinese authority. The treaty was composed in the form of the Indian ambassador in Beijing, N. Raghavan, addressing a detailed memorandum explaining all the terms and conditions of the new relationship between India and Tibet, to Chang Han-fu, China's Vice Foreign Minister, and Mr Chang writing back on the same day to say he agreed, and that the agreement would come into force immediately. Thus ended the half century of British-Indian patronage of Tibetan autonomy and the legitimation of the resurgence of Chinese authority. The Tibetans were not consulted.

The dramatic nature of the shift in Indian policy became clear when Nehru addressed the *Loksabha* a fortnight later and told his fellow parliamentarians,

> *A very important event to which I would like to draw the attention of the House is the agreement between India and China in regard to Tibet. That agreement deals with a large number of problems, each one of them not very important in itself perhaps, but important from the point of view of our trade, our pilgrim traffic, our trade posts, our communications there, and the rest. It took a considerable time to arrive at this agreement, not becasue of any major conflict or difficulty but because of the number of small points were so many and had to be discussed in detail. The major thing about this agreement to which I would like again to draw the attention of the House is the preamble to the agreement.*[22]

Nehru spelt out each of the five principles which were to guide future relations between India and China. Putting the best spin on the retrenchment which had been forced on Delhi's Tibet policy, Nehru offered a global vision of peace and security modelled on the Sino-Indian agreement.

> *These principles indicate the policy that we pursue in regard to these matters not only with China but with any neighbour country (sic). What is more, it is a statement of wholesome principles, and I imagine if these principles were adopted in the relations of various countries with one another, a great deal of the trouble of the present-day world would probably disappear.*
>
> *It is a matter of importance to us, of course, as well as, I am sure, to China that these countries, which have now almost 1,800 miles of frontier, should live on terms of peace and friendliness, respect each other's sovereignty and integrity, and agree not to interfere with each other in any way, and not to commit aggression on each other. By this agreement, we ensure peace to a very large extent in a certain area of Asia. I would honestly wish that this area of peace could spread over the rest of Asia and indeed over the rest of the world.*[23]

Optimism appears to have been laced with the anxiety to appease China so that India was not faced with a military and political debacle. Neither in the text of the agreement itself nor in any explanatory commentary issued by the Government of India was there any hint of the unhappiness expressed in the many notes sent by Delhi to Beijing in late 1950 and early 1951. Nor was there any suggestion that India was concerned with the adverse consequences of China's military occupation for the people of Tibet. The *volte face* was achieved without any apparent recognition of contradiction between the policy prior to the signing of this accord and that following it.

This was pragmatic realism at its best and this became clear in the following months and years. India now openly cultivated China's Communist leadership. Premier Zhou En-lai became a relatively frequent visitor to Delhi. At a banquet given in the visitor's honour on 26 June 1954, Nehru once again referred to the agreement and said, 'I hope that our two countries will stand for peace and human advance as they have done for the past two thousand years of human history.'[24] Hyperbole aside, hearty slogans shouted across India to welcome the Chinese visitor, '*Hindi Chini Bhai Bhai*' (Indians and Chinese are brothers) came to represent the popular view of Sino-Indian relations in the mid-1950s.

Two other developments had cast their shadows on the centre-periphery drama in South Asia in the meanwhile. In December 1953, US and Chinese delegates met for their first formal negotiations in Geneva. Protracted talks dealt with questions of US prisoners in China and Chinese expatriates detained in the US, as well as more general issues relating to peace and conflict-resolution in Asia. The talks were to last until August 1954. It was during one of these sessions that the US Secretary of State John Foster Dulles pointedly refused to shake Premier Zhou En-lai's extended hand. This relatively minor footnote to Cold War history did not help the self-confidence and sense of pride of the elite in power in Beijing. It is possible that Washington lost an opportunity to make contacts with the Chinese leadership and merely hardened the latter's position in subsequent encounters. The US may also have failed to identify and exploit a possible breach between Moscow and Beijing. Focusing on the apparently monolithic nature of Communism, US officials did not appear to grasp that Beijing sought to emerge as its own master rather than perform forever as an appendage of the Soviet Union.

The other development had a more direct impact on the subcontinent. In May 1954, less than a month after the *Panchshil* agreement had been signed in Beijing, the US and Pakistan signed a Mutual Defence Assistance Agreement in Karachi. The agreement had seven articles: the first talked about the *materiel* the US would transfer on the basis of this agreement, and spelt out where and in what circumstances this military hardware could be employed. The essentially defensive nature of the accord and the focus on collective security too were pointed out. The two governments also assured each other that both, but especially Pakistan, the recipient, would ensure the security of all material, information and funds thus exchanged. The second article dealt with questions of exchanging technical information and patents and ensuring necessary safeguards. Article three stated that Pakistan would provide the US with rupee funds with which the US military assistance team to be deployed to that country would carry out local administrative functions, the amount of this fund being determined by mutual negotiations. It was also stated that all material, equipment and items of property imported into Pakistan under this agreement would be accorded duty-free status; tax relief was to be granted to all American expenditure in Pakistan under the terms of this accord. The fourth article described the status of immunity to be enjoyed by members of the US military assistance team to be deployed to Pakistan who would be exempted from having to pay export or import duties on goods and services they required during their stay in Pakistan on duty. The fifth article demanded that Pakistan make its contribution to world peace and physically support the Charter of the United Nations by offering military service in the interest of global peace – this being largely effected by increasing its own armed strength, and assisting the United States with supplies of raw and semi-processed materials when such supplies were mutually agreed upon. According to article six, Pakistan agreed to join the US in controlling trade with 'nations which threaten the maintenance of world peace.'[25] Article seven stated that the agreement would continue in force until one year after receipt by either party notification of termination from the other. In short, consolidating the basic military alliance which the US and Pakistan had established in 1950, this agreement secured Karachi's position as Washington's avowed client in the subcontinent. South Asia's strategic map had thus become even more complex now that Delhi was tied to Beijing in a treaty defining their borders and consequent changes to their relationship, and Washington and Karachi had developed a collaborative linkage which could be, perhaps very incorrectly, construed to be poised against it.

## From Kashmir to Formosa

Delhi did, however, continue to play a role as a mediator and a conduit in the many transactions between the US and China but its rhetoric now suggested far greater sympathy with Beijing's cause than its declared policy of non-alignment would allow. In July 1954, visiting US Supreme Court judge, Justice William O. Douglas, had lunch with Nehru in Delhi. It is not clear if he was acting as an emissary of Washington but the two spent some time discussing Sino-Indian relations. Nehru 'spoke at length regarding Zhou En-lai's visit (in June 1954)'. He appeared to put a postive gloss on bilateral relations, maintaining the only difference between the two neighbours was over their borders. However, Nehru was not prepared to discuss the issue with Zhou and it did not come up in his meetings with his Chinese counterpart. India had, however, posted security checkpoints along the McMahon Line.[26] The US was understandably keen to obtain as much information about the Communist Chinese leadership from the Indians as possible. In mid-July, Ambassador George Allen met the Indian Vice President Radhakrishnan and asked him about the Vice President's impressions of Zhou. 'Radhakrishnan said Zhou was "reasonable about everything except the United States." Zhou said as long as US was determined to put Chiang Kai-shek back in Peking, his government had no alternative but to maintain its military strength at highest possible potential.'[27] Despite this collaboration at the highest levels in providing information, explanations and analyses regarding the Chinese leadership which Washington would not find anywhere else, Delhi was extremely unhappy about US regional security policy. Washington's recently concluded military assistance agreement with Pakistan and one with the Republic of China under discussion at the time were both seen as sources of major concern. Such concern was acknowledged by sections of the Department of State[28], but others felt the wider strategic interests being served by the alliance with Pakistan and Taiwan were of higher priority than assuaging Delhi's fears.

The autumn of 1954 proved to be trying for all the parties. As discussions of a security link-up between Washington and Taipei became more intense, and anti-Communist guerrilla activities grew more extensive, the war of words led to actual violence. On 3 September, PLA artillery units deployed to the coastal belt began shelling the disputed Quemoy island under KMT military occupation, triggering a major crisis. In october, it escalated further when PLA gunners began lobbing shells on the neighbouring Matsu island too. Eager not to get involved in a second Eastern theatre at a time when events on the Korean peninsula were far from settled, and Europe looked potentially turbulent, Washington sought indirect means of bringing pressures to bear on Beijing to force it to back off without offering pretexts for general escalation. The options appeared to be limited to covert operations. But these were not producing any spectacular results. The CIA's own assessment, presented in the form of a National Intelligence Estimate in mid-September, acknowledged that 'Organised guerrilla groups on the China mainland are few, small, and generally unimportant in spite of some local success.'[29]

Operations in Tibet now lost some urgency and priority as hostilities became a distinct possibility along the Chinese coasts. In late October, the Secretary of State reported to the NSC that current US policy vis-a-vis Communist China and the Republic of China was: encouragement of Chinese Nationalists' harassing operations by sea and air against Communist shipping, and against certain mainland targets of opportunity. For security reasons, the location, number and nature of these targets were not specified, but the report suggested that the latter element was partially and provisionally in suspension.[30] This caution was one of two contradictory strands to the US policy vis-a-vis China at the time. The Department of State sought, despite its unhappiness with the apparently monolithic communist power, to exercise circumspection in challenging the 'Marxist adversaries'; 'teeth services' such as the various intelligence organs and the armed forces, on the other hand, recommended a more robust policy to arrest, even roll back the 'spread' of communist control. One day after the

Secretary of State's report to the NSC, the Joint Strategic Survey Committee filed a memorandum to the Joint Chiefs of Staff which said 'Current United States policy applicable to Communist China and the Soviet bloc in general provides, in part, that the United States "undertake selective, positive actions to eliminate Soviet-Communist control over any areas of the free world. In the absence of further Chinese Communist aggression, or a basic change in the situation, the policy of the United States toward Communist China should currently be to seek, by means short of war to reduce the relative power position of Communist China in Asia".'[31] The Establishment's division between 'hawks' and 'doves' was underscored in numerous discussions in Washington around this time. One contemporary NSC document refined the Government's policy to state that it was to 'Reduce the power of Communist China even at the risk of but without deliberately provoking war.'[32] Given US belief at the time that China was an instrument of Moscow and Washington's determination to avoid a general war with the Soviet Union, this caution was understandable. At the 221st meeting of the NSC on 2 November, the President approved action recommended by his advisers. What was not clear from the debates between the Department of State and the Pentagon, for instance, and between various sections within the diplomatic and defense establishments, was where the limits of US activism would eventually be drawn, and who would ensure that executive decisions were implemented as originally intended.

While the CIA and the Joint Chiefs of Staff embarked on their covert and not so covert operations to threaten and challenge Beijing's authority, officials in Washington were absorbed in exercises aimed at clarifying and articulating their own positions underpinning these operations. In December, the National Security Council submitted two policy proposals to the President. The first, issued on 10 December, recommended that the US 'utilize all feasible overt and covert means, consistent with a policy of not being provocative of war, to create discontent and internal divisions within each of the Communist-dominated areas of the Far East, and to impair their relations with the Soviet Union and with each other, particularly by stimulating Sino-Soviet estrangement, but refrain from assisting or encouraging offensive actions against Communist China or seaborne commerce with Communist China'.[33] This suggested that while landborne assistance to the Tibetan guerrillas across the Indian Himalayas was safe and reasonable, Taiwanese seaborne raids on the Chinese mainland and on Communist shipping in the Taiwan Straits were not. The need to strike a balance between reducing Communist Chinese effectiveness and avoiding direct hostilities which could escalate to a general war involving the Soviet Union engrossed NSC staff for months and possibly years in the 1950s. They were endlessly finetuning phrases which would reflect the subtleties of a nuanced approach, getting their suggestions to the right mix of activism and restraint. Their efforts culminated in

December in the signing of a US-Republic of China Mutual Defence Assistance treaty, an alliance which angered Beijing and annoyed Delhi, but delighted Taipei and reinforced Washington's ability to respond urgently to crises like the one over the islands of Quemoy and Matsu in the autumn. At the end of the year, the NSC presented yet another policy proposal which recommended:

'Continue covert operations . . . .

Continue military assistance and direct forces support for the Government of the Republic of China (GRC) armed forces to enable them . . . to contribute to non-Communist strength in the Far-East and for such other actions as may be mutually agreed upon under the terms of the Mutual Defense Treaty.

Continue co-ordinated military planning with the GRC designed to achieve maximum co-operation from it in furtherance of overall US military strategy in the Far-East.

Continue programmes in which Formosa serves as a base for psychological operations against the mainland.' [34]

The agreement between Washington and Taipei, and NSC 5441 which followed, brought US-Taiwanese collaboration against China into a formal framework. Officials from the two sides now met regularly to co-ordinate covert operations across the Himalayas. Although New Delhi was not pleased, the US and India tacitly worked together in the sense that they collaborated in their mutual silence. US operatives did not go out of their way to inform Delhi what they were doing, mostly from their operational control centre in Dhaka, the capital of Pakistan's eastern province, and from the tiny state of Sikkim which abutted on Tibet and had traditional cultural, religious and other ties to Lhasa. Geography ensured that some of these operations crossed Indian territory but Delhi's administrative reach in these distant ramparts was so attenuated that India could claim with some honesty that it had no knowledge of any foreign activities in the region. However, the honesty of such claims was only partial. As early as March 1952, Nehru had explained the threats to Indian security emanating from China's military control of Tibet to the Indian Intelligence Bureau (IB), sanctioning 'intelligence activities' in both Tibet and China.[35] A year later, Nehru authorised the Director, Intelligence Bureau, to meet the Dalai Lama's brother in Darjeeling, instructing Mullik to 'help the Tibetan refugees in every way possible.'[36] Tibetan refugees were already conducting logistical operations from Kalimpong to assist the resistance in eastern Tibet. Despite the growing warmth of Sino-Indian relations in 1954 and a clear commitment to respect the territorial integrity and sovereignty of China, especially Chinese control of Tibet, Nehru assured the Director, Intelligence Bureau, that same year that, 'even if these refugees helped their brethren inside Tibet, the Government of India would not take any notice and, unless they compromised themselves too openly, no Chinese protest would be entertained.'[37] Around the time of the conclusion of the *Panchshil* treaty between Beijing and Delhi, Nehru told his principal intelligence aide that the only way to 'raise Tibet again on her feet was to make India strong. It was only through India's strength that Tibetan autonomy could be re-established.' But Nehru was aware of India's weak military circumstances and he said he 'needed time to build up India.'[38]

It is difficult to reconcile these contradictory signals the documentation hints at. Events in 1954 proved to be particularly intriguing. Nehru visited both China and the US and was received with considerable warmth in both countries. His government spewed fire against US alliance-building efforts with Pakistan and Taiwan, and India itself signed an agreement with China reversing its fifty-year tradition of maintaining considerable influence in Tibet. Using the US-Pakistan Mutual Defence Assistance agreement as a pretext, Nehru reneged on his pledge to hold a plebiscite to determine the future of the disputed Jammu & Kashmir state and thereby removed whatever opportunity there was of establishing a measure of normalcy in the subcontinent. To mitigate Indian concerns with the consequences of US military supplies to Pakistan, Washington entered into a substantial agreement with Delhi in September 1954. This secret accord committed the US to transferring 'end-items' ie, military hardware and ordnance, and offering 'direct forces support' in the form of communications gear, transport equipment and training facilities worth $350 million over the next three years. Had the agreement been implemented with the expected degree of promptness, India may have been persuaded to maintain its position as a loyal client. In the event, Washington transferred the promised goods and services very slowly indeed and the Indians appear to have lost both patience and faith. And yet, as far as Tibet was concerned, Delhi did nothing to stop US and KMT operations being mounted from bases in East Pakistan and Sikkim through Indian territory, and, in fact, Indian intelligence itself became an active if secretive collaborator in the Tibetan national resistance. In terms of official rhetoric, however, Delhi steadily moved to the left of the US. Given the view prevailing in Washington at the time, this was not too hard to do.

India did not entirely pull out of its proximity to Washington in its role as a conduit to Beijing. In November, the US was especially troubled over the fate of American prisoners of war, mostly from the Korean war, detained by the Chinese. According to Washington's own estimates, 944 POWs were unaccounted for when Beijing announced plans to put 11 airmen captured from a downed B29 bomber on trial on charges of espionage and other serious crimes. Indian officials contacted their US counterparts to offer help in negotiating with the Chinese on what clearly was a sensitive issue for the Americans. The leader of India's delegation to the United Nations General Assembly, Krishna Menon, a close confidante of Nehru, too pitched in, presumably with the Prime Minister's authorisation. Seeking an appointment to see Secretary of State Dulles, Menon asked the latter if he, Menon, could be useful in connection with the US POWs in China. Menon pointed out that India held the chair of the 'neutral nations repatriation committee', an organisation established at the time of the Korean armistice. He said he believed there were possibilities of repatriating the POWs as part of a 'comprehensive settlement' between China and the US. This offer was not considered too helpful by Dulles; he said most POWs were members of the UN Command and the UN had a responsibility in securing their release. Menon, on the other hand, suggested that he did not think 'much good would come from UN.'[39] So, while India and the US did appear to slide apart on the question of US military assistance to Pakistan, on broader questions of dealing with China, Nehru and his colleagues still maintained their proximity. Department of State documents suggest that Krishna Menon sought to ingratiate himself with the Washington elite, especially the President and the Secreatry of State, with a view to making himself useful in helping the US secure the release of American prisoners from Chinese detention. In this, Menon was not very successful since he was treated with a greater degree of patience and tolerance by his US hosts than seriousness. Ironically, it was to be Pakistan's role to build bridges between the US and China, but that still lay many years in the future.

# CHAPTER 4

# Covert Collaboration in Diplomacy and War
## 1955–1957

The US-Pakistan Mutual Defence Assistance Agreement signed in May 1954 reinforced Washington's ability to persuade Karachi to do things considered important by US policymakers. It affected the perceived regional balance of power between the two client states Washington cultivated in the subcontinent, and as a result of Indian reaction, caused a measure of flux. As we have seen, Nehru was not mollified by Eisenhower's assurances to the extent of the latter's offers to supply India weapons of the variety being given to Pakistan. While disappointed over Delhi's response, Washington was determined to build up Pakistan's military capacity, and its economic strength to support that military capacity, with a view to protecting Middle Eastern oil fields from possible Soviet moves. In January 1955, the US and Pakistan signed a Defence Support Assistance Agreement which enabled Washington to offer considerable economic aid to Pakistan and free up its domestic resources for strengthening the military modernisation process set in train in 1954. The agreement enabled Pakistan to receive $60 million in the first six months of the year, and larger sums in subsequent annual tranches, but it also required Pakistan to provide equivalent amounts in local currency to be spent by mutual consent, ie, as advised by US consultants and economic advisers. The agreement made considerable resources available to the Pakistani authorities but also increased the role of their American patrons to both formulate policy and execute it.[1]

This development in US-Pakistani relations, to the extent that it was the consolidation of a trend, could not have pleased Jawaharlal Nehru and his government in Delhi. Angered by Washington's apparent lack of concern with Delhi's anxieties, Nehru now embarked on an exercise in ambivalence. On the one hand he continued co-operating with US operatives active in north-eastern India in their assistance to the Tibetan national resistance; on the other, he initiated a mediatory enterprise, seeking to bring Washington and Beijing close together in an effort to defuse tensions which had led to large-scale military preparations across the Taiwan Strait. As will be seen, he had only limited success in this enterprise.

The formalisation of the US-KMT alliance against China in late 1954 allowed the US to provide Taiwan with greater access to US *materiel* and intelligence resources in the KMT's ongoing struggle with Beijing's Communist rulers. As a *quid pro quo*, Washington was now better placed in calling the shots as to where these resources went. Because of Beijing's apparent leverage in the form of the fairly large number of US and other Western prisoners, detainees and downed airmen and agents in custody, the US was wary of the KMT's commando operations at sea and along China's south-eastern coasts. These high profile raids and ambushes, when detected, or on occasion when they went wrong, proved costly for Washington. On the other hand, the KMT was serving US interests in hitting Communist 'soft spots'! Washington and Taipei appeared to have reached a compromise by agreeing on reducing the profile of covert operations in and around the South China Sea, and instead, focusing on Tibet where the Chinese stake was relatively lower, and Beijing's ability to retaliate, more limited. Nonetheless, the importance of covert operations as an instrument of diplomacy vis-a-vis China was paramount since other options did not appear to be effecive. This was underscored in a policy statement issued by the US National Security Council (NSC) in mid-January 1955. To a large extent, US views were coloured by fears of possible Communist occupation of off-shore islands under KMT control.[2] The overwhelming nature of the PLA's superiority along the coasts meant that Chiang Kai-shek's forces would not be able to hold on to these in the face of a determined assault, and the US was reluctant to get directly involved in another confrontation with the Chinese so soon after Korea. The focus of the indirect approach thus shifted from China proper to Tibet.

India, whose territory had to be crossed, to get aid to the Tibetans in Kham and Amdo, was at this time something of a problem for the US. Unhappy over the US-Pakistan treaty and the US-Taiwan agreement, both signed in 1954, Delhi had openly moved to make peace with Beijing. Nehru and his close confidante, Krishna Menon, spearheaded an attempt by several newly-independent Afro-Asian countries to establish a 'third force' of non-aligned states, a group which would support neither the US and the West, nor the Soviet Union and its Communist allies. Nonetheless, Nehru was considered a helpful source of information and advice; when in early 1955 he attended the Commonwealth Prime Ministers' conference in London, US Ambassador to the UK, Winthrop Aldrich, sought Nehru's advice on possible moves in the Far East to resolve tensions around Taiwan. Vijaya Lakshmi Pandit, Nehru's sister, then the Indian High Commissioner in London, was present at this meeting. Nehru pointed out that India recognised Mao Tse-tung's government; hence it was impossible for India to consider Chiang's claim to Formosa legitimate. Nehru 'reiterated statement that history had passed Chiang Kai-shek by and compared his position to Indian princes. Nehru said that in his own interviews with Mao Tse-tung he had not found him unreasonable.'[3] Despite an apparently basic disagreement on the questions of the legitimacy of the Chinese government, Nehru assured the ambassador 'He would do everything in his power to be helpful.'[4]

Meanwhile, a group of successor states coalesced around India, Egypt, Indonesia and Yugoslavia. The group met at Bandung in Indonesia in the spring of 1955, where the five *Panchshil* principles enunciated a year ago in the preamble to the Sino-Indian agreement over Tibet, became the cornerstones of what came to be called the Non-aligned Movement, NAM. However, Nehru and Menon went on to exploit their NAM credentials with a view to securing the confidence of the authorities in Washington. At the end of April 1955, just back from Bandung, Menon informed US ambassador John Sherman Cooper in Delhi about the 'long hours' he had spent talking to Zhou En-lai and about his conviction that China was 'not expansionist'. Menon 'said Communist China appeared not to desire hostilities at this time but would not be "bullied" . . . Menon's tone was moderate. Nevertheless it seems clear to me that he accepts Chinese Communist position re sovereignty over Taiwan and holds that ultimate settlement would require ousting nationalists.'[5] Around this time, Nehru announced that Menon would visit Beijing within ten days to continue his talks with Prime Minister Zhou En-lai concerning the 'Taiwan situation' begun at Bandung.[6] Menon again met Cooper a few weeks later, certainly with Nehru's permission, after returning from his consultation with Chinese officials in Beijing. He advised the US ambassador that the freedom of US detainees in China could be secured with the release of Chinese nationals detained in the US. Menon also said US airmen would be released by Beijing if their relations were allowed to travel to China to see them.[7] He was told this second term was not acceptable.

Bandung generated another embarrassment of diplomatic riches for Washington. Despite having signed the Manila Pact, the precursor to the South East Asian Treaty Organisation, an overtly anti-Communist alliance sponsored by the US, Pakistan had been invited to attend the Afro-Asian summit in Bandung. The Pakistani Prime Minister, Mohammad Ali, met Zhou on 25 April and briefed the US ambassador in Jakarta, Hugh S. Cumming, the following day. According to Ali, Zhou had said to him that China had 'made a gesture and the United States had not responded.' Zhou invited Ali to visit Beijing, and Ali asked Cumming for US views on the advisability of his accepting the invitation and 'pursuing further his conversations with Chou on subject Taiwan'.[8] At the end of April, the Secretary of State sent a message to the US ambassador in Karachi where some of Washington's impatience with South Asian diplomatic initiatives came to the surface. The telegraph said,

'Following is for your guidance in event Mohammad Ali requests your views.

We should not encourage Ali accept Chou's invitation or seek definitely to dissuade him since either course might be misunderstood and possibly misused by him. Decision must essentially be his own, after consideration all factors. We are concerned implications visit by Ali at this time since it would be first visit Peiping by Asian leader whose Government clearly aligned with anti-Communist camp and party to Manila Pact. As such would be feather in Chou's hat since important objective his performance Bandung was to elicit public evidence Peiping's acceptance in community of nations. We assume Ali aware these factors and will give them consideration.

With regard to Prime Minister's offer mediate he may be informed we have given most careful consideration to his offer and deeply appreciate his willingness be of assistance. While we do not believe necessary utilize at this time, we will keep in mind his desire to be of assistance. You are also authorized inform Prime Minister United States is not utilizing services of any intermediary at present and specifically Krishna Menon's prospective trip Peiping not undertaken at our request or with our knowledge. Dulles.'[9]

The Pakistani initiative fizzled out quite quickly, but the Indian one did not.

Menon's repeated overtures failed to elicit the kind of response from Washington which Delhi may have hoped to secure. As though to reinforce Menon's missives, Nehru himself wrote to President Eisenhower on the day he received Menon's report on the latter's return from Beijing. Nehru explained his government's interests in helping the US and China to resolve their disputes. The letter was delivered to the President by the Indian ambassador Gaganvihari Lallubhai Mehta on 27 May 1955. Nehru said although India did not represent either party to the dispute, as a friend of both, it was aware of the positions of the two antagonists and because of this, he felt he could act as an intermediary. Following recent exchanges, particularly with Chinese leaders, Nehru now suggested specific steps for the US to take which would reduce tensions and lead to the reciprocal release of US nationals detained in China and Chinese nationals detained in the US. To prove his credentials as a conduit, he specified the date and timing of forthcoming announcements to be made by Beijing in this regard. Nehru went on to suggest a timetable and framework for further negotiations between the US and China, presumably with a continuing role for India as an honest broker, although this was not specified per se.[10] In his immediate response, Eisenhower instructed that his 'gratitude', and an invitation to Krishna Menon to visit the White House for private and informal talks, be conveyed to Nehru and this was done by Ambassador Cooper.[11] Dulles too wrote a letter to Nehru soon afterwards to thank him for the efforts he had made for securing the release of the US prisoners detained in China.[12]

Washington officials appear to have been taken aback by the extent of the initiative taken by Nehru and Menon on their behalf. While gratified by the latter's success in securing the release of four of the US airmen detained in China, US policymakers felt they could not allow Indian leaders to shape the course of events to such an extent that Washington would be obliged to act in response to a *fait accompli* designed in Delhi and Beijing. In early June, after Delhi had informed Washington that Menon would be leading the Indian delegation to the United Nations, and during his visit to the US, would very much like to meet the President and the Secretary of State, Acting Assistant Secretary of State for Far Eastern Affairs William J. Sebald wrote to the Secretary of State about possible responses to Nehru's initiatives with the Chinese. He suggested that the US tell Menon Washington's aims were to:

(i)   secure early release of remaining US airmen and if possible, of civilian detainees,
(ii)  extend present tacit avoidance of hostilities in Taiwan area,
(iii) convey sincerity of US desire to seek peaceful solutions to troublespots including Taiwan, and
(iv)  avoid specific commitments which might limit freedom of action of the Chinese Nationalist Government.[13]

Sebald's advice appears to have provided the basis for Washington's response to the flurry of meetings with Menon which followed.

President Eisenhower received Menon in the morning on 14 June 1955 at the White House. Dulles and Indian ambassador Mehta were present at the meeting. Menon said he was not an 'authorised representative of Communist China or the United States' but that he was merely 'trying in a friendly way to prevent a tense situation from becoming worse and developing into a war'. He briefed the President on his talks in Beijing with Zhou and other Chinese officials, and asked to see the President once again. The latter agreed 'if this would serve a useful purpose', but not before early July. Menon said 'he would be prepared to wait that long.'[14]

That same afternoon, Dulles received Menon and the Indian ambassador at the Department of State. Menon said he was trying to ascertain if there was a possible basis for agreement on entering into direct negotiations between the US and China, what conditions should be established precedent to such negotiations, and what form such talks should take. 'In a general exposition of the point of view of Prime Minister Nehru and himself, Menon quite intently explained that India wanted to help increase and promote the prestige of the United States throughout Asia and that India was not opposed to the United States.'[15] Menon met Dulles the following day in New York where both were attending the United Nations General Assembly. This time around they met alone and Dulles himself recorded the proceedings. Menon said the families of the US airmen should be allowed to go to China and so should US journalists and broadcasters. He also asked if they could discuss the hypothetical situation if the prisoners-of-war were released. He wanted to know if he could be officially informed that the Chinese students in the US wanting to go back to China were free to leave. Dulles told him the US would accept no conditions whatever and demanded the immediate release of all US detainees held in China. Menon 'asked if he could see me again in San Francisco (where the UN session would be moving). I said that if he were out there, we could probably set up some time'.[16]

Once in San Francisco, the President and the Secretary of State were once again approached by the Indian mission with requests to see Menon. On 19 June, Eisenhower and Dulles met alone to discuss their quandary. Once again, Dulles recorded the minutes. He wrote 'I told the Prez (sic) that Menon was troublesome, because he was mixing up the channels of communications; and no one knew quite where we stood, particularly (UN Secretary-General Dag) Hammarskjold and the UN. The Prez agreed, but said he did not see that we could do any less in view of the personal plea from Nehru.'[17] It was clear that Eisenhower, and perhaps to a lesser extent, Dulles, saw Nehru as an ally whose pleas, unlike those from the Pakistani Prime Minister, could not be sidestepped or ignored. Menon was to see both Eisenhower and Dulles once again.

Meanwhile, following his discussions with the President, Dulles met British Foreign Secretary Harold Macmillan on 20 June when they both agreed that on China, 'Menon was messing things up'. But the Americans 'had seen him because Nehru had written both the President and me urging that we do so.'[18] This explanation was necessary since it was the British, working through the Foreign Secretary himself, who were at the time providing the principal channel of communications between Washington and Beijing. It is not clear from the documentation why the Chinese allowed Nehru and Menon to convince themselves that they alone enjoyed Beijing's confidence as a conduit to Washington. It is possible that the Chinese wanted to keep their options open so that if one intermediary failed, there was a fallback. Alternately, Beijing may have sought to neutralise India's position as an ally of the US in the covert warfare that not only continued in eastern Tibet, but in the mid-1950s, was beginning to spread and challenge the effectiveness of Chinese control over large stretches of the plateau. While the motives driving the various actors remain somewhat unclear, their actions were better recorded.

Menon saw Dulles in Washington on 1 July when the latter said that five or six people were claiming to represent Zhou En-lai and it was difficult to identify China's real emissary. He said a competition was building up over the handling of the release by China of US prisoners. Menon said he had no wish to get involved in any competition and 'If our efforts have been harmful, we can withdraw.' Dulles said Indian intent was good but the outcome of Menon's labours nullified Dag Hammarskjold's work. Menon said the US public had an incorrect idea of China which was quite different from Russia. He said in China different political parties operated, and Beijing was not happy to remain dependent on one great power – this is why China wanted good relations with the US. Menon also expressed concern over US and KMT military build up around the Quemoy and Matsu islands, saying both he himself 'and his Prime Minister were anxious, he said, to avoid such loss of prestige by the United States.'[19] Dulles replied he had seen no evidence of China's goodwill and he could not negotiate the evacuation of Quemoy and Matsu. Menon asked for another appointment and Dulles promptly fixed 6 July at 11 AM. This second meeting did not go very well either, with each side arguing their respective case. Dulles asked the Geneva talks should be upgraded to ambassadorial level; Menon suggested the talks be shifted to Delhi or Moscow. Menon said the US should treat trade with China at par with trade with Russia; Dulles said that was effectively the case. Menon repeated that Zhou was 'a reasonable man' who wanted good relations with the US and that US passport-holders visiting China would be treated 'properly'; Dulles said the US could not rely on third countries to protect US citizens. Menon 'repeated that his government's position in opposition to the use of force was well known. The Secretary said he had always thought that was India's position. He did not believe that India would use force, for example, to take Goa. Mr. Menon said that was entirely correct.' Towards the end of the meeting Menon, hinting perhaps at near-desperation, said, 'If you could let us impress Peking that we had access to your mind, we could be more effective.'[20] The minutes do not reveal Dulles's response to this plea. When Menon asked for another appointment on the 12th or 13th of July, his host said he was busy. However, Menon was allowed briefly to see the President on the same day, ie, 6 July. There is no record of that meeting in any Department of State documents. Only Eisenhower's diary has a short entry. It says the President told Menon China must release all US prisoners and not bargain over their freedom. The diary entry says, 'This Menon does not accept.'[21]

Perhaps to reinforce the hands of his emissary, Nehru, at the time on a long trip across Europe and North Africa, had written to Eisenhower on 27 June broadly along the lines that Krishna Menon had been pursuing in Washington, New York and San Francisco. Dulles drafted a reply on Eisenhower's behalf in which the President thanked both Nehru and Menon for their efforts to help but reminded the Indian Prime Minister that at Bandung Zhou had expressed hopes for holding direct talks with the US and that ' I am inclined to think that the best step now to take is to explore this course.'[22] Nehru replied on 11 July using the US embassy in Cairo. Eisenhower saw this letter on the following day. Nehru said Zhou had informed him that diplomatic talks between the US and China at Consular level held in Geneva 'served little purpose'. Nehru also said that 'it might be possible to discuss other issues'.[23] By the time Eisenhower replied to Nehru, the latter had returned to Delhi. He said he was keen to raise the level of talks in Geneva if that would help.'We are quite prepared to make it clear in our communication to Chou En-lai that if our Geneva talks were conducted on a more authoritative level, this could facilitate further discussion and settlement of certain other practical matters now at issue between the two of us.'[24] In short, Washington was turning down Nehru's offers at mediation as gently as it could. Four days later, Dulles asked Macmillan to convey to Zhou the message that the US would raise the Geneva talks to ambassadorial level from 1 August, if he agreed. Zhou did. On 25 July, Washington and Beijing made simultaneous announcements of beginning 'negotiations through the diplomatic channels of the United Kingdom' on 1 August 1955 in Geneva.[25] Nehru's reaction to this development is not documented, but once his failure to secure a position of significance in Washington's calculations vis-a-vis Beijing became clear, he made another dramatic move in India's foreign policy formulation. Taking up an invitation extended some time ago, Nehru decided to visit Moscow.

## Peace Efforts and Covert Operations

The Chinese authorities in Tibet, meanwhile, had embarked on far-reaching steps to 'liberate' the people of Tibet. Perhaps the most significant measure was to build a network of motorable roads linking various parts of the plateau with China proper and with Xinjiang. Given the rugged nature of the terrain and non-availability of engineering gear and materials other than rocks, in Tibet itself, this was a considerable venture. Beijing appears to have understood that without the ability to move large bodies of men and shipments of *materiel* rapidly across the plateau, occupation would be difficult, and 'democratic reforms', impossible. The first motorway ran from Lake Kokonor in the north-east through Amdo to Lhasa. The other was a much more ambitious project aimed at linking Kanting/Kangding to the south-east across Kham with Lhasa. These were completed by the end of 1953 when the Chinese began extending additional roads, especially one which followed the tracks used by PLA units moving from Xinjiang, crossing the Aksai Chin snowy-desert in the north-eastern tip of Kashmir's Ladakh region into south-western Tibet, thus completing the pincer movement which militarily encircled the plateau in 1950. Once the motorways enabled the PLA to take physical control of towns, villages and nomadic settlements, 'reforms' would begin.

The PLA was methodical in its approach to effecting change. The 1951 agreement with the Dalai Lama's emissaries provided a juridical basis for Chinese activities in Tibet. The ruling elite, both lay and clerical, were assured that they had nothing to fear and indeed, in many committees which were set up to advise the Chinese on local matters, many lords and abbots were co-opted. Khampa leaders of Chamdo, Batang and Dergue were thus persuaded to co-operate with the PLA. But the Khampas in the eastern border districts were subjected to very different treatment. Public meetings were held in every village and the villagers were classified into five categories – capitalists, landowners, middle-class, smaller peasants and finally, agricultural labourers and servants. Members of the lowest classes were encouraged to denounce 'reactionary serf-owners' at long and abusive 'struggle sessions.' The Chinese were often surprised to find that despite the apparently primitive feudal social structure of Tibet, class-hatred was not as pronounced as they would have expected. This failure often led to frustration which, in turn, saw acts of barbarous conduct. In the Khampa districts of Apha, Kandze and Liangsham, for instance, the PLA soon gave up all pretension to legality and began treating the landowning Khampas like animals, riding them like ponies, in an effort to crush the spirit of these families and lowering their image before their neighbours. When this failed to impress the locals, a number of wealthy Tibetans were rounded up and shot in public view. In the Amdoa township of Doi, three hundred 'serf-owners' were shot in the head before a horrified crowd.[26] The PLA was soon providing protection to a large influx of Han-Chinese mainlanders who were given land taken away from Khampa landlords, and cattle confiscated from unfriendly pastoralists. When the Chinese tried to disarm the traditionally militant Khampa tribesmen, rebellion broke out. Out-manned and outgunned by the PLA, the rebels were often a disorganised mob of horsemen trying to attack the local Chinese garrison in a fit of frenzied outrage. Often the Chinese suffered some casualties in the first raid; but they soon recovered and hit back. The rebellion thus burst forth in one spot, was crushed soon afterwards in a bloody confrontation, then exploded somewhere else. The PLA was soon engaged in firefighting missions all over the eastern districts of Kham, and in parts of Amdo.

Communications being what they were, and all modern technology being under Chinese military control, news travelled slowly. But the PLA was not able to control all movements. The Pangda Tsang brothers, wealthy, influential and ambitious merchant-princes of the Po Dzong in the Markham district of Kham, decided to act. Rapgya Pangda Tsang, a former governor of the Markham district and an erstwhile communist-sympathiser, travelled in secret to Lhasa to mobilise elite opinion in the capital against the Chinese. In this he failed. The Dalai Lama and the National Assembly had just been forced to dismiss the two co-prime ministers, and the older of them, Lukhangwa, was so angry with the Chinese that he crossed the Himalayas into Kalimpong where he set about organising resistance. The Pangda Tsang brothers had a large establishment in that town, with offices, mules and horses in large stables, and spacious warehouses to store large quantities of commodities being exported and imported across the mountains. These facilities were now made available to Lukhangwa and his supporters. But in Lhasa itself, life under Chinese occupation remained calm. In fact, it was so calm that the Dalai Lama agreed to travel to Beijing to meet Mao Tse-tung and attend the 1954 session of National People's Congress there. While the Dalai Lama's party was making its slow progress across the mountains of Kham, a more organised rebellion broke out.

In August, reports citing Taiwanese sources, stated that 40,000 Tibetan farmers had challenged the PLA and in the conflict which followed, most were killed.[27] The gravity of the situation became clear when it was learnt that the PLA's 18th Army, rushed to help defeat the rebels, was not faring too well and that Soviet reinforcements had been deployed to 'advise' the Chinese.[28] Meanwhile, in Beijing, the Dalai Lama was persuaded to deliver an address eulogising the fraternal relations between his Tibetan subjects and other Chinese peoples. He had also met Mao in mid-September, and reportedly proclaimed his fidelity to the People's Republic. Despite the god-king's apparent satisfaction with the status quo, his devotees in eastern Tibet were increasingly restive. In late October, reports arrived of a major reverse suffered by the Chinese and their Soviet advisers; the PLA was said to have handed over the administration of the Lithang district to the powerful abbot of the Lithang monastery, and then departed to safer grounds.[29] This autumn revolt was, however, largely restricted to the regions east of the Yangtse. West of the river, the Khampas still pursued their traditional lives since the PLA had not yet put them under the kind of pressures being applied to their compatriots in the east. But the fear for the Dalai Lama's safety in Chinese hands was almost universal; late in 1954, three thousand Tibetan monks, including many in Kham, teamed up to write a petition sent via Kalimpong to Nehru asking him to press Beijing for the return of their living-god. The Dalai Lama returned in the spring of 1955. Enroute, he stopped at Chamdo where he advised his Khampa devotees to show moderation and desist from violence. Many Khampas found this advice no longer practical. Even in Lhasa, some people were beginning to get restive. The PLA began discouraging Tibetans from visiting monasteries. Interference in their religious devotions was not something Tibetans could accept. Rapgya Pangda Tsang slipped across the Himalayas into Kalimpong where he contacted both US operatives, and along with the Amdoa resistance leader, Gompo Sham, sought help from the Taiwanese agents based there.[30]

The Chinese were not pleased by this turn of events. In early November 1954, they had formally vested all military authority in Tibet in General Zhang Zing-wu. Zhang now began a major reinforcement-and-enforcement operation in eastern Tibet. The next step was to get the Tibetan members of the Chinese-sponsored 'Chamdo Liberation Committee' to approve of immediate implementation of what the Chinese called democratic reforms throughout Kham. The Chinese did wish to give the appearance of getting decisions taken democratically and put great store by such collective processes. They were, however, surprised when the Committe, and other local leaders, rejected the reform programme in unison. Committe members were next invited to the large Jomdho Dzong fortress some miles from Chamdo for considering matters of 'vital importance'. Once the conclave of Khampa leaders was safely closeted within the walls of the great Dzong, the Chinese commanders pointed out that armed sentries guarded all entrances and exits and that the prisoners were expected to endorse reforms or face indefinite detention. After a fortnight of discussions, the Khampas opted to act together and pretended to be persuaded by the Chinese arguments in favour of the 'liberation' of the masses. Once their agreement to Beijing's plans was secured, the PLA detachment relaxed its vigil. On the night of the fifteenth day of imprisonment, members of the Chamdo Liberation Committe surprised their Chinese guards and broke out of the Dzong. Some were killed in the ensuing firefight, but the rest escaped. From several accounts it appears that 23 of them gathered later, sending out messages to tribal and clan leaders across Kham, seeking unity of the Khampa people against the Han. Despite communication difficulties, the clans of Nangchen, Nakchu and Rakshi Gumpa, the Horpas of Kandze, the Chengtreng nomads and the dozen tribes of Markham abjured their blood-feuds and rose up in arms. Almost overnight, a guerrilla army of tens of thousands of Khampa warriors materialised across south-eastern Tibet, this time west of the Yangtse. They were joined by an estimated twenty-thousand strong band of the much feared Goloks from Butsang, Khangring, Khangsar and Tsangkor. The PLA was deployed across Kham in platoon and company-strength garrisons along the motorways trisecting the region. The guerrillas began attacking these in raids and ambushes, inflicting severe casualties on the Chinese forces. By the end of 1954, what would eventually become the National Volunteer Defence Army (NVDA), originally called the *Tensung Dhanglang Magar* (The Volunteer Army to Defend Buddhism) and *Chushi Gangdruk* (Four Rivers, Six Ranges – an ancient name of Tibet) had established pockets of 'liberated' areas where the PLA could not enter without taking grave risks. However, the fluid nature of guerrilla resistance meant that the NVDA was unable to hold territory and had to engage the PLA in a mobile campaign in the tradition of the people's war which the PLA's own Red Army precusror had refined in the 1940s.

The PLA had a very considerable advantage over the resistance. On Christmas-day in 1954, the Qinghai-Tibet and the Xikang-Tibet highways were declared open. This meant that all military resources freed up by the Korean armistice could be redeployed to Tibet from China using the PLA's large fleet of trucks along the motorways. The guerrillas could not match the PLA's *materiel* strength or its trained manpower. But they were fighting on their own land, and often fighting for their lives. Some of their detachments were receiving modest military assistance from their Taiwanese,

Indian and US supporters, but most of their ordnance came from investments made by Khampa merchant-princes like the Pangda Tsang brothers of Po and Gompo Tashi Andrugtsang, the Lithangwa leader who subsequently assumed command of the NVDA. A large quantity of ordnance was also procured from secret government arsenals to which sympathetic Lhasa officials gave them access.[31] The guerrillas' motivation was stronger and they frequently destroyed small, isolated, PLA detachments with little loss to themselves. Only when the two sides met in positional clashes did the PLA prevail. The most intense period of fighting began in the winter of 1955–1956 when an uprising centred around the town of Dartsedo or Kanting spread rapidly to become the 'Kanting rebellion'. Kanting was the Chinese administrative headquarters for the whole of eastern Tibet, and for several months in early 1956, the Khampas and allied tribes of Tibetans forced PLA units out of much of the region. Residual Chinese forces sought shelter in Drugmo Dzong in Nyarong district; the Tibetan resistance failed to capture this fortress despite several costly attempts.

Sometime later, PLA reinforcements from Kandze, Drango and Thawu relieved the besieged Chinese and the Nyarong guerrillas were forced to disperse. Casualty figures or orders of battles are not known, but the scale of combat might be gauged from some estimates: according to one author, the Chinese lost around 40,000 men dead in 1956–1959 while Tibetans from Khampa, Amdowa, Golok and other militias and resistance fighters from U Tsang and Loka may have had suffered 65,000 killed in the same period.[32] The PLA had deployed elements of two armies throughout Tibet, with concentrations around Lhasa, and in eastern Tibet. They had the support of their Soviet allies who provided advisers, combat troops and military hardware. The guerrillas, organised in disparate militias and operating without a coherent structure, brought together anywhere from 50,000 to 200,000 men, most of them ill-equipped and untrained in modern warfare.[33] They received modest help from small, secret cells within the Lhasa administration, who opened up arsenals hidden away in mountains and monasteries, and granaries originally stockpiled to meet the Tibetan government's needs. Some NVDA elements also received air-drops of arms, ammunition, explosives and other ordnance provided by the Taiwanese using airfields in Thailand, and the CIA's covert airlines operating from Thailand, Dhaka, and the various Indian airfields covered by the agreements signed in the late 1940s.[34] While the Indian government had indicated its reluctance to allow US aircraft carrying no combat or support markings to operate from Indian bases, the CIA solved this problem by either operating aircraft carrying Air Force markings, or having USAF aircraft baled to the Agency under the Tab-6 scheme. This was not special to the US operations in Tibet; similar devices were employed by the CIA in Indonesia, Laos and in Africa too.[35] It appears that the CIA carried out around 200 sorties overflying Tibet and western China, initially using its own aircraft carrying either no markings, or for those using Indian facilities, carrying USAF markings. Subsequently, the CIA engaged aircraft flown by its subsidiary, the Civil Air Transport (CAT) company, for these operations.[36]

### India's Diplomatic *Volte Face* and The Moment of History

While war raged in eastern Tibet and the Tibetan-populated districts of Szechwan, an almost equally dramatic event took place in India. Having failed to secure for Delhi a position of significance in the US strategic policy-making mechanism, Nehru went to Moscow. This visit, the first by the leader of a country militarily aligned with the US, was another indication of Nehru's interpretation of non-alignment. Nehru had administered a shock to the US with the Sino-Indian *Panchshil* Treaty at a time when the Indian Intelligence Bureau had been, under his instruction, assisting the Tibetan resistance. Now, when the CIA was operating covert airborne operations against the Chinese in Tibet from Indian airbases,[37] as well as from Dhaka, he turned to the post-Stalinist Soviet Union to assert India's independence. The mid-1950s saw Cold War tensions peak between the super powers. The pronounced shift hinted at by this visit needs to be understood in the context of all that had gone on in South Asia and in the realm of US policymaking with regard to the subcontinent until then. The US had indicated support for the holding of a plebiscite in Kashmir, thus reinforcing a UN Security Council resolution widely seen in India as supportive of Pakistan's position; Washington had rejected Delhi's offer to mediate with China despite protracted efforts by Menon and Nehru himself; and perhaps more painful for Delhi, the US had persisted in its attempts to shore up Pakistan's military and economic build-up, ignoring Indian protests. It appears Nehru felt he needed to demonstrate that while Washington needed India's assistance in the pursuit of its Containment of China, Delhi could consort with Washington's rival and thereby strengthen its own bargaining leverage with both. It may have been a non-traditional interpretation of the concept of non-alignment, but it was pragmatism at its best,and effective in securing India's perceived national interests.

Khruschev and Bulganin were pleased to receive the leader of the most prominent of the former colonial successor states and one that carried some influence in both the Afro-Asian circles and Western capitals. Agreements were signed to help India economically and technologically; the Soviet Union also came out openly supporting India's claim to Jammu & Kashmir. Nehru had every reason to feel his visit had been a great success and a victory for India. The Soviet leaders returned the compliment in November–December 1955 when they spent a month travelling across India with Nehru, and made a pointed visit to Srinagar, the capital of

Kashmir. Everywhere they went, the Soviet visitors were treated to a tumultuous and emotional welcome. Both the Congress and the Communist Party of India (CPI) organised rallies and receptions and Nehru made full use of the visitors' presence in India to spell out what he sought from India's superpower patrons. Addressing a civic reception at Calcutta in honour of the two Soviet leaders on 30 November 1955, the Indian prime minister said, perhaps with pragmatic tongue in strategic cheek,

> *We should keep ourselves free from military or like alliances and from the great power groups that dominate the world today. It is in no spirit of pride or arrogance that we pursue our own independent policy. We would not do otherwise unless we are false to everything India has stood for in the past and stands for today. We welcome association and friendship with all and the flow of thought and ideas of all kinds, but we reserve the right to choose our own path. That is the essence of Panchshil.*[38]

The US was clearly disappointed with the Indo-Soviet entente, especially at a time when the CIA, the Indian Air Force and the Indian Intelligence Bureau were working so closely together in their covert operations in support of the Tibetan resistance with high-level co-ordination being provided by the Prime Minister's Secretariat. But official US reaction was subdued and pained rather than overt or noisy. On 30 March 1956, the Operations Co-ordinating Board, a subcommittee of the US National Security Council (NSC), submitted a progress report on South Asia. The key points were the Soviet campaign 'to woo India and Afghanistan' which caused deep concern, the (Portuguese colony in) Goa issue which had 'seriously strained' US-Indian relations, and Pakistan's adherence in September 1955 to the Baghdad Pact alliance which marked 'a major step' forward.[39] The report described in some detail the Soviet leaders' visit to India and the various economic and diplomatic prizes offered to Delhi, the consequences of Washington's support for Portugal's claim to Goa (as well as the smaller enclaves in Daman and Dieu), and the border clashes between Indian and Pakistani forces which had underscored the volatility of relations between the two US client-states in the region. Despite these difficulties with India, the report noted several positive developments: General Maxwell Taylor had visited India and the Chief of the Indian Army Staff had reciprocated by visiting the US, the Indian Atomic Energy Commission had been presented with a library carrying a significant collection of nuclear research documentation. In addition, 17 C-119G cargo aircraft were delivered to the Indian air force to strengthen Delhi's ability to supply its own military forces, and presumably allied units, along the Tibetan borders; the Indian army and air force were permitted to procure hardware worth $33 million; and to obviate a proposed purchase by India of around 60 Soviet bombers, the US had released control over its

Green Satin radars installed on UK-built Canberra bombers to be sold to the Indian air force. Washington had also offered substantial economic assistance to India: a grant of $50 million had been released, 20,000 tons of wheat and rice had been given as flood relief, 500,000cc of Gamma Globulin had been given to Delhi as a gift, and Washington was planning a 3-year package for providing $400 million in foodgrains via the PL-480 programme.[40] What was not mentioned in the report but may have influenced Nehru's decision-making was Washington's failure to honour a commitment to provide much more substantial military assistance to India than has been reported elsewhere. In March 1956, Assistant Secretary of State Herbert Hoover visited Delhi and reviewed bilateral relations with senior Indian officials. This was part of the Administration's attempt to find out exactly what had gone wrong. In his report to Secretary of State Dulles, Hoover explained Delhi's disillusion with US reliability as an ally. 'A three-year commitment for end-items and direct forces support, now estimated to cost $350 million, was entered into in September 1954. With the period almost half gone, in early 1956, we have delivered only $21 million of hardware and little if any direct support. The same situation appears to exist in many other countries.'[41]

The report on Pakistan was shorter and more positive. It was noted that US-Pak co-operation had become much closer since 1953, and especially so since Pakistan joined the Baghdad Pact in September 1955. The US was now providing increasing flow of money and *materiel* in support of Pakistan's military modernisation and economic developmental goals. In fiscal 1955, Washington had supplied commodities paid for by its Defense Support funds; in fiscal 1956, $56.43 million was budgeted for Defense Support, and $6 million for Technical Co-operation. Obligations in March 1956 exceeded $35 million.[42] The report noted that Pakistan had been encouraged to strengthen its anti-Communist publicity and propaganda campaign. The report hopefully concluded that US assistance to the armed forces of both India and Pakistan had improved the latter's quality 'and the defense of the Free World was strengthened thereby in some measure.'[43] The optimism expressed in that report was, however, somewhat reduced by the nature of actual negotiations at that time being conducted between the US and Pakistan. Washington acknowledged the importance of Indian sensitivities vis-a-vis US military assistance to Pakistan at a time when the Kanting rebellion across the Tibet-Szechwan border demanded greater co-operation between the US and its collaborators among the executive agencies of the Indian government. The main concern expressed by Delhi was that Karachi would redeploy the hardware received from the US against India at the earliest opportunity and that Pakistan was not really concerned about Communist threats from the north. While still happy with Karachi's assertions of its anti-Communist motivations, Washington was troubled enough by Delhi's protestations to impose strenuous terms and conditions on Pakistani use of American hardware. The winter of 1955–1956 which saw the *Chushi Gangdruk* come into its own against the PLA and the Chinese administration in eastern-Tibetan areas also saw the beginning of the cooling off of the initial ardour of the US-Pakistan alliance. In March 1956, Dulles assured Nehru that should Pakistan attack India, presumably using US-supplied hardware, Washington would come to India's assistance. Following this assurance, Washington demanded and obtained Karachi's agreement on the pre-eminence of US wishes in determining how weapons and equipment supplied to Pakistan under the Mutual Defence Assistance Agreement of 1954 were to be used. On 15 March 1956, US ambassador Horace A. Hildreth wrote to the Pakistani Foreign Minister Hamidul Huq Chowdhury a letter that summarised bilateral talks on the subject and served as a draft agreement.

Hildreth asked that Pakistan 'report to the Government of the United States such equipment or materials as are no longer required or used exclusively and effectively for the purposes of and in accordance with Article I, paragraph 2 of the Mutual Defence Assistance Agreement. The Government of the United States may also draw to the attention of the appropriate authorities of the Government of Pakistan any equipment or materials which it considers to fall within the scope of these arrangements.'[44] Pakistan was left in no doubt that should the use by Pakistan of any item supplied by the US did not satisfy Washington, such hardware would be recalled and withdrawn, or even 'The Government of the United States may accept title to such equipment or materials for transfer to a third country or for such other disposition as may be made by the Government of the United States.'[45] The draft also laid down that should any transferred material be scrapped, only the US Government would determine how much of it could be salvaged and how the salvaged material should be disposed of. The documentation does not reveal the reasons behind the stringency being imposed, but the Pakistanis were concerned enough to agree to all terms and conditions, and perhaps thereby allay US suspicions, to have the letter countersigned by their foreign minister on the same day, and have it returned to Hildreth so that the letter became effective as a US-Pakistan agreement. If it was intended as a rebuke, it seems to have worked; there is no further evidence of comparable US misgiving until the 1960s. If it was designed to reassure India, it may have been only partially successful; Indo-US co-operation was to continue at the tactical-strategic level, ie, against the Chinese in Tibet, but at the truly strategic level, Delhi was pursuing a bi-alignment that would eventually establish Moscow as the pre-eminent external influence in the shaping of India's global security policies.

That Delhi's claims of Pakistani motivations contained some truth became evident when Vice President Richard Nixon visited Karachi in the summer of 1956. He had a meeting with President Iskander Mirza and Prime Minister I I Chundrigar. Nixon's hosts sought assurances of rapid US military operations if the Soviet Union attacked the Gulf. Mirza also asked for help with raising an additional infantry division so that the modernised Pakistan army would have a total of five infantry and half an armoured divisions. When talks veered to Tibet, Mirza pointed out that the Chinese were popular in Pakistan owing to 'good cotton business'. 'The Chinese were effective and intelligent people with wonderful manners.'[46] Eventually, discussions focused on India. Chundrigar complained that Canada and the US were helping India to build a $14 million nuclear reactor whereas Washington had offered only $350,000 to Pakistan for meeting half the cost of a small reactor. The Pakistanis also sought assistance with foodgrain buffer stocks and commercial credits. Mirza additionally expressed interest in procuring light bombers. He said 'in 1951 India did not attack Pakistan largely because they knew of six Halifax bombers in Pakistan. Mirza felt a light bomber squadron would be very helpful in deterring Afghan aggression as well as threats from India.'[47]

1956 was a year of intense activity, both diplomatic and covert-military. The Tibetan resistance continued to engage the PLA across a wide stretch of territory and its allies in India, Taiwan and the US worked ceaselessly to provide assistance. Beijing may have been taken aback by the ferocity of the opposition and its response was brutally violent, but the efficacy of the secret network of support stretching from the US through Hawai, Saipan, Guam, Taiwan, Chiang Mai, Dhaka, Dum Dum, Barrackpore and Kalimpong meant there was little evidence to support its complaints of 'imperial intervention' in Chinese affairs. However, overwhelming force eventually told on the guerrillas and by the end of 1956, the Chinese leadership was able to announce, if somewhat prematurely, the demise of 'the reactionaries and serf-owners and imperial agents'. Early in the new year in 1957, the 308th meeting of the NSC saw some lively exchanges where the diplomatic vs.military divide came to the fore. The Joint Chiefs of Staff wanted the President to assume a more activist stance, using NSC-5409 to enable him to take military action if a South Asian country other than Pakistan, ie, India, sought help to counter a Communist attack without having to go to the Congress first.[48] Eisenhower decided against such a policy-statement saying he would not have his hands tied down by such a pronouncement. The Chief Executive was clearly opposed to any move which might make it easier for the executive branch of government to launch overt military operations. He was also quite critical of the fact that the US was doing 'practically nothing for Pakistan except in the form of military aid.' Eisenhower said it was 'a terrible error, but we now seem hopelessly involved in it.'[49] The NSC recognised that any more aid to Pakistan in response to Karachi's intermittent pleas would lead India to expect more aid as well. When it was pointed out that compared to Pakistan, India was more 'neutral', the President said he was not too unhappy with the kind of neutrality India was pursuing because to turn

India into a 'positive ally', the US would not have the money India would require as a US ally.[50]

For India too, 1956 turned out to be a year of intense action. With Yampel and Rapgya Pangda Tsang at Kalimpong and Topgay Pangda Tsang in Kham moving large amounts of Chinese silver dollars to India and buying considerable volumes of ordnance for the resistance, with the CIA and the IB operating a growing network of links between the NVDA and its sub-montane supporters, and with the 2500th anniversary of Goutam Buddha's birth approaching, Delhi was a hive of activities. The Dalai Lama had been invited to attend the anniversary festivities in various parts of India but did not receive Chinese permission to travel until very late in 1956. India, keen to play the role of an honest broker, certainly to the world and especially to the Beijing leadership, also asked Zhou to visit Delhi at the same time. Nehru was troubled when the Dalai Lama asked to stay on in India and not suffer the indignity and pain of seeing his ancient kingdom and its people being subjected to continued Chinese brutality. Nehru consulted Zhou and asked the latter to reassure the Tibetan god-king that peace and harmony would be restored to the plateau. Despite the overtly religious nature of the Dalai Lama's visit, both Nehru and Zhou fully utilised the opportunity to secure respective diplomatic and security interests. For several weeks in November and December, the three leaders met separately with each other – the Dalai Lama politely demanding that Zhou assure an end to PLA barbarity, Zhou offering such assurance with all the charming sincerity at his command, and Nehru ensuring that Delhi was seen by both visitors as a friendly and reliable mediator. Judging by the outcome of these discussions, all three succeeded.

For Washington though, concern with South Asia remained topical for a number of reasons, not least because both Indian and Pakistani delegations to the United Nations were in New York at the time and the leaders of both delegations had asked to see the US envoy. The latter needed Washington's advice. The Indian mission, once again led by Krishna Menon, this time around focused on the Kashmir issue. Menon told the US mission that even if a plebiscite was held in Kashmir, Pakistan could only win it by fanning religious sentiments which could lead to another round of rioting. Menon also insisted that Ladakh would never go to Pakistan and would rather secede to Tibet, ie, Communist China. That could then trigger secessionism in other Buddhist areas in Northern India and 'move Communist China strategically into South Asia.'[51] Menon reflected Delhi's concern that should the UN Security Council pass another resolution demanding that its earlier injunction regarding a plebiscite be implemented, India could be left in a difficult position. He met Henry Cabot Lodge again and said the Security Council should take no action on Kashmir; India was not prepared to give up any of its legal position on Kashmir. He repeated Delhi's position that the entire State had formally acceded to India 'in proper form' at the time of partition by agreement between the UK, India and Pakistan, and the Indian constitution, like that of the US, did not have any provision for secession. He said 'if Kashmir were allowed to secede this might disrupt unity of Indian state in as much as over 500 other states and principalities had acceded to India in same fashion as Kashmir'.[52] Menon reassured Lodge that 'India had no military intentions re areas they did not control . . . best indications of lack of Indian military intentions was fact it had done nothing about East Bengal and Goa. He said East Bengal would fall to India if India blew hard and Goa could be taken by six policemen.'[53] Having issued this none-too-subtle hint for Pakistan and its allies, Menon said the Indian position was based on two fundamental points – the legality of Kashmir's accession and problems of military security. He said he could not publicly talk about security aspects of the Kashmir issue. He also expressed concern about Pakistan's stability – there was 'much leftist tendency in Pakistan and Moslems were very susceptible to Communist doctrines. Pakistan had conservative government now, but it was questionable how long it would last. Next year government might be leftist and following year Communist.' This would cause great concern in India and India had to take special precautions for its security. Menon also repeated his comment of Ladakh going to Tibet should a plebiscite be held and Pakistan won it. 'On plebiscite Menon said that if India were ever foolish enough to agree it would produce communal riots in India and upset Indian efforts to be secular state.'[54]

The drive behind Menon's rather hard-headed approach is not revealed by the documentation. His failure to elicit a positive response from his US interlocutors in the previous year and Nehru's consequent frustration may have made a contribution; the new warmth between Delhi and Moscow may have strengthened Indian resolve to stand its ground, especially on Kashmir; Washington's increasing dependence on India for the Tibet operations too may have been a factor; Delhi's recent success in persuading the US to clamp restrictions on the use of US-supplied military hardware down on Pakistan might have boosted the confidence of its chief delegate to the UN. Menon may also have been encouraged by the fact that Nehru had accepted an invitation to visit the US and his prospective hosts were keen to make up for whatever had been lost to Moscow.

Nehru was due to arrive in mid-December, 1956, and throughout November and early December, correspondence between the Department of State and the US embassy in Delhi underscored the anxiety afflicting Washington to get it right. The most detailed set of recommendations came in the form of a memorandum from Counsellor Frederik P. Bartlett who was standing in for ambassador John Sherman Cooper who was ill. Bartlett began with a backgrounder on India's economic difficulties, especially potential inflation, foreign currency shortfalls, and the danger of India falling behind China in economic progress posed by failure of the Five Year

Plan. He went on to suggest that the recent loss of prestige of the Soviet Union and the UK – presumably over Hungary and Suez respectively, although Bartlett did not specify these – the US now had an opportunity to strengthen its diplomatic influence over Delhi. Bartlett suggested greater economic assistance to India and efforts to woo the US Congress so that American public perception of India became more friendly which, in turn, would persuade Nehru to pay greater attention to US sensitivities and help narrow gaps on such issues as China's role in the international system, military assistance to Pakistan, US military bases and pacts, and nuclear tests. Bartlett also reassured Washington that Zhou's extended visit to India notwithstanding, Delhi was deeply concerned over Chinese activities.[55] It is very likely that like most of his Foreign Service peers, Bartlett knew nothing about the 1951 Indo-US Military Assistance Agreement or their covert collaboration against China in Tibet. He saw India as a natural counter-weight to China and underscored the rationale behind an alliance between the US and India on a strategic level. He concluded, 'We feel strongly that "moment of history" has arrived which if seized and exploited, can give US much firmer anti-Communist and anti-Red China counterpoise in India . . . If India were convinced of our enduring interest in seeing her through the critical years ahead, India might be expected to ameliorate some of her present objections to American policy, especially as regards Pakistan, SEATO, the Baghdad Pact. Risks are involved but it appears to us that the risks are greater of losing India through failure to exploit the opportunities now presented.'[56]

In Washington, Nehru was lionized. There were a number of public and private engagements, meetings and receptions at which mutual admiration was much in evidence. He also spent a fair amount of time discussing bilateral relations with President Eisenhower. Several of these sessions were unattended by aides. Records of the proceedings of these discussions have not been released, but given the background, it can be surmised that talks focused on strategic issues, especially those relating to the US and Indian perceptions of the threats and opportunities presented by the Soviet Union and China. While differences remained on the question of US military aid to Pakistan, Washington's imposition of restrictions on the latter was reassuring. On China too, there was increasing convergence not just at the tactical level but also in the belief that Beijing did pose considerable potential threat to India's territorial integrity. The Administration was able to announce a large tranche of both immediate and medium-term economic assistance to India. The visit was, to that extent, a mutual success. Nehru's address to his hosts, the US public, was broadcast on radio and television on 18 December. He concentrated on the great moral principles shared by the founders of the two countries. 'Our two Republics share a common faith in democratic institutions and the democratic way of life and are dedicated to the cause of peace and freedom. We admire the many qualities that have made this country great, and, more especially, the humanity and dynamism of its people and the great principles to which the fathers of the American revolution gave utterance. We wish to learn from you and we plead for your friendship, and your co-operation and sympathy in the great task that we have undertaken in our own country.'[57]

Whether Eisenhower seized Bartlett's 'moment of history' or not, the breach was healed and Indo-US relations were restored to their earlier health. Mutual reassurance and convergence on 'the Chinese threat' led to a significant increase in the range and scope of covert operations across the Himalyas. Nehru is likely to have urged his hosts to reduce the activities of the KMT on Indian soil and from early 1957, the Taiwanese slack in supporting the NVDA was taken up by the CIA. The outcome of discussions between Nehru and Eisenhower was summed up in a memorandum prepared by NSC staff shortly after Nehru's departure. It said 'It is in the United States national interest that the genuine independence of India be strengthened and that a moderate, non-Communist government succeed in consolidating the allegiance of the Indian people . . . A strong India would be a successful example of an alternative to Communism in an Asian context . . . In view of the intensified threat to Free World interests in Asia posed by the rapid growth in Chinese Communist power, should our basic objective toward India be stated more correctly as "the development of a strong India, more friendly to the United States, and better able to serve as a counterweight to Communist China?"'[58]

There was now such a spurt in the Tibetan resistance that across large swathes of eastern Tibet, Chinese administration was reduced to beleaguered PLA garrisons waiting for relief and reinforcement. In Tibetan-populated Qinghai, Gansu and Szechuan, the PLA rushed around 150,000 troops to contain the rebellion and to ensure the guerrillas did not break out of the proposed Tibet Autonomous Region (TAR).[59] This reaction to Beijing's attempts at 'liberating' the people of Tibet persuaded Mao Tse-tung that the Central People's Government did not yet have the means of converting the Tibetans to socialism. On 27 February 1957, he delivered a speech 'on the Correct Handling of Contradictions Among the People' in which he for the first time admitted to facing difficulties in Tibet. He said conditions there were not yet 'ripe' for 'democratic reforms', ie, identification and elimination of the 'reactionary serf-owners and capitalists', confiscation of land, animal-herds and other property from the former, collectivisation of economic activities by redistributing confiscated property among poorer Tibetans and the growing army of Han settlers, and the destruction of the power and status of the Lamaist clergy, replacing these with the authority of the Chinese Communist military and civil administration. Mao conceded that these reforms could be implemented 'only when the great majority of the people of Tibet and their leading public figures consider it practicable.'[60] Mao announced that reforms in Tibet would not be implemented in the forthcoming Second Five Year Plan-period, ie, in 1958–1962. This was as close to an admission of defeat as the Great Helmsman was going to make.

The restoration of Indo-US friendship was so effective in weakening Beijing's hold over Tibet that at the 327th meeting of the NSC in June 1957, Director of Central Intelligence, Allen Dulles, noted the withdrawal of large numbers PLA units 'from Tibetan land, possibly in the face of Tibetan resistance and economic problems'.[61] The DCI's asessment suggested that Beijing would perhaps change its military method with a view to gaining Tibetan loyalty. President Eisenhower asked if the deployment of PLA units to Tibet had not also been intended to increase pressure on India; Dulles agreed that it was. The evident effectiveness of heightened Indo-US collaboration was reviewed at an Operations Coordinating Board (OCB) meeting in early July. The OCB laid down special operating guidelines for all executive agencies of the Administration in dealing with India. Delhi's strategic significance in the pursuit of US national interests, and the dilemma of supporting a regional great-power aspirant, were highlighted in these guidelines, which are being quoted at some length here.

> *It should be borne in mind in dealing with India that it is not merely the largest of the less developed countries, but is very important in itself to US policy. It is one of the leading powers of the world and stands pre-eminent among the free Asian-African countries. Communist China's tacit yet certain rivalry with India is one of the basic facts of Asian politics. Its implication to US policy and operations lies in the inevitable comparison that will be made between the two countries' progress – the one depending upon totalitarian controls and devices, and the other relying on democratic processes and methods. The outcome of the race could have a very considerable effect on the other and much smaller Asian countries. India is deeply and officially committed to an 'independent' foreign policy amounting to neutralism between the Communist bloc and the West. Equally, if not more important, the US is committed to support its ally Pakistan against Communist aggression, and India has interpreted this commitment as a potential danger to India's security. The intensity of India's resentment of this alliance is a reflection of age-old communal tensions between Hindus and Muslims, greatly exacerbated by the partition of the subcontinent and the ensuing, bitter Kashmir dispute. There appears to be no easy 'out' to the dilemma, but with patience there may be a chance eventually to persuade India that its oft-expressed fears of the misuse of US military aid to Pakistan in aggressive action against India are unfounded and harmful to India's aspirations for a reputation of objectivity.*

> *In spite of the conflict between certain United States and Indian policy objectives, there are many lines of parallel action: to stand against further Communist expansion; to limit Chinese Communist influence in South and Southeast Asia; to limit Soviet influence in the Near East and Africa; and to foster regional co-operation among the non-Communist countries of both continents. India of course hopes to extend and strengthen its ties with its smaller neighbours generally. While an Indian 'sphere of influence' would not necessarily be consistent with United States aims, no serious problem is posed to present American policy so long as India remains non-Communist and democratically oriented. On the contrary, Indian influence contributes to the stability of parts of Free Asia.[62]*

The documentation does not reveal the degree of access OCB staff enjoyed to CIA operational information which would have made it clear to them that the current level of success in 'bleeding' the PLA in and around Tibet would have been impossible without close co-operation of the Indian government at its highest level irrespective of the differences dividing Washington and Delhi. Indo-US support for the *Chushi Gangdruk* now reached new heights. Intelligence officers working for the CIA and the IB began recruiting large drafts of Tibetan guerrillas from among the exile community in Sikkim and India's North-Eastern Frontier Agency, especially the Tawang Tract. Sturdy young men in the employ of the Pangda Tsang brothers at Kalimpong too would be inducted. Initially, most of them would be brought down to the Cooch Bihar area of West Bengal where they would be given a change of clothes similar to what the Bengalis of East Pakistan normally wore. At the border, they were asked to walk into a selected stretch of Pakistan's Dinajpur district where they would be received by officers from a detachment of Pakistan Military Intelligence's 'Geo-survey Unit'. Occasionally, CIA liaison officers too would be in the small reception teams. The recruits would sometimes be asked to walk across country to Dhaka, the sleepy capital of East Pakistan where aircraft of the US National Military Establishment would fly them out to Taiwan, Guam or Saipan via Chiang Mai in Thailand for training. The guerrillas would be given basic training in weapons-handling, signal communications, survival techniques, close-quarter battle and unarmed combat, sabotage using explosives, and parachute drops. Once Nehru became confident that more direct Indian involvement was in Indian national interest, some Tibetan recruits began being flown out of Dum Dum airport just outside Calcutta. The best of the guerrilla trainees were flown across the Pacific to Camp Hale in Colorado where advanced training lasting several weeks was designed to turn angry Khampa fighters into commanders of the resistance. The induction of the Lockheed C-130 Hercules long-range cargo aircraft into the USAF and subsequently, the CAT and other CIA-owned operations, increased the range of what the Tibetans' allies could do for them and how frequently. The late 1950s were the only period in the Tibetan saga when many guerrillas could almost realistically believe in the ultimate success of their struggle.

The PLA was under intense pressure across much of the plateau. When Under Secretary of State Christian Herter visited Taiwan in the autumn of 1957, Chiang Kaishek informed him that the Chinese Communists were facing considerable difficulties and not only in Tibet. According to the KMT's intelligence, anti-communist resistance had burgeoned in Xinjiang and Mongolia as well as in Tibet. Since May 1957, these movements had become especially powerful and active, forcing Beijing 'to take drastic action'. Chiang urged the US to take serious steps to exploit these opportunities. He warned Herter of 'the serious repercussions for the Government of Republic of China and the US if we let this movement die down'.[63] Chiang had submitted an ambitious plan in late 1956 for the US to train a large number of KMT paratroopers so that Taiwan could drop these troops in areas 'liberated' by resistance forces as a first step in a process of 'liberating China'. In the end, the US agreed to train several thousand KMT paratroopers in addition to the Taiwanese Airborne Regiment, but there is no indication that the US seriously believed in being able to 'liberate China' by deploying large numbers of paratroopers, Taiwanese or otherwise. Washington was now counting on India to provide an effective counterpoise to China. The Administration closely monitored Delhi and toward the end of the year the President was reassured by a National Intelligence Estimate which stated 'India is unlikely to make any significant change in its policy toward Communist China as long as Nehru heads the government'.[64] Given the degree of co-operation between the two governments and their intelligence organs, this stable predictability was welcome news for Washington.

Meanwhile, as the year drew to a close, in Washington, a rather unusual and intriguing line of thinking emerged in one section of the Department of State. Robert McClintock of the Department's Policy Planning Staff drafted a review of US policy toward China in which he made certain radical recommendations. McClintock appeared to build upon Nixon's comments following his Far Eastern tour three years earlier and said the emergence of the People's Republic of China as the legitimate Chinese authority was inevitable and that the US should prepare itself for this development. He suggested that Washington negotiate a settlement with Beijing over the next decade at the end of which the US and China would sign a 'Pacific Pact' under which Vietnam and Korea would be militarily neutralised and unified and China would be admitted to the United Nations. With regard to the trans-Himalayan battleground, McClintock wrote, 'Tibet would be neutralized, its independence and territorial integrity guaranteed by the limitrophe states, the USSR, China, India and Nepal. Simultaneously,

Chinese troops would be withdrawn from Tibet. Tibet, if it desired, would be admitted to the UN.'[65] Given the context of the reality in which the Policy Planning Staff operated, McClintock's New Year's Eve proposal was too radical, even visionary, for being implemented. It seemed to challenge the very basis on which US policy toward the Far East generally and China in particular was premised. A whole architecture of strategic alliances had been erected at considerable cost in pursuit of the Containment objective; the support of numerous states had been secured, often bought, to that end. Much blood, treasure and 'face' had been invested in that enterprise and thousands of Tibetans had been encouraged to sacrifice their lives, limbs and property in that endeavour. What's more, the project seemed to be succeeding. Early in the year Mao had come close to conceding defeat and postponed 'democratic reforms' in Tibet for another six years. Surely this was no time for a *volte face*! As it turned out, Washington did persist in its 'bleeding' operations for over a decade after McClintock drafted his remarkable review. It would take years before Richard Nixon would refashion the world's strategic centre with China as a partner, but by pointing the way, McClintock may have seized 'the moment of history' in a manner not intended in the Bartlett memo.

# CHAPTER 5

# War Clouds Gather

By the end of 1957, the *Panchshil Treaty* was in tatters. India and China had come out openly with differing claims of the alignment of the Himalayan boundaries between Tibet and northern Indian territories. Beijing and Delhi had published maps showing claims and counter-claims, and worse still, there had been occasional instances of border guards crossing the undemarcated, and often undelimited, borders uninvited. The Indians claimed that the frontiers inherited by Delhi from the British were legitimate and mutually accepted by all the properly constituted authorities concerned; the Chinese, on the other hand, appeared to maintain that the British imperial authorities had forcibly extracted a lot of concessions from the Chinese in the eighteenth, nineteenth and even the twentieth centuries, and the fruits of that extortion, in Beijing's view, should not be enjoyed by post-colonial India,and that Beijing was determined to restore its own rights and claims anyway.[1] The border dispute provided the pretext for increasingly bitter exchanges between the two neighbours. The Chinese also made clear in some of their official notes that they believed India was not only permitting the Tibetan resistance to make use of Indian territory as sanctuary but also allowing anti-Communist Western powers, ie, the US, to operate from Indian soil against Chinese interests. Delhi consistently rejected this claim, often with an expression betraying hurt and surprise.

Early in 1958, Delhi asked Washington substantially to increase the transfer of *materiel* to both the Tibetan resistance operating from bases in north-eastern India, and to India's own Intelligence organs and the Indian armed forces deployed to the northern borders. Washington responded positively to this request in the face of Beijing's growing cantankerous approach to India. However, it also directed its *Charge' d'Affaires* in Delhi to secure confirmation from the Government of India that the new hardware, support material and information would not be used in any offensive operations, presumably against Pakistan, the US's other client-state in the region, but also perhaps against China with which the US was very reluctant to get involved in a direct engagement. Such clashes carried the potential of drawing Moscow in and thereby escalate out of hand. The

US *Charge'*, Winthrop G. Brown, wrote to Nehru on 16 April 1958, asking for assurances that US military and intelligence assistance to India would be used in accordance with the stipulations of the Mutual Defense Assistance Act of 1949, as amended, and that these strictures were 'to be applicable also to equipment, materials, information and services furnished under the Mutual Security Act of 1954, that Act as amended from time to time, and such other applicable United States laws as may come into effect.'[2] Nehru did not reply. In fact, Delhi would not formally respond to this note for eight months. But given the progressive intensity of clashes between the Chinese and Indian forces, closely monitored by US diplomats and intelligence officers stationed in India, Washington felt compelled to provide all the assistance it could inspite of Delhi's unwillingness or inability to respond at the time. It had good reasons.

By the summer of 1958 Mao and his colleagues had determined that Beijing had no alternatives to meeting force, as represented by the growing strength of the Tibetan resistance with larger drafts of guerrillas being recruited, trained and armed by the US and India, with some sort of a show of force. PLA border guards in southern Tibet began crossing the barren, windswept and frequently snowclad ramparts of the McMahon Line in the east and the Karakoram mountains in the west, penetrating the often uninhabited and inhospitable suspected base areas of the NVDA, ambushing unsuspecting Indian patrols and raiding small border posts. The resulting exchange of protest notes painted a picture of a downward spiral in relations. Between 2 July and 10 December, 1958, Delhi and Beijing wrote to each other about six major incidents.

On 2 July, the Indians told Beijing, 'The Government of India has received information that troops of the Government of the People's Republic of China crossed into Indian territory and visited the Khuranak Fort (latitude and longitude were given) which lies within the Indian frontiers of the Ladakh region of Kashmir and occupied it . . . The Government of India propose to send a reconnaissance party to the area with clear instructions that the party will remain within the Indian side of the frontier.'[3] The Chinese reposted a month later in a note complaining 'Since 8th July 1958, more than twenty Indian personnel entered into Wu-Je of the Tibet Region of China, bringing with them wireless communication apparatus, arms etc . . . The Chinese Government cannot but lodge a protest and demands that the above-mentioned Indian personnel withdraw immediately from China's territory Wu-Je.'[4] In its very detailed reply handed over six days later, Delhi explained that the United Provinces Revenue Department had despatched several senior officials to the border region of Barahoti on 8 July. The ownership of the region was admittedly disputed but negotiations between Chinese and Indian representatives throughout June and July had failed to resolve the question as both sides held fast to respective claims. 'The Government of India, therefore, are of the view that the Government of the People's Republic of China can have no legitimate cause for protest against the action taken, particularly in view of the fact that the sending of Indian officials to any part of Indian territory is an internal domestic matter.'[5]

While this unhappy drama was unfolding across the Himalayan highlands, Washington's attention was drawn to events slightly closer to home. US policymakers still believed that the Communist 'threat to the Free World' actually emanated from Moscow, which they saw as the sole fountainhead of Marxist beliefs and practices controlling a unified Communist adversary. To them, Beijing was still a secondary player essentially marching to the tunes played in the Kremlin. In this worldview the source was far more fundamentally threatening than the agencies of execution could ever be. Following the untidy ending of the Suez crisis in 1956 and the consequent turbulence in that region, Washington had been increasingly anxious to secure both the source of energy lying beneath Middle-Eastern sands and the commercial lifelines linking that source with the heartland of the Western industrialised world. Growing Soviet activism and Moscow's apparent willingness to apply coercive pressures in its own 'anti-Freeworld' interests, persuaded the US to enagage in discussions with Britain and several regional actors so as to strengthen the network of security alliances enmeshing the Gulf region. For much of the spring and early summer of 1958, US officials met their counterparts from Turkey, Iran and Pakistan in London. The British Government were hospitable hosts, but given the unpleasantness of Suez, they would not be seen to be joined in as direct participants in this endeavour. Washington succeeded in signing up Turkey, Iran and Pakistan to what came to be called the London Declaration on 28 July 1958. This agreement was central to US efforts to put in place a significant regional miliatry alliance to deter, and if necessary, counter, possible Communist threats to the oilfields of the Gulf. All three countries in question had already signed up bilateral agreements with Washington, and now it was for the US to build on this core the Central Treaty Organisation, CENTO. Engaged in this alliance-building endeavour, Washington may have given the appearance of underplaying the significance of the growing rift between another ally, India, and a Communist opponent, the People's Republic of China. Documentation from the period shows that the latter states' bilateral relations were taking on an increasingly malignant character.

The bitterness of complaints and countercomplaints manifest in the notes exchanged in Delhi between the Ministry of External Affairs and the Chinese Embassy focused on the border dispute. However, that the source of the trouble, certainly from the Chinese point of view, lay in Delhi's US-aided covert operations on the plateau, can be better gauged in the more lengthy, and detailed, notes exchanged in Beijing. In one such note handed to the Indian embassy by the Chinese Foreign Office on 10 July, Beijing accused Delhi not only of providing indirect assistance to the Tibetan resistance and its US and Taiwanese sponsors in violation of bilateral agreements, but also of engaging its own 'local special agents' in a covert campaign against Beijing's authority. 'According to reliable material available to the Chinese Government the American Chiang Kai-shek clique and local special agents and Tibetan reactionaries operating in Kalimpong have recently stepped up their conspiratorial and disruptive activities against the Tibet region of China. Using Kalimpong as a base they are actively inciting and organising a handful of reactionaries hidden in Tibet for an armed revolt there in order to attain the traitorious aim of separating the Tibet region from the People's Republic of China.'[6] The Chinese placed special blame on the two brothers of the Dalai Lama, Thubten Norbu and Gyalo Thondup, who were referrred to in the note as Thubten Nobo and Gyalodenju, and on the former Prime Minister Lukhangwa and chief delegate, Shakabpa. That Thubten Norbu had been to the US and back in India at Washington's behest during the Dalai Lama's visit to India in late 1956 was known to Beijing, as indeed was the collaboration between US, Taiwanese, Tibetan 'reactionaries' and Indian 'local special agents'. Despite this knowledge, Beijing appears to have appealed to Delhi's non-aligned and *Panchshil*-inclinations in seeking to prevent these 'subversive and disruptive activities'. The note reminded Delhi, 'China and India are co-initiators of the five principles of peaceful co-existence, to uphold and propagate which the Government of India has made unremitting efforts. The Chinese Government is confident that the Government of India, pursuing a consistent policy of defending peace and opposing aggression, will accept its request and take effective measures'.[7] Although the missive ended on a benign note, Beijing sought to insert an element of caution in its message to Delhi. It said, 'The Chinese Government regards the criminal activities of the above-said reactionaries and special agents as a direct threat to China's territorial integrity and sovereignty and yet another malicious scheme of United States imperialists to create tension in Asia and Africa. It cannot be overlooked that in using Indian territory adjacent to China to perpetrate disruptive activities against the People's Republic of China, the American and Chiang Kai-shek clique special agents have also the hideous object of damaging China-India friendship. In order to shatter the underhand schemes of the United States imperialists, defend China's territorial integrity and sovereignty and safeguard China-India friendship, the Chinese Government hereby requests the Government of India to repress the subversive and disruptive activities against China's Tibet region carried out in Kalimpong by American and Chiang Kai-shek clique special agents.'[8] The point, made as explicitly as diplomacy allowed, was not lost on the recipients. The Indian Ministry of External Affairs handed an equally elaborate response to the Chinese embassy in New Delhi on 2 August.

Delhi expressed pained surprise at the Chinese claims and said 'the statements contained in this note must have been based on a complete misunderstanding of facts. The Government of India have no evidence that the United States Government and the Kuomintang regime are using Kalimpong as a base for disruptive activities against China's Tibetan region. The Government of India will never permit any portion of its territory to be used as a base of activities against any foreign Government, not to speak of the friendly Government of the People's Republic of China.'[9] India assured China that the six persons named in Beijing's note were under observation and some of them had been warned 'that if their activities, political or other, are such as to have adverse effect on the relations between India and China, the Government of India will take the severest action against them. The Government of India have no definite evidence that these persons have been indulging in unfriendly activities. Even so, the Government of India propose to warn them again.'[10] The note went on to deny any anti-Chinese activities being conducted by any Indian, US, Taiwanese or Tibetan persons or organisations from Kalimpong, or indeed from any other part of India. Delhi ended the note on a reassuring note, saying 'The Government of India reiterate their friendship for the people and the Government of the People's Republic of China. They have no doubt that the Chinese Government's note is based on misinformation and express the hope that, in the light of the facts now mentioned, the Government of the People's Republic of China will feel assured that India does not and will not permit any activities on its territory directed against the People's Republic of China and the Government of India are determined to take action under the law of the country against those who indulge in any such illegal activities.'[11] It is not clear how reassured the Chinese were because the following day, the Chinese ambassador in New Delhi called on the Indian Foreign Secretary and made a formal statement which claimed that expatriate Tibetans living in north-eastern India were actively engaged in specific anti-Chinese operations:

> *Tibetan reactionary elements have recently set up in Kalimpong an organisation named 'Committee for giving support to resistance against violence'. The organisation is now engaged in a signature movement. At the end of July nearly all the Tibetan aristocrats in Kalimpong, rebels from Sczedchuan and Sikang provinces, the Lamas and nearly all the members of the Tibetan Association and the Indian Tibetan Association put their signatures on a petition. Some of the signatories were compelled to give their signatures.*
>
> *On the 29th July, fifteen aristocrats and rebels from Tibet held a meeting. The following are the names of some of the persons who were present:*
>
> *1. Khan Chung Sagapa.*
> *2. Avang TumJun.*

3. *Sokhang Khen Chung.*
4. *Chiang Pa Wang Tui.*
5. *Chiang Pa Tsin Liang.*

*They passed a resolution at that meeting in favour of sending an appeal to various countries in the world. The meeting decided to send out the appeal on the 18th June according to the Tibetan calendar, which corresponds to 3rd August, i.e., today. It is stated that after the appeal has been sent, a demonstration will be organised. The main contents of the appeal are a request to the various countries to give assistance and support to the independence of Tibet. In the appeals there would be slanders against China and against the People's Liberation Army.*[12] *– 3 August 1958*

On the point of the Tibetan resistance operating with US and KMT help from Indian territory, Delhi remained adamant in its rejection of all Chinese complaints. It did, however, soften its stance in relation to the possibility of some Tibetans, resident in and around Kalimpong, being hostile to Chinese rule in Tibet, and repeatedly assured Beijing of being tough on them, but only in so far as this was permitted under Indian law. It is not clear from the documentation if India at this stage elected to go on a diplomatic offensive on a slightly different tack to counter the Chinese allegations, but the focus of the exchanges between the two governments now shifted to the disputed nature of the Himalayan boundaries between India and Tibet. By the late summer of 1958, Delhi was concentrating on what in its view was unacceptable Chinese claims on territories clearly delimited as Indian. The Ministry of External Affairs handed over a protest note to the Chinese Embassy on 21 August which said,

*The attention of the Government of India has been drawn to a map of China published on pages 20–21 of the 'China Pictorial' magazine (No.95 – July 1958) in which the borders of China have been indicated by a thick brown line. Though this map is on a small scale, there are clear inaccuracies in it in so far as China's border with India is concerned. The border as depicted in the map includes as Chinese territory*

 (i) *four of the five Divisions of India's North-Eastern Frontier Agency;*
 (ii) *some areas in the north of the State of Uttar Pradesh and*
 (iii) *large areas in eastern Ladakh which form part of the State of Jammu & Kashmir.*

*It appears that the entire Tashigang area of Eastern Bhutan and a considerable slice of territory in north-western Bhutan have also been included as Chinese territory.*

2. *In the past, similar inaccurate maps have been published in China. The matter was referred to His Excellency Premier Chou En-lai by His Excellency the Prime Minister of India when the latter visited China in October 1954. His Excellency Chou En-lai had at that time replied that current Chinese maps were based on old maps and that the Government of the People's Republic of China had had no time to correct them. The Government of India recognised the force of this argument. Since, however, the present Government of the People's Republic of China has been in office for so many years and new maps are being repeatedly printed and published in China the Government of India would suggest that necessary corrections in the Chinese maps should not be delayed further. In this particular case, the map has been published in a magazine, which is printed in an official press and is distributed by an official agency.*

3. *The Government of India are, therefore, drawing the attention of the Government of the People's Republic of China again to this matter. They trust that the necessary corrections will be made soon. The northern boundary of India is clearly shown in the Political Map of India – 3rd edition, 1956 (scale – one inch to seventy miles), which is freely available on sale. The Government of India will be happy to supply a copy of this map to the Government of the People's Republic of China.*[13] *– 21 August 1958*

This shift in focus, and the more robust approach taken by Delhi, were reflected by events on the ground. China's new motorway linking Xinjiang with western Tibet across the Aksai Chin 'snow-desert' claimed by India and shown in all Indian maps as part of the Ladakh division of Jammu & Kashmir, became the scene of clashes. On 8 September, the Chinese ambushed and detained an Indian border patrol on a stretch of this road. A second patrol, sent out to look for the first, was also taken by surprise and taken into custody four days later. Delhi launched air-reconnaissance sorties to try to locate the troops. The latter were eventually repatriated on 22 October. These incidents marked an escalation in both the field and diplomatic exchanges. Shortly after deporting the Indian border-guards, Beijing wrote to Delhi in response to the latter's note of 21 August, claiming how it was still saddled with old, 'pre-liberation' maps. It also pledged that 'consultations with neighbours' will take place before finalising the precise layout of borders and surveys would be conducted in consultation with neighbours. However, Beijing also added a stern message in describing what it saw as 'Indian intrusions'. It said, 'The above mentioned unlawful intrusions of Indian armed personnel and aircraft into Chinese territory and territorial air to conduct reconnoitring and surveying activities are inconsistent with Sino-Indian friendly relations and the five principles of peaceful co-existence initiated by the two countries.' Beijing sought from

Delhi a guarantee that such 'unfriendly acts' would not be repeated.[14] The Indian reply to this note was equally cool. Delhi expressed surprise that Beijing claimed ownership of the Aksai Chin area too. The Indian Government also took exception to the fact that its men had been kept in detention by the Chinese for five weeks without giving any information to Delhi and then sent back without giving India any prior information, thereby posing a grave risk to the personnel because of the severe winter conditions in the region at the time.[15]

As the correspondence continued, the shrillness of mutual recrimination built up. On 10 December 1958, the Ministry of External Affairs issued another note to the Chinese mission in New Delhi. It was long and much of it recounted Indian complaints from the recent past. It recalled that Delhi had asked as early as in August 1955 that the two neighbours 'neutralise' the Barahoti area and that in response, Beijing had suggested that 'both sides might refrain from sending troops into the Wu-Je area.' In aides memoire issued in October 1956, India had agreed to this proposal. And in February 1957, a Chinese note had said Beijing would not despatch any troops to that area 'this year'. India too had agreed to desist from despatching any troops to Barahoti/Wu-Je for that year. According to the Indian note, in October 1958, after several sessions of talks, the Chinese were apparntly building structures in Barahoti and changing the situation on the ground there. Delhi also complained that the Chinese had occupied two Indian border posts at Lapthal and Sangcha Malla south of the Balcha Dhura Pass from which Indian troops withdrew in the winter. India claimed that the border in this region was based on 'traditional' delimitation and that China had made no previous claims here.[16]

The notes exchanged between the two governments neither resolved any of the specific disputes nor cleared the air of suspicion and mistrust which was steadily creating a sense of growing hostility. In mid-December Nehru himself intervened, addressing a long letter to Zhou En-lai that reminded the Chinese leader of the commitments Zhou was said to have made during his visit following the *Panchshil Treaty*, and then once again, two years later when the Dalai Lama sought asylum in India for the first time and the Chinese Premier, with Nehru's help, managed to dissuade the Tibetan god-king.

> . . . 7. You told me then that you had accepted this McMahon Line border with Burma and, whatever might have happened long ago, in view of the friendly relations which existed between China and India, you proposed to recognise this border with India also. You added that you would like to consult authorities of the Tibetan region of China and you proposed to do so . . . I then mentioned that there were no disputes between us about our frontier, but there were certain very minor border problems which were pending settlement. We decided

*that these petty issues should be settled amicably by representatives of
the two Governments meeting together on the basis of established
practice and custom as well as water-sheds . . . .*[17]

Several weeks were to pass before Zhou responded. In the meanwhile,
pressures on the Indian border security forces increased. The political
leadership was pressed by a boisterous parliament, and a vocal right-wing
opposition, to take firmer measures against what was frequently described
in these circles as 'unreliable' neighbours. Delhi had set in train a modest
rearmament programme to equip its forces but as tension rose, demands
rapidly outstripped supply. India could no longer delay responding to the
US's demands that it provide written assurances without which a new
Mutual Defense Assistance Agreement renewing the 1951 Agreement and
reinforcing the security bonds linking Delhi with Washington could be
formalised. India sought a renewal of that first Indo-US Mutual Defense
Assistance Agreement in the spring of 1958. Washington, in the form of a
letter from the US *Charge' d'Affaires* in Delhi to Nehru dated 16 April,
demanded fresh assurances regarding the purely defensive use of the
requested military hardware. It was not until 17 December, that the Indian
Foreign Secretary, Subimal Dutt, writing on behalf of his Minister,
addressed a reply to the recently accredited US Ambassador, Ellsworth
Bunker. He confirmed 'that the assurances contained in the Agreement
between our two Governments effected by an exchange of notes signed at
Washington on March 7 & 16, 1951 are applicable also to supplies and
services furnished to the Government of India by the Government of the
United States of America under the Mutual Security Act of 1954 as
amended from time to time. I am to add that in fact, as is well known, the
firm policy of India is to work for international peace and on no account
does the Government of India even consider the possibility of aggression
against any other State.'[18] This note, in conjunction with the earlier one
addressed to Nehru in April, constituted the second Indo-US security
agreement. Armed with the material, juridical and psycho-strategic
consequences of the agreement, Delhi could now face Beijing's increasing
animus with reasonable equanimity.

The opportunity to do so came towards the end of January 1959 when
winter snow had closed most Himalayan passes and the two border forces
had been frozen out of their proximity in 'eyeball-to-eyeball' confrontation.
Unlike Nehru who had addressed Zhou as 'My dear Prime Minister', the
Chinese leader addressed his Indian counterpart as 'Dear Mr Prime
Minister'. In diplomatic nuance, this overtly formal tone underscored a
hardening of the Chinese stance. Zhou recounted a position Beijing had
maintained for long although it had not articulated in its missives to Delhi
in recent years. And, more worrying for Delhi, the Chinese leader for the
first time formally repudiated the validity of the McMahon Line which

provided India with the basis on which to draw the latter's northern and north-eastern frontiers.

> *. . . The Sino-Indian boundary has never been formally delimited. Historically no treaty or agreement on the Sino-Indian boundary has ever been concluded between the Chinese central government and the Indian Government. So far as the actual situation is concerned, there are certain differences between the two sides over the border question.*
>
> *. . . It was true that the border question was not raised in 1954. That was because conditions were not ripe for its settlement and the Chinese side, on its part, had had no time to study the question . . . The McMahon Line was a product of the British policy of aggression against the Tibet region of China and aroused great indignation of the Chinese people. Juridically, too, it cannot be considered legal. I have told you that it has never been recognised by the Chinese central government.[19]*

Zhou went to express 'the Chinese people's anxieties' over a recently published Indian map showing the western reaches of the Sino-Indian borders and reiterated the view that a settlement of the dispute required surveys of the border and mutual consultations. To prevent repetation of 'minor border incidents', Zhou asked Nehru that the two sides maintain the status quo pending negotiations and surveys.

Washington was concerned over the clear downturn in Sino-Indian relations, but all the documentation suggests that the Administration was also delighted at the rapidity with which Delhi was shedding its overtly neutralist stance and showing signs of recognition that simultaneous friendship with both the US and Communist China was not a viable option in the late 1950s. Washington felt confident that trans-Himalayan tensions would strengthen the pragmatic and realist forces within India's ruling elite under Nehru and create conditions conducive to India becoming even more closely aligned to the US than it already was. In any case, the 1958 US-Indian Mutual Defense Assistance Agreement provided a juridical basis for increased US military and security assistance to India against both domestic threats to security and growing Chinese bellicosity. The trend was, therefore, a welcome development from Washington's point of view and the latter now felt able to concentrate on countering aspects of what it saw as the immediate 'core' threat, ie, Moscow's machinations in areas of vital strategic significance such as the Middle-East. And the central plank in that endeavour was the quadrupartite linkage binding Turkey, Iran and Pakistan with the US.

Following the signature of the London Declaration on 28 July 1958, Washington conducted detailed bilateral negotiations with the governments of the three regional client-states. These led, in early March 1959, to the signature of a further 'Agreement of Cooperation Between the Government of the United States of America and the Government of Pakistan' and with the Governments of Turkey and Iran. The US-Pakistan treaty, while reinforcing Washington's *cordon-sanitaire* around the Gulf oilfields, also deepened its commitment to the defence of Pakistan. That was a price Washington considered worth paying since the security of the Gulf was vital and the role Pakistan was expected to play in the scheme would reduce direct US involvement, especially in terms of the need to deploy US troops and suffer casualties in any regional conflict, to an acceptable level. For Pakistan's insecure elites, such an assurance of US protection was crucial to the very sustenance of the Pakistani experiment. In short, the 1959 treaty appeared to be what future management-specialists would call a 'win-win' arrangement. The preamble stated,

> *The Government of the United States of America and the Government of Pakistan, Desiring to implement the Declaration in which they associated themselves at London on July 28, 1958;*
>
> *Considering that under Article I of the Pact of Mutual Cooperation signed at Baghdad on February 24, 1955, the parties signatory thereto agreed to cooperate for their security and defense, and that, similarly, as stated in the above-mentioned Declaration, the Government of the United States of America, in the interest of world peace, agreed to cooperate with the Governments making that Declaration for their security and defense;*
>
> *Recalling that, in the above-mentioned Declaration, the Members of the Pact of Mutual Cooperation making that Declaration affirmed their determination to maintain their collective security and to resist aggression, direct or indirect;. . . .*
>
> *Desiring to strengthen peace in accordance with the principles of the Charter of the United Nations;*
>
> *Affirming their right to cooperate for their security and defense in accordance with Article 51 of the Charter of the United Nations;*
>
> *Considering that the Government of the United States of America regards as vital to its national interest and to world peace the preservation of the independence and integrity of Pakistan;*
>
> *Recognizing the authorization to furnish appropriate assistance granted to the President of the United States of America by the Congress of the United States of America in the Mutual Security Act of 1954, as amended, and in the Joint Resolution to Promote Peace and Stability in the Middle East; . . . Have agreed as follows:*[20]

The text of the Agreement had six articles. The first reiterated Washington's pledge to assist Pakistan in case it was faced with aggression. It said, 'The Government of Pakistan is determined to resist aggression. In case of aggression against Pakistan, the Government of the United States of

America, in accordance with the Constitution of the United States of America, will take such appropriate action, including the use of armed forces, as may be mutually agreed upon and as is envisaged in the Joint Resolution to Promote Peace and Stability in the Middle East, in order to assist the Government of Pakistan at its request.'[21] Article II assured Pakistan that the US would continue to provide it with significant military and economic assistance. In Article III, Pakistan gave assurance that the assistance provided by the US would be used strictly in conformity with the terms of the London Declaration of July 1958. In Article IV the US and Pakistan promised to work in concert with the other signatories to the London Declaration, ie, Turkey and Iran, in developing collective defense. Article V assured both parties that this new treaty did not adversely affect their collaboration on the bases of other agreements. Article VI laid down that the treaty would come into immediate effect and would only be terminated a year after either party received a written notice from the other to that effect. Signed in Ankara, this Agreement sealed US-Pakistan relations which, in South Asian security literature, would from now on brand Pakistan as 'the most allied of allies'.

## A Climax for the Tibetan Resistance

While the forces of international diplomacy and politics swirled around them, the Tibetan resistance and its Chinese adversaries continued to wage their bitter struggle at the margins of the central Containment drama. By the second half of 1958, the Chinese had completed their network of all-weather motorways linking most parts of Tibet with the centre of Beijing's military administration in Lhasa, the more accessible parts of western China where the base areas for medium-term logistic support lay, and Xinjiang from which border-province reinforcements could be deployed to western Tibet far more quickly than they could be from central or eastern Tibet. The PLA was now able to mount major counter-offensives against the NVDA.[22] However, since the Resistance itself had gained in combat experience, organisational cohesion and command expertise, as well as in supplies of ordnance and communication equipment, the clashes were becoming more protracted and bloody. Intense fighting in Amdo and Kham saw an influx of refugees displaced from highland hamlets into the capital where, presumably, there would be food and shelter as well as protection in the presence of, or proximity to, the Dalai Lama. In the autumn of 1958, the NVDA was advised to take cover of this refugee influx and infiltrate into Lhasa in preparation for a dramatic operation of some sort although the precise nature of this operation was not, for obvious security reasons, made clear to rank and file.

The Chinese military authorities inadvertently aided the process by which support for the Resistance grew in and around the capital. They took several steps which led to further alienation of the Tibetan elite, even those sections of it which had sent sons to Beijing for education. In October, Beijing's representatives had sought to prepare the ground for 'democratic reforms' by issuing leaflets which denigrated the Buddha as a reactionary. Outraged, the Dalai Lama protested and the Chinese withdrew many of the leaflets from circulation, but the damage had been done. In November, the PLA began house to house searches in Lhasa to detect and eliminate suspected NVDA pockets and soon sporadic fighting began close to the capital. Perhaps the first major encounter took place late in August 1958 near a village named Nyemo Dukhak Sumdo. According to Tibetan claims, around 200 Chinese and 40 guerrillas were killed.[23] Many Lhasan aristocrats, converted to the belief that only active resistance to the Chinese had any chance of restoring the honour of their faith, customs and possibly social organisation, joined the guerrillas. This infusion of new leaders both strengthened the NVDA and caused organisational stresses. The Chinese were understandably determined to wrest control over the capital's environs from the Tibetan fighters and reinforcements were rushed in from outlying districts. According to the principal Indian adviser to the resistance, the guerrillas were faced with almost insuperable odds and the NVDA's commander-in-chief, Gompo Tashi Andrugtsang, was forced to disperse his forces, the best-organised elements of a resistance-army perhaps 80,000-strong, from their bases in Jhang in the north and move south to Drigu, close to the Indian border and sanctuary provided by Delhi's officials.[24] Despite the Chinese pressure against the NVDA command structure from the growing PLA strength around Lhasa, a large number of guerrilla subunits remained dispersed in the Lhoka region south of the capital. Indian Intelligence estimated that Chinese troop concentration around Lhasa in February 1959 had risen to 200,000 all ranks.[25] By this time, the Dalai Lama himself appears to have been convinced that given the brutal nature of Chinese measures against suspected guerrillas in Amdo and Kham, a peaceful settlement was no longer possible.

Early in February, even before the Dalai Lama had responded to the Chinese invitation, Radio Beijing announced that Tibet's god-king would be attending the forthcoming session of the National People's Congress in Beijing. This announcement is likely to have raised fears and suspicions in Tibetan minds that the focus of their veneration and the symbol of their national identity might be held against his will to secure Tibetan allegiance to China. On 16 February, the resistance approached the Dalai Lama, sending a religious delegation led by the revered abbot of the Jeykundo monastery which had been reduced to rubble by PLA bombers. The delegation painted a grim picture of the bloody combat raging in Kham and Amdo, seeking the Dalai Lama's blessings for the NVDA's 'war of independence'. Unable to endorse violence, the Dalai Lama urged moderation upon the combatants. The guerrillas, having lost virtually everything, could not now give up their struggle and were disappointed in their failure to secure the Dalai Lama's blessings. However, other Lhasa officials were more sympathetic, and NVDA men were often able to take over the contents of government armouries and granaries in various parts of the country without too much trouble.

The *Monlam* (Tibetan New Year) festival in the spring of 1959 provided the climax to the steady build-up that had gone on over the past couple of years. The CIA, operating primarily out of Dhaka with some activities in Calcutta and Kalimpong, monitoring and assisting a force of perhaps 14,000 Khampa guerrillas and providing supplies to them by flying converted C-130 Hercules longrange transporters[26] from Thai bases, appears to have set its mind on 'rescuing' the Dalai Lama from Tibet. Given the messages contained in letters sent out by US diplomats to the Tibetan leader over the years, this was understandable. The fact that Gompo Tashi Andrugtsang was far away from the capital engaged in defensive operations against his PLA pursuers for most of March 1959 and only heard reports of the events of mid-March in an All India Radio broadcast on 22 March[27] suggests that what happened in Lhasa in the second and third weeks of March had nothing to do with operational plans laid out or executed by the NVDA's formal leadership structure. Accounts of these events have appeared in numerous publications, not least in the Dalai Lama's own autobiographies.[28] From an historical perspective, the latter of his two accounts may be considered a more credible source of information. However, in the light of the secrecy that still surrounds official US and Indian discourse on the subject[29], these accounts could by no means be comprehensive.

The god-king took his final theological tests following the *Monlam* festival. These were rigorous and extremely demanding and yet essential to the Dalai Lama's office. Preparation for these tests had taken the better part of two years and the young Dalai Lama was understandably looking forward to crossing these last formal hurdles to the fulfilment of his metaphysical and intellectual enlightenment. It was during this period that representatives of the PLA Political Commissar in Lhasa, General Zhang Jing-wu invited the Dalai Lama to visit the local garrison and see the performance of a visiting Chinese military dance troupe. This invitation may have been timed by the Chinese to show respect to the 'fully qualified' Dalai Lama, as it were, in an attempt to rebuild Tibetan-Han amity in the capital, or, as the Resistance claimed, to kidnap the Tibetan leader and hold him hostage to the NVDA's good conduct. Apart from these extreme views, the possibility that the PLA might simply have wished the Dalai Lama's presence at its headquarters as a demonstration of his endorsement of the military administration, and its offshoot, the Preparatory Committee for the Autonomous Region of Tibet, PCART, of which the Dalai Lama himself was the formal head, can not be ruled out. Once the exams were behind him, the Dalai Lama was once again approached by the Chinese who wanted to know when he might be able to see the performance; he told them 10 March 'would be convenient.'[30] A few days before that proposed visit to the garrison, the commander of the god-king's bodyguard, the *Kusun Depon,* was told by the Dalai Lama's Chinese Military Advisor, PLA Brigadier Fu, that during the forthcoming visit, traditional formalities would be dispensed with, no armed escorts would be allowed into the PLA garrison and the Dalai Lama would be accompanied by only two or three unarmed Tibetan guards, that too if considered necessary by the Tibetan court. Fu also instructed that the *Kusun Depon* maintain strict secrecy over the entire event. These unusual strictures caused alarm among the guard. Night-long discussions among the Dalai Lama's advisers eventually leaked out into the general populace, and presumably, to NVDA contacts active in and around the capital.

Rumours of a Chinese plot to kidnap the Dalai Lama swept Lhasa. In the morning, large, noisy crowds of Tibetans surrounded the Norbulingka palace where the Dalai Lama was in residence, presumably to prevent the god-king from being taken away. When crowd violence led to the death of a visitor and serious injury to another official, the Dalai Lama sent word both to the Chinese and to the growing crowds around his residence that he would not be visiting the PLA headquarters. But the citizens of Lhasa, organised into new versions of the older *Mimang Tsongdu,* demanded that the Dalai Lama promise never to go to the Chinese garrison. When these assurances were given, the leaders left the palace grounds to organise meetings in the capital, but the crowds did not leave. The Dalai Lama sent senior emissaries to the PLA General Tan Kuan-sen who accused the Tibetan government of secretly organising anti-Chinese agitation and warned that the treachery of 'imperialist rebels' would not be tolerated. Meanwhile, several senior Lhasa officials and advisers joined a number of Tibetan Officers of the Bodyguard and popular leaders of the movement in the 'Jewel Garden' on the palace grounds, demanding the formal scrapping of the 'Seventeen Point Agreement' between Tibet and China. Executive authority was slipping out of the god-king's hands and he sought to persuade these ardent followers to tone down their language and help lower tension in the capital. He did not succeed. Over the next few days, General Tan Kuan-sen and the Dalai Lama exchanged letters in which the general asked that the Dalai Lama move into the garrison for 'his own safety', and the latter kept up the correspondence trying to mollify the PLA commanders in Lhasa and buying time. Eventually, General Tan appeared to be tiring and demanded that the *Kashag* order the crowds to dismantle all the barricades they had put up around the palace and across Lhasa. This suggested to the recipients of the PLA's demands that the latter planned to bring in reinforcements for a violent showdown with the crowds of civilians. On 16 March, the Dalai Lama received general Tan's last letter which came with an appendix written by Ngabo Ngawang Jigme, the leader of the Tibetan delegation to the talks in Beijing in 1951, and now a senior official in the PCART, currently ensconced in the PLA garrison. Ngabo informed the Dalai Lama that the PLA planned to launch an assault on the Norbulingka and if the Dalai Lama returned a map of the palace marking exactly where he would be, the PLA artillery would ensure their shells did not land on his quarters. Given the violence about to be visited upon the unarmed citizens of Lhasa, the Dalai Lama decided that it was time to leave. He writes that the honoured oracle Dorje Drakden now changed his instruction to the Dalai Lama to stay on in the capital and advised him to 'Go! Go! Tonight!'[31]

Once the decision to leave had been taken, initially for the southernmost town close to the Indian border, the Dalai Lama asked his Lord Chamberlain, an official named Phala, who was in touch with the resistance, and other close advisers,for making preparations.

He then met the leaders of the popular movement and asked for maximum co-operation and secrecy. On the night of 16 March, dressed as a junior soldier of the Tibetan army, the Dalai Lama left the Norbulingka and after a tense but otherwise uneventful journey across the Kyichu river, joined up with a detachment of the resistance. Travelling on ponies, the Dalai Lama's small entourage, comprising several senior officials, tutors and members of his immediate family, as well as a small detachment of guards, soon crossed the Che La. Once that 16000-foot pass had been crossed, the group was in difficult country home to the guerrillas; the Dalai Lama was safe. His escorts were heavily armed and even his cook was a CIA-trained guerrilla armed with an anti-tank weapon. The CIA had also deployed a radio-operator to accompany the group and maintain contact with operational headquarters.[32] The Tibetan leader mentioned the flight of an unidentified aircraft over the group when it was close to the Indian border and he feared that this might have been a Chinese aircraft trying to locate the fugitives. While this is possible, given the Chinese anger at the Dalai Lama's flight and Beijing's willingness to assault centres of resistance, and monasteries, with squadrons of attack aircraft, it is more likely that this was a CIA sortie providing support to the god-king's escort. The Dalai Lama says his plans were to halt at Lhuntse Dzong, a fortress not far from the Indian border, repudiate the 17-Point Agreement, re-establish his administration as the legitimate government of Tibet, and try to reopen negotiations with the Chinese. However, less than a week out of Lhasa, he received news of the PLA's crackdown on the capital's civilian population, the reduction of the Norbulingka to a shelled ruin and the general bloodbath visited upon all Tibetans suspected of opposition to Chinese rule. So, although at Lhuntse Dzong the Dalai Lama did formally repudiate the 1951 Sino-Tibetan Agreement and proclaim his administration to be Tibet's legal government, negotiating with the Chinese was not considered an option and the decision to seek asylum in India followed. Delhi's permission came promptly.[33]

At the Indian border, the Dalai Lama was received by representatives of the Indian Government one of whom handed the Dalai Lama a telegram from the Prime Minister. The message said, 'My colleagues and I welcome you and send greetings on your safe arrival in India. We shall be happy to afford the necessary facilities to you, your family and entourage to reside in India. The people of India, who hold you in great veneration, will no doubt accord their traditional respect to your personage. Kind regards to you. Nehru'.[34] This telegram was, perhaps coincidentally, drafted around the time when Nehru also wrote to Zhou En-lai in response to the Chinese Premier's letter received a month earlier. In this reply, Nehru too adopted the more formal address 'Dear Mr Prime Minister', and wrote,

> . . . *I am somewhat surprised to know that this (Sino-Indian) frontier was not accepted at anytime by the Government of China. The traditional frontier, as you may be aware, follows the geographical principle of watershed on the crest of the High Himalayan Range, but apart from this, in most parts, it has the sanction of specific international agreements between the then Government of India and the Central Government of China.*[35]

Nehru referred to the Anglo-Chinese convention of 1890 which delimited the Tibet-Sikkim boundary which was jointly demarcated on the ground five years later. With regard to the Ladakh-Tibet borders, Nehru recalled that these had been agreed in the 1843 treaty between the Emperor of China, the 'Lama Guru of Tibet', and the ruler of Kashmir and that in 1847, the Government of China had accepted that agreement as 'sufficient'; that a Chinese map published in 1893 showed the area currently being claimed by Beijing as part of India. Referring to the McMahon Line, Nehru mentioned the 'Tripartite Conference' held at Shimla in 1913–1914 during which the Tibetan delegate, Lonchen Shatra, said he had received instructions from Lhasa accepting the proposed boundary. Nehru also recalled that in January 1957, Zhou had himself, during his visit to Delhi, agreed to this High Himalayan boundary. Nehru also protested the establishment of an armed camp at Barahoti by the Chinese.[36] However, that the main issue was the growing strength of the Tibetan resistance operating from the security of its Indian sanctuary, rather than the disputes over the Indo-Tibetan boundary, was in a way conceded when on 30 March, Nehru addressed the parliament. Drawing the *Loksabha*'s attention to Beijing's repeated complaints, the Prime Minister said,

> . . . *On two or three occasions in the last three or four years there were references* (by Beijing) *to Kalimpong and to some people in Kalimpong carrying on propaganda and like activities. Our position*

*has always been – and we have made it quite clear to people who come from Tibet – that they were welcome to come here, but we could not allow Indian soil to be used for subversive activities or even aggressively propagandist activities against friendly Governments. That general policy of ours applies to every embassy and to every foreigner here. **It may be that they sometimes overstep the mark. It may be that we did not object when we might have objected.** On two or three occasions, some leaflets came out in Kalimpong, which we thought was undesirable, and we told people who had brought it out that they should not do that kind of thing from Indian soil. Our instructions and warnings had effect. We are not aware of any activity in Kalimpong in the last many months. It is wrong to say that Kalimpong was a kind of centre from which activities were organised. We have very good control of our check-posts and over people coming and going between Tibet and India. In Kalimpong itself, nobody can easily come and go.*[37]

The following day, the Dalai Lama and his entourage crossed the border into India. The Indian Foreign Secretary informed this to the Chinese ambassador in Delhi on 3 April. By then, the very tired and rather ill Tibetan leader had been moved away from the vicinity of the border and taken to safer precincts. Three weeks later, amid reports of considerable violence by the Chinese forces in and around Lhasa, the Indian Foreign Secretary made a formal statement to the Chinese Ambassador. This latter statement was an elaboration of the preliminary report. The envoy was given details of the arrival of the Dalai Lama and his entourage at the Indian border, how the armed Tibetans were disarmed, and how the Tibetan leader reached the hill-station of Mussoorie on 21 April where Nehru met him three days later. The statement also rejected Beijing's claim that the Dalai Lama had been brought out of Lhasa under duress and pointed out that the latter had assured Nehru he had left Lhasa of his own free will. Delhi also assured Beijing that 'India has had, and has, no desire to interfere in internal happenings in Tibet. Because of old contacts, recent tragic events in Tibet have affected the people of India considerably, but it has been made clear by the Prime Minister that there is no question of any interference in the internal affairs of Tibet.'[38]

Meanwhile, the Dalai Lama had issued a statement to the press repudiating the 17-Point Agreement, thereby seemingly refuting whatever legal claims Beijing may have had to its control of Tibet. At first, the statement was scripted in the third person and issued on behalf of the Tibetan leader. When this caused some confusion, and when Beijing claimed that this statement had been imposed by Indian authorities and 'imperialist' agents, the Dalai Lama issued a second statement scripted in the first person. Beijing appears to have been more outraged than mollified by this sequence of events. In his address to the parliament on 27 April, Nehru explained these events from Delhi's point of view not only for domestic consumption, but perhaps also to reinforce the message given to the Chinese ambassador a few days earlier. The Prime Minister reported, 'Soon after entering India, the Dalai Lama indicated his wish to make a statement. We were later informed that this statement would be released at Tezpur . . . I should like to make it clear that the Dalai Lama was entirely responsible for this statement as well as a subsequent briefer statement that was to be made by him from Mussoorie . . . In these days of the Cold War, there has been a tendency to use unrestrained language and often to make wild charges without any justification. We have fortunately kept out of the Cold War and I hope that on this, as on any other occasion, we shall not use the language of Cold War'.[39] Nehru informed the House the Dalai Lama had told him that he agreed to leave Lhasa only after the PLA artillery unit's shells fell on a pond near his palace. He also pointed out that the Khampa rebellion against the Chinese had been in progress for over three years and given that backdrop to the resistance, Kalimpong could not be held responsible for events in Tibet.[40] Nehru may have convinced his parliamentary colleagues, but he was less successful with the Chinese.

Having unleashed a crackdown on Lhasa of a degree of brutality until now reserved for guerrillas in Kham and Amdo, Beijing found it impossible to accept any of Delhi's arguments. The premise that Tibet and Tibetans deserved special consideration which seemed to underlie Indian commentary on the subject was rejected out of hand by the Chinese government. Delhi's repeated denials of any responsibility for the NVDA's operations across much of Tibet too was viewed as unacceptable. The disputed nature of the border, especially the fact that while India claimed there was no dispute and China demanded control over land shown in Indian maps as Indian territory and neither being willing to concede, made for a combustible mix. In mid-May, the Chinese envoy in Delhi made a formal statement to the Indian Foreign Secretary. In it, he said 'Since March 10, 1959 when the former Tibet Local Government and the Tibetan upper class reactionary clique unleashed armed rebellion, there have appeared deplorable abnormalities in the relations between China and India. This situation was caused by the Indian side, yet in his conversation on April 26, 1959 Mr. Dutt, Foreign Secretary of the Ministry of External Affairs of India, shifted responsibility on to the Chinese side. This is what the Chinese Government absolutely cannot accept . . . Did not the impressive welcome extended to the Dalai Lama by the Indian Government and the talks Prime Minister Nehru himself held with him mean giving a welcome to a Chinese rebel and holding a meeting with him? All these statements and actions of the Indian Government, no matter what the subjective intentions might be, undoubtedly played an objective role of encouraging the Tibetan rebels . . . The facts themselves have completely overthrown the allegation that there is no Indian interference in China's internal affairs . . . The Dalai Lama was abducted to India by the Tibetan rebels. A most strong proof of this is the three letters (sic) he wrote to General Tan Kuan-san, Acting Representative of the Central People's Government in Tibet, before he was abducted out of Lhasa.'[41] The ambassador told his host that the main threat to China was the US in the east and Beijing did not wish to have to fight on two fronts. He then asked the rather ominous if rhetorical question – shouldn't India too avoid opening up two fronts?[42] It is not clear if Beijing wished to threaten Delhi with the possibility of extending support to India's regional rival Pakistan or to India's own rebellious highlanders in the north-east. But in the light of subsequent developments it appears as though China was aware of the potential cards it held against India and wished to alert Delhi to such future dangers.

## The New 'Great Game'

Meanwhile, Washington saw the Dalai Lama's flight, Delhi's grant of asylum to the Tibetan leader, the subsequent insurrection around Lhasa, violent repression by the PLA and the rapid decline in Sino-Indian relations as a great success of strategic policy-making. In frequent meetings of the National Security Council, most of them chaired by the President himself, there was considerable excitement and much satisfaction at the turn of events. The opportunities presented by developments were not lost upon the Administration; however, there were cautious notes too. The minutes of one such meeting concluded with the remarks, 'Secretary McElroy thought that Tibet should be treated as a new Hungary and it seemed to him that the Tibetan situation was in fact getting out of the front pages. It was in our interest to keep it there. Secretary Herter cautioned that we must be careful that we ourselves do not appear to stimulate reactions to the Chinese Communists' action in Tibet but rather covertly assist the Asian peoples themselves to keep the Tibetan action prominently before the world. Mr. Dulles promised to get to work on this problem.'[43] Allen Dulles, the Director of Central Intelligence, was an effective controller of the US intelligence operations across the world. If there was any success in Tibet, credit as seen in Washington, largely went to the efforts made by his organisation. His teams were energized into expanding their secret mission by raising the level of training to be given to the Tibetan guerrillas. It was decided to select the very best of the fighters for special training in the United States itself. A secluded barracks in the Rocky mountains at Camp Hale, Colorado, was selected for this purpose. Amidst great secrecy, select bands of Tibetans, future commanders of the Tibetan forces and the elite of the new Tibet, were brought into Colorado, given exhaustive training in not just guerrilla warfare but in command and leadership, and then flown back across half the world to be dropped into Tibet. Between 1959 and 1962, about 170 resistance leaders were processed through the school.[44] The facility was closed to Tibetans for about a year in 1962 when the US may have decided to offer Mountain Warfare training to Indian regulars although this has not been confirmed. The CIA reopened the Tibetan training school following the Sino-Indian war but it was finally closed down in 1964.

However, the Tibetan drama was not a simple act of executive agencies and undercover agents working in great secrecy against considerable odds against the powers of a major actor, it was also one in which secret diplomacy played a major role. One of the actors on that less covert stage was Taiwan, or the Republic of China, as it was then popularly called. The Taiwanese envoy to the US, Dr. George K.C. Yeh, was a frequent caller at the Department of State. His government was pleased with events in Tibet in so far as they suggested Beijing's control was being challenged with some effect, but Taipei was anxious lest Nehru agree to hand the Dalai Lama back to Beijing in exchange of Chinese recognition of the McMahon Line.[45] US officials asked that Taiwan renounce Chinese suzerainty over Tibet. Dr. Yeh pointed out that the Chinese constitution barred any territorial changes to China without the support of two-thirds of the members of the Legislative Yuan or three-quarters of the membership of the National Assembly and in its currently reduced circumstances, the Taiwan-based legislature was not able to undertake such a task. However, in a speech delivered on 26 March, President Chiang Kai-shek had promised that once the Republic recovered the mainland, it would help the Tibetan people to realise their aspirations in keeping with the principle of self-determination. Despite considerable US pressure, the Taiwanese would not renounce suzerainty over Tibet.

Towards the end of April, the CIA submitted a detailed 'Review of Tibetan Operations' for the President. Most of the ten-page memorandum remains classified, but the parts that have been declassified give some indication of the scope of the CIA's activities in the region. The sequence of the narrative, especially of the pages and paragraphs deleted from the text when seen in the context of the preceding and succeeding pages and paragraphs, tells the story of the CIA's close involvement in the manage-ment of some key elements of the organised segments of the resistance.[46] The review also suggests that while the CIA did play an important role in some aspects of the Tibetans' struggle, it had no control over or contribution to many others. In some key areas, it was merely an interested observer, and its inability to help the guerrillas in time of their most serious need became clear towards the end of the memorandum. The concluding paragraph stated, '8. Later intelligence from [*less than 1 line of source text not declassified*] Tibet – the last message was received today, April 25 – reports that the Tibetan resistance in the South has been heavily engaged and decimated, and is tragically short of food and ammunition.' The documentation does not report the President's response. The seriousness of the guerrillas' plight became clear only some years later when a detachment of fighters based in the remote enclave of Mustang in northern Nepal ambushed a PLA convoy and captured official Chinese documents showing PLA calculations that between March 1959 and September 1960, 87,000 Tibetans had been killed in clashes with the Chinese.[47] The dire strait of the resistance was commented upon by the Taiwanese ambassador in Washington, Dr George Yeh, when he met the Assistant Secretary of State for Far Eastern affairs, Walter S. Robertson, on 29 April. Dr Yeh said that the very large number of refugees who had fled to India following the Dalai Lama's flight from Lhasa 'could only mean that the Khamba tribesmen, who had been the main anti-Communist fighting force in Tibet, had fled to India. He thought it was vital to set up some organization which would enable these people to rally around the Dalai Lama.'[48] The minutes did not record US response to this suggestion. On the question of Taiwan's recognition of Tibet's independence, however, despite US persistence, Dr Yeh's superiors were no more flexible now than they had been in the past.

On the following day, at the 404th meeting of the National Security Council, the Director of Central Intelligence Allen Dulles briefed the Council on developments in and around Tibet. He said the Chinese had been mopping up the rebels and had sealed off the Indo-Tibetan border. 'As a result, organized Tibetan resistance had disintegrated. The rebels had initially made the mistake of fighting in large groups; from now on they would probably discover the essence of guerrilla warfare consists of fighting in small bands. In Lhasa many Tibetans had been killed and the young men had been rounded up and apparently headed for concentration camps.'[49] While commiserating with the Tibetans, President Eisenhower nonetheless saw these developments as an opportunity for the US to build bridges between its two regional clients. Taking the wider view, 'The President said that the present situation should promote a better understanding between Pakistan and India. Pakistan had always maintained that it was arming because of the danger from Communist China, but Nehru had pooh-poohed this contention. Now, however, Nehru must recognize that Communist China is getting tough and might start trouble in Nepal next. The President thought that in this situation the U.S. should work quite actively toward promoting a better understanding between India and Pakistan.'[50] The President could not ignore purely Tibetan affairs, however. On the very day, acting Secretary of State Douglas Dillon sent him a paraphrased translation of a letter addressed to the President by the Dalai Lama and delivered by his brother Gyalo Thondup on 23 April 1959. In the letter, the Dalai Lama requested continued assistance to the Tibetans in their desperate struggle against Beijing's massive military superiority and asked for US recognition of 'the Free Tibetan Government'.[51] Dillon provided a backgrounder on past US response to Tibetan request for recognition of independence. His suggestion was to wait for other Asian states to recognise Tibet's independence first. However, with regard to the provision of *materiel*, his views reflected the general, sympathetic, reaction to the Tibetans' plight. The Director of Central Intelligence Allen Dulles assured the President on 7 May 1959 'I wish to advise that preparations are under way . . . These preparations were inaugurated following your approval of the memorandum shown you by Mr. Gordon Gray on 30 March 1959 . . . However, the recent setback which befell the Tibetan resistance forces south of Lhasa following the flight of the Dalai Lama has resulted in a delay . . . pending receipt of fuller information as to the continuing existence and location of active resistance forces. Every effort is being made to identify and establish communications with such forces; . . .'.[52]

The following day, on 8 May, 27 senior officials from the Department of State and the Joint Chiefs of Staff (JCS) met to discuss a range of issues. The first point on the agenda was Tibet. Here, after many years of convergence, the difference in emphasis between the diplomats and the soldiers became apparent. It was made clear by the former that while considerable assistance was to be provided to the Tibetans, 'it was important that to avoid an indication of U.S. Government involvement and to keep the aid and assistance on a private voluntary basis.'[53] The generals and admirals from the JCS, on the other hand, 'expressed the hope that the U.S. would be able to take affirmative and positive action in support of the Tibetan people.' But Department of State officials were more concerned with the views of Asian countries and their leaders, especially of India and Nehru, regarding Tibet. Deputy Under Secretary of State Murphy described the difficulties Washington would face if it established itself as the protector of the Dalai Lama and the Tibetan people. 'He thought it was important that Nehru not be able to place the Tibetan problem in the context of the Cold War and thereby find it possible to wash his hands of the matter.'[54] The meeting went on to discuss the current state of Indo-Pakistan relations and the prospects for settling the Indus water dispute between the two neighbours. It appears that the Eisenhower Administration was convinced that the achievement of Indo-Pakistani amity was not only an important strategic objective for the US but also a realistic and attainable one.

Tibet featured in the 409th meeting of the NSC on 4 June 1959 at which a senior official commented, 'there existed very strong feeling in some parts of the Department of Defense that our current U.S. "hands off" policy with respect to Tibet needed re-examination . . . The President commented sharply that he thought the State Department should take the lead in such matters.'[55] Ever alert to the danger of encroachments by the 'military-industrial complex' on the civilian executive's policy-making prerogative, Eisenhower may have also wanted to avoid getting the NSC involved in discussions of highly classified operational matters the Director of Central

Intelligence communicated about with him directly. Despite the expression of Presidential ire, the Pentagon did not stop sending memos to the Department of State, the NSC and the CIA asking for a more activist role in Tibet. In mid-June, for instance, Deputy Secretary of Defense Thomas S. Gates sent up a memo from the Chairman of the 'Collateral Activities Coordinating Group' which supervised covert operations by the US armed forces in which he said 'we believe that the United States should openly proffer assistance to the Tibetans in every way possible in order to capitalize on the present climate in Asia . . . Inaction, at this time, by the West can be interpreted by the Asians as an indication of weakness, indifference, and a lack of dynamic leadership. We are convinced that the question of the security of India and the remaining free nations of Asia is at stake.'[56] Given the degree of covert co-operation between Washington and Delhi since 1951, it appears that the Pentagon was either not aware of the level of US support being given both to India and to the Tibetan resistance, and nobody in the Administration felt the need to brief the Department of Defence about collaborative projects already in hand, or, the more likely probability, the military sought a very much greater involvement of its own personnel and resources in the enterprise.

Meanwhile, around 26 May 1959, the Dalai Lama had handed a letter addressed to Eisenhower to Gyalo Thondup which was then sent on with an undated covering memorandum from Allen Dulles to General Good-paster. The letter was translated and summarised at the State Department and on 16 June, acting Secretary of State Douglas Dillon forwarded the summary to Eisenhower. The Dalai Lama once again sought US support in his claims to Tibetan independence and in preventing the entry of Communist China to the United Nations. Dillon proffered detailed advice to the President as to the legal and geopolitical ramifications of possible US responses to the Dalai Lama's request.[57] Dillon maintained the Department of State's circumspection while asking Eisenhower to write an encouraging reply to the Dalai Lama. His suggestion was for the President to assure the Tibetan leader that the latter's concerns were close to the President's heart and that the Tibetan people's 'couragous struggle against Communist tyranny' would always receive US support. Also, the US would continue to unequivocally oppose the entry of Communist China to the United Nations. Initially, an oral response was communicated, and on 6 July, at Tibetan insistence, the President wrote a letter to the Dalai Lama confirming that the earlier message did indeed carry his own views.

In the late 1950s, especially since the launch of the Sputnik satellite, Washington was not concerned simply about Chinese activities in Tibet and along the Sino-Indian borders; it was also anxious about Soviet technological advances and their security implications. The US-Pak Agreement signed in March saw the deepening of an alliance that was already transferring considerable *materiel* into West Pakistan. Now, in

May, Washington devoted some efforts to the appreciation of the dynamics shaping Pakistani elite-perceptions. The Administration, in its continued inability to grasp the fundamental character of the schism dividing the subcontinent,[58] strove mightily to fashion a South Asian alliance against the 'Communist threat'. The CIA's intelligence estimate of 'The Outlook for Pakistan' issued in early May underscored the Agency's essential optimism regarding the region: 'Relations with Communist China are not likely to expand. Pakistan's governments have in the past apparently flirted with the idea of trying to use Communist China as a counterweight to India. However, the military regime (under General Mohammad Ayub Khan, who had taken over in October 1958) is probably more aware . . . that West Pakistan, as well as India, shares a Himalayan border with Communist China and that the potentially dangerous indigenous Communist movement in East Pakistan is particularly susceptible to encouragement by Peiping.'[59] The CIA was wrong; Pakistani officials were already making secret attempts at establishing friendly contacts with Beijing although the Chinese at this stage showed little interest. This may have been caused by the jubilation with which Pakistan flaunted its alliance to the US. While Karachi basked in its links with Washington, Delhi went out of its way to conceal the equally strong bonds tying it to the Administration. Despite the transfer of considerable US *materiel*, information and other services to India being underway, when Ambassador B.K Nehru called on Douglas Dillon at the Department of State in early May to discuss the relatively innocuous question of US aid to Indian agriculture and industry, he insisted on strict secrecy. Dillon's minutes of the exchange noted, 'Mr Nehru opened the conversation by requesting that this discussion be off-the-record.'[60] For many US officials this Indian coyness was both irritating and troubling.

Washington's preoccupation with establishing a South Asian counterweight to China was highlighted in a planning paper on the subcontinent produced by NSC staff in late May: 'The possibility of (indo-Pakistani) rapprochement has been somewhat enhanced by the deterioration of Indian-Communist Chinese relations as a result of the Tibetan revolt and the general re-evaluation of relations with the Communist Chinese regime occasioned throughout South Asia by that development. In this connection, the U.S. might discreetly utilize the Tibetan revolt and its impact on South Asia in order to improve the general position of the United States in this area.'[61] In response to the US's efforts to cajole the South Asian client-states into an anti-Communist alliance of their own, both India and Pakistan, but especially Pakistan, appeared to seek to milk the patron state for all it was worth. When negotiations were underway for Pakistan to provide base facilities for launching US U-2 strategic reconnaissance sorties over the Soviet Union, and also to install a 'Communications Unit' in north-west Pakistan from which US military intelligence personnel would monitor Soviet missile telemetry and other electronic emissions, Karachi secured assistance in establishing a Special Services Group commando unit for its army with its base at Cherat, not too far from the proposed site of the Communications Unit at Badaber. Ayub Khan told the US ambassador that both India and the Soviet Union felt that US-Pak collaboration was over a tactical missile site and that this misperception raised major new security threats for Pakistan which the US was morally responsible for redressing. The General wanted the US to replace 30 of the older F-86 Sabrejet fighters in Pakistani inventory with more modern F-104 Star-fighter interceptors.[62] Three days later, the Pakistani Ambassador in Washington, Aziz Ahmed, saw Assistant Secretary of State William Rountree to reinforce Ayub Khan's plea. When Rountree raised the question of affordability, Ahmed pointed out that unless threats to national security were met early on, greater costs could be imposed. Rountree asked when the Tibet issue was bringing India and Pakistan 'closer together', wouldn't the induction of these high-peformance jets inflict new tensions? Ahmed said Pakistan had proposed 'joint defence' to which the Indian response was indifferent. Pakistan's view was 'the danger of overt invasion of the subcontinent was not great but Tibet might become an offensive base for bringing various pressures on India and Pakistan.' There was not enough time for strengthening the 'northern tier' for the two neighbours to compose their differences and jointly face the common foe; in short, Pakistan wanted the fighters urgently to protect itself.[63] After some more exchanges which did not endear the two parties to each other, Washington did agree to replace two squadrons of F-86s with F-104s. This opened the way for finalizing the agreement on the US Communications Unit in north-western Pakistan.

On 18 July, Pakistan's Foreign Minister Manzur Qadir wrote to the US Ambassador, James M. Langley, confirming his Government's decision to make available land and physical protection for the installation of the Unit. US personnel would be able to bear arms and operate in 'secure areas' where only 'authorized persons' would have entry. Equipment of the Unit and personal effects belonging to its staff would be brought in and out of the country duty-free and these personnel would effectively enjoy the status of US diplomatic staff. Washington would be able to bring in construction material and equipment so as to be able to construct the proposed facilities in accordance with the terms and conditions set out in the bilateral Military Defense Construction Agreement signed in Karachi on 28 May 1956 which led to the US building a number of military facilities in Pakistan for the latter's revamped armed forces. The agreement would remain in force for ten years and unless either party issued a written notice a year before a proposed date of termination, would be extended for another ten years.[64] The Ambassador and Minister exchanged several notes on the same date which formalised Pakistan's agreement to grant the US Military Judicial system the right to try US personnel should they be arrested by Pakistani police on charges of violating Pakistani law. The agreement thus provided the US with extra-territorial authority in Pakistan not dissimilar to those enjoyed by the British in Tibet until August 1947, and then by the Indian authorities until 1954. But the transfer of modern fighter aircraft to Pakistan at a time when Washington was seeking to reduce tensions in the region and bolster India in the face of growing threats from China caused considerable criticism of Pakistan within the Administration. Pakistani ambassador Aziz Ahmed called on Acting Secretary of State Douglas Dillon in late July to assure him that Indo-Pakistani tensions had been born with the birth of the two countries long before the arrival of any military assistance from the US. He reminded US officials that these tensions centred around the state of Jammu & Kashmir, and the division of Indus waters.[65]

Meanwhile in Tibet, residual NVDA units had been rejuvenated by their leaders in a superhuman effort to continue the struggle against Beijing's military control. The CIA's deliveries of supplies were bearing fruit now that India felt just a little less constrained in its collaboration with its US partners, and a small nucleus of US-trained leaders was assuming command and control, raising the level of professional competence of the combatants. These developments took place painfully slowly while the PLA raised its numbers across Tibet with a view to eliminating all challenges to Beijing's authority. Given the loss of face following the Dalai Lama's flight and the international furore over the bloody destruction of any semblance of Tibetan autonomy and civil society, Beijing appeared to have adopted a power-based approach to the Tibetan issue. More troops were deployed to towns and villages and along the principal routes to dominate nodal points. By flooding the vulnerable and key points with soldiers, the PLA wrested back most of the NVDA's tactical gains. But the cost was enormous; by the beginning of 1960, the Chinese would have to deploy around 100,000 troops in Amdo and Kham, a similar number in central Tibet, and thousands more along the Indian border.[66] This sledgehammer approach was brutally successful but since the nearly-barren plateau was largely bereft of any extractable surplus, the PLA had to rely on trucking most supplies from China proper or Xinjiang across guerrilla-infested stretches of Tibet.

The Department of State, at a meeting held on 28 July 1959 decided to extend its total support to the Dalai Lama's efforts to raise the Tibet issue at the United Nations General Assembly session in the fall. The suggestion was to advise the Dalai Lama to focus on the massive violation of Tibetan human rights by Chinese forces rather than on the issue of Tibet's independence and sovereignty preferred by the Tibetan leader. This was communicated to Secretary of State Herter by the Assistant Secretary of State for Far Eastern Affairs and his International Organization Affairs counterpart on 5 August.[67] The fact that on 25 July, the Geneva-based International Commission of Jurists had published their report titled 'The

Question of Tibet and the Rule of Law' giving out details of the barbaric nature and extent of the Chinese atrocities in Tibet was considered to have strengthened the case for making a 'human rights approach' at the General Assembly. Herter was also informed that in the third week of July, the Dalai Lama had expressed 'his desire to establish a formal connection with our Ambassador in New Delhi to facilitate consultation on matters of joint concern'[68] and the authors' advice was that should the Tibetan leader wish to see the US Ambassador or *Charge' d'Affaires* in Delhi, they should be happy to meet him. While Tibet and the Dalai Lama remained a source of concern in some segments of the Administration, the focus continued to be on the subcontinent itself and the problems of collectively confronting 'Chinese Communist threats'. However, India and Pakistan insisted on pursuing their individual, often contradictory, policy lines. Washington's troubling failure to forge a more useful bond between its two South Asian clients received attention at the NSC's meeting on 21 August. Recommendations emerging from this review were to guide US policy toward the subcontinent until the mid-1960s. Although the Kennedy Administration's priorities and emphases would be shaped by events, its South Asia policy would see continuity.

The NSC still saw Communism as a monolithic threat: 'The rapid growth in Chinese Communist power and the intensification of the Soviet economic offensive in South Asia . . . underline the importance of developing in South Asia, particularly in India, a successful alternative to Communism in an Asian context. In the nations of India, Pakistan and Ceylon, there is considerable potential for achieving this goal.'[69] The NSC was troubled over Delhi's vocal opposition to some US policies despite close Indo-US collaboration in sensitive areas, but it suggested 'It is in the US national interest that the independence of India be strengthened and that a moderate, non-Communist government succeed in consolidating the allegiance of the Indian people. A strong,increasingly successful India will add weight to this (non-aligned) opposition (to the US) occasionally. Over the long run, the risks to US security from a weak and vulnerable India would be far greater than the risks of a strong, stable, even though neutral, India.'[70] Delhi was to become the recipient of the largest share of US economic aid. The NSC saw Pakistan as a resolute ally too, assistance to whose military build-up was a major factor in maintaining stability, 'thereby contributing to the Free World strength in the area . . . It is in the US national interest that Pakistan remain an active ally of the US, continue its economic progress, improve its internal stability and maintain its defensive capabilities.'[71] However, given the Pakistani generals' attempt to exploit the alliance to continue expansion of their armed forces beyond levels considerd necessary, the NSC recommended against making any further commitments on the Military Assistance Programme designed for Pakistan.[72] Taking a global perspective in its regional review, the NSC suggested that the Administration make continuing efforts to persuade India and Pakistan that the greatest threats to their individual and collective security came not from each other, or indeed from any other quarter, but from 'the increasing menace of Sino-Soviet power.'[73] This message, issued so earnestly, was to fall on deaf ears.

Along the Indo-Tibetan borders, however, there was now little reason for doubting where threats to security came from. The summer of 1959 saw several 'incidents' in which Indian and Chinese troops crossed various 'lines', occupying ground claimed by the other side, jostling each other and firing shots in anger. At the end of August, there was so much publicity of 'Chinese incursions' that Nehru was constrained to address both Houses of parliament on the subject. He told the *Loksabha* that Chinese forces had indeed intruded into Indian territory several times over the past two or three years.[74] Beijing had accused Indian troops of shelling Chinese positions in June at Migyitun on the North East Frontier Agency (NEFA)-Tibet border and then joining up with bands of 'Tibtan bandits'. Following Delhi's rejection of this allegation, 200 PLA men crossed the border at Khinzemane in the Kameng administrative Division on 7 August. The PLA company pushed an Indian detachment from its border check-post two miles south of the McMahon Line, and then returned to its original position north of the Line. On 25 August another PLA detachment entered NEFA's Subansiri Division and opened fire on a picket manned by the paramilitary Assam Rifles. The picket was captured by the Chinese but eight of the twelve men escaped and returned to the Indian post at Longju. The Chinese then began firing at the Longju post forcing the Assam Rifles to abandon it. The following day, Delhi placed the border under the army's control. Until now, perhaps reflecting the ambiguity of the nature of India's acquisition of the region, NEFA had been administered by the Ministry of External Affairs; this too was to change now. But there had also been clashes in the west. Indian patrols had been arrested in the Ladakh area and worse still, the Chinese had built a motorway through Ladakhi territory linking Gartok in western Tibet with Yarkand in Chinese Turkestan/Xinjiang. Nehru explained that this road cut through an Indian spit of land called the Aksai Chin, a very remote area which it 'takes weeks and weeks to march and get there.'[75] Here it was the Kashmir-Tibet and Kashmir-Chinese Turkestan borders which were disputed. The Sino-Indian border was 2,500 miles long and difficult to demarcate because of remoteness and lack of central interest until now, etc.

The Prime Minister's explanation did not allay parliamentary disquiet and three days later, Nehru told the *Rajya Sabha*, the Upper House,that the Chinese had aggressively pursued their own objectives in the western sector for several years: 'According to an announcement made in China, the Yehcheng-Gartok Road, which is also called the Sinkiang-Tibet Highway, was completed in September 1957. Our attention was drawn to a very small-scale map, about 2¼ × 1¾ inches, published in a Chinese newspaper, indicating the rough alignment of the road. It was not possible to find out from this small map whether this road crossed Indian territory although it looked as if it did so. It was decided, therefore, to send reconnaissance parties in the following summer to find out the alignment of this road. Two reconnaissance parties were accordingly sent last year. One of these parties was taken into custody by a superior Chinese detachment. The other returned and gave us some rough indication of this newly constructed road in the Aksai Chin area. According to their report, this road enters Indian territory in the south near Sarigh Jilganang lake and runs north-west leaving Indian territory near Haji Langar in the north-west corner of Ladakh.'[76] Nehru reminded the House that the entire Ladakh area including Aksai Chin had become part of Jammu & Kashmir State as a result of the 1842 treaty signed by representatives of Kashmir's Maharaja Gulab Singh, 'the Lama Guru Sahib' of Lhasa and the Emperor of China. Nehru pointed out that for 100 miles, the road ran across Indian territory and Chinese rejection of this Indian claim was at the heart of the dispute in the west. The record shows that at least one *Rajyasabha* member asked the Government to consider bombing the road and oust the Chinese troops from Indian territory but the Prime Minister rejected that option outright. As if to underscore the need for a more robust response from India, around this time, another Indian patrol was captured by the Chinese at Chusun, detained briefly, and then released. Indian troops were under strict instructions to operate purely in self-defence.

Nehru's known aversion to overt violence notwithstanding, following the signing of the 1958 Indo-US Mutual Defense Assistance Agreement, the Indian forces had received orders to secure forward positions to prevent further Chinese occupation of what Delhi saw as its inheritance. This activist policy paid off in terms of obviating Beijing's encroachments, but by altering the status of a largely uninhabited and non-militarised land into a series of defended positions, it appears to have provoked a strong Chinese reaction. The clashes were a consequence. Taking the opportunity of the difficulties the Chinese appeared to be inflicting on his Indian allies, Eisenhower sought to bring Nehru out of what the US President saw as a dangerous lapse. Visiting France in early September, Eisenhower wrote to Nehru from Paris,[77] expressing sympathy for the victims of the Chinese 'attacks'. He said he had met Mrs Vijaya Lakshmi Pandit, then the Indian High Commissioner to the UK, in London during his stopover there on 1 September, and heard from her about the situation along the Indo-Tibetan border, although no record of that conversation has been found. Nehru's reply to Eisenhower has not been traced either, but Zhou En-lai's letter to the Indian leader a week later suggested Nehru could use a little sympathy.

Taking nearly six months to respond to a note sent By Nehru in late March, Zhou wrote, 'I find from your letter that there is a fundamental difference between the positions of our two Governments on the Sino-Indian boundary question. This has made me somewhat surprised and also made it necessary for me to take a longer period of time to consider how to reply to your letter.'[78] Zhou repeated Bejing's contention that the British-imposed border was 'an outcome of colonial-imperial expansionist policy' which led to 'aggression against China'. He said Beijing rejected both the 1842 and 1914 treaties and pointed out that China claimed 90,000 square kilometres of territory Delhi considered Indian. He also reminded his Indian counterpart that Delhi took effective occupation of the region south of the McMahon Line only in 1951. Zhou rejected India's right to discuss China's border with Bhutan and Sikkim and once again refuted the validity of the McMahon Line. He also accused India of 'intrusions' in ten different areas in the west, linking the border dispute with Indian links to the Tibetan resistance. 'Since the outbreak of the rebellion in Tibet, however, the border situation has become increasingly tense owing to reasons for which the Chinese side cannot be held responsible. Immediately after the fleeing of a large number of Tibetan rebels into India, Indian troops started pressing forward steadily across the eastern section of the Sino-Indian boundary. Changing unilaterally the long existing state of the border between the two countries, they not only overstepped the so-called McMahon Line . . . but also exceeded the boundary drawn in current Indian maps which is alleged to represent the so-called McMahon Line, but which in many places actually cuts even deeper into Chinese territory . . . It is merely for the purpose of preventing remnant armed Tibetan rebels from crossing the border back and forth to carry out harassing activities that the Chinese Government has in recent months dispatched guard units to be stationed in the south-eastern part of the Tibet Region of China. This is obviously in the interest of ensuring the tranquility of the border and will in no way constitute a threat to India.'[79] In short, although China saw its differences with India on the border question as 'fundamental', the US-Indian proxy-war in Tibet was the key to the current Sino-Indian confrontation.

Nehru sent an unusually detailed reply three weeks after receiving Zhou's note. He did not mention the issue of alleged Indian role in the Tibetan resistance, instead focusing on the relative merits of the two sides' claims on the border. The main theme running through was a sense of distressed amazement: 'I had no idea that the People's Republic of China would lay claim to about 40,000 square miles of what in our view has been indisputably Indian territory for decades and in some sectors for over a century . . . We did not release to the public information which we had about the various border intrusions into our territory by Chinese personnel since 1954, the construction of a road across Indian territory in Ladakh, and the arrest of our personnel in the Aksai Chin area in 1958 and their detention . . . I can refer, for example, to the construction of a 100-mile road across what has traditionally been Indian territory in the Aksai Chin area, the entry of Chinese survey parties in the Lohit Frontier Division in 1957, the establishment of a camp at Spanggur in 1959, the despatch of armed personnel to Bara Hoti in 1958 and stationing them there in winter against customary practice and last, but not least, the use of force in Longju.'[80] The record suggests this was the last long letter written to each other by either Nehru or Zhou; from this point on, the correspondence tended to be short and sharp, underscoring the bitterness and sense of betrayal each seemed to feel. While Washington and its emissaries in South Asia laboured over the best method of bringing up the Tibet issue at the UN General Assembly without the US having to sponsor it in any way, and the Dalai Lama engaged in frantic diplomatic efforts to secure support for Tibetan independence,[81] without success as it turned out, China and India became robust contenders along their disputed border. On 21 October, the General Assembly adopted Resolution 1353 (XIV) by a vote of 45 to 9, with 26 abstentions including that by India and the UK, expressing concern at reports to the effect that 'the fundamental human rights and freedoms of the people of Tibet have been forcibly denied them', and called for 'respect for the fundamental human rights of the Tibetan people and for their distinctive cultural and religious life'.[82] It fell far short of the Dalai Lama's repeated pleas to raise the issue of China's violation of Tibetan sovereignty and independence,[83] but the Tibetan leader was gracious enough to send his brother Gyalo Thondup to Washington to thank the Administration for its help and support.[84]

On the day that the General Assembly passed this resolution and following through its argument that as China was not a member of the United Nations, such resolutions were ineffectual and hence pointless, India abstained, Indian and Chinese troops clashed again. Deputy Chief Intelligence Officer Karam Singh of the Intelligence Bureau was leading a patrol near Kongka La close to the Chang Chenmo river when the group was ambushed. Several Indian personnel were killed and the others were detained. Delhi protested but the group was not released before three weeks had passed. In subsequent discussions, the Indian army was critical of the IB's border activities, accusing it of pushing India into a situation for which neither the country nor its army might be ready.[85] In independent India, the military's status had been lowered considerably as the Congress adminis-tration sought to build a civilian state-structure; also, development priorities meant the services did not receive the budgetary allocations pre-independence forces did. More significantly, Nehru had employed the IB in covert operations to which the military was not privy but could only conjecture about. The army feared it would be called upon to clear up the IB's proverbial mess along the borders and this might lead to serious conflict with the PLA for which the commanders felt the army was neither properly armed and equipped nor trained.

Meanwhile, Tibet kept impinging on Indian foreign policy initiatives. President Eisenhower was scheduled to visit India towards the end of the year; the Dalai Lama asked US Ambassador Ellsworth Bunker to arrange an informal meeting with the President when he was in Delhi. Bunker advised Foreign Secretary Subimal Dutt and was told that such a meeting could only add strains to Indo-US relations. Bunker himself felt 'I believe policy we have followed here has paid off as it relates to Tibetan situation and ChiCom aggression and it would be unfortunate to offset substantial advantages already secured.'[86] Getting Delhi to adopt a more overt anti-Beijing stance was so important that it could not be risked for making the Tibetans happy. Aware of the delicate balance Washington would have to maintain to strengthen its alliance with Delhi on the one hand and not betraying the Tibetans' trust on the other, Secretary of State Christian Herter instructed Ambassador Ellsworth Bunker to personally deliver a letter, 'written on official stationery and signed by yourself as Ambassador to India', to the Dalai Lama before President Eisenhower's arrival in New Delhi. In this letter, the Administration assured the Tibetan leader 'The United States Government is prepared, when a suitable opportunity presents itself, to make a public declaration of its support for the principle of self-determination for the Tibetan people.'[87] But Washington would not support the Tibetan claim to independence, merely its claim to autonomy under Chinese suzerainty. Now, presumably, Eisenhower could focus on his main mission.

For the President, the key objective of this visit appeared to be to persuade Nehru and Ayub Khan to either resolve their differences peacefully, or barring that, to lay them aside for the moment and concentrate their collective energies to the threat so clearly visible and growing across the Himalayas. Although during an official visit, heads of states have to get through a great deal of formal activities, Eisenhower spent much of 10 December talking to Nehru about the 'waste' of human and material resources and the opportunity costs imposed on India and Pakistan by their military approach to the Jammu & Kashmir dispute. Nehru agreed that the belligerency of massive deployments was wasteful, but he was afraid of a Pakistani 'stab in the back.'[88] After much discussion with his guest, Nehru proposed that he and Ayub Khan either make a joint declaration or issue simultaneous statements promising that 'all questions between India and Pakistan would be settled for the indefinite future by peceful negotiations' and that resort to force and war would be excluded. Eisenhower asked if Nehru meant **all** disputes, ie if the Kashmir dispute too was to be included in this framework; Nehru replied it was.[89] Eisenhower instructed the US Ambassador in Karachi to see Ayub Khan as soon as possible and convey Nehru's proposal as a personal message from the President of the United States to the President of Pakistan. There, the initiative stalled. The envoy was reminded that Nehru had made similar offers in the past, the first on 22 December 1949, nearly a year after the first ceasefire in Kashmir had become effective, and again in June 1959 when mounting tension with China made preventing a parallel conflict with Pakistan rather urgent for India. Ayub Khan said Pakistan's fear was that under the cover of such a declaration, India would consolidate its military gains in Kashmir and never think about the United Nations Security Council resolution calling for the holding of a plebiscite to ascertain the opinion of the people of Jammu & Kashmir. What Ayub Khan wanted was a specific timetable for the resolution of that dispute; as long as Indian forces occupied the 'vital Jammu & Kashmir areas', any joint declaration with India would be 'a disaster for his regime' at home.[90] In short, no Indo-Pak rapprochement could be established before the Kashmir issue was resolved. Cold War compulsions of the global centre had to take a backseat to the national and regional imperatives afflicting the South Asian actors. The asymmetry in patron-client relations made no visible dent in the fundamental disputation dividing the regional subsystem.

The approach of 1960 saw a hardening of the trends. Indian and Chinese border guards confronted each other following the spring thaw and each complained about the other's intrusions and encroachments. Patrols clashed and both sides suffered casualties. Sharp, short and bitter protest notes were exchanged. The US speeded up its deliveries both to Indian forces and to the Tibetan resistance. India and Pakistan remained at daggers drawn over Jammu & Kashmir, but Washington was eventually successful in getting a World Bank sponsored plan to develop a large and significant infra-structural project for redistributing the waters of the Indus river system between India and Pakistan. This was a major diplomatic, financial and engineering feat, but it essentially left the Kashmir dispute untouched. Washington did, however, chalk up some other successes. The main one was the reorganisation of the Tibetan resistance. By the beginning of 1960, the remnant guerrilla groups had been identified, rejuvenated, armed, equipped and provided with highly trained and dedicated leaders. By the end of January, when Chinese troops were stretched on the snowbound plateau, the NVDA was busy attacking small PLA posts and ambushing Chinese supply convoys. The re-emergence of the NVDA as a vital force fighting the PLA was the main point of discussion at a session of the National Security Council chaired by the President on 4 February. The Director of Central Intelligence proposed the launching of a new operation called 'Project Clean Up'. The idea was to build around the nucleus of the Tibetan guerrillas who had been able to set themselves up in cohesive bands in northern India despite the horrors in the wake of the Dalai Lama's flight, and mount a sustained campaign against the PLA in Tibet. Once again, key elements of the briefing remain classified but the general outline is clear: 'Mr Dulles briefed the group on CIA operations in support of the Tibetan resistance. He covered the history of the program [*1 line of source text not declassified*] and he described the high quality of the resistance fighters and their strong motivation. The DCI requested approval for the continuation of the program [*less than 1 line of source text not declassified*] to the resistance elements so far identified and to those which he expected to be contacted in the future [*3–½ lines of source text not declassified*]. The President wondered whether the net results of these operations would not be more brutal repressive reprisals by the Chinese Communists who he felt might not find continued resistance tolerable. Mr. FitzGerald pointed out that there could be no greater brutality than had been experienced in Tibet in the past. The President asked the Secretary of State whether he was in favour of proceeding as recommended by Mr. Dulles. The Secretary responded that he was so in favour after full consultation with appropriate persons in his department. He felt not only would continued successful resistance by the Tibetans prove to be a serious harassment to the Chinese Communists but would serve to keep the spark alive in the entire area. He felt that the long-range results could mean much to the free world apart from humanitarian considerations for the Tibetans . . . The President gave his approval for the continuation of the program as outlined.'[91]

Having obtained presidential approval, the CIA reorganised the new NVDA located outside Tibet as a unified force several thousand strong. It could not operate from Indian territory without risking discovery now that Chinese forces had been deployed along much of the disputed stretches. The militia established a base of operations in Mustang, a tiny principality in the remote northern mountains of Nepal[92] south of the Tibet-Xinjiang motorway, all the easier to mount ambushes upon PLA supply convoys. Here Kathmandu's writ ran only in theory and the guerrillas operated with almost total freedom presumably with Delhi encouraging the Nepali authorities to turn a blind eye to the NVDA's activities. Andrugstang Gompo Tashi, the Commander-in-Chief of the NVDA, appointed Baba Yeshi, a guerrilla leader of repute from Bathang in Kham, the commander of the Mustang forces. The CIA began making supply drops to the Mustang-based guerrillas in Tibetan territory with its C-130s in mid-1960. With detachment commanders trained in Guam, Saipan and Colorado, Baba Yeshi's men hit PLA targets with considerable success. Their deep-penetration raids into southern Tibet forced the Chinese to deploy large pickets along the Tibet-Xinjiang motorway. The next two years would bring many trophies to the NVDA's soldiers. One such booty carried the documentary confirmation that the PLA had killed around 87,000 Tibetans in and around Lhasa in the months following the Dalai Lama's flight.

Meanwhile, India and China had sought to make one more attempt at reconciliation. Zhou En-lai, writing to Nehru on 17 December in response to Nehru's letter of 16 November, offered a summit meeting on Boxing day, 1959, and Nehru accepted. Just before Zhou's arrival, though, Nehru expressed grave pessimism regarding the prospects, as he saw them, for a negotiated settlement of the Sino-Indian border dispute. He told senior officials from the Indian Intelligence Bureau and other security services 'The northern frontier had, for the first time in history, become live and dangerous. It would remain dangerous unless China broke up, which was not going to happen easily.'[93] This prognostication did not bode well for the talks. Nehru obviously could see beyond the immediate issues and discern the procsses shaping the structure of Sino-Indian relations. What he saw was unlikely to have filled him with joy. Zhou's visit was not a warm and friendly repetation of past trips. The two sides remained divided over their mutually incompatible claims, challenging as Zhou did the validity of the very treaties which shaped his hosts' perception of where the Indo-Tibetan borders lay. As for a possible way out of the impasse, at least one source suggests that Zhou made an offer: Delhi should accept Aksai Chin as part of China; Beijing would accept the McMahon Line as the legitimate boundary in the east.[94] Over the next four decades, this was to emerge as the de facto solution to the problem, but in 1960, Delhi could not countenance a proposition that invalidated all the arguments in which India had invested so much of logic, and perhaps equally important, 'face'. More significantly, however, documentary evidence confirming this offer has not been traceable. The two leaders did agree to initiate official-level talks during which both sides presented historical evidence supporting respective arguments. When the final reports were published at the end of 1960, it was apparent that the wide gulf separating the two sides was now no narrower.

As the Sino-Indian borders became increasingly 'active', there were pressures on the Indian government to strengthen its defenses with the help of great powers. Political forces from the Indian right demanded that Delhi now openly sign up as a Western ally, just as Pakistan had done. Similar pressures appeared at the Bangalore conference of the Indian National Congress in mid-January 1960. Curiously, Nehru continued to maintain what can only be described as his ambivalence between declaratory stance and actual policy. Although India had renewed its Mutual Defense Assistance Agreement with the US just a year earlier, Nehru persisted with his familiar non-alignment. He challenged those who suggested building an alliance relationship with greatpowers:

*What does this business of military pacts mean? Does it mean foreign armies, in large numbers, marching across our territory? Is the idea feasible? It is not. We will not have foreign armies on our soil, and we will not make any exception to this, whatever be the consequences. We have had enough of them in the past – we should at least learn from experience. If we enter into military alliances, we may derive some advantages, like getting some kind of military equipment. That is a possibility. But it is open to us to get that from any country we choose. What happens when we go and line up as faithful standard-bearers of this group or that group, except that India ceases to have any individuality and ceases to stand on its own feet? It does not take us forward. SEATO and CENTO and all the odd things that have arisen in the last few years have done no good to anybody . . . Do we expect foreign armies to come and sit on the Himalayan peaks to defend our country? The moment the Indian Army and the people cannot defend its borders, and we rely on others to do this, India's freedom is lost . . . So, from any point of view, opportunist, practical or idealistic, we arrive at the conclusion that it would be very wrong and harmful for countries to align themselves with power blocs or have military alliances for the purpose of ensuring their security.*[95]

With guerrilla operations proceeding rather better than before and Washington's assistance flowing with greater munificence, both Nehru and the Dalai Lama may have felt less despondent than they did in 1959. Having failed to meet Eisenhower during his visit to India in December 1959, the Dalai Lama wrote to Secretary of State Christian Herter on 5 January 1960 seeking the US's open endorsement of the Tibetan claim to independence. This plea was discussed among the Department's senior officials. Herter wrote back on 20 February reiterating the US position: support for Tibetan autonomy and self-determination under Chinese suzerainty, yes.[96] The question of offering possible US support for Tibetan independence was not mentioned. The Dalai Lama was to write to Herter two more letters before sending Gyalo Thondup to meet the Secretary requesting support for Tibetan self-determination. As the U.N. General Assembly session approached, the Dalai Lama wrote to the Secretary of State on September 13 and 16. It appears he was now reconciled to the impossibility of securing support for Tibetan independence. Herter sent a thoughtful reply on 11 October, offering to extend all help to the Tibetans and also to Malaya and Thailand, the two countries sponsoring a resolution on Tibet. He assured the Dalai Lama, 'The American people continue to admire the heroic struggle of the Tibetan people to maintain their religion and culture in the face of ruthless efforts to Communize them by force. I am certain that free men everywhere continue to hope that the brave Tibetan people will survive their present ordeal and that they will eventually be able to live a life of their own choosing in peace.'[97] Two weeks later, Gyalo Thondup called on Herter with a message from the Dalai Lama thanking the Secretary and the US Government for all the support and assistance extended to the Tibetan people. Thondup and Herter discussed the Tibet resolution being sponsored by Malaya and Thailand and whether it might be possible to insert a clause supporting Tibetan self-determination. Herter felt the item should be so scripted that it won the maximum possible support in the General Assembly. 'Mr. Thondup thanked the Secretary for his opinion. He said that before taking leave he would again like to convey the Dalai Lama's request for U.S. support of the cause of Tibetan freedom. The Secretary said that, as Mr. Thondup knew, we had been helping in every way we can and would continue to do so.'[98]

The US did provide considerable assistance to its South Asian clients in the early 1960s. The Indian army raised two new divisions in 1960, improved many of its older, smaller airfields and built several new ones for combat and logistic support operations, and the air force received and commissioned C-119 Packet cargo aircraft from the US and An-12s from the Soviet Union to provide support to units deployed in difficult areas such as along the northern borders.[99] And many Tibetan refugees were engaged as high-altitude road builders with the new Border Roads Organisation. Other Tibetans, former guerrillas and prospective ones, were to be absorbed into several paramilitary forces, the best known ones being the Indo-Tibetan Border Police, and the Special Frontier Force. However, the Chinese were active too. Faced with repeated reports of continued road-building by the Chinese in border areas and probing patrols into Indian territory, Defence Minister Krishna Menon called a meeting with the Chief of the Army Staff, Defence Secretary, Foreign Secretary, and the Director, Intelligence Bureau at the end of May 1960. Having reviewed the situation, Menon ordered the establishment of a number of new border posts to prevent further Chinese incursions. In September and November, the IB issued further reports of continuing Chinese activities in the Ladakh area. In November 1960, the Defence Minister called another meeting to review progress on the lines taken at the May meeting. China and India appeared to be headed toward a confrontation as both sides continued their build-up across the border. The degree of Indian concern at the way things were going was reflected at a meeting Ambassador Ellsworth Bunker had with the Indian Foreign Secretary towards the end of November. It was a formal meeting and in his report to Washington, Bunker wrote,

'*Foreign Secretary Dutt called my attention to GOI White Paper covering Indo-Chinese Communist relations from period March-October 1960 in which India had protested repeated violations of Indian airspace by Chinese Communist planes. Chinese Communist reply asserted twice no Chinese planes over Indian territory but these American planes based Formosa which had been dropping arms, agents and equipment to Tibetans. Dutt added by way of comment that four Tibetan refugees recently arrived Ladakh had US arms but I pointed out that most arms this area war surplus to which he agreed. Dutt said he of course did not know whether we had dropped supplies in Tibet but he wished inform me GOI planning take vigorous action shoot down planes violating Indian territory. Therefore he hoped that if we planning air drops in future we would not fly over Indian territory. If US plane shot down it would create 'tremendous furor'. Dutt added GOI preparing further documentary evidence against Chinese Communists.*

*Comment: I believe Dutt's statement indication that while GOI not averse to aid being rendered Tibetans, fearful that if US planes brought down over Indian territory it would greatly weaken Indian position vis-a-vis Chinese Communists, lend color to Chinese Communist assertion rebellion instigated by US, pull rug from under severe critics of Chinese Communists in press and parliament, and turn public opinion against US, which GOI most anxious avoid.[100]*

Bunker'

As India's Foreign Secretary, Subimal Dutt was the custodian of the most confidential information relating to the country's diplomacy and national security. He had represented his Government in correspondence with the US regarding the Indo-US Mutual Defence Assistance Agreements, and indeed had signed the 1958 agreement on Delhi's behalf. He was the closest and perhaps Nehru's most influential confidante in so far as Sino-Indian relations were concerned. It is very unlikely indeed that he did not know about the covert operations being mounted by the CIA and the IB in Tibet. However, diplomatic nicety demanded that charades be played, and both Bunker and Dutt played them. Delhi may, in fact, have wished to communicate a sense of deep anxiety, perhaps even a measure of desperation, over Chinese activities and Dutt's message may have been a plea for help, subtly nuanced so that only those with the diplomatic code-keys, as it were, knew what was being transmitted. As the year ended, India and China appeared headed for an inevitable denouement, and the US, as the principal patron to one of the main actors in this Himalayan drama, needed to be kept aware of developments. Delhi and Dutt apparently were seeking to ensure that it was.

# CHAPTER 6

# The Denouement

For the US-Sino-Indian security triangle, 1961 began almost the way 1960 had ended. The US was concerned that mounting Chinese pressures along the Indo-Tibetan borders could seriously threaten the subcontinent's safety unless India and Pakistan overcame the bitterness of their mutual inscurities and worked together in concert with Washington. Delhi was increasingly anxious about the gravity of the threat posed to it by the PLA's growing confidence in Tibet following the marginalisation of the NVDA on the plateau, but the Indian ruling elite could not see a way out of the apparently zero-sum dispute over Kashmir with Pakistan. The military government of Field Marshal Ayub Khan, on the other hand, sought to consolidate its alliance with Washington so as to build up a military capability that alone appeared to offer some protection from what was seen as 'the Indian threat'. Additionally, Pakistan's anxieties following disclosure of the delivery of US *materiel* to Indian forces triggered further Pakistani efforts to establish a *modus vivendi* with Beijing. These efforts focused on the stretch of Kashmir-Xinjiang border which had fallen under Pakistani control after the January 1949 ceasefire ending the first Indo-Pak war over Kashmir. Meanwhile, the PLA in Tibet mounted a series of tactical moves mirror-imaging the 'forward deployments' by Indian border guards so that once the winter snows thawed in April-May 1961, the two sides were once again deployed in eyeball-to-eyeball confrontation at a number of accessible points in both the eastern and western stretches of the Himalayan fastnesses. According to confidential accounts issued by New Delhi, by mid-1961, the border dispute had become so acute that Chinese forces had penetrated 150 miles into Indian territory in some areas.[1] These intrusions were not reported to the Indian public, but New Delhi's anxieties were conveyed to its American allies at a series of high-level meetings.

Nehru had attended the United Nations General Assembly session in New York in September 1960 at which he reiterated Delhi's declaratory position on the wasteful futility of coercive measures in resolving disputes. His speeches underscored the view that conflict at thresholds above actual violence was best avoided, and although he only made tangential references to Kashmir and Tibet, the points he was making were not lost upon his audience. During this visit to New York, Nehru held detailed discussions with US Under-Secretary of State-designate, Chester Bowles. They reviewed not only bilateral relations but also the regional implications of Sino-Indian and Indo-Pakistani tensions. Although not much changed owing to these meetings, they did reinforce Indo-US amity and reinvigorate strategic collaboration. These discussions were resumed in early August 1961 when Bowles visited Delhi to chair a gathering of US envoys in South Asian capitals. He met Nehru three times on 8th and 9th August. This time around they discussed the situation in Berlin, Congo, and Latin America, the Belgrade conference on non-alignment at which Nehru had played a leading role, as well as China and Tibet. But the latter received most attention since by this late summer along the Himalayan ridges, China's military strength was making its presence felt far more robustly than in the past. This was reflected in Bowles's report to Washington:

> *Nehru stated that China was in an arrogant mood and the greater her internal difficulties, the greater her arrogance was likely to become. He described with considerable bitterness Peking's refusal to negotiate the border question in spite of the fact that Chinese forces had pushed 150 miles within Indian territory. As in my talk with him last September in New York he referred with considerable awe to Mao Tse-tung's boasts that China could absorb 300 million casualties in a nuclear war and still survive as a nation. Nevertheless, Nehru felt as did U Nu that the Chinese Communists were unlikely to provoke a war in Mao's lifetime. They would press forward wherever possible, but it was unlikely that they would undertake any massive military moves.*
>
> *I then said although he did not believe the Chinese Communists would move militarily, under present circumstances, the possibility of such a move in the next ten years could not be denied. Although India and America might be unable to co-operate fully in planning to cope with such a possibility, we should at least be able to discuss the subject in confidence and to understand each other's limitations and potentials . . . The only other long range hope of controlling Chinese pressure that I could see was through the development of an indigenous Asian power-balance which would depend only indirectly on the United States military. Such a balance, as I had suggested to him on other occasions, could be provided over the long haul only by India, Pakistan and Japan.*
>
> *I asked Nehru about Chinese progress in Tibet. He replied that he had mixed reports, but that he was inclined to feel that the Chinese hold had been pretty well-established, that the Khamba revolt had largely been suppressed, (although sporadic fighting continued in*

*some areas) and that there had been some relaxation in regard to the Chinese control of the monasteries. He said the Chinese had built a network of roads which had greatly improved their military position. Nevertheless, he doubted that the Chinese would attempt to breakthrough in this area. If this should occur, he felt that the Indians and the Pakistanis (who regardless of present differences would be forced into some degree of co-operation) could provide formidable opposition.*

*Comment: Nehru seemed in excellent spirits, confident, **ready and anxious to exchange confidences, very favourably inclined toward the United States**, while frankly concerned that we would again become so absorbed in Europe that Asia would receive less attention. I had assumed that the question of Pakistan-India relations would come up naturally. But it was not mentioned, and I did not think it wise to introduce the explosive question of Kashmir.*[2]

This level of understanding and amity was, however, tested following the United Nations General Assembly session in the autumn at which India and the US pursued contrary lines especially on the conflict in Vietnam. Washington had already got quite deeply involved in South Vietnam's internecine struggle over ideological supremacy and power between the right and the left. Krishna Menon, once again leading the Indian delegation, asked President Kennedy to see him later on in Washington. Nehru too had asked Kennedy that Menon be given some time. Menon was invited to the White House on 21 November. He and the President discussed the effectiveness and future direction of the UN system as well as prospects for peace in Laos and Vietnam. It appears that Menon was seeking to establish the degree of familiarity he had secured with Eisenhower and Dulles, but the record shows that his encounter with Kennedy was more fraught than had been the case with Eisenhower. The President was more forthright in his rejection of the points made by Menon on Vietnam.[3] Judging by the tone and content of the correspondence between Delhi and Washington over the following months, the warmth of the Eisenhower era had come to an abrupt end.

If the Indian leadership faced a difficult introduction to the new US Administration, the Pakistanis appeared to have a slightly easier run. Ayub Khan attended the UN General Assembly session in New York in September and visited Washington where he was met by Secretary of Defense Robert McNamara. Their discussion focused on US military assistance to Pakistan. Ayub said he did not seek any expansion of the agreed force base or any additional assistance; however, he hoped that delivery of agreed supplies could be improved. McNamara said that FY 1962 deliveries had been slowed down by the crises in South East Asia and Berlin and he assured his guest that FY 1963 deliveries would be at least twice, perhaps two-and-a-half times that achieved in the preceding year. The two sides agreed that the ongoing Military Assistance Programme authorised the delivery of a submarine to the Pakistani navy not earlier than FY 1964. Plans to deliver four C-130 cargo aircraft and 130 tanks, chiefly M-48s, were on schedule and a survey team from the US Air Force was to visit Pakistan to establish the latter's need for additional airlift capacity. No new deliveries of fighter aircraft were planned, but attrition of existing F-86 Sabrejets and F-104 Starfighters would be met with physical replacement of aircraft by Washington.[4] The Kennedy Administration appears to have been aware of the Indian sensitivities regarding US military assistance to Pakistan. While reassuring Ayub Khan, the Administration did not wish to be faced with any adverse reaction from India either. The Department of State instructed the Embassy in New Delhi to advise the Indian government that Ayub Khan's discussions in Washington did not lead to any increase in military supplies to Pakistan but merely reiterated previously agreed deliveries. The Embassy was asked to inform New Delhi, if the latter asked, that the submarine being supplied to Pakistan was intended to help Pakistani naval personnel in anti-submarine warfare training. If Ayub Khan went to the press and claimed that Washington had agreed to provide additional military assistance to Pakistan, the ambassador was authorised to release to Indian officials the contents of the minutes underscoring the fact that no additional deliveries were either requested by the Pakistanis or approved by the Americans.[5]

Meanwhile, as superpower tensions deepened over differences in Europe and other flashpoints, it became clear that a coherent pattern of policies could not be maintained by any of the actors in an environment affected by the interplay of numerous variables whose consequence was often unpredictable if not uncontrollable. This feature would characterise the Himalayan drama as 1961 drew to a close. The Kennedy Administration's efforts to maintain a degree of balance in its treatment of India and Pakistan was severely tested by Nehru's decision to take over the Portuguese enclaves of Goa, Daman and Dieu in December 1961. The dispute over these enclaves between Portugal and India had simmered for several years and Washington had, in the recent past, extracted a commitment from Delhi that the Indian approach would be peaceful. But Indian forces surrounded and occupied Goa in mid-December. There was little resistance and none of it effective, but this apparent breach of good faith infuriated the US Administration, especially after it had assured its NATO ally, Portugal, that Delhi would not employ force. Kennedy's outrage was expressed in a series of telegrams sent to the Embassy in Delhi by the Department of State. On 29 December, Nehru sent an eight-page letter to the President justifying the forcible absorption of the colonies.[6] Judging by subsequent correspondence, Kennedy may have been only partly mollified. Alarmed by Delhi's successful intervention, Ayub Khan wrote to Kennedy in the new year expressing deep concern and using the Goan experience as a possible indicator of Indian plans for Jammu & Kashmir.[7] It is not clear if this note had any significant impact on the presidential mood, but on 18 January, Kennedy sent a fairly stern reply to Nehru in which most of the latter's arguments were robustly nullified.[8] The US leader was concerned that by applying military force to a territorial dispute, India had not only set a poor example and lowered its own position in the eyes of the world, but had also contributed to the worsening global security situation which had suffered from rising tensions between Washington and Moscow over several flashpoints. Nehru appears to have taken these complaints into serious account. In his response to Kennedy sent on 30 January, he said he had indeed considered many of the President's concerns and then taken what he saw as necessary action which to his mind, was 'the lesser of the two evils'. This appears to have partially calmed passions in Washington.

Meanwhile, troubled by India's successful absorption of the Portuguese enclaves and what this might portend for Kashmir, Pakistan's rulers decided to pre-empt a possible Indian move in the north by raising the Kashmir question in the UN Security Council. The near-panic gripping Rawalpindi was underscored in two letters Ayub Khan wrote to Kennedy in quick succession. The first, dated 18 January 1962, informed the US President the Government of Pakistan's plans to raise the Jammu & Kashmir issue at the Security Council[9] seeking implementation of the 1950 UNSC resolution demanding the holding of a plebiscite to determine the wishes of the people of the state regarding their political future. Ayub Khan pointed out that Washington had played a leading role in securing the passage of the original resolution and he now hoped that the Administration would remain steadfast as an ally in ensuring that the resolution was implemented by the two parties, India and Pakistan. The documentation does not make it clear if Ayub Khan received a reply from Kennedy to this 'Eyes Only' message. His second letter, dated 20 April, was couched in a language of urgency,[10] and sought US assistance in tabling and securing passage of the proposed resolution on Jammu & Kashmir. This letter was forwarded to McGeorge Bundy, Kennedy's Special Assistant for National Security Affairs. Pakistan's pleas now received a more sympathetic hearing because of the Indian decision to establish a strategic military relationship with the Soviet Union. The logic of strengthening economic and diplomatic co-operation between Moscow and Delhi, initiated by Nehru in 1955, led to a significant development in the military field. Following the induction of F-104 Starfighters into Pakistan Air Force, Delhi had sought to commission a countervailing capacity in its own interceptor fleet. The US offered to deliver F-104s and France, Mysteres; but Delhi chose to procure MiG-21s from the Soviet Union. This was a declaration of independence of sorts that evoked much delight in the Kremlin and considerable unhappiness in Washington. Ambassador Galbraith was outraged, especially by what he saw as Delhi's lack of sensitivity at a time when it was receiving $500 million from the US in economic assistance, and another $280 million in food aid.[11] Galbraith and the Indian Defence Minister, Krishna Menon, had an unpleasant encounter[12] a few days later. Galbraith expressed the Administration's anger at this apparent slap in the face administered by Delhi at a time when the Cold War confrontation between the US and the Soviet Union was becoming worrisome. Krishna Menon defended Delhi's non-aligned stance, its rejection of the zero sum nature of Cold War alliances, and its right to choose the sources of its military supplies. Indo-US relations dipped rapidly as the perceptions of the fundamental premises underpinning these relations began to differ widely in Washington and New Delhi.

To complicate matters, in May 1962, Pakistani and Chinese officials signed a draft 'interim agreement' about the borders between north-western reaches of Kashmiri principalities under Pakistani control and the Chinese province of Xinjiang. This caused consternation in both Delhi and Washington. It was against this backdrop that Kennedy wrote to Ayub Khan in late May. The US President expressed general sympathy with Pakistan's case in the Jammu & Kashmir dispute and assured support[13] when the proposed resolution was tabled. A resolution, tabled by Ireland on 22 June at Washington's behest, urged India and Pakistan to begin direct negotiations on the Kashmir dispute, especially regarding means of implementing the 1950 stricture about holding a plebiscite. The resolution was supported by seven members of the Security Council led by the US and the UK while two members including the Soviet Union opposed it; two others abstained. US support for what was widely interpreted as a pro-Pakistan proposal and the Soviet veto against it imposed the cleavages born of the Cold War on what was a purely local issue. The global centre thus reinforced regional fissures, deepening and widening them. US efforts to create a subcontinental strategic unity focused against 'the communist threat' had collapsed. On 23 June Nehru expressed 'deep regret and sorrow' that the US and the UK should 'almost invariably be against us' on subjects like Goa and Kashmir. He said the Kashmir debate at the Security Council had 'hurt and injured' India, and had created 'doubt in our minds about the goodwill' of the US toward India.[14] The Administration was not, however, totally united regarding the validity, or the feasibility, of the plebiscite option.

Ambassador Galbraith himself considered the holding of a plebiscite an unrealistic objective, and hence best discarded rapidly. In a message to Washington, he talked about 'Myths, such as possibility of plebiscite, no more desirable here than elsewhere.'[15] Galbraith suggested that he issue a statement saying Washington was flexible on the plebiscite issue and willing to explore other options to resolve the Kashmir dispute, and thereby arrest the rapid chilling of Indo-US relations. This view did not go down well with the Administration. The following day, a telegram from the Department of State advised the ambassador that the President and the Department were 'energetically averse to your making a statement to the effect that the US believes that plebiscite question dead, and Kashmir settlement has to be found in other directions.'[16] This message was reinforced in a telegram sent by Bundy who stressed the importance of the Administration speaking with one voice. Referring to the Department of State's telegram issued on 2 July, Bundy wrote 'State's NIACT 6 to you does reflect the President's own sentiments. He practically dictated the telegram to Carl (Kaysen, Deputy Special Assistant to the President for National Security Affairs), along with some other comments that are too hot even for this channel.'[17] Under Presidential dictum, Galbraith was obliged to take a firmer line on the Jammu & Kashmir dispute with Delhi but his heart did not seem to be in it. Nonetheless, it was clear to Indian leaders that the Kennedy Administration was not willing to be taken for granted despite the pressures mounting along the Indo-Tibetan frontiers. Early in August, Nehru made one last attempt at salvaging Indo-US relations. He wrote a letter to President Kennedy in which he sought to reassure Washington about the basic fidelity of his government to the ties forged between the two states over the past decade: 'My colleagues here and I are particularly anxious to have the friendship of the United States in the great tasks that confront us. I believe today this friendship is good not only for our two countries, but also for the world . . . I can assure you, therefore, that whatever might happen, our attitude will continue to be to encourage friendly relations between our two countries.'[18]

Nehru's rather plaintive letter reflected a measure of pragmatic realism few critics have credited the Indian leader with. It also proved timely. Following Delhi's decision in the spring of 1962 to either stop or push back Chinese forces in Ladakh, the late spring and summer had seen an intensification of clashes between Indian and Chinese forces. It was increasingly clear to Delhi that Beijing would neither negotiate nor give up either claims to or occupation of disputed territory in the North-Eastern Frontier Agency in the east and Ladakh in the west. In August Delhi took another diplomatic initiative issuing several notes to Beijing proposing 'preliminary talks' for the purpose of creating conditions in which talks on the border could be initiated. Subsequently, under pressure from the parliament, Nehru demanded that the objectives of the negotiations should be to restore 'status quo of the border', ie withdrawal of Chinese forces from Indian-claimed land. Beijing offered to hold talks 'without pre-conditions', ie without any withdrawals or acceptance of the Indian position that the border was delimited. Eventually, the Chinese suggested that talks be held in Beijing on 15 October and that both sides withdraw 20 kilometres from present positions to facilitate exchanges. Delhi agreed to the date and place of talks, but only on their 'own terms'. Given these differences, diplomacy did not offer much hope. The confrontation took on a serious turn in early September as both sides sought to improve respective positions before the approaching winter. It appears that faced with the possibility of a Chinese attempt to 'break out' along the Indo-Tibetan frontiers, the Administration now turned around and decided to do everything possible to bolster Delhi in accordance with the strategic plans worked out over the years since the first Indo-US Agreement was signed in 1951.

The first significant clash took place in early September near the banks of the Chip Chap river in Ladakh in which four Chinese troops were reportedly killed. But then the focus of the fighting shifted to the east. Delhi claimed that on 8th or 9th September some 300 to 400 Chinese troops crossed the McMahon Line to threaten Indian posts near Dhola although according to the Department of State, it was not clear if the point of ingress actually lay north or south of the McMahon Line.[19] On 20 September the two sides began sustained firing at each other with a view to dislodging the adversary. This shooting match remained relatively light with limited casualties on either side until 10 October when the exchanges became heavy. On 12 October, Nehru announced that two days earlier, the Chinese had suffered nearly a hundred casualties and the Indians, just seventeen.[20] The Prime Minister also said he had ordered the army to clear Indian territory in the NEFA of 'foreign intruders.' Reversing its stance with regard to weapons procurement, Delhi made three approaches to Washington after operations began in and around Dhola. On 2 October, the Indian Foreign Secretary asked Ambassador Galbraith to help procure spares for C-119 transports operated by the Indian Air Force. The US Air Force moved swiftly and flew out the requested parts to keep the airborne supply train linking the Indian forward positions to the base areas functional. On 3 October, the US Embassy in Delhi informed Washington that the Indian Defence Ministry had asked the Indian Embassy in Washington to buy 250 ANGRC-9 radio units for use along the Indo-Tibetan borders. Even before a formal request arrived from Delhi, the US Army was directed to work out availability of the sets in advance. On 4 October, the Indian Embassy in Washington requested that the US divert two Caribou short-take-off-and-landing (STOL) aircraft ordered for the Pentagon from De Havilland of Canada, suitable for operating in mountainous territory, to the Indian air force. This the US did and the aircraft were transferred to India in late October. In anticipation of further Indian requests, the Departments of State and Defense began working out in advance the early availability of transport aircraft, communications gear, 'and other military and quasi-military equipment on terms which would be likely to be acceptable to India.'[21] In mid-October, as fighting spread along the McMahon Line, Ambassador Galbraith suggested a set of guidelines for the US policy toward India to formalise the relationship that had already developed:

1. *We have natural sympathy for the Indians and the problems posed by the Chinese intervention.*
2. *We will be restrained in our expressions in the matter so as to give the Chinese no pretext for alleging any American involvement.*
3. *We hope for a settlement acceptable to India. We should be careful to avoid any suggestion that Chinese trouble may force a reconsideration of India's foreign policy. If there is such reconsideration it will obviously begin with Indians.*
4. *We will not offer assistance. It is the business of the Indians to ask. We will listen sympathetically to requests. Where, as in the case of the C-119 spares or the Caribous the request is one to which we believe we should accede, we shall move with all promptness and efficiency to supply the items. Mission feels that recent Washington reaction on spares and Caribous was especially impressive to the Indians.*[22]

Washington also moved to secure a degree of compliance from Pakistan to present a united regional front if not a coalition against the Chinese. On 16 October, Pakistan's Foreign Minister Mohammad Ali met Secretary of State Dean Rusk and President Kennedy in Washington. Although they discussed a number of security issues, the focus was on Sino-Pakistani border talks which Pakistan had initiated in 1961 and the Chinese had agreed to hold once tensions with India along the Ladakh-Tibet frontiers spilled over into sustained violence. Ali told Rusk that the US needed to apply effective pressure on India to force it toward settling the Kashmir dispute; the latter doubted if Washington could apply effective pressure, and instead speculated on the possibility of action by the Commonwealth and the United Nations. Rusk promised to 'have another look at the problem', but Kennedy gave no such assurances. He insisted that the primary threat to both India and Pakistan came from Chinese Communists. Ali said all Pakistan sought was to remove the threat of border trouble with China; but he also said 'my enemy's enemy is my friend'[23] suggesting that Pakistan was using these talks as an instrument of leverage against India. Kennedy 'Admitted that all countries do not view danger alike and it important that those who do work together even though others like neutrals were getting "a free ride". Mohammad Ali welcomed this point of view which he said Pakistan shared.'[24] Dean Rusk asked Ambassador McConaughy in Karachi to persuade President Ayub Khan to maintain the momentum on negotiations with the Afghans and also utilise the 'excellent opportunity' presented by recent Indian overtures for holding Ministerial-level discussions on outstanding Indo-Paksitan issues.

Anxious to prevent the Sino-Indian confrontation from becoming a more general conflict, the Government of Ceylon (later on, Sri Lanka) had taken an initiative under the Commonwealth rubric to bring the two sides together. In mid-October, Nehru went to Colombo to attend a summit meeting of interested countries. Given the gulf separating Delhi and Beijing, little progress was made. Galbraith met Nehru shortly after the latter's return from Colombo. Nehru told Galbraith that India had taken the decision to drive the Chinese out of Indian-claimed territory whether it took one year, five years or ten. The favoured method was to maintain steady pressure on the Chinese by Indian forces, rather than open warfare, and this intention applied to Ladakh as well as to NEFA. Weather, terrain and supply problems favoured the Chinese who came in with better winter-protection for their troops. With regard to the Indian supply-train, Nehru said 'We learned too many complicated things from the British.'[25] Air-delivery of gear was sustaining heavy losses forcing resort to slower overland supply. Nehru was concerned with the Chinese occupation of Longju 'but noting its location immediately on border he discounted its importance.' The realist in Nehru worried about the imbalance in forces between the two sides along the Himalayan borders. 'He expressed deep alarm about the prospect of war in this area and his discontent with those who had described efforts to avoid it as appeasement'[26] Galbraith expressed Washington's sympathy with Delhi and informed Nehru that Secretary of State Dean Rusk had personally made similar reassurances to Mrs. Indira Gandhi during her recent visit to Washington as Nehru's emissary. Nehru told Galbraith that US policy was correct and sound 'and certainly it was much appreciated by the Indians.'[27]

## The Sino-Indian Catharsis

Dean Rusk was concerned not to appear to be focused solely on Delhi's problems in South Asia. Pakistan's border dispute with Afghanistan was threatening to get bigger unless the Shah of Iran's mediation with Washington's support made some headway. Rusk urged Ambassador McConaughy in Karachi to press Ayub Khan on sustaining diplomatic efforts with the Afghans while the Embassy in Kabul was asked to do the same with the Afghan government.[28] In the end, though, Beijing's action proved to be the issue demanding most urgent attention. On 20 October, Chinese forces launched a major offensive across the border in Ladakh and south of the McMahon Line in NEFA. All along the disputed frontier, Indian forces were forced to fall back, abandoning posts and forward positions. Casualties were heavy and many Indian troops were taken prisoner. Rusk was now concerned to assist Delhi in concentrating all efforts against the Chinese without any distraction from the Pakistanis. Immediately after receiving news of the Chinese offensive, he instructed Ambassador McConaughy to convey to Ayub Khan 'the undesirability of any action which would prevent India from concentrating on the Chinese attack and to suggest to Ayub that he propose a mutual understanding with

Nehru to keep the border between India and Pakistan calm during the crisis.'[29] McConaughy felt the Pakistanis 'might react adversely to any suggestion that they alone were responsible past border difficulties with India.'[30] Rusk agreed that such adverse reaction was undesirable; the Ambassador was now asked to 'stress our view that Sino-Indian border developments have taken such a serious turn as to threaten security of entire subcontinent.'[31] He was asked to explore with Ayub Khan 'what useful gestures GOP might make that would help Nehru and GOI psychologically . . . We are exploring on urgent basis what further steps we might take to encourage parties get together in this and other connections.'[32]

Despite considerable diplomatic efforts by the US on India's behalf, the situation on the ground rapidly deteriorated in so far as Delhi's interests were concerned. The Chinese moved south and captured Tawang, a communications centre in NEFA about 20-air miles from the McMahon Line. Foreign Secretary M.J. Desai met Galbraith on 24 October; Finance Minister Morarji Desai too discussed the situation with the US Ambassador on 25 October. Both men said a formal request for US military assistance was 'inevitable and imminent.' Morarji Desai said 'the Indians are fighting with vastly inferior weapons. They have World War I rifles vs. the modern automatic weapons of Chinese, few mortars, inadequate machinegun support . . . in view of the military and political situation it is plain that we may have to act with utmost urgency when the request is made.' Galbraith's explanation of the absence of a formal request for aid until then was Delhi's hope that Moscow would restrain the Chinese, and also Krishna Menon's reluctance to 'confess the total defeat of his hopes and policy.'[33] Galbraith suggested that Washington begin contingency planning to airlift infantry weapons and ammunition for two divisions-plus operating under mountain conditions so that the arms could be moved to Indian bases in NEFA 'within hours after request.'[34] Menon featured in confidential correspondence too. Possibly on 25 October, Ambassador Galbraith sent a letter to Kennedy using 'the private channel', as distinct from the diplomatic channel used by US missions and the Department of State. Galbraith wrote that the US was certain to be asked to supply military assistance to India in considerable volume. He suggested that Washington make clear that 'any help will require Indians, in their own interest, to be more considerate of our political and public opinion than in recent past.' He sought guidance on how vigorously he should play his strong hand: 'The immediate question concerns Menon. Does important American assistance require his effective elimination from the Defense-UN scene?'[35] President Kennedy was briefed by his Deputy Assistant for National Security Affairs, Carl Kaysen, on the following day. Kaysen informed Kennedy 'The Indians are in retreat along a wide area of their border in both the Northwest and the Northeast. The Chinese have occupied some inhabited places. They are now beyond the territory they had previously claimed. The Chinese offer of a cease-fire and mutual retreat of 20 kilometers from the present line of battle was rejected by the Indians.'[36] Quoting *Pravda* as saying that this was a reasonable offer which the Indians should accept, Kaysen suggested that at least for the moment, Moscow was tacitly supporting Beijing. He sought Kennedy's approval of three specific and immediate measures:

a. *Help the Indians with arms and equipment on a military assistance basis if they ask for it. Up to now, we have been dealing with them on a cash sale basis.*

b. *Make a public statement through Galbraith that we recognize the McMahon Line as the traditional border between India and China.*

c. *Approach Ayub with the suggestion that he recognize the danger and make some significant gesture; for example, breaking off in a public way his own negotiations with the Chinese about the border.*[37]

Kennedy approved these steps and Galbraith was immediately authorized to state that the US recognized the McMahon Line as the traditional and generally accepted international border and fully supported India's position in this regard.[38] On the same day, Ambassador B K Nehru saw Kennedy at the White House to deliver a letter from the Indian Prime Minister. Describing the nature and extent of 'Chinese aggression', Nehru expressed the confidence that in this hour of crisis, India 'shall have your sympathy and support.'[39] Kennedy told the Ambassador that India definitely had US sympathy and support and the Administration was prepared to demonstrate this in practical ways. The Ambassador insisted that the President's reply to the Prime Minister 'contain no reference to arms or to aid.'[40] Kennedy agreed and said Galbraith would be asked to discuss India's needs with Prime Minister Nehru and other Indian officials. Kennedy's comments on the Indian Defence Minister reflected Washington's collective impatience. 'President asked Ambassdor what would be effect on Krishna Menon's future of Indian reverses. He said that Krishna Menon was an Indian problem and that we were not going to say anything about him but added that he was not an Indian asset. Ambassador replied that political considerations would undoubtedly require that Krishna Menon be kept on as nominal Defense Minister. On basis of his information he judged that PriMin had in fact taken over Defense Ministry and would run it with assistance of defense advisory group composed of senior military officers, all of whom opposed Krishna Menon.'[41] Following these discussions between President Kennedy and the Indian Ambassador, Galbraith was informed that a letter from Kennedy addressed to Nehru was being sent to him for delivery to the Indian Prime Minister.

Meanwhile, Washington also maintained its contacts with Rawalpindi (the new seat of the Government of Pakistan). On 26 October, Ambassador

McConaughy delivered a letter from President Kennedy to Ayub Khan in which Kennedy explained the basis of the US response to the Cuban missile crisis then reaching a climax. Kennedy also indicated his desire to work in close concert with US allies in responding to 'threats to the free world'. Ayub Khan responded by strongly endorsing US actions.[42] On McConaughy's other, more immediate, point, however, the Pakistani leader was less helpful. The US envoy described in some detail the advances made by the Chinese forces against Indian defenders and how they now posed major threats not only to India but also to Pakistan. Ayub Khan was advised about the benefits of a message from him to Nehru reassuring the latter that Pakistan would not take advantage of India's adversity. Ayub Khan rejected this line of thinking out of hand. 'Basically, Ayub indicated little sympathy for Indian position. He felt Indians had handled situation badly, issuing rash and boastful statements on intentions push back ChiComs, giving ChiComs some excuse for countermeasures and then proving totally incapable of handling subsequent military actions.'[43] Ayub Khan also rejected the view that Beijing posed a fundamental security threat to the region and refused to send any message of sympathy to Nehru. He said such a message was not warranted by Delhi's determination to deploy the bulk of its forces along the Indo-Pakistani borders when the situation along the Chinese border had become desperate, and also that such a message would not strengthen India's military position. Instead, he sought US pressure on Delhi to resolve the Kashmir dispute with Pakistan. McConaughy, disappointed with this response, nonetheless came away with an assurance that Pakistan would not seek to take any military advantage of India's difficulties with the Chinese.[44]

Washington kept up communications with Karachi with the hope of persuading Ayub Khan to 'lift his sights above present restricted frame in which he now views Pak-Indian relations and Sino-Indian crisis.'[45] But the Pakistani leader was unwilling to budge from his basic position. Rusk advised McConaughy that while delivering a letter from Kennedy to Ayub Khan on 29 October, the Ambassador should 'Reiterate our view that Sino-Indian border conflict is second in importance only to Cuba in present global confrontation between the Free World and the Sino-Soviet Bloc. We expect our allies in both areas will do all they can to meet the Communist challenge.'[46] McConaughy was also to urge Ayub Khan to send a message of assurance to Nehru, or to Generals Cariappa or Thimayya then in command of the Indian army, adjourn border talks with Beijing, and issue guidance to the Pakistani press for taking a 'positive approach' in its treatment of India. Rusk's basic message to Ayub Khan was that 'In all candor Paks now have an unparalleled opportunity to transform basic relationships in the subcontinent.'[47] Getting Ayub Khan to grasp this opportunity was a challenge.

Washington felt the presence of Krishna Menon as India's Defence Minister not only weakened India's military position vis-a-vis China but also made it difficult for Pakistan to make any conciliatory gestures toward India. Carl Kaysen, Bundy's Deputy, advised Galbraith that subtlety was of the essence; Washington wanted to provide substantive military *materiel* to Delhi without any credit for this redounding to Menon: 'We again urge the importance of avoiding the slightest appearance of U.S. initiative and responsibility in removing Menon. Our efforts with Ayub will be such as to prepare the way to take advantage of Menon's disappearance without requiring it as a condition of forward motion . . . By timing of your moves after you deliver the President's letter to Nehru, you can help to bring about the results you desire.'[48] In fact, Kennedy wrote to both Nehru and Ayub Khan almost simultaneously, the latter letter being issued before the former.

Kennedy wrote to Ayub Khan about the dangers posed by the Chinese offensive to not only India but the whole subcontinent.[49] He expressed disappointment that the press in Pakistan was vehemently anti-Indian at a time when 'a unique opportunity exists for laying the basis for future solidarity . . . You, on your part, are in a position to make a move of the greatest importance which only you can make.' Kennedy informed Ayub Khan that Washington planned to 'give the Indians such help as we can for their immediate needs. We will ensure, of course, that whatever help we give will be used only against the Chinese.'[50] Kennedy went on to reiterate his earlier message about the appropriateness of a private message from Ayub Khan to Nehru reassuring the latter that Pakistan had no plans or intention to take military advantage of India's moment of crisis; this would enable Delhi to redeploy the bulk of its forces from the Indo-Pakistani borders to the active front in the north. Kennedy said given his understanding of the history of the Kashmir dispute, he did not make this suggestion lightly but that 'This crisis is a test of the vision of all of us, our sense of proportion and our sense of the historic destiny of the free nations.'[51] Despite the eloquence of this Kennedyesque flourish, the US now could only wait to see what Ayub Khan's response would be.

The President's letter to Nehru[52] was briefer and relatively prosaic, but no less supportive and reassuring for that:

*Dear Mr. Prime Minister:*

*Your Ambassador handed me your letter last night. The occasion of it is a difficult and painful one for you and a sad one for the whole world. Yet there is a sense in which I welcome your letter, because it permits me to say to you what has been in my mind since the Chinese Communists have begun to press their aggressive attack into Indian territory. I know I can speak for my whole country, when I say that our sympathy in this situation is wholeheartedly with you. You have displayed an impressive degree of forbearance and patience in dealing with the Chinese. You have put into practice what all great religious teachers have urged and so few of their followers have been able to do. Alas, this teaching seems to be effective only when it is shared by both sides in a dispute.*

*I want to give you support as well as sympathy. This is a practical matter and, if you wish, my Ambassador in New Delhi can discuss with you and the officials of your Government what we can do to translate our support into terms that are practically most useful to you as soon as possible.*

*With all sympathy for India and warmest personal good wishes. Sincerely, John F. Kennedy*

Galbraith was instructed to tell Nehru, when he saw him to deliver Kennedy's letter to him, that President Kennedy believed that a letter from the Indian Prime Minister to the Pakistani President would strengthen President Kennedy's hand in persuading Ayub Khan to act in a way helpful to India during the crisis.[53] It appears that Defence Minister Krishna Menon, in an effort to salvage his own position, asked to see Galbraith, presumably to ask for US military assistance and thereby take the credit for making a dramatic shift in India's overt security policy. Galbraith responded that he had to deliver President Kennedy's letter to the Prime Minister and could see Menon only after that. At his meeting with Galbraith, Nehru 'made definite request for US military assistance'.[54] Galbraith then called on Menon who reaffirmed Delhi's request for US military assistance, especially the urgent need for automatic weapons and long-range mortars. Menon said a list of the required items would be delivered to the US Embassy 'tonight or tomorrow.'

In terms of strategic security diplomacy, this was Washington's victory against Delhi's neutralist tendency which had, until now, prevented Nehru from securing an open military alliance with the US. Once the Indian leadership had decided that it was in its immediate interest to dispense with the rhetoric of non-alignment and secure significant military assistance from the only foreign patron that could provide countervailing weightage against China, there was a dramatic shift in aid flows. The arrival of US military advisers and *materiel* was considerable enough to trouble Ambassador Galbraith himself. He asked Washington to exercise caution in its efforts to help Delhi: 'In the days ahead I see a new danger. That is that in our natural desire to help the Indians we will overwhelm them. They do not want to break quickly with their past beliefs. Words like nonalignment still have great evocative power. Phrases like military blocs, military alliances, even Pentagon still have a bad sound. In particular a large influx of American military personnel however well-intentioned could have a most damaging effect. And numbers could quickly get beyond my power to control and guide our political posture and response.'[55] The Administration had delegated the responsibility of working out the modalities of providing immediate military assistance to India to the Pentagon. The Chairman of the Joint Chiefs of Staff General Maxwell Taylor selected Major General John Kelly to head an 'observation group' of around 20 officers. This group was assigned to work as part of the 'Country Group' operating under Galbraith's direction.[56] Washington took Galbraith's concerns seriously enough to give him the overall responsibility of managing the physical implications of the transformation of Indo-US relations. Nonetheless, there were other aspects of this strategic shift beyond Galbraith's ken. Perhaps the most significant of these was the subordination of US-Pak relations to the rapidly growing Indo-US alliance. This entailed costs to Washington's regional endeavours as Carl Kaysen explained to Kennedy early in November: 'We are now faced with the necessity of making the Pakistani (sic) realize that their alliance with us had been of immense value to them. This comprises not only the substantial economic and military assistance we have given, but also the general support that the alliance provides in their relations with India. They are obviously the weaker power, and they have been able to maintain as strong a line on Kashmir as they have in part because of the existence of our support in the background. We are now beginning to confront them with the fact that we are really not able to support their demand for a settlement via plebiscite, and that their best opportunity for settlement on terms something like ratification of the status quo may be passing from their grasp. This will be a difficult and painful process, but it is one we must push through.'[57]

The Department of State's 'Report on Current Activity on the Sino-Indian Border and Estimate of Future Developments' issued in early November underscored the urgency of substantially strengthening the Indo-US alliance. Chinese forces had occupied Indian territory 15 miles south of the McMahon Line at a number of points, and in Ladakh, the main Indian bases were being threatened by PLA advances. Here, about 6,000 Indian troops faced about 10,000 Chinese, and in NEFA, some 30,000 Indian troops opposed an 'estimated 15,000 Chinese invaders, with another 20,000 Chinese in reserve across the border.'[58] Indian casualties totalled around 5,000. Having occupied territory claimed in 1960, Beijing appeared to be planning to hold on to its successes. The impact of these reverses on Indian political thinking was as profound as those on military strategy. Non-alignment and expectations of Soviet support against China had been discredited, and the demotion of Krishna Menon to the Ministry of Defence Production was an immediate outcome. Washington had taken practical steps to assist the Indian war effort: 'After deliberately waiting for the Prime Minister's request, the United States initiated an air shipment on November 1 of military supplies to India designed to reinforce Indian resistance on the border to the Chinese Communists. These initial shipments include:

```
    40,000  Anti-personnel Mines
 1,000,000  Rounds caliber .30 ammunition
       200  Caliber .30 Machine Guns with mounts and accessories
        54  81 millimeter mortars with mounts and accessories
   100,000  Rounds 81 millimeter ammunition
       500  ANPRC-10 radios
       250  ANGRC-9 radios'59
```

Washington also increased the flow of intelligence on Communist China to Delhi and encouraged countries such as the UK, France, Canada and Turkey to provide military assistance. Despite the generally positive tone in describing the improvement in Indo-US links, the report was modest in its assessment of the prospects. 'We shall have to define a new relationship with India. Our military assistance is designed to help a friend, not win an ally . . . We can expect the Indians to redefine their nonalignment policy, but we do not expect them to abandon it.'[60] It was with regard to Pakistan that the Department expressed deep concern. It admitted that efforts to get Pakistan to lay the foundations of improved Indo-Pakistani relations had failed, and also apprehended 'a temporary widening of the breach between Pakistan and India, a Pakistani reassessment of the value of its alliance with the United States and increased political tensions within the country . . . This situation bears the closest watch because Pakistan is, in fact, going through a traumatic experience almost equal to that of India.'[61]

This was confirmed at a two-hour meeting between President Ayub Khan and Ambassador McConaughy on 5 November. Ayub Khan expressed deep unhappiness at the US delivery of military assistance to India without prior consultation with this ally, and with US pressure on Pakistan to make concessionary overtures toward India such as withdrawing troops from the border and assuring Delhi of harbouring no ill intent. He also expressed doubts about the gravity of the Chinese threat to India and suggested that Beijing's objectives, from a military point of view, given the timing and terrain of the operations, could only be limited.[62] He was bemused by the supply of hardware by the US which the Indians not only had adequate stocks of but themselves manufactured. As the Pakistani leader held forth on Pakistan's 'right of self-defense', expressing unease about possible use by India of US military equipment against Pakistan, McConaughy formally handed over an aide-memoi're assuring Pakistan of US assistance to the latter in case of an Indian attack: 'The Government of the United States of America reaffirms its previous assurances to the Government of Pakistan that it will come to Pakistan's assistance in the event of aggression from India against Pakistan.'[63] Ayub Khan asked that these assurances be made public, and on 17 November, the Department of State issued a press release noting that Washington had assured Rawalpindi that if US assistance to India were 'misused and directed against another in aggression, the United

States would undertake immediately, in accordance with constitutional authority, appropriate action both within and without the United Nations to thwart such aggression.'[64]

Kennedy was troubled by McConaughy's report on this meeting with Ayub Khan. He asked the NSC what had been done to keep Pakistan informed about military supplies to India, and the exact volume of such deliveries todate. He was informed Pakistan's Ambassador Aziz Ahmed had been provided with an idea of the type though not the quantity of equipment transferred; further details would be provided soon. As regards volume, Kennedy was advised that between 1 November and 9 November, about 800 tons of *materiel,* worth about $3.5 million,[65] had been airfreighted to India. Kennedy's apparent softening toward Pakistan at this point disturbed senior NSC staff. They had worked hard at winning the great South Asian prize, India, as a strategic security ally, in Washington's confrontation with world Communism; now that prize had been won, the President could not be allowed to lose it through any sentimental attachment to past expressions of solidarity with Pakistan. Robert Komer of the NSC staff wrote to the President, 'The Pakistanis are going through a genuine emotional crisis as they see their cherished ambition of using the US as a lever against India going up in the smoke of the Chinese border war. . . Given Pak bitterness, our pitch should be sympathetic understanding and no pressure. We can let the facts themselves work for us. But I urge equally strongly that there be no give in our position. We have no need to apologize. If we compensate Ayub for our actions vis-a'-vis India, we will again be postponing the long-needed clarification of our position, and this at a time when we've never had a better excuse for clarifying it . . . So if we can weather the current shock, we should be able to hold on to our assets in Pakistan, while still emerging with the sub-continent-wide policy toward which we aim.'[66] The Administration was particularly pleased with the departure of Krishna Menon from India's policy-making hierarchy. Shortly after the outbreak of war, Nehru had moved Menon to the secondary Ministry of Defence Productions, and now, on 7 November, Nehru announced that Menon had resigned from the Indian cabinet. Washington felt it would now be easier to deal with Delhi.[67]

When Ambassador Aziz Ahmed called on Kennedy to hand over a letter from Ayub Khan, the President was sympathetic but firm. He said he understood Pakistan's view that what was happening to India was 'result of its own foolish policies. On the other hand, US cannot stand by idly while China tries to expand its power in Asia.'[68] The gulf between the Administration and its Pakistani allies became evident in Ayub Khan's letter. Ayub Khan reiterated his position that India did not take the Chinese operations seriously since eighty per cent of Indian forces were still deployed along the Kashmiri ceasefire line and Indo-Pakistani borders. He also explained why he believed Beijing's military objectives were limited and did not merit the type and volume of aid India was now receiving. His rejection of Washington's pleas for a sympathetic approach to Delhi's problems was stark: 'although India today poses as an aggrieved and oppressed party, in reality she has been constantly threatening and intimidating,in varying degrees, small neighbouring countries around her. Let me assure you that in the eyes of many people in free Asia, Indian intentions are suspect and the Indian image as a peace-loving nation has been destroyed.'[69] This vitreol was not unexpected, but the fact that a letter dated 5 November was delivered on 12 November suggested that Ayub Khan had lost much of his faith in the utility of Pakistan's alliance with the US. And while this was the outcome of a combination of circumstances, it also reflected Washington's belief that India was by far the bigger prize in terms of strategic security calculations, and if winning and securing that prize imposed the cost of losing Pakistan's friendhip, that was a price worth paying. However, India had not been fully won, certainly not yet.

This is what Galbraith wrote to Kennedy in a detailed, personal, report to the President on 13 November. Galbraith had perhaps played the key role in persuading Washington that sacrificing Pakistan was a necessary step and he was delighted with developments in India. But he also urged caution. He feared 'there is still a role here for a Rasputin. And all of this is apart from Menon's utter incompetence as a Defense Minister and his deeply divisive political influence on the Army . . . The departure of Menon is an enormous gain. I have little doubt that in recent years he was an immediate and efficient channel of communications to the Soviets and possibly even to the Chinese. His departure means, among other things, that we can work with the Indians on sensitive matters – things which I resisted before because of the insecurity involved.'[70] Galbraith accused Menon of arranging 'some shooting on the East Pakistan border' and 'the march on Goa last year' as diversions from the Chinese penetration along India's northern border and the 'anti-Chinese syndrome which was developing as a result'.[71] Now that Menon had disappeared from view, Washington could engage Delhi in serious negotiations to renew the 1958 Military Assistance Agreement not only to take care of the immediate threats from the north but as a basis for a significant deepening of the strategic alliance. However, Galbraith's optimism about the future of Indo-US relations was moderated by his anxiety about the extent of the consequent burden: 'If the Chinese should really come down the mountain in force, there will be more political changes here. Much so-called nonalignment went out the window with Menon. In his pro-Soviet manoeuvers and his articulate anti-Americanism he was the counterbalance for five ordinary pro-Western ministers. Popular opinion and our military assistance has worked a further and major impairment (sic). The problem in face of a really serious attack would be how we would react to the prospect of a new, large and extremely expensive ally. I personally hope that the Chinese do not force this choice. The Indians are busy worrying about the end of nonalignment. It is we that should be doing the worrying on this.'[72] Galbraith did realise the difficulties faced by Pakistan but he focused on the 'big picture' of the strategic shift in US security fortunes and saw the Kashmir issue in that context. In a way, Galbraith reminded the President that he, Galbraith, had been right about the way forward on Kashmir, and Kennedy had been wrong, but he was civilised about it: 'Eventually but not too soon the Indians must be asked to propose meaningful negotiations on Kashmir. This should not incidentally raise the question of a plebiscite, an idea in which there is no longer any future. The only hope lies in having a full guarantee of the headwaters of the rivers. Each side should hold on to the mountain territory that it has and there should be some sort of shared responsibility for the Valley. I really don't think that a solution on these lines is impossible. It may be wise incidentally when the time comes to have the British do it as a Commonwealth exercise.'[73]

It was against this backdrop that an exchange of notes took place in Washington on 14 November between Assistant Secretary of State Phillips Talbot and the Indian Ambassador B.K. Nehru. The exchange laid a formal basis for the military assistance provided by the US since 3 November. Talbott's note pointed out that US military assistance was designed to help defend India against 'outright Chinese aggression'. The other condition was that US representatives be allowed to observe the use of the *materiel* being provided and that any excess supplies be returned when no longer needed for the stated purpose.[74] B.K. Nehru confirmed that Delhi fully agreed to all the terms and conditions laid down. Following the agreement, the Administration turned its attention to medium-term concerns. Meanwhile, Prime Minister Harold Macmillan of the UK and President Ayub Khan exchanged letters, Macmillan essentially taking the position adopted by Washington vis-a-vis the need for Indo-Pakistani amity at a time of regional crisis in the face of the 'Communist threat', and Ayub Khan repeating his response to Kennedy. At Galbraith's instance, Nehru too wrote to Ayub Khan, explaining the latest situation along the Sino-Indian border as seen from Delhi and assuring the Pakistani leader of India's general goodwill towards its neighbour. None of this correspondence mollified Pakistan. In fact, Ambassador McConaughy was so troubled by the reaction of his hosts to the increasing weight of US military supplies reaching India that Carl Kaysen told Kennedy 'McConaughy obviously is somewhat frightened and thinks the situation is out of hand.'[75] Nonetheless, Kaysen and his colleagues advised the President to hold firm and maintain the course of building up India's military capability. To this end US officials contacted their British and other Commonwealth counterparts with proposals to raise and 'equip a force of about five divisions and their supporting formations. A preliminary guess is that the equipment involved might cost as much as

$50 million. The associated supplies, especially ammunition, might be equally or more expensive . . . The rationale of the program is that, with such assistance, the Indians would be capable of holding the Chinese where they are now. If the Indians wish to reconquer the Chinese-occupied area, they would have to use half to two-thirds of the forces they now have on their border with Pakistan.'[76] The Administration moved swiftly to deliver equipment necessary for raising five infantry divisions capable of engaging in protracted combat in mountainous terrain.

While negotiations continued between the Administration and its allies in the UK and elsewhere with regard to stepping up assistance to India, the Chinese advanced deeper into Indian-claimed territory, threatening to cross into the Brahmaputra valley in Assam. One major Chinese pocket at Walong in NEFA threatened to break out into the plains. Against that backdrop, Galbraith appeared to have been disturbed by Washington's short-to-medium term plans. He felt events were pushing the US far beyond the need to help India contain the Chinese offensive at the current line of contact and resist further Chinese penetration into the submontane regions. In a detailed reaction to the NSC's suggestion to limit immediate military assistance to the raising of five mountain-divisions, he underscored Washington's dilemma. He pointed out that in the Walong area the PLA appeared to have attacked Indian positions with nearly a division, and reported the very large volume of military assistance being sought by Delhi: 'Any Indian Government must be prepared for the contingency, of a long-continuing forward Chinese military policy in NEFA, the border countries, UP, Kashmir and it must assume that this will be combined with flexible claims as to what is Chinese territory. In light of our past lecturing on the aggressive designs of the ChiComs, we cannot now reverse the field and tell them to confine their preparations as we will confine our help in accordance with the assumption that the Chinese are basically lambs.'[77] Galbraith said Washington must adopt a policy to help Delhi build up its forces beyond five new divisions: 'we should, I believe, help the Indians on a very substantial scale to organize their continuing defenses and build the supporting industry so far as this is clearly within their capacity . . . The Indians now want, in fact, an intimate and confidential relationship with the United States . . . We stand on the edge of great opportunity here-reconciliation between India and Pakistan, security for the whole subcontinent, a decisive reverse for communism in its area of its greatest opportunity.'[78] Galbraith also laid down a few conditions on which the new, intimate, security links should be forged with India. 'Our help must be related to a sense-making defense plan which reflects the realities of the military situation, does not commit the Indians to impossible tasks (e.g. the recovery of all the Aksai Chin), involves a realistic view of the weaponry and is related to actual as distinct from our imagined capacity to assist. There must be a clear understanding that India (not the US) will take up the

Pakistan problem. Pakistan in the past has been regarded as an American problem. Now it is serious Indian business.'[79]

Washington was troubled by the implications of Galbraith's message. Dean Rusk's reply highlighted the Administration's anxiety especially on the Pakistan issue, but also on the problems of perception faced by patron-states vis-a-vis the limits of effective power: 'India must understand the limits upon our capacity to influence Karachi. We ourselves cannot prevent a Pakistan-Peiping side deal and a withdrawal of Pakistan from CENTO and SEATO if Pakistan becomes determined, however irrationally and recklessly, to pursue that course. Delhi would not be the first capital to make the mistake of believing that we have unlimited power of persuasion in every capital other than its own.' Rusk said he was not arguing Pakistan's case, merely 'emphasizing utter seriousness your fourth recommendation.'[80] The depth of Rusk's anxiety was reflected in his detailed message to Ambassador McConaughy issued a few hours later: 'It clear that Paks have whipped themselves into near hysterical state and that next few weeks will be very difficult for all of us. In view legacy Indo-Pak relations strong reactions to our aid to India were to be expected. We can tolerate and are prepared for considerable buffeting but obviously wish avoid dramatic reversals of policy.'[81] Rusk pointed out the various occasions when, via meetings with Pakistani Ambassador Aziz Ahmed in Washington, the letter from Kennedy to Ayub Khan, another from Rusk himself to his counterpart Mohammad Ali, and a press release issued by the Department on 3 December, the Administration had provided repeated reassurances to Pakistan that the US would not tolerate any aggression against it using US arms supplied to India. Rusk instructed McConaughy to warn his hosts of the dangers of consorting with China: 'Our policy continues to be not to object to legitimate GOP efforts make boundary settlement. However, to help GOP avoid errors, you will wish to make clear that U.S. would not understand entente between two and such action would be viewed most seriously here. At time when ChiComs attacking subcontinent we do not expect nation which allied with us against communist expansionism give aid and comfort to Chinese.'[82]

These exchanges on high policy did not affect the course of combat on the Himalayan slopes, however. Despite the arrival of considerable military assistance from Western allies and friends, Indian forces found themselves being pushed southward along wide stretches of the north-eastern borders. The extent of India's plight was underscored for President Kennedy at a meeting of the NSC on 19 November. The meeting was intended to secure the President's approval of the US-UK Memorandum of Understanding on medium-to-long term strategic assistance to India which had gained added urgency because of the rapid deterioration of the situation on the ground. Senior CIA officials briefed the NSC on the latest Chinese gains. The PLA was thought capable of supporting around 300,000 men in the fighting area including 170,000 combatants. This would require the deployment of 35,000 of the 200,000 trucks in Chinese inventory. McNamara suggested that the JCS quickly send out a fact-finding team of 10–15 officers to 'size up the situation.' Although initially keen to see the UK take an initiative in this regard, Dean Rusk acknowledged that the Assam Valley could fall to the Chinese in a week and that C-130s and spares for C-119 transport aircraft should be sent out quickly while a more systematic evaluation of Indian needs was made. Kennedy felt the UK should be persuaded to take the lead in building up the 5-division package. The NSC also discussed the possibility of a Sino-Indian deal. It was pointed out that Nehru had proposed that the Chinese return to the November 1959 line and offered an Indian withdrawal to the 8 September 1962 line; it was said that Nehru had not formally declared war with the Chinese in the hope of eventually striking a deal on these lines. The President was reminded that the 'gentleman's agreement' with the Congress on aid to India would be violated if military supplies exceeded $25 million in FY 63. Kennedy did not wish to go to the Congress but he 'decided that we should: (1) get a mission off to Delhi; (2) send some C-130s; (3) take care of the C-119 spare parts; and (4) push the UK to get the Commonwealth in.'[83]

These efforts by the Administration were unable to prevent what in Delhi appeared to be an imminent disaster of cataclysmic proportions. Prime Minister Nehru, himself commanding the war effort, felt constrained on 19 November to write two urgent letters for immediate delivery to Kennedy. Ambassador B.K. Nehru took both to the White House.[84] It appears that Nehru consulted only the Foreign Secretary M.J. Desai in writing these two letters. Both carried the same message, the second sounding slightly more urgent than the first. Nehru described the situation as 'really desperate' and requested the immediate despatch to India of at least 12 squadrons of all-weather supersonic fighter-interceptors to be flown by US airmen. He also asked for the immediate installation of a radar communications network to be manned by US personnel for the airdefence of Indian cities from Chinese attack until Indian staff had been trained to take over from the Americans. There was a further request for the deployment of US-operated aircraft to assist the Indian Air Force in engaging the Chinese in combat in Indian air space. Nehru also asked for the despatch of two squadrons of B-47 strategic bombers to enable India to attack Chinese bases and air fields but these would be flown by Indian crew whose members were to be immediately sent to the US for training. Nehru assured Kennedy that 'All such assistance and equipment would be utilized solely against the Chinese.'[85] As a political backstop to these requests, Nehru sought a strategic alliance with the United States which would not only transform Indo-US relations, but also force a major realignment of regional, perhaps even global, partnerships forged as part of Washington's Containment policy.

Shortly after sending Galbraith a copy of Nehru's second letter to Kennedy, Rusk, presumably having consulted the President, sent Galbraith an 'Eyes Only Ambassador' telegram. He agreed that the US-UK programme designed to raise and equip five mountain-infantry divisions was no longer sufficient but underscored the need for information regarding Delhi's plans and capacity for meeting the new situation. He advised Galbraith of the immediate despatch of a high-level team with senior officials from the US Army and Air Force as well as the Department of State and the CIA. The team 'may wish to visit scene of action on frontier.'[86] Rusk also advised that the team headed by General Kelly already in India supervising US supplies was being enlarged. A squadron of twelve C-130 Hercules transports was being sent out immediately for helping with troop movements in Assam and Ladakh as was a 'Special airlift team'. Galbraith was asked to provide 'earliest estimates men and tonnage involved.' Rusk did say that supplies considered urgent should 'not be delayed despite lack of clear picture.' He felt one item Delhi might require without delay were the bombs which the UK had been asked to deliver. Rusk instructed the US Embassy in London to check with Whitehall the availability of British 'air shipment capabilities.'[87]

Meanwhile, few senior Administration officials at the White House, the State Department, the Pentagon and the CIA were getting much sleep. Many were analysing the ramifications of the strategic alliance Nehru had sought to erect in his second letter to Kennedy. Shortly after midnight, Rusk sent a Top Secret response to Galbraith which reviewed Nehru's request and explained why the US could not, under the circumstances defined by Delhi's actions in the military, political and diplomatic arenas until then, make a positive response to the plea for establishing the degree of strategic intimacy Nehru sought: 'As we read this message it amounts to a request for an active and practically speaking unlimited military partnership between the United States and India to take on Chinese invasion India. This involves for us the most far-reaching political and strategic issues and we are not at all convinced that Indians are prepared to face the situation in the same terms.'[88] In the telegram drafted by Rusk himself and cleared by the President, Rusk now effected a *volte face* and claimed that India needed to enlist the support of Pakistan by 'some kind of satisfaction of Pakistan's interest in the Kashmir question.' Rusk also expressed disappointment that India showed no signs of trying to mobilise support from the Commonwealth and the United Nations, nor from the countries in southern and south-east Asia against the Chinese threats to its security. He was also determined to extract a minimal *quid pro quo* from Delhi for any deepening of the alliance: 'Latest message from PriMin in effect proposes not only a military alliance between India and the United States, but complete commitment by us to fighting a war. We recognized this might be immediate reaction of a Government in a desperate position but it is a proposal which cannot be reconciled with any further pretense of non-alignment. If this is what Nehru has in mind, he should be entirely clear about it before we even consider our own decision.'[89] Rusk pointed out other reasons why Washington 'should not appear to be the point of the spear in assisting India in this situation.' He felt that if the US role became too obvious, the Soviet Union might feel forced to come out with open support for China. Rusk wrote Washington had indications that Moscow too was 'very much worried about the dangerous possibility' of escalation of the current conflict. Rusk sought Galbraith's views on Washington's opinion that 'India must mobilize its own diplomatic and political resources, seek the broadest base of support throughout the world and, more particularly, enlist the active interest and participation of the Commonwealth'[90] before Kennedy replied to Nehru's urgent and top secret letters.

Meanwhile, highly charged rhetoric inside and outside the legislature was shaking Pakistan. The National Assembly and the press fulminated against US military assistance to India, describing it as a 'betrayal' of the US-Pakistan alliance, and the Government of Ayub Khan did little to discourage such vituperation. Ambassador McConaughy met Foreign Minister Mohammad Ali to deliver a letter from Secretary of State Rusk and to ascertain the Pakistan Government's official position. He was reassured to learn that 'GOP had reached decision adhere to present basic foreign policy orientation, including pacts, and to support U.S. leadership, largely because no alternative to this policy at present.'[91] McConaughy's assessment was that the rapidity and extent of Chinese military victory had given the Pakistanis cause for a sober reappraisal of their own position, and that Ayub Khan himself was a moderate but public opinion as represented by the National Assembly, was still volatile in its anti-US sentiment. He recommended that Washington not pursue a 'tougher line' in its dealing with the Pakistani Ambassador, Aziz Ahmed.

Later that day, events took a dramatic turn as Beijing announced that Chinese forces would unilaterally begin observing a ceasefire along the entire Himalayan frontline from midnight; PLA units would be withdrawn and checkpoints would be established; if the Indian Government reciprocated with corresponding measures, Beijing would be willing to enter into negotiations with Delhi with a view to resolving the conflict.[92] This unexpected move gave Indian forces a badly needed respite and Delhi an opportunity to review its options. Washington too was relieved, but the Administration decided to press on with all the activities which had been planned, begun or were under execution. A high-powered delegation led by Assistant Secretary of State for Far Eastern Affairs Averell Harriman and including Paul Nitze, Carl Kaysen, Roger Hilsman and General Paul D. Adams left for Delhi on schedule to arrive there on 22 November. Shortly after hearing of the Chinese ceasefire announcements, Kennedy wrote to Nehru[93]

*Dear Mr. Prime Minister:*

*I was on the point of responding to your two urgent letters when we received news of the Chinese statements on a cease-fire. I, of course, wish your assessment of whether it makes any change in your situation. I had planned to write to you that we are ready to be as responsive as possible to your needs, in association with the United Kingdom and the Commonwealth. We remain prepared to do so.*

*We had already organized a small group of top U.S. officials, who would arrive in New Delhi Friday, to help Ambassador Galbraith in concerting with your government how we can best help. It seems useful to go ahead with this effort as planned and we will do so unless you think it inadvisable.*

*With warmest personal good wishes.*
*Sincerely, John F. Kennedy*

Kennedy's letter was handed over by Galbraith early on 21 November. Nehru replied the same afternoon, thanking the US President and government for all the help they had extended and were still extending, and expressing fervent hopes that the process of strengthening Indo-US ties currently underway would be consolidated despite the Chinese declaration of ceasefire.[94] Like his two earlier letters issued on 19 November this letter too was an emotive missive seeking profound US commitment to long-term Indian security. All three letters underscored Delhi's total dependence on Washington's material assistance, moral and diplomatic support and substantive advice on strategic security issues. Kennedy had already briefed Harriman as to how far the US could proceed on the basis of what Delhi appeared able to do for itself. Now, Rusk sent a Top Secret message to the American envoys on Kennedy's instruction: 'Eyes Only for Harriman and Galbraith from the President. Messages from New Delhi show your watchfulness on the matter but I want to emphasize again that I think it is important that we neither push the Indians forward nor hold them back in the present phase. We do not wish to be responsible either for war or for truce. We should be ready to cooperate with them, subject to obvious limits to our capabilities, in whatever course they choose, but it must be for them to make the choices. Obviously we should not hesitate to give advice against more obvious forms of political or military rashness and our calmness should be a counterpoise to shaken Indian confidence. But we cannot allow them to put off on us the basic responsibilities which must remain Indian.'[95] Galbraith's response the following day showed that at least on the fundamentals, he shared Kennedy's views: 'There are few matters on which I have been so clear as the need to avoid either cheering the Indians on to battle or telling them to make peace, each with its attendant responsibilities for blame.' Galbraith also noted that Harriman agreed with him.[96]

Harriman met Nehru four times between 22 November and 28 November. Initial talks focused on the Indian perception of the Chinese truce offer and prospects for peace. Nehru stressed the point that Beijing's objective had been to humiliate Delhi and having achieved this, China would now withdraw from much of the territory captured in the war. When Harriman asked if Nehru still expected the urgent air-support he had asked for on 19 November, the Prime Minister said he did not apprehend another Chinese attack for at least several months, and the urgency of that request had dissipated.[97] In later meetings, Harriman focused on the need for India to initiate negotiations with Pakistan especially on Kashmir. Nehru said because India had been humiliated by China, public opinion would not permit any further concessions, and certainly not on Kashmir. When Harriman pressed Nehru on this, the latter expressed fears that concessions could trigger communal rioting 'endangering lives of 40 million Indian Muslims.' Nehru rejected giving half of Kashmir to Pakistan or offering independent status to the state, but he agreed that some compromise acceptable to Indian opinion and interests would be necessary on Kashmir. It took a lot of persuasion from Harriman to secure the Prime Minister's agreement to holding negotiations with Pakistan; however, Nehru was still primarily concerned with the threat to Indian security posed by China.

Once Delhi acquiesced in the ceasefire, the urgency of India's desperation gave way to more deliberate and sober reflection on options and opportunities for the short-to-medium-term future. The focus for Nehru's administration remained China's military profile along the Sino-Indian frontiers, but for the US Administration, the import of forging a regional superstructure to security relationships was restored to its position of pre-eminence. While India rapidly expanded its armed forces with US and other Western assistance and consolidated its positions along the ceasefire line, Washington began reviewing its linkages to regional security arrangements. Harriman was advised to visit Pakistan and brief Ayub Khan on how, in Washington's view, the war had altered the subcontinet's position in the American strategic perspective. Kennedy reminded Harriman: 'We have had to look at this situation in terms of Free World security and we regard it as a major test of our alliance ties as well as Ayub's statesmanship whether he does so too.'[98] Kennedy regretted that Ayub Khan had elected to use the war as an instrument of leverage on Washington so as to force the latter to press Delhi on resolving the Kashmir dispute and encouraged Harriman to talk frankly to Ayub Khan about how far Washington would tolerate this attitude. At the end of his long advisory, Kennedy laid down specific objectives for Harriman: 'Your mission will be an unqualified success if we can get the following from Ayub: (1) recognition that he must start re-educating his public before things drift too far; (2) indications of his willingness to respond to Indian overtures, so that we can encourage Nehru to **make** them; (3) minimizing of attacks on the US, which only redound to

Pak disadvantage; and (4) cutting off his flirtation with Peiping on matters other than their own border problem. In return we can assure Ayub that we will take full account of Pak interests in our dealings with India.'[99]

It was a tough message to be taken to a very unhappy ally, but Harriman was helped by the presence in the region of Duncan Sandys, Prime Minister Harold Macmillan's envoy and the UK Minister for Commonwealth Relations. Sandys had informed Ayub Khan of Nehru's willingness to begin negotiations regarding Kashmir without preconditions and had proposed a preliminary Ayub Khan-Nehru summit in Delhi since Nehru had visited Karachi for signing the World Bank-sponsored Indus Water Agreement in 1960. Harriman arrived in Rawalpindi on 28 November and was advised that Ayub Khan wished to dine with him and Sandys alone that evening. Sandys briefed Harriman on his recent discussions with the Indian and Pakistani leaders before they met Ayub Khan for dinner. At this meeting Sandys produced a draft communique' to be issued by Ayub Khan and Nehru after their proposed preliminary meeting. Ayub Khan said if they were to agree upon a communique, why not do that via correspondence between the two leaders rather than by a visit? Harriman and Sandys agreed to this and the three came up with a draft communique to be issued after Nehru had approved it:

> *The President of Pakistan and the Prime Minister of India have agreed that renewed effort should be made without delay to resolve the Kashmir problem so as to enable their two countries to live side by side without anxiety.*[100]
>
> *In consequence, they have decided to open negotiations at an early date with the object of reaching an honourable and equitable settlement.*
>
> *The negotiations will be conducted initially at the ministerial level. At the appropriate stage direct talks will be held between Mr. Nehru and President Ayub.*

Sandys and Harriman briefed Ayub Khan on the changes wrought in India by the war and how resolution of outstanding problems with Pakistan had assumed a higher priority in Delhi. Ayub Khan insisted that Kashmir be described as *the problem*. 'Both Sandys and I made it plain that it would be impossible to have a plebiscite, that the Vale as such could not be transferred to Pakistan, but that there was an understanding in India that they had to make certain concessions beyond the present cease-fire line. We both told him we had not discussed details and did not know how far the Indian Government was ready to go at the present time. Ayub accepted this situation and recognized that the negotiations on Kashmir might last a long time'.[101]

The discussions were wide-ranging and touched on both Cold War issues of global proportions and regional concerns. Over dinner, Ayub Khan sought an explantion of 'this assistance you are giving to India.' Harriman summarised the supplies being delivered and suggested that these were less than the assets lost by the Indian 4th Infantry Division. However, he also advised Ayub Khan that Delhi had embarked on a long-range military build-up designed to counter any future Chinese attacks. Harriman said General Paul Adams would provide greater details to the President on the 29th. Ayub Khan felt that given Khruschev's Cuba exercise which left him with an option to withdraw from brinkmanship, 'Red China was more reckless.' However, he was keen to reach an agreement with Beijing on the Hunza-Xinjiang border. The dinner meeting was followed by a one-on-one session between Ayub Khan and Harriman the following day. Harriman inquired how strong Ayub Khan felt his political position was now that he had started constitutional processes and he commanded the support of only a part of the National Assembly. Ayub Khan said his support base was better than a half of the membership and that for the moment, the democratic experiement would be limited since 'in the East people didn't understand it.' Harriman said Kennedy and Rusk 'wanted to do all we could to help strengthen his position and asked what we might do. He replied three things:

1. Use our influence to get a Kashmir settlement.
2. Don't press him for disengagement with India in the meantime.
3. Go slow on urging joint defense of subcontinent. This would come automatically with the Kashmir settlement.'[102]

Ayub Khan also suggested that Harriman tell the press 'Circumstances force us to give military aid to India but emphasize that Pakistan is our close friend and ally. We realize Kashmir is Pakistan's major problem.' Harriman pointed out that speculation about the imminence of a non-aggression pact between China and Pakistan was damaging 'Pakistan's goodwill in the U.S. He said to pay no attention to such talk, it was unthinkable for him to do such a thing.' During this meeting Sir Morrice James, the British High Commissioner, was ushered in with a message that Nehru had accepted the draft communique worked out by Ayub Khan, Harriman and Sandys. Harriman viewed this as 'a first test of Nehru's sincerity in starting discussions.'[103] Harriman's delegation returned to Washington on that positive note. Harriman submitted a report on his commission's sub-continental trip to the NSC on 3 December.[104] The report was discussed by the Executive Committee of the NSC on the same day.[105] Harriman reported, among other things, that India recognized 'Red China' as its principal, long-term, enemy but was less clear about the threats from the Soviet Union; the majority of Pakistanis considered India their primary enemy with the exception of Ayub Khan and some of his aides; Pakistani leaders were partly responsible for the dramatic reaction to US aid to India, motivated by domestic political drives; only a settlement of the Kashmir dispute could change Pakistani attitude to India and such an attempt ought to be encouraged and assisted by the US and the UK; post-war changes to the Indian leadership had removed 'malevolent influence (of) Krishna Menon' and weakened Nehru's authority – this process should be encouraged so as to bring up younger leaders to positions of influence; India was determined to build up its armed forces and a settlement with Pakistan would strengthen the subcontinent against China; in case of future Chinese attacks, India should be able to use 'tactical air' which would involve 'certain contingent arrangements for supplemental US and preferably Commonwealth air activity'; Indian propaganda efforts had been ineffective, and the US and the UK 'should discreetly assist'. Harriman expressed satisfaction with the way India's 'non-alignment policy' was undergoing 'considerable substantive reinterpretation', but recommeneded against a formal alliance between India and the West since such a formal linkage could ensure a break between India and the Soviet Union and strengthen the currently weak bonds between China and the Soviet Union.

At the meeting of the NSC Executive Committee chaired by President Kennedy, the discussions led to the question of sharing costs of building up Indian defenses in the ongoing 'emergency phase'. The British were said to have agreed to provide £10 million and were thought likely to offer another £5 million; Australia and Canada had offered modest help. Secretary of Defense McNamara feared this might impose a burden of $120–150 million on the US. Kennedy said the US and the Commonwealth should split the costs equally. He repeated this proposal in a letter to Prime Minister Harold Macmillan. Kennedy said Washington should pay $60 million for providing 'emergency' military aid to India and he hoped that 'you and the Commonwealth countries will be prepared to operate with a similar ceiling, and that we can act so as to share the burden roughly equally between us.'[106] Kennedy also proposed that the US and the UK directly help Indian air defense capacity against the much-feared threats of Chinese air attacks: 'In view of the great expense and the long interval of the time required to provide the Indians with their own air defense capability, as well as the possible repercussions in Pakistan, it seems to me that we would do well to consider the extent to which we could agree to provide a certain amount of air defense operated by our own forces should the Indians need it. I would suggest that we undertake to provide the radar and other ground equipment necessary while you and some of the Commonwealth countries accept the commitment to send an appropriate number of fighter squadrons to India should the need arise.'[107]

To maintain the momentum of the process begun by the Harriman mission, Kennedy followed this up with similar letters to Ayub Khan and Nehru. These encouraged both to make efforts at addressing mutual anxieties and take steps to negotiate a settlement of the Kashmir dispute, making it possible for them to forge a regional coalition, even if tacit and informal, against the 'Communist threat'. To Ayub Khan he wrote 'Governor Harriman has told me of your appreciation of the threat that Chinese Communist aggression against India poses to Pakistan and, with the settlement of Kashmir, of the long term need of a combined plan for the defense of the subcontinent. Your discernment in this matter, going beyond the passions of the moment, is of the highest importance for your country and the whole free world.'[108] Kennedy reiterated the assurance that Western military aid to India was specifically aimed at the the Chinese alone. To Nehru, Kennedy wrote, 'We appreciate how difficult it is for you at this moment, when the memory of the recent Chinese attack combines with the prospect of a further one, to turn your attention to the old and troublesome problem of Kashmir. Yet an effective defense against the Chinese threat to India depends on your ability to concentrate your full resources on meeting their aggression. Further, since the threat extends to the whole subcontinent, ultimately the efforts of the whole subcontinent will be necessary to meet it. A full commitment of your own resources and unity of effort against the Chinese can be reached if the issues which divide India and Pakistan, the most important of which is Kashmir, are settled.'[109] This persuasive effort continued on the ground with mixed results. The first reaction was to come from Delhi; Nehru would write two letters to Kennedy in quick succession, on 8 and 10 December. The Pakistani response was apparently more deliberate and somewhat more relaxed. Ayub Khan would not reply before 17 December, the letter being delivered several days later. And in addition to writing about regional security issues, he wrote a second letter seeking Kennedy's help in implementing the large Tarbela hydro-electric and irrigation project.

Ambassador McConaughy delivered Kennedy's letter to Ayub Khan and informed him that Washington had, by then, shipped some 5,000 tons of military equipment to India. Ayub Khan indicated that this 'emergency assistance' could be taken in stride but he expressed 'strong concern' about the implications of a major build-up of Delhi's military capability. On the impending negotiations on Kashmir, Ayub Khan appeared to be 'open-minded and compromising' but he was concerned about the potential impact if the talks failed.[110] When Ambassador Galbraith delivered Kennedy's letter to Nehru, the latter discussed the contents with the envoy. Regarding the difficulties facing efforts to resolve the Kashmir dispute, Nehru felt giving up the Valley to Pakistan or 'to countenance its internationalization', posed serious political and strategic problems for India which 'rendered such solutions impossible.'[111] Following this exchange, Galbraith reported that he saw 'little prospect for negotiations to settle the dispute'.

Dean Rusk appreciated the linkages between the central, global, strategic need for forging a regional response to the 'Chinese Communist threat' on the one hand and a settlement of the fundamental dispute dividing India and Pakistan, and the depth of the misgivings and mutual insecurity between the two making such a settlement extremely difficult at best on the other. He wrote to both Galbraith and McConaughy: 'Most pressing immediate needs on Kashmir are to maintain momentum generated as result Sandys-Harriman initiative, and to keep responsibility firmly fixed on India and Pakistan for working out solution. Because of Commonwealth ties, and less close British identification with previous efforts to move this problem towards solution, we believe British should be kept in forefront of this effort.'[112] Galbraith was instructed to 'continue remind Nehru at suitable occasions' the fact that Washington could not continue extension of military aid to India for long if Delhi was 'expending efforts on quarrel with Pakistan', and that the US believed it was better for it to have both South Asian countries as friends rather than just one. Galbraith was also advised to try and brief such senior ministers and politicians as Morarji Desai, Lal Bahadur Shastri, S.K. Patil, Y. B. Chavan, Kamaraj Nadar, P.C. Sen, and Sanjiva Reddy. Galbraith was asked, at his discretion, to 'encourage President Radhakrishnan urge Nehru be prepared make concessions necessary for agreement.'[113] Equally significantly, Rusk wrote, 'Similar missionary work should be carried out among senior officers of the Indian military establishment where direct relationship between US capacity extend military aid and Kashmir settlement should be easy to explain.' To McConaughy, Rusk's advice was: 'we should point out this is probably most opportune time since independence for Pakistan obtain settlement from India. In future India may become less disposed to compromise. Paks should take advantage of opportunity of the moment; to ask too high a price might dissipate chance. By pressing Delhi to come to negotiating table on Kashmir, US is fulfilling promise to make new effort bring solution. This is most opportune moment and we may not again be able to help.'[114] Rusk instructed that the Ambassador also brief senior Pakistani political and military figures on the need to move swiftly on Kashmir. He also suggested that a British mediator be identified and kept in readiness, if necessary, to shuttle between the two capitals, to encourage the negotiating process. Rusk told both ambassadors 'Since we believe present circumstances offer best prospect for Kashmir solution in recent years, we are prepared to undergo some risk to bring it about. It is not our desire seriously to weaken either Nehru or Ayub and we count on both Embassies to warn us if this likely happen.'[115]

Meanwhile, the South Asia subcommittee set up by the Executive Committee of the NSC, formalised the proposals Kennedy had made to Macmillan. The basic points were that the 'emergency phase' of immediate military assistance to India should have a total ceiling of $120 million and should be completed over the next 2–3 months; it should be shared between the US on the one hand and the UK and the Commonwealth and other countries on the other on 'as close to a 50–50 basis as possible; the US ceiling of $60 million should not include the air defence element but should include the $22.8 million committed until then.[116] The proposed US-UK air defence package, under which the US would provide a radar network and ancillary equipment and the UK and the Commonwealth would provide manned aircraft, would be elaborated on separately. Discussions would be held with Delhi to work out the status, remit, privileges and immunities of the various US military and security teams operating in India under General Kelly and other senior officials. Two days later President Kennedy approved[117] the subcommitte's recommendation pending UK endorsement of the burden-sharing clause, and these became official US policy vis-a-vis India for the immediate future.

Ambassador Galbraith, understandably stressed by the strains of the past few months, was asked to return to Washington on home leave and for consultations. Just before his departure, the Indian Ministry of External Affairs requested him to personally carry Nehru's reply to Kennedy's recent letter to Washington. Galbraith handed the letter to the Indian Ambassador, B.K. Nehru, to formally deliver it to President Kennedy.[118] Nehru was deeply appreciative of all the military, political, diplomatic and moral support Kennedy and the Administration had extended. However, he also pointed out the great difficulties his government faced in working out any compromise over Kashmir that would be acceptable to the people of India. He expressed the hope that Kennedy would understand India's difficulties and continue to assist Delhi in its days of tribulation. The overwhelming emphasis in the letter was on the continued urgency, in Nehru's view, of ensuring adequate air defence against the possibility of future Chinese attacks on Indian formations, positions and installations. To consider these and other issues, Kennedy had arranged a summit with Macmillan and the two were due shortly to meet at Nassau in the Bahamas. The British leader sent a Top Secret reply to Kennedy's letter offering his preliminary thoughts on Kennedy's proposals. He agreed that the immediate costs of the aid to India should be shared equally, and he gave the details of India's needs. 'Some five or six divisions are likely to be used against the Chinese in the mountains. All these forces should be equipped not on the scale of continental armies with tanks and armoured cars and all the rest of it for fighting in the plain, but as mountain troops. Some two brigades have lost all their equipment and the rest of the three divisions were badly mauled. The initial task is to re-equip these and supplement the equipment of the rest of the force.'[119] He did not believe this would cost $120 million. Macmillan felt as a staunch member of the CENTO and SEATO pacts, Pakistan deserved to have its concerns addressed while the US and UK pressed the South Asian neighbours to settle the Kashmir dispute. He had doubts if democratic governments in India and Pakistan would ever be able to muster the resources needed to adequately face a major Chinese assault.

'This leads me therefore to conclude that what we must aim at is getting first the two parties to agree on the joint defence of the sub-continent as a whole and then perhaps to get them into one of the regional military pacts. This would mean that the Chinese, like the Russians, would hesitate before making a massive attack for they would never be sure that they would not draw down upon themseves the nuclear reply.'[120] Macmillan underscored the difficulties of getting the two countries to take complex and painful political steps but he had no doubts as to who had the main responsibility. 'It is the Indians who must make the first move. If they show a disposition to compromise, we can bring pressure on the Pakistanis to abate their extreme demands.' With regard to India itself, 'We have one important card in our hands, namely India's dependence on the West for military aid. But if we overplay the hand we could easily destroy the favourable atmosphere which recent events have created. It will obviously be unwise for us to threaten the Indians with the withdrawal of military aid if they fail to reach agreement with Pakistan.'[121] Macmillan felt the flow of visiting senior figures from the US and the UK to India and Pakistan, offering informal advice to the leaders there, would be more effective than having a designated person as a possible middleman. Macmillan said he and Kennedy could, from time to time, despatch squadrons of fighters to India as a symbol of support and a demonstration of Western willingness to defend Indian airspace, but he recommended against making any formal commitments since that would offer India greater protection than that afforded other states which had become members of CENTO and SEATO.

The Harriman report triggered activity on various levels. The Joint Chiefs of Staff conducted their own study and General George W. Anderson, acting Chairman of the JCS, reported the findings to McNamara. The JCS felt a degree of material support to Indian defence was appropriate but 'providing a completely self-sufficient air defense capability to the Indian armed forces is militarily, politically and economically unsound.'[122] The JCS recommended that the US install three fixed radars in the Assam-Bihar area by the end of 1963, provide three mobile radars and retro-fit three squadrons of Indian fighter aircraft with Sidewinder air-to-air missiles. It also recommended that the UK, Canada and Australia provide command and control, communications and fighter modernisation including air-to-air missiles for three squadrons with training support and operational assistance. The JCS wanted the Department of State to ask the UK and the Commonwealth to assure India on the provision of interim air defence in case of renewed Chinese attack, but its basic position was that Washington ought to offer air defence support should Delhi ask for it in the event of a Chinese offensive.

The NSC too reviewed these issues and presented the President with a detailed analysis in a pre-summit briefing paper. Robert Komer of the NSC suggested that Kennedy take the following line with Macmillan:

1. *We should press Ayub and Nehru to avoid above all the pitfall of a breakdown in the talks, arguing that this could dissipate the last chance for an amicable solution and would inevitably color US/UK support of both countries. You could send letters to both parties along these lines.*

2. *Perhaps the best result obtainable would be if the talks ended with a communique' expressing: (a) recognition of both parties that an early settlement is imperative; (b) determination to keep talking until one is reached; (c) explicit recognition that any settlement will involve a compromise in some respects unsatisfactory to both parties; (d) intent to create continuing organs of consultation, i.e. technical committees; and (e) agreeing on certain interim steps toward a solution. Galbraith and McConaughy should press this theme.*

3. *State's idea of technical committees is good but, by itself, does not entail sufficient momentum toward a solution to satisfy public opinion, especially in Pakistan. So we should examine what 'interim steps' might be feasible in addition. I have in mind mutual withdrawals from the cease-fire line, trade concessions, etc. To the extent that such moves had a joint character, they might (though billed as interim expedients) actually start a trend toward a European-type solution by getting people used to it.*[123]

Komer added that providing aid to India was so inexpensive that 'let's divert MAP (Military Assistance Program funds) from elsewhere if necessary.' He pointed out that it was becoming increasingly clear that Beijing 'never contemplated a major attack on India', and as US-UK support for Delhi became visible, Chinese activities were unlikely to escalate. Komer's optimism was reflected at the meeting of the Executive Committee of the NSC on 17 December. Although South Asia was on the listed agenda, it was not discussed; Cuba and Congo were. However, President Kennedy did see Ambassador B.K. Nehru that very day at the latter's request. The ambassador had been instructed to present Delhi's views on the Kashmir issue just before the President's departure for the Nassau summit with Macmillan. Delhi was extremely unhappy with the abusive reports published in the Pakistani press which suggested that Rawalpindi was not serious about negotiating with India. Delhi presumed that Washington had made no commitment to hold US aid to India ransom to Pakistan's satisfaction; if that were the case, the US should make this point clear to the Pakistanis. Kennedy observed that Nehru's recent statement in the parliament denying any plans to 'give up' Kashmir was unfortunate as it suggested that Delhi was not sincere about the talks. Kennedy felt the next few months would be very difficult for everyone and the best option was to enter the dialogue seriously and ignore all the unpleasant commentary for the duration. He assured B.K. Nehru that 'we get a lot of abuse, as India feels it does.' But Ayub Khan was the only man in Pakistan 'who can carry off a settlement that involves heavy compromise of Pakistani claims and it may be that Nehru is the one man who could do the same in India.'[124]

On the day that B.K. Nehru visited the White House, Ayub Khan wrote a letter to Kennedy in response to the latter's letter of 5 December. Ayub Khan said he found no difficulty in working out with Harriman the joint communique' which announced the forthcoming ministerial meeting on Kashmir, scheduled for 26 December in Rawalpindi and that he was serious about the talks. He felt it was 'unfortunate' that Nehru should make his *Loksabha* statement on the day after the communique was published. But his primary concern, as before, was with the continuing flow of *materiel* into India. 'You must be aware, Mr. President, that there is considerable alarm in this country in regard to the arms aid that has been sent to India. Should the volume of aid to India increase without settlement with us, it would result in serious disadvantages to us and is bound to cause greater alarm and criticism in Pakistan.' Ayub Khan went on to claim that India was using the military aid to build up two armies 'one of which would be concentrated against Pakistan and the other could also be deployed against us when they should want to do so. Surely this cannot be the object of American policy.'[125] Ayub Khan pressed that Washington robustly persuade Delhi to negotiate a settlement of the Kashmir dispute and also not to launch a 'military adventure' against China since such an effort could embroil the region in a major conflict. The Pakistani leader's message was one of deep anxiety over the perception of rapidly growing military imbalance and consequent threat to national security, especially since the Kashmir dispute remained a source of potential confrontation. 'That is why I have been urging that until the Kashmir question is satisfactorily resolved, there can be no disengagement between India and Pakistan in order that we may both live free from anxiety from each other. It is, therefore, most important that your efforts should be directed to the early settlement of the Kashmir question and I would strongly urge that any further supply of arms to India is made contingent on this settlement.'[126]

President Kennedy would not see this letter for several days; he was on his way to Nassau where he conferred with Macmillan from 18 December to 21 December. Their talks were wide-ranging and covered many issues other than the South Asian situation. In the end, it focused on nuclear defence systems. Two sessions on 20 December concentrated on the Sino-Indian confrontation and the Indo-Pak initiative. At the first plenary session, much concern was expressed at the stalemate in Indo-Pak discourse and the Western shift of focus from China to Kashmir. On the positive side, it was confirmed that the US-UK team had agreed that the US and the Commonwealth would each give 'emergency' military assistance worth $60 million to India. Six Indian divisions would be converted to 'mountain' status although India could well raise several additional divisions on its own. On air defence, it was agreed that a specialised team would go out to explore the requirements regarding radar installations. Four fighter squadrons from the US and Commonwealth air forces would be deployed to India on a rotational basis and their role would be air defence against Chinese attacks. There was much debate on the implications of basing Western interceptors for defending India. The fact that a still theoretically non-aligned state was being offered greater security than that afforded formal allies was a source of considerable anxiety, especially on the British side. Macmillan said what 'worries him is that, as so often before, we support the people who are troublesome, such as Nehru and Krishna Menon, and abandon the people who support us.'[127] Kennedy agreed that Nehru's recent letters to him and to Macmillan were intended to persuade them to delink continued military assistance from progress on the Kashmir front. He wondered whether the two of them should contact Nehru to impress upon him the need to proceed vigorously with the Indo-Pak negotiations over Jammu & Kashmir.

In the second session on the same day, Kennedy and Macmillan agreed on a series of steps to be taken with regard to countering the Chinese threat to India. McConaughy said massive assistance to India, a failure to resolve the Kashmir dispute, and a Chinese pull back from the Indian border would weaken the Western position in Pakistan. Duncan Sandys said if India received MiG fighters from Moscow on top of Western aid Pakistan would certainly leave CENTO. Kennedy asked what would be 'so disastrous' if Pakistan did indeed leave CENTO. Sandys replied that it would be 'a slap in the face to the West and that Iran would doubtless follow.' Kennedy asked what the alliance got from Pakistan. McConaughy replied that Pakistan had offered to help in the Laos crisis and in the 1950s 'had offered to send two divisions to Korea if we would guarantee the defense of Pakistan in the meantime.'[128] Lord Home too feared that air defence assistance to India would force Pakistan to leave the alliance. Macmillan said it was a question of balance; 'there has been a great turning to us in India, and we must not repel it. On the other hand, he judged that it is quite clear that Chinese won't attack India seriously. If we do all that is proposed for the Indians and they do not settle Kashmir then we will have lost the last opportunity and the Pakistanis will turn against us.'[129] He asked if there was any chance of Nehru's moving on Kashmir. Galbraith said if both countries continued to demand possession of the Valley, there was no chance. In the end the summit led to a formalisation of the measures already discussed and agreed between London and Washington.[130] There was no breakthrough to talk about.

Nonetheless, considerable energy had been expended in trying to devise a framework which the Western leaders could suggest and which India and

Pakistan could live with. Directly after returning from Nassau, Kennedy wrote to both Ayub Khan and Nehru giving indications of the summit's outcome. To the former, he reiterated earlier assurances that India was being given only modest, defensive, assistance to protect itself from further Chinese attacks: 'We agreed on a reasonable and frugal program of military assistance designed solely to enable India to defend itself better should the Chinese Communists renew their attacks at an early date. To deny India the minimum requirement of defense would only encourage further Chinese Communist aggression, an aggression we both see as posing as grave an ultimate threat to Pakistan as to India.'[131] Kennedy assured Ayub Khan that Macmillan and he agreed that no step would make a greater contribution to the security of the subcontinent than a resolution of the Kashmir dispute, and despite 'the probably painful and time consuming process required, we look forward with confidence to real progress . . . .'[132]

Kennedy's letter to Nehru, in terms of both form and content, was more prosaic and to the point. The President informed the Indian leader that following the receipt of Nehru's letters of 8 and 10 December, Kennedy had 'thought a great deal about the problems of the defense of the subcontinent';[133] and at the Nassau summit, these issues had featured prominently. He informed Nehru that Macmillan and he had agreed to send out a joint team to appraise India's air defence needs but his emphasis was on a regional approach to security, and the significance of efforts at intra-regional conflict resolution: 'Protracted and time consuming as these talks may have to be, we were confident that you and President Ayub will be able to work out solutions. Nothing could contribute more to the security and progress of the subcontinent.'[134] Galbraith met Nehru on 27 December and handed over Kennedy's letter to the Prime Minister. He noted the US-UK joint plans to send out a military team to India to review India's air defence needs, and reiterated the bilateral agreement between Kennedy and Macmillan to fund the conversion of six Indian Army infantry divisions into mountain warfare divisions. Galbraith told Nehru that the question of longer term military assistance to India would have to be based on the results of further assessment of Chinese designs and intentions, and the larger issue of assuring regional defence of the entire subcontinent.[135]

McConaughy met Ayub Khan on 27 December at Murree, a hillstation north of Rawalpindi close to 'Azad' Kashmir, the north-western third of the state of Jammu & Kashmir under Pakistani control. Ayub Khan was 'relaxed, cordial and very friendly' during the meeting. He did not protest when McConaughy confirmed that the US and the UK had agreed to complete an emergency military assistance programme for India worth a total of $120 million, tacitly agreeing that this aid contributed to the deterrence of further Chinese attacks on India. He also appeared reconciled to the fact that this aid could not be tied to progress in the Indo-Pak talks on Kashmir. But 'throughout conversation Ayub made clear that he still felt

Nehru would not be moved to negotiate Kashmir settlement except under pressure from United States and United Kingdom. While he did not contest our view that emergency arms aid could not be witheld as a condition for progress in Kashmir negotiations, he pointedly asked whether we felt failure to make this aid conditional would harden Indian position in forthcoming ministerial talks.'[136] McConaughy said Washington did not believe that to be the case. Ayub Khan gave the impression that 'his reaction to our emergency arms aid program would ultimately depend on Indian attitude at ministerial talks and that his current tolerant and non-committal reaction could harden if it appeared Indians were taking unwarranted comfort from our continued unconditional provision of emergency aid.'[137] On the whole, McConaughy felt his meeting with Ayub Khan had gone 'better than I dared hope.' The Pakistani leader showed considerable confidence in the warmth of US-Pakistani relations, and the envoy appeared to reciprocate that cordiality.

The year thus ended on a slightly more positive note than it had begun on. But clearly, a great deal was riding on the Indo-Pakistani ministerial talks. The first round of these was held in Rawalpindi on 26–29 December. The Indian delegation was led by Sardar Swaran Singh, Minister for Railways; the Pakistani side was headed by Zulfikar Ali Bhutto, Minister for Industries, National Resources and Works.[138] The Ministers met five times over four days and at each of these sessions they restated their respective, well-established, positions on the Kashmir question. Bhutto pressed for the implementation of the longstanding UN Security Council resolution which asked that a plebiscite be held under UN auspices; Swaran Singh asserted that as a secular republic India could not countenance acceding to a plebiscite organised on the basis of confessional differences. Thus the fundamental disputation between the two neighbours born of their mutually exclusive founding principles had come full circle. The talks were adjourned on 29 December without making any progress, but at least the two sides were now talking. The Ministers agreed to meet again, in Delhi, in mid-January 1963. The prospects for peacemaking looked a little bit more realistic as 1962 drew to a close. But as events were to prove, such hopes were misplaced and, in fact, in just over two years, India and Pakistan would embark on their own little war, the second one since gaining independence, on the vexed question of the ownership of Jammu & Kashmir.

# CHAPTER 7

# Epilogue

Indo-Pakistani ministerial talks on Kashmir held in Rawalpindi towards the end of December 1962 were the product of much tenacious diplomacy by US and UK envoys to both Nehru and Ayub Khan. Sardar Swaran Singh's arrival in the Pakistani capital itself was seen as a success of sorts. However, a jarring note came on 26 December when Pakistan announced that agreement in principle had been reached with Beijing over the demarcation of the Himalayan frontiers between northern Kashmiri territories under Pakistani control and Xinjiang. Foreign Minister Mohammad Ali would work out the details during a trip to Beijing in the near future. Swaran Singh told the press in Rawalpindi that Pakistan's agreement with 'India's enemy' on the eve of ministerial talks did not bode well for a mutually satisfactory resolution of the Kashmir dispute.[1] In the event, the two sides agreed to meet again in Delhi, in mid-January, but Ayub Khan pointedly declined an invitation to visit India. This caused embarrassment for the US, the principal sponsor of the talks, but more so for India since Delhi had not only publicised its invitation to the Pakistani leader, but had also been responsible for 'jumping the gun on announcement acceptance'[2] before receiving a formal response. While disappointed with these activities, Washington instructed US envoys to encourage positive action from the wings: 'Our role in this process should continue to be one of exercising influence from sidelines. When either side makes faux pas, we should call attention to the effect on atmosphere in other country . . . While playing this watchdog role we should not, however, become directly involved in preparations for Jan 15 talks.'[3] Washington did not wish to tie military aid to India with progress on Kashmir, but insisted that there was a long-term linkage between the two. The Pakistanis too were advised that continued aid to India would not be allowed to be used against them. The latter themselves were to continue to receive both military and economic aid from the US and Washington would push for a resolution of the Kashmir dispute acceptable to Pakistan. US diplomacy in South Asia was thus driven by the perceived need to reconcile apparently irreconcilable demands of its two clients.

Meanwhile, Nehru wrote to Kennedy stating his Government would welcome the proposed visit to India by a joint US-UK air defence team to assess India's needs: 'the earlier it comes, the better.'[4] Kennedy proposed to Macmillan that the US officers go to London around 15 January and the joint team travel to India a few days later.[5] Macmillan asked that the visit be postponed until the conclusion of the Indo-Pak ministerial talks in Delhi[6] so as to avoid upsetting the Pakistanis. In the event, the latter were not appeased. Ayub Khan wrote to Kennedy: 'Our assessment of the situation in the context of the Sino-Indian conflict has already been conveyed to you. The trend of the exchanges between Peking and New Delhi as well as the recent statements of Prime Minister Nehru clearly indicating his intention of reaching a negotiated settlement with Communist China, would seem to confirm our own conclusions as to the deeper reasons behind India's request for massive military assistance from the West . . . Only a speedy and just Kashmir settlement can give us any assurance that the contemplated increase of India's military power is not likely to be deployed against Pakistan in the future.'[7] Ayub Khan ended by saying that if US arms supplies were 'so regulated as to' encourage India toward a peaceful solution of the dispute, then he was confident of a positive outcome of the dialogue set in motion by Washington.

Such a linkage between US military assistance to India and progress on the Kashmir question was reflected in the National Security Council's decision to call its South Asia subcommittee the 'Subcommittee on Military Aid to India, and Kashmir'. The group filed a status report to the NSC early in January. It dealt with technical, even tactical, aspects of US efforts in the subcontinent. According to the report, the US-UK Joint Air Defence Team was going ahead with its visit to India in the second half of January. The Pentagon was despatching a separate team from the Army Materials Command to explore possibilities of boosting India's defence production in armaments and such secondary fields as textiles and communications equipment. Meanwhile, Britain was urging Canada, Australia and New Zealand to help Indian forces materially; Washington sought similar collaboration from France, West Germany and Italy. The US had shipped *materiel* worth $22 million to India between 3 November 1962 and 6 January 1963. The initial airlift between 3 and 14 November carrying urgently needed infantry kit was worth $7 million. A much heavier consignment of ordnance worth $12.4 million was sent by sea on three ships arriving in India in January. Two Caribou transport aircraft and aircraft spares, 50,000 pairs of snow goggles and 25,000 sets of high altitude winter clothing worth another $2.6 million had either arrived in India, or were enroute. The cost of the 12 C-130 Hercules transports operating along the Himalayan borders was not included in these figures.[8] The report cited difficulties being caused by the $60 million ceiling on aid to India in the FY laid down by the Congress. It was feared that the ceiling would soon be breached and 'We are, therefore, initiating consultations with the Congressional leaders regarding the ceiling.'[9] The NSC was also advised that the subcommittee was assessing US-UK collaboration on aid to India, India's long-term military and economic needs, the implications of Pakistan's increasingly warm relations with Beijing, and ways of improving 'our intelligence regarding Communist China as it relates to the Sino-Indian conflict.'[10] The authors of the report expressed deep concern over the effect on the Indo-Pak talks of 'increased Pakistani flirtation with the Chinese Communists', and reported that Ambassador McConaughy had already been instructed 'to speak firmly' to President Ayub Khan about these developments.

Washington's anxiety over the prospects for the second round of talks came across in Dean Rusk's instructions to Galbraith on the eve of that meeting. Galbraith was to convey to both sides that 'we are not prepared see negotiations break down, certainly not at forthcoming talks. Hence, you should continue to urge respective Governments (1) explore any and all proposals; and (2) at minimum agree to continue ministerial-level talks, and be prepared in advance with communique' which will assure this.'[11] In case the Delhi talks collapsed, Rusk instructed Galbraith to advise both sides that the US, in conjunction with the UK, but alone if necessary, would very soon put forward its own proposals, and therefore, both sides should agree to continue discussions early on. Rusk told Galbraith he knew Delhi preferred a bilateral approach to problems with any country and that its initial reaction to a proposal from Washington was likley to be cool, but Rusk wanted to serve notice that if Delhi did not proceed seriously in bilateral talks, Washington would make proposals demanding equal sacrifice from both sides. These would be tabled only after the US had reviewed the progress made at the Delhi talks.

The progress in the event was modest. The two sides, led by Swaran Singh and Zulfikar Ali Bhutto, met from 16 January to 19 January and agreed on a joint statement of objectives. The parties stated that they sought a political settlement of the Kashmir issue without prejudice to their respective basic positions; they agreed to examine proposals for an 'honorable, equitable and final boundary settlement' on the basis that both India and Pakistan sought delineation of the international boundary in Jammu & Kashmir; Pakistan urged consideration of the composition of population, control of rivers and their headwaters, respective defence requirements and the acceptability of future arrangements to the people of the state; India asked that any territorial readjustment take into account geography and administration, and involve the least possible disturbance to the life and welfare of the people of the region. Both countries agreed that disengagement of their forces in and around Kashmir was an essential part of any settlement which should also embody the determination of the two peoples to live side by side in peace and friendship, resolving problems peacefully and to mutual benefit. The parties agreed not to publicise the statement of objectives and keep it confidential. This last decision underscored the sensitivity of any suggestion of mutual compromise and the delicate and difficult nature of the tasks ahead. The next round was expected to be held in Karachi around 8 February. And the agreement on continuing the talks itself was seen as something of a success by the Kennedy Administration. The latter appeared to believe that only a dialogue offered opportunities for compromise.

Washington was also concerned over diplomatic efforts undertaken by the 'Colombo group' of Afro-Asian states – Burma, Ceylon, Ghana, Indonesia, Cambodia, and the United Arab Republic – which had met in Colombo on 12 December 1962 with a view to coming up with a set of proposals to peacefully resolve the Sino-Indian dispute. The group's view was that the existing *de facto* ceasefire to which India had not formally agreed but was adhering to anyway, be taken as a starting point for further bilateral talks between the two belligerents. The Indian parliament was due to discuss the 'Colombo proposals' on 23 January. India's non-aligned past and neutralist proclivities could, Washington feared, drag it back into a compromising stance *vis-à-vis* Beijing. Partly to obviate such a possibility, Kennedy wrote to Macmillan asking that the joint US-UK Air Defence team be sent to India on 24 January, the visit being announced before the parliamentary debate in Delhi. 'I am still persuaded that adding to Indian confidence vis-a'-vis the Chinese is more likely to help promote a Kashmir settlement than to make the Indians more intransigent. It appears that Nehru is unlikely to settle Kashmir with too obvious a gun at his back. By the same token, we feel strongly here that Pakistan's rather transparent flirtation with Peiping is harming rather than helping its case.'[12] Kennedy despaired that if Sino-Pakistani 'flirtation' continued, India could have an excuse to claim making any concessions on Kashmir would be too humiliating under the circumstances. Kennedy sought Macmillan's help in trying to persuade Ayub Khan not to send Foreign Minister Mohammad Ali to Beijing to discuss border issues. Macmillan responded the following day. He agreed to everything Kennedy had written but he did not think Ayub Khan was in a position to abandon, at that rather late stage, a border treaty already agreed in principle with the People's Republic of China.

The Pakistani position, seen from Rawalpindi, may have become even more vulnerable following the appearance of reports in the American press that a medium-term security support arrangement being negotiated between Washington and Delhi could lead to a $3,000,000,000, 5-year military modernisation scheme for the Indian forces with US hardware, training facilities, logistic backup and secondary industrial support. These reports both alarmed and outraged the Pakistani leadership. Pakistan's move towards closer ties to Beijing was widely promoted as a defensive balancing act by the insecure. While that point was not specifically made, the context was highlighted in a letter from the Pakistani Foreign Minister Mohammad Ali to Secretary of State Dean Rusk. Written on 21 January 1963 in response to Rusk's letter dated 19 November 1962, this note summarised the Pakistani complaint of allies being marginalised while neutrals were being treated generously by the US. Mohammad Ali essentially went over old issues:

> . . . You, in your letter, have dealt with Chinese objectives in Sino-Indian dispute. It appears that you seem to view it 'as stepping stone to next objective.' Whatever ultimate objectives of parties concerned may be, we consider that up to present, Sino-Indian dispute is limited to question of their borders.
>
> Our President in his letter of 5th November 1962 to your President has already thrown light on consequences of massive military aid to India. It is our firm conviction that this aid would either be used in resuming hostilities on Sino-Indian border with its enormous repercussions on all neighbouring countries or consequent military build-up in India might well be used against us in absence of Kashmir settlement. You have correctly been informed of adverse public reaction in Pakistan to your assistance to India. I may add that talk in American press concerning $3 billion, five-year arms aid programme to India has further alarmed people of Pakistan.
>
> I have given thought to assurances contained in your letter that U.S. military assistance to India will not be used against Pakistan. Government of India, however, appears to be committed to a policy of self-sufficient defence establishment. 'The aid to which we attach greatest importance,' said Prime Minister Nehru according to the Washington Post of January 1, 1963, 'is aid which enables us to develop ourselves, to manufacture, to make armaments that we need, because that is permanent help in making us self-reliant in that respect . . . That means additional machines for our armament factories and our ordnance depots.' Should India be able to acquire such a military capability with foreign assistance, I wonder how any power would be able to refrain her from using output of her own defence establishment in any manner she deems fit. The current U.S. military aid to India, in above context, is therefore cause of genuine concern to all of us.
>
> I avail myself of this opportunity to reaffirm that we attach great importance to our long-standing friendship with the United States and our common membership in CENTO and SEATO. We are also grateful for the assistance we have received from the United States. We do believe in you when you say that in recent weeks you have kept in fore-front of your minds interests and concerns of Pakistan. I would, nevertheless, in all frankness as desired by you, like to point

> *out that there is genuine fear among our people that your Government's preoccupation with Chinese motivations may preclude you in long-run to pay adequate attention to vital interests of Pakistan which, it is needless for me to stress, has always given unstinted support to the United States.*[13]

That there was an element of tension between Washington's emphasis on alliance building efforts as the mainstay of its Containment policy on the one hand, and its willingness to treat some 'neutrals' or 'anti-alliance states' more favourably than some allies on the other, became clear on 22 January when the Director of Central Intelligence, John McCone, made a policy review for the National Security Council. Talking about the choices available to the Administration in framing US policy towards neutrals generally and towards India in particular, he said:

> *There is criticism about our lack of difference between the Allies and the neutrals. The Pakistanis are critical, but we must recognize the importance of the Indians. If they joined the Chinese we would have no free South Asia. The Pakistanis are struggling against the Indians and the Afghanistans (sic). They will use or attempt to exploit our power. Our interest is to make a strong sub-continent. We will use the country that can help further that aim. We have used India lately. We do not like their present leadership, but we can use them. While doing this we have moved away from the Pakistanis and they are moving closer to the Chinese and against the Indians. We have not been able to persuade the Pakistanis or the Afghanistans (sic) to change their policy on India. These forces were there long before we came on the scene and we cannot do much about it – we cannot settle all the disputes, but we want to keep them free from the Communists. We cannot permit those who call themselves neutrals to be completely taken into the Communist camp. We must keep our ties with Nassir (sic) and others, even though we do not like the leaders themselves.*[14]

McCone's statement, superficially speaking,may have betrayed a somewhat loose grasp of the Indo-Pak-Afghan dynamics, but it also highlighted the dilemma of super power-politics. In the new 'great game' being played out in the High Himalayas the stakes appeared to be so high, the risks so considerable and the prizes so grand that issues of consistency and coherence, not to speak of the apparent irrelevance of principle, became secondary. Once the identification of gaining the dependence of India, rather than the Containment of China, was settled upon as the prize *per se* of the exercise, the nature of the game itself stood transformed. For Pakistan the shock of what it perceived as betrayal was too much to bear, and forces hostile to friendship with the United States gradually started asserting themselves in the domestic political milieu. China was now increasingly seen as a countervailing force on which to rely as a balancing factor vis-a-vis a strengthening India. The Indo-Pak ministerial talks would continue over the year, a total of six sessions being held, all led by Swaran Singh for India and Zulfikar Ali Bhutto for Pakistan, but in the end, they failed to break the stalemate. The process which had begun, certainly for the United States, and perhaps for Britain too, as a mark of hope and progress, fizzled out without any changes in the stalemated *status quo*.

While Kashmir remained a key plank to Washington's South Asia policy, the strategic focus was on the Sino-Indian borders. These priorities became clear during a special session of the NSC titled a 'Presidential meeting on India'. Held on 25 April 1963, the proceedings of this meeting drew the parameters of subcontinental policy Washington would pursue for the remainder of the Kennedy administration. McCone's intelligence briefing at the outset suggested that the threat of another Chinese attack was small for the next two to three years. He felt Beijing could field no more than 2,30,000 armed men to the Tibet-Ladakh region of whom only 1,20,000 would be frontline combatants. Such a force would require the use of 40,000 trucks and 40 per cent of China's 1962 gasoline supply to maintain it in readiness. India needed an army of 12–14 divisions to cope with such a hostile force, and with reserves, the Indian order of battle could reach 16 divisions with three independent brigades, adding up to 6,50,000 all ranks.[15]

Secretary of Defense Robert McNamara unhappily noted that India now planned to build up an army of 1.4 million all ranks, a $1.8 billion annual defence budget with domestic resources, and $1.6 billion in US military assistance over three years. He felt 'All this is quite unrealistic.'[16] Asked what he considered to be realistic, McNamara said he felt the grant of a maximum of around $300 million to be funded jointly by the US and the UK over three years, possibly a half of that sum, would be a realistic figure. But he was concerned about the impact of military assistance of such magnitude on the current efforts peacefully to resolve the Kashmir dispute. President Kennedy wondered aloud if $300 million would be enough[17] to modernise the Indian forces. The Special Assistant to the President for National Security Affairs, McGeorge Bundy, asked if the danger to subcontinental security posed by the possibility of a Chinese envelopment via Burma had been considered. McCone discounted this particular threat. Despite the uncertainty over Britain's willingness to share the costs of further modernising Indian forces, Kennedy was clear as to the next step forward. He said 'Let us not be penny wise about India; let us not get them into a position where they feel that they cannot cope with the Chicoms and Paks on top of their other problems . . . India is the important thing, not the UK.'[18] As for the efforts to resolve the Kashmir dispute, 'the President thought the chances were almost nil.' Washington's priorities and compulsions were laid out in the closing paragraphs of the minutes. 'The

President . . . felt we must make clear to Ayub we were doing our best on Kashmir but could not hold off indefinitely on aid to India. Rusk agreed and said we must tell the Paks we could not subordinate our larger interests to their quarrel with India over Kashmir. The President . . . asked whether we were likely to get thrown out of our base in Pakistan if we went ahead with aid to India. Rusk thought it would be rough; we might lose our Pakistani base unless the Chicoms attacked again . . . The President thought we ought to go ahead on air defence and work on Congress to this end. Congress would be much madder if India went Communist.'[19]

That last comment explained the manner in which the Administration pursued its South Asia policy for the remainder of 1963: boosting India's immediate defensive capacity by transferring *materiel*, building up Delhi's medium-to-long term domestic capabilities by transferring technology and capital, and encouraging India and Pakistan to continue the process of discussing the thorniest of their disputes at regular, high-level, meetings so that the deployment of forces along their mutual borders was no longer seen as either necessary or useful. In this enterprise, Washington gained only partial success. By the time of Kennedy's assassination in November 1963, Indo-US security co-operation had blossomed to the point that the CIA was no longer running its Tibetan operations from Dhaka but from Delhi, with residual NVDA guerrillas being reorganised into a compact force to be based in the remote Mustang region of northern Nepal. Plans to establish a substantial, clandestine, surveillance system on Himalayan peaks to monitor Chinese activities in Tibet were beginning to gell. However, US-Pakistani relations, and Indo-Pakistani talks, were clearly failing, and Pakistan was making a determined move to recoup some of its tactical losses by forging a new, strategic, alliance with China. Despite occasional rumblings of rhetoric between Beijing and Delhi, mirrored by troop movements on either side of the McMahon Line, and in Ladakh, no shooting war was to break the peace of the snowbound Himalayan heights. But violence and coercion continued on other levels. The Chinese crackdown in Tibet intensified to reach a peak in the mid and late-sixties as the Red Guards unleashed their revolutionary fervour on the plateau, and overt hostility was channelled into covert collaboration with dissenters in both India and China by rival intelligence services. In fact, one consequence of the Sino-Indian conflict and the nature of US participation in it was the apparent legitimisation of clandestine attacks on the vitals of rival states by proxy across Southern Asia.

## A Plethora of Proxy Wars

According to Indian intelligence sources, at least half of the 50,000 Tibetan guerrillas trained by their foreign patrons and allies had received training and support from Indian intelligence services.[20] Once the Sino-Indian war had transformed South Asia's strategic map and its linkages to the global centre, alignments were redrawn as state and sub-state actors adjusted to the changed circumstances. Pakistan was the first to make a move independent of the Cold War activities in pursuit of its own regional interests. Moving from supporting Indo-US secret operations in aid of the Tibetan resistance, Pakistani intelligence began extending support to the 'Naga National Army', a guerrilla band operating under the rebellious 'Federal Government of Nagaland'[21], since the late 1950s. The Nagas would threaten Delhi's control over large swathes of north-eastern India for decades. Pakistan's Inter-service Intelligence Directorate (ISI), would offer sanctuary, arms and training to Naga guerrillas at base-camps established in East Pakistan's Chittagong Hill Tracts. The conflict between Naga insurgents and the Indian security forces received a further boost in the late 1960s when Beijing agreed to provide training and arms to the Nagas. Several thousand Naga guerrillas travelled to training camps in China's Yunnan region where courses lasted several months, and returned to join the war via Burma. Despite several peace agreements being signed between Delhi and leaders of one or another Naga group, one major faction, and several minor ones, of armed Nagas continued their violent struggle into the late 1990s.

A much wider proxy war was to develop in the north-western quadrant of the Himalayan slopes. Shortly after Nehru's death in 1964, Pakistan launched a major covert operation in the Indian-controlled Jammu & Kashmir. Pakistani commandos and *Azad Kashmiri* fighters were infiltrated into the valley to instigate a major uprising. This abortive 'Operation Gibralter' collapsed in 1965 when India escalated its counter-insurgency operations into 'Operation Grand Slam', an armoured thrust into Pakistani Punjab, thereby beginning the 1965 Indo-Pak war. Washington formally disengaged from its overt security linkages to the region at the outbreak of this war, although secret contacts were to persist between US and Indian intelligence organisations until 1970. In the diplomatic vacuum left behind, Moscow entered the subcontinent as an honest broker and worked out 'the Tashkent Declaration' which restored a measure of normalcy between India and Pakistan in 1966. However, behind the scenes, both neighbours continued their efforts to subvert each other. Indian intelligence responded to pleas from Bengali nationalists from East Pakistan[22] to help them in their still quiescent struggle against Pakistan's authoritarian military government while Pakistan's ISI Directorate proffered assistance to guerrillas of the Mizo National Army from India's Mizoram state. In the end, Delhi was able to co-opt the leaders of the Mizo nationalist movement[23], but Pakistan's military response to Bengali nationalism led to a civil war which, through the instrument of Indian intervention, contributed to the secession of East Pakistan and the creation of independent Bangladesh. China supported the Mizos and offered them similar facilities to the assistance given to the Nagas, and stood behind Pakistan in its efforts to crush the Indian-aided separatist campaign mounted by Bengali nationalists. Beijing also provided training and hardware to Meitei 'socialist' guerrillas fighting Delhi's authority in north-eastern India's Manipur state,[24] but there is little evidence of Pakistani support for the Manipuris. Even in the 1980s and 1990s, India and Pakistan traded accusations against each other. Pakistan accused India of aiding Sindhi separatists and *Muhajir*[25] nationalists active in Pakistan's Sindh province; India accused Pakistan of aiding Sikh separatists in Punjab, masterminding the Kashmiri insurrection in Jammu & Kashmir, and sponsoring bombing campaigns by Muslim extremists in Maharastra and Tamil Nadu states.

Persistent denials by all sides notwithstanding, proxy wars and covert operations in support of dissidents active in unfriendly neighbouring states have become the norm in the subcontinent since the initially successful bleeding of the Chinese in Tibet. Apart from the examples linking India, Pakistan and China, there have been other instances of covert operations that have enmeshed Bangladesh and Sri Lanka. Following the violent internal changes which bloodied Bangladesh in the mid-1970s, Indian intelligence provided sanctuary and arms to the supporters of the fallen awami League administration. *Kader Bahini* guerrillas, operating from camps in India's Meghalaya state, once occupied by *Mukti Fauj* combatants fighting the Pakistani forces in 1971, launched attacks across the border into Bangladeshi territory. This force was disarmed and disbanded[26] only after a new government took power in Delhi in 1977 and dramatically, if all too briefly, shifted its stance towards all neighbouring states. Indian intelligence also patronised the *Shanti Bahini*, a Montagnard militia fighting Bangladeshi forces for autonomy in the Chittagong Hill Tracts in south-eastern Bangladesh.[27] Ironically, the nucleus of this guerrilla band was provided by tribal *Chakma* youth recruited and armed by Pakistani intelligence in the 1960s to protect training camps established for Naga and Mizo rebels from India. Many of the Chakma fighters had fought alongside Pakistani forces against Bengali nationalists and Indian regulars in the 1971 war. Once the internal tables were turned in Bangladesh, however, these tribal guerrillas became the recipients of Indian largesse and sanctuary. Only in early 1998 following the surrender of arms by a large group of the jungle-fighters under their leader, Jyotirindra Bodhipriyo Larma, did this particular episode come to an end.

The bloodletting in another minor if much more vicious and destructive drama, however, continued unabated as the new Millennium approached. The Tamil minority in norhern and north-eastern Sri Lanka, threatened by the increasingly majoritarian tendency of the Sri Lankan government in the late 1970s, engendered several militant groups. Many of these were based in India's Tamil Nadu state across the narrow Palk Strait separating Sri Lanka from the mainland. There, the state government and Indian intelligence gave them not just sanctuary but money, arms and training. The group which emerged as the most vigorous and violent, the Liberation Tigers of Tamil Eelam (LTTE), received the most support from Delhi's covert operators.[28] However, when Prime Minister Rajiv Gandhi worked out a peace deal with President Junius R. Jayawardene of Sri Lanka in 1987, virtually imposing a *Pax Indiana* on the island, the LTTE turned against its erstwhile patrons. It gave the Indian regulars of the Indian Peacekeeping Force (IPKF) deployed to the island a bloody nose, persuading Delhi eventually to withdraw all its military units from Sri Lanka. In the end, an LTTE suicide-bomber allegedly operating under orders from its supreme leader, blew up Rajiv Gandhi during an election campaign rally in 1991. Since then, former Indian patrons of the Tamil guerrillas have become hostile to their erstwhile proteges. The CIA and the Indian Intelligence Bureau might have ended their direct support for the Tibetan national resistance in the 1970s, but the aftereffects of those clandestine operations – a culture of clandestine subversion of neighbours – have continued to reverberate across the region.

While the state-actors have adapted their policies and shifted ground in pursuit of changes to respective elite-perceptions of their own interests, the consequences for the Tibetan people generally and suspected activists in particular have been truly tragic. This is not to say that the Tibetan resistance should have quietly acquiesced in their brutal fate into which the PLA delivered them, but the role played by their trans-Himalayan allies and mentors – US, Indian, Pakistani and Taiwanese intelligence agencies, and their national executives, need to be questioned. The latter's motives, the pursuit of national self-interest as defined by respective ruling elites, is clear enough. The moral arguments underpinning the rather abrupt abandonment of the guerrillas by their former sponsors in 1970–1974, when the Nixon-Kissinger worldview transformed the global centre, dramatically altering the regional strategic alignments, is less clear. The cost of what can only be described as the heroic struggle by the nationalists against insurmountable odds in the 1950s is one indication of what the Tibetan people have experienced. Even the Chinese authorities acknowledge the scale of the revolt. Seen from Beijing shortly after the Dalai Lama's flight from Lhasa,

> *Their rebellion was engineered by the imperialists, the Chiang Kai-shek bands and foreign reactionaries. The commanding centre of the rebellion was in Kalimpong; and their leader is the dismissed Sitzub Lokongwa Tsewongrouten. Many of their arms were brought in from abroad. The base of the rebellion to the south of the Zangbu River received air-dropped supplies from the Chiang Kai-shek bands on a number of occasions, and radio stations were set up there by agents sent by the imperialists and the Chiang Kai-shek clique to further their*

179

*intrigues. Between May and June last year, on the instructions of the Tibetan Local Government and the upper-strata reactionary clique, the rebel bandits intruded into Chamdo, Dinching, Nagchuka and Lhoka, destroyed communications, ravaged the people by plunder, rape, arson and murder, and attacked agencies and army units of the Central People's Government there. Guided by the spirit of national unity, the Central People's Government repeatedly enjoined the Local Government of Tibet to punish the rebel elements and maintain social order. But the Local Government of Tibet and the upper-strata reactionary clique took the Central People's Government's attitude of maximum magnanimity as a sign of weakness. Their talk was of this sort: The Han people can be frightened off; in the past nine years, the Han people have not had the courage to even lay a finger on our most wonderful and sacred system of serfdom; if we attack them, they can only defend and not hit back; they dare not suppress our rebellion, but only entreat us to suppress the rebellion; if we bring a large group of rebel forces to Lhasa from other places to hit them with, they will surely runaway; if not, we can abduct the Dalai Lama to Lhoka and gather forces for a counter-attack to take Lhasa back; if we fail, we run to India; India sympathizes with us and may help us; there is the powerful United States which may also help us; President Chiang Kai-shek in Taiwan has already given us active help; the Dalai Lama is god, who dare not obey him? . . . They blatantly abducted the Dalai Lama from Lhasa and launched an all-out attack on the People's Liberation Army units stationed in Lhasa on the night of March 19. The hope of a peaceful settlement was extinguished. The reactionary forces of Tibet finally chose the road to their own extinction.*[29]

According to this account, Beijing ordered the PLA units in Lhasa to crush the rebellion at 10.00 AM on March 20. This was achieved after 'more than two days of fighting.' By 23 March, the Chinese claimed to have captured more than 4,000 rebel troops along with 8,000 small arms of various types, 81 light and heavy machine guns, 27 mortars, six mountain guns and ten million rounds of ammunition. Chinese estimate of the number of 'rebellious bandits' stood at 'only 20,000' out of a total population of 1.2 million Tibetans in the region west of the Drichu River but including Chamdo.[30] Beijing had underscored its determination to eliminate all vestiges of nationalist resistance by making clear that 'In order to wipe out the rebel bandits thoroughly, the State Council has ordered the Units of the Chinese People's Liberation Army stationed in Tibet to assume military control in various places in Tibet.'[31] The results of that exercise have been described elsewhere. Whether the scale of the tragedy and the intensity of the savagery visited upon the Tibetan populace would have been any different had the US and India acted differently, by either providing very much greater and perhaps overt support to the Tibetan cause, or not providing warmaking assistance at all, is a contrafactual conjecture without practical value. But the recent discovery of the '70,000 Character Petition' filed by the late 10th Panchen Lama to Zhou En-lai in May 1962 in which the author gave an account of the horrors inflicted on the Tibetans by the Han in 1959–1962 makes these questions unavoidable. This is especially so because directly following the Dalai Lama's flight from Lhasa, Beijing had ordered the PLA to establish Military Control Committees to take control over all of Tibet 'except for Shigatse which is under the leadership of Panchen Erdeni, where it is not necessary to set one up.'[32] The Panchen Lama's role in Tibet's recent history is an oft-neglected aspect that could provide an understanding of the complexities of the situation. Seen by many as a pro-Beijing 'anti-nationalist' Quisling, the Panchen Lama has been an enigma until now.

## The Costs of Resistance

Lobsang Trinley Lhundrub Choekyi Gyaltsen was born to Amdoa parents in Chinghai in 1938. Following a series of controversial decisions by various factions of the Tibetan religious elite, he was selected as the reincarnation of the 9th Panchen Lama in June 1949 and enthroned as such in Kumbum monastery in August that year. Following the advent of the Communist government in Beijing, the 10th Panchen Lama was taken by it under its wings. He was a guest of the Government in Beijing from April to June 1951 during which visit he met both Premier Zhou En-lai and Chairman Mao Ze-dong. The Panchen Lama met the Dalai Lama for the first time in April 1952 in Lhasa where he spent nearly six weeks enroute to Shigatse. In June, he took residence at the Tashilhunpo monastery, the traditional seat of the Panchen Lamas. He and his retinue were supportive of the 'liberation' of Tibet by the Chinese Communist Party and the People's Liberation Army. In 1954, the Panchen Lama was elected as a member of the Standing Committee of the National People's Congress in Beijing. During this visit to Beijing the Panchen Lama not only had a formal audience with Mao, but also met him privately. When the 7th Plenary Meeting of the State Council passed the decision to establish the Preparatory Committee for the establishment of the Tibet Autonomous Region (PCART) in March 1955, it also appointed the Dalai Lama as its Chairman, and the Panchen Lama as its Vice-Chairman. Over the years, Beijing patronised the latter and apparently exploited the traditional rivalry between the Lhasa and Shigatse elites to divide the authority and reduce the effectiveness of the rulers of Tibet. When the spring 1959 rebellion rocked Lhasa with considerable violence in Kham and Amdo preceding it, Shigatse and the region under the Panchen Lama's control remained calm. After the PLA crackdown following the flight of the Dalai Lama, the Panchen Lama

181

telegraphed Mao endorsing Beijing's military response to the rebellion. Early in April 1959, the Panchen Lama was asked by Beijing to take over the Chair of the PCART in Lhasa from the absent Dalai Lama. This he did. He then proceeded to Beijing to attend the second National People's Congress. When he returned to Lhasa, the Panchen Lama was the senior-most Tibetan combining in his person the region's highest station in both spiritual and temporal realms. He was also seen as the most loyal Tibetan dedicated to the success of the 'democratic revolution' sweeping the plateau at Beijing's behest. His briefings to Mao and other senior Chinese figures regarding events in Tibet were likely to have been taken seriously. It is in this context that the Panchen Lama's 70,000-character secret report[33] to Zhou and Mao is such a remarkable document.

The Panchen Lama had been, and had been seen by people within Tibet and without as, supportive of Beijing's actions in Tibet, especially in response to the resistance. But following his visits to the affected regions across the plateau and in Tibetan areas of the provinces of Qinghai, Sichuan, Gansu and Yunnan the Panchen Lama appeared to have been devastated by the suffering he saw being indiscriminately and brutally visited upon all members of the Tibetan nationality: 'When dealing with captured rebels, cadres adopted vengeful, discriminatory, casual and careless methods. Because they did not investigate the circumstances of the rebels with sufficient thoroughness or depth, they had no way to make rational distinctions in their treatment . . . There were some people who were labelled as rebels because, during the rebellion, they lived in an area where the rebellion was taking place, went to such an area or, passing through such an area, they stayed there for a short time. As regards relationships with the rebels, they indiscriminately labelled as collaborators with the rebels all those who during 1957 and 1958 had new or old contacts or dealings with people from Kham and Amdo, even those who had provided accommodation for people from Kham and Amdo who were passing through . . . the majority of people whom it was unnecessary to label as rebels and many good people who should not have been labelled were all unjustly labelled, arrested and jailed, their property was confiscated and they were dealt with in the same way as the chief criminals of the rebellion.'[34] The Panchen Lama spoke of Communist cadres bent on a policy of *San Guang*, ie, the 'burn all, kill all, loot all' policy associated with the Japanese invasion of China, in their treatment of suspected Tibetans. He mentioned the fate of his own father, Gonpo Tseten, whose only crime was to have travelled from Lhasa to Shigatse of his own accord, acknowledge past errors from his property-owning days and apologising to the masses. He was subjected to vicious beating by the cadres for his troubles.[35] The 'struggle sessions' which suspects were subjected to were often violent and sometimes ended in mutilation, even death.

*Once the struggle had started, there were some shouts and rebukes, and at the same time there was hair pulling, beating with fists and kicking, pinching people's flesh, pushing back and forth, and some people even used a large 'lun shi' (an iron weapon like a bill-hook) and clubs to beat them fiercely. This resulted in bleeding from the seven apertures in the heads of those who were being beaten and in their falling down unconscious and in their limbs being broken; they were seriously injured and there were even some who lost their lives during the struggle . . . Many innocent people fled to foreign lands, some who were unable to flee ended up in the unfortunate and terrible situation of throwing themselves into rivers or using weapons to kill themselves.*[36]

The Panchen Lama made a distinction between the 'correct policies' of the Chinese Communist Party and of Chairman Mao on the one hand, and the activities of the Chinese cadres in Tibet on the other. But he underscored the loss of peace and self-respect, of confidence in the future of their families and their country, of livelihood and of life itself afflicting very large numbers of Tibetans. His comments on the scourge of famine that swept across Tibet as Chinese Communist 'reforms' transformed the processes of both production and distribution hit hard at the system and structure he himself represented: 'Because at that time (when Communist cadres forcibly collected grains from Tibetans) there was a shortage of grain, people who lacked grain could not obtain it from else-where. Consequently, in some places in Tibet, a situation arose where people starved to death . . . Because the amount of grain was not enough to feed even those with the lowest requirements, the fire of bitterness and hunger was ignited, and so dregs of fat, grain husks, and so on which formerly in Tibet were fodder for horses and donkeys, bulls and oxen, became hard to get and were considered nourishing and fragrant foods. Also, in order to make the food appear more and to dispel one day's hunger and bitter-ness, the responsible people in the canteens, apart from gathering together a lot of grass, which was more or less edible, even gathered together tree bark, leaves, grass roots and grass seeds, which really were not edible. After processing this, they mixed it with a bit of foodstuffs, made it into a thin gruel like pig food and gave it to people to eat, and even this was limited in amount and could not fill their stomachs . . . In some places, many people directly starved to death because the food ran out; therefore, in some places, there was a phenomenon of whole families dying out.'[37] The report was equally scathing on the Chinese Communist treatment of the Lamaist Buddhist faith and religious institutions in Tibet:

*Before democratic reforms, there were more than 2,500 large, medium and small monasteries in Tibet. After democratic reform, only 70-odd monasteries were kept in existence by the government.*

> *This was a reduction of more than 97% . . . In the whole of Tibet in the past there was* (sic) *a total of about 110,000 monks and nuns. Of those, possibly 10,000 fled abroad, leaving about 100,000. After democratic reform was concluded, the number of monks and nuns living in the monasteries was about 7,000 people, which is a reduction of 93% . . . Those who have religious knowledge will slowly die out, and religious affairs are stagnating, knowledge is not being passed on, there is worry about there being no new people to train, and so we see the elimination of Buddhism which was flourishing in Tibet and which transmitted teachings and enlightenment. This is something which I and more than 90% of Tibetans cannot endure.*[38]

Such candid and vigorous criticism, not of the principle of 'democratic reform' but of its practice, from Tibet's most loyal leader must have troubled Zhou and Mao. The latter is known to have made critical comments about the Panchen Lama at a private meeting in the summer following the latter's delivery of his petition, but formal complaints were not aired until the end of September. In October he was informed that he had made serious mistakes and although he retained his formal posts in the PCART, he was not allowed to attend its meetings. He was compelled to stay at Shigatse for nearly two years. In September 1964, a PCART meeting turned into a 50-day session of criticism of the Panchen Lama. He was subjected to *Thamzing*, ie, struggle, which he had been so critical of in his report. In November, he was labelled as 'anti-Party, anti-People and anti-socialism'. In December, the Chinese NPC voted to remove him from the post of Vice President. He was kept under house arrest in Beijing from early 1965 until his release in October 1977. Two years later, he was back in the NPC, first as a deputy for the Tibet Autonomous Region to the 5th NPC, and then, as a Vice Chairman. In 1980, the Panchen Lama met Deng Xiaoping, now China's 'paramount leader'. This was not as remarkable a reversal as it might appear; after all, Deng had already met Gyalo Thondup, the Dalai Lama's elder brother, in March 1979. The Panchen Lama was able to lead a reasonably 'normal' life after this, never buckling under pressure. He continued to speak out for the oppressed people of Tibet whenever an opportunity presented itself. He did this until his death at the Tashilhunpo monastery in 1989.

## Centre-Periphery Linkages and the Small Nations

In Southern Asia, the central could not escape, and was indeed shaped by, the regional. Neither the US nor China presumably had any essential interest one way or another as to how India and Pakistan approached or resolved their dispute over the State of Jammu & Kashmir. However, as we have seen, the local actors could not avoid the consequences of the fundamental, even philosophical, disputation caused by their mutually exclusive founding principles on the bases of which they had been fashioned out of Britain's Subcontinental empire.[39] And in its efforts to engage its two regional client states to erect a regional counterpoise to Communist China, the US too was sucked into this apparently insoluble dispute. Washington's endeavours to create a South Asian bulwark against what was seen as a Communist attempt at breaking out eventually ran into the sands of the Kashmiri quagmire. For China, Kashmir had a more physical, if somewhat subordinate, interest. Beijing's efforts to secure control over Tibet almost inevitably led to increasing reliance on its coercive capability. Given Tibet's topography, a motorway from Xinjiang to Lhasa cutting across the Aksai Chin plateau in the north-eastern corner of Ladakh made eminent military sense although this violated territory claimed by India. In addition, the disputed nature of Kashmir's northern boundaries with Xinjiang, in the context of the very much greater intensity of the Indo-Pakistani and Sino-Indian confrontations, served as an incentive for Pakistan to engage in the *Kautilyan* realpolitik of forging a tacit alliance with China. This was solidified in the 1970s when Chinese and Pakistani military engineers constructed the Karakoram Highway linking Kashgarh with Karachi along an alignment said to follow the legendary 'silk route' of medieval Central Asian trade. The KKH, as it came to be called, not only established a Chinese stake in the configuration of the Kashmiri boundaries, but also provided a marker of Beijing's interest in Pakistan's continued survival. In the end, South Asia emerged as a land of survivalist struggles where local actors engaged in subverting each other's legitimacy and even existence, and the bigger drama involving the global centre became a sideshow to that regional phenomenon.

Washington's unpublicised tie-up with Jawaharlal Nehru's pre-independence security establishment was its first strategic success in the region. The agreement signed in July 1947 allowed the US to continue, even expand, its aerial missions in China in support of Chiang Kai-shek's KMT forces against Mao's Red Army. The US Army Air Forces, and subsequently, the US Air Force, replaced the Royal Air Force as the principal user and beneficiary of the network of airfields and related ground facilities built up across the region before and during the Second World War. India itself thus effectively became an overseas air base for US air combat units fighting their first 'Containment' battles in Asia. Pakistan, on the fringes of the Indian heartland, entered the fray slightly later, in the early 1950s. Its drives were more immediate, the main purpose being to 'borrow power' to ensure its continued existence in the face of what its elites saw as 'the Indian threat', rather than for any anti-Communist proclivities as such. But once it became a client state, Pakistan too joined in the covert operations mounted by US, and KMT as well as Indian, intelligence services against Beijing's authority in Tibet. By the mid-1950s, Pakistani facilities in Dhaka were being used in

185

support of the Khampa and Amdoa resistance, and those in Badaber and Peshawar, in support of surveillance operations by US forces monitoring the Soviet Union. While Pakistan became 'the most allied of allies', India ironically pursued its 'non-aligned' policy of overt friendship with Moscow and Beijing, and covert collaboration with the CIA and the DIA. Successive US Administrations sought to wean Delhi away from its declaratory non-alignment, and in particular, its close economic-diplomatic links to the Soviet Union and fraternal ties with Mao's Beijing. The continuation of this trend was to make India the recipient of the single largest share of US economic aid in the 1960s.

Delhi, however, remained extremely sensitive to the possible domestic and external consequences of its clandestine proximity to Washington; Indian envoys often requested that discussions be kept 'off-the-record' even when the agenda dealt with such innocuous issues as US technical assistance to Indian agriculture. Eisenhower's personal relationship with Nehru was especially warm and his exchanges with the Indian leader exuded that warmth. However, his administration appeared to be more concerned with the defence of the Middle-East from perceived Soviet threats in which Pakistan's putative role sundered Indo-US ties on the overt level, leading to Nehru's decision to initiate dramatic openings to Moscow which were to last until the collapse of the Soviet Union. The Kennedy Administration was more formal in its approach to Delhi, but despite its concentration on Cuba and Berlin, it identified a possible alliance with India as 'the big prize' in Asia. Indeed the coincidence of the Sino-Indian war and the Cuban missile crisis would not lower the profile of the former in Washington's deliberations. As trans-Himalayan tensions spiralled downward into a major military confrontation, and then, armed conflict, Washington responded with alacrity to Nehru's urgent appeals for help. It was more cautious when Nehru urged an immediate, and dramatic, deepening of the hitherto covert security links into a formal military alliance, but the pursuit of that goal became a key plank of the US's Asian security policy. Both Administrations saw, like their British counterparts, South Asia as an indivisible strategic actor whose cantankerous components appeared to be behaving like siblings riven by irrational rivalry. Washington believed it was both reasonable and realistic to bring India and Pakistan together into a collaborative relationship with itself in a collective security endeavour against Communist encroachments into the region. This effort did not succeed; in fact, such effort repeatedly led to a parting of the ways. In the mid-1950s, India struck out on its own, first signing an agreement with Beijing handing over its powers and privileges in Tibet, and then building up warm relations with the Soviet Union; in the early 1960s, Pakistan forged close ties to China which too would last. Washington's apparent failure to recognise the fundamental nature of the Indo-Pakistani disputation reduced the long-term effectiveness of its alliance-building efforts.

186

The most glaring instance of this failure was the outcome of its emphasis on the resolution of the Kashmir dispute as an adjunct to the US-UK initiative to build India up as an anti-Beijing bulwark. Washington's perseverance resulted in six sessions of ministerial discussions over a year which generated virtually no movement. That Kashmir represented, or came to represent, elemental contradictions characterising the Subcontinent's political configuration appeared to have been lost on Washington, and even London, not to speak of the South Asian elites themselves. The latter appeared to view Kashmir as a zero-sum game in which the slightest compromise would be no less than defeat, something neither could concede. US and British policy-makers, on the other hand, appeared to view the dispute as a colonial loose-end that needed to be tied up through mutual discussions before India and Pakistan could get down to the serious business of erecting a Subcontinental strategic alliance co-sponsored by London and Washington. That the nature of the Partition and the premises on which the successor states had been created made this virtually impossible until most if not all collective memories had been wiped clean by generational change did not dawn on any of the actors, regional or extra-regional. Not much appears to have changed since then.

For much of the 1950s, while Indian air force ground crew helped USAF personnel in servicing and maintaining their aircraft on Indian airbases, Delhi pursued a policy of overt friendship with Beijing's Communist rulers. This unusual lack of consistency, given that US air combat effort based in India was directed against Chinese Communist authorities, could be interpreted as masterly pragmatism on Nehru's part. He appeared to be pursuing a policy of independence with regard to his warmth towards Mao and Zhou, especially the latter, a frequent visitor to Delhi, while at the same time offering clandestine support to the US as a balancing act, a strategic card up the sleeve, in case relations turned sour with Beijing. This happened in the late 1950s when overt and immediate US support became essential to the survival of the cohesion of the Indian elite and the state it had fashioned. Non-alignment notwithstanding, Nehru had, in fact, identified Communist China as a potential threat to Indian security in 1950 following the PLA's march across the Drichu River. The following year, he instructed his sister, Vijayalakshmi Pandit, then the Indian ambassador in Washington, to sign up to the first formal military assistance agreement between India and the US which enabled Delhi to secure Washington's covert assistance against Chinese power in Tibet. Nehru also ordered the Indian Intelligence Bureau to extend 'all possible help' to the Tibetan national resistance, and indeed, to build up that resistance. This duality, or apparent asymmetry, between declaratory policy and *realpolitik* was pragmatism par excellence.

If Nehru's realism was unsuccessful in the end, it was not because of his failure to grasp the nearly inevitable nature of the confrontation between his country and China; it was because within the Asian subordinate system there were factors beyond his capacity to mould. India did not have the time to build up its internal capabilities to stand up to a China commanded into a homogenising model by its authoritarian rulers. India was a diverse empire being fashioned into a federal polity by a leadership which had largely internalised liberal-democratic and pluralist values. A disparate subcontinental proto-state could not extract the surplus or muster the resources necessary for matching the strength of the nearly-monolithic Communist China. The asymmetry between the two rival actors could perhaps partially explain the paradox of Nehruvian Non-alignment on the one hand and India's secret anti-Chinese alliance with the US on the other. The management of this very complex and difficult combination of appearances and reality in the end failed Nehru and his colleagues, but the basic premise, given India's circumstances and the global strategic environment, could hardly be faulted. In sum, India was born into an environment characterised by insecurity bred by political uncertainty and military fluidity without an inherent ability to pursue its perceived national interests. To that extent, its independence was circumscribed. To a large extent, if only demonstrating a relatively lower level of sophistication, Pakistan too pursued similar objectives, playing an even weaker hand. Both actors, seeking autonomy in a hostile environment, grasped at whatever opportunities the nascent Cold War threw at them. In the process, they were incorporated into the confrontation shaping the global centre and lost whatever measure of independence they might have had in designing their immediate environs. Both client-states tried to exercise some freedom – India by vocally condemning alliances and chastising Pakistan for doing what it was itself guilty of, and Pakistan by moving towards a security tie-up with China when the latter was in a position to seriously threaten India. However, these attempts restored neither country's autonomy.

For Washington, the 'loss' of China to the Communists had been a severe blow, and the Administration's efforts were directed not only at making life difficult for the victors but also at ensuring that India, perhaps the only other Asian power with comparable long-term potential, was not similarly lost. The US was additionally determined to protect the interests of the residual KMT regime in Taiwan but this determination was moderated by an anxiety lest Chiang Kai-shek's forces precipitated a general conflict with the mainland which the US would inevitably get sucked into. Washington was keen to 'contain' all Communist powers including China, but it was equally eager to avoid getting embroiled in a general war which could drag the Soviet Union into a nuclear confrontation with it. The Washington establishment saw China as a mere appendage to the Kremlin's 'global designs'. With the exception of Vice President Richard Nixon and isolated mid-level officials, few US policymakers could visualise 'normal' relations between Washington and Beijing and a stable environment in the Far-East. Domestic right-wing tendencies exerted pressures on the elites for much of the 1950s, but US leaders demonstrated little strategic vision or imagination in being able to build on speculations of possible changes. Traditional patterns and conventional assumptions shaped policies. The 1950s were a period marked by mediocrity and stolid perseverance along well-trodden paths. The American national genius displayed little of the adventurous spirit that had brought the US to the position of the premier global power at the end of the first half of the century.

It was in this context that the Tibetan nationalists of assorted ilk were encouraged by the evidence of support extended to their cause by Washington. The assumption appeared to be that since Taiwan, India, Pakistan and the US were willing to aid the resistance, there must be a reasonable prospect for success in the struggle against the Chinese. Many Tibetan authors have made the point, quite accurately, that Tibetan nationalism was an indigenous phenomenon and had little to do with the minimal support it received from external patrons. However, without the assistance it did receive from across the Himalayas, it is difficult to see how the NVDA and other guerrilla units could have persisted for so long against the massive superiority in numbers and firepower deployed by the Chinese to Tibet. Seen against the almost mindless brutality and violence Beijing's agencies unleashed on the small populace of Amdo, Kham, the Tibetan inhabited districts of the four 'brother provinces', and eventually, in Lhoka, U Tsang, and elsewhere in the plateau, the import of external input in the longevity of the resistance becomes apparent. The US and India withdrew from active involvement in Tibet in the early 1970s as they found alternative means to pursue their interests. For Washington, the strategic calculus had changed altogether. As the Nixon Administration erected a triangular edifice of great-power relationships at the global centre, Tibet lost whatever significance it had held in the eyes of the US security establishment. Pakistan, only marginally involved in the Tibetan drama, found its association with China more fruitful in terms of the role it could play as a conduit and a bridge between Washington and Beijing. For physical and geopolitical reasons, Delhi could not entirely wash its hands of Tibet; former NVDA guerrillas soon found their place in such Indian forces as the Indo-Tibetan Border Police and the Special Frontier Force. However, the possibility of the India-based nationalist elements 'liberating' Tibet from Chinese occupation remains as distant as that of the Pakistan-based Kashmiri nationalists freeing the Vale of Kashmir from Indian control. Unless dramatic shifts occur within the domestic political dynamic of occupying powers, or in the global strategic environment, small nationalities like the Tibetans and the Kashmiris are likely to continue to exercise only marginal influence on the gory drama sweeping their lands and blighting their lives.

# Appendices 1–12

## APPENDIX 1

**Government of India agrees to the continuance of United States Army Air Forces operations to and across India on a Special Mission basis.**

Source: Department of State, United States Treaties and other International Agreements [USTIA]-1951, Vol.2, Part 2, Washington, D.C., USGPO, 1952, pp. 568–574.

An agreement between the Governments of the United States of America and India on the temporary stationing of ground crews to service aircraft/ groups or units; not expected for more than two weeks [in individual instances]

a) Agreement effected by an exchange of notes signed at New Delhi, July 1 and 5, 1947; entered into force on July 5, 1947.

b) An amending agreement effected by an exchange of notes dated at New Delhi, April 22 and May 3, 1948; entered into force on May 3, 1948.

I. *US Ambassador [Henry F Grady] to the Indian Member for External Affairs and Commonwealth Relations [Jawaharlal Nehru]; 1 July 1947*

[The US Ambassador seeks continuation of the following facilities after India becomes independent]

1. Temporary stationing of American service personnel to service US aircraft,

2. Facilities to be made available at Maripur [Karachi], Agra, Barrackpore and/or Kharagpore. US aircraft entering Indian airspace from the west would land at Maripur, those entering Indian airspace from the east would land at Barrackpore or Kharagpore. Agra would be used for intermediate staging in flights across India; in an emergency, US military aircraft would be able to land anywhere in India.

3. Night landings would be made only at Palam near New Delhi; after Palam became a civil aviation facility, a new, alternative night-landing airfield would be designated.

4. US authorities would provide 48-hours notice of projected arrivals to the Air Headquarters.

5. Services, maintenance, accommodation, messing and transportation facilities available to the Indian air forces at these airfields would be made available to US aircrew and aircraft.

6. Customs, health and passport regulations which applied to Royal Air Force personnel and aircraft would apply to US Army Air Forces personnel and aircraft.

7. These facilities would only be extended to aircraft with official US markings. These facilities would, in the first instance, be extended until October 24, 1947; thereafter, further consideration would be given to the arrangements.

8. The agreement would be extended for two years in the first instance; each side would give the other six-months termination notice. [pp. 568–570]

## II. *Member for External Affairs and Commonwealth Relations [Jawaharlal Nehru] to H E the Ambassador of the United States [Henry F Grady], New Delhi; 5 July 1947*

Whereas in the Ambassador's letter the original proposition is, 'refuelling will be done by "a commercial petroleum company" under the "Jupiter-scheme"', Mr Nehru demands that the Government of the United States pay for POL [petroleum, oil and lubricants], maintenance, servicing, spares, and repairs by Indian staff. Costs of accommodation and messing to be charged. Accounts to be maintained by the US air attache stationed in Delhi. [pp. 570–572]

## III. *The Indian Minister for External Affairs & Commonwealth Relations to the American Ambassador, New Delhi; 22 April 1948*

Ministry of External Affairs and
Commonwealth Relations
Dated, New Delhi 3, The 22nd April, 1948

The Minister for External Affairs & Commonwealth Relations presents his compliments to His Excellency the Ambassador of the United States of America and has the honour to refer to his letter no.249, dated the 24th September 1947, regarding flights across India by United States military aircraft and the facilities to be accorded to such aircraft while within Indian territory.

2. As suggested in paragraph 2 of the letter under reference, the Government of India agree to the revision of numbered paragraph 2 of the arrangements already reached. The Partition of the country, has further necessitated the amendment of certain other arrangements, and the Government of India therefore consider that the numbered paragraph 2 should read as follows:-

'2. Facilities for these flights transiting India are to be available at Bombay (Santa Cruz), Agra, and Dum Dum. The aircraft should land, for customs and health examinations, at

(i) Bombay (Santa Cruz) airport if it enters India directly from the West without landing at Karachi, OR

(ii) Palam if it has already been cleared by the Health authorities,

(iii) Dum Dum if it enters India from the East. Agra can be used for intermediate landings, and any aerodrome can be used in an emergency.'

It may however be noted that facilities pertaining to servicing, accommodation, messing and transport cannot be provided at Dum Dum airport. These may possibly be obtained by the United States Military authorities by arrangement with Pan-American Airways. Facilities will not also be available at Barrackpore as no unit of the R.I.A.F. [Royal Indian Air Force] will be located there.

3. The second sentence of clause 7 of the arrangements already reached should now be deleted as the privilege thereby conferred expired on the 24th October 1947. It is considered that fare-paying passengers, if requiring international air transport, should be carried by civil airlines and not on State aircraft.

4. Throughout the agreement, the words 'Royal Air Force' or 'R.A.F.', wherever used, should be substituted by the words 'Royal Indian Air Force' or 'R.I.A.F.'.

[SEAL]

To
His Excellency the Ambassador of the
United States of America
New Delhi
[pp. 573-574]

### IV. *The American Charge' d'Affaires ad interim to the Indian Minister for External Affairs and Commonwealth Relations, New Delhi; 3 May 1948*

American Embassy
New Delhi, India, May 3, 1948

The Charge d'Affaires ad interim of the United States of America presents his compliments to the Honourable Minister of External Affairs and Commonwealth Relations and has the honour to refer to his note No.

D.1750-FEA/48 dated April 22, 1948, regarding amendments to an arrangement dated July 5, 1947 with respect to flights across India by United States military aircraft.

The revisions suggested in the aforementioned note are satisfactory to the United States Government, which now regards the previous arrangement as amended accordingly.

The United States Government agrees, as a matter of general principle, that fare-paying international passengers should be carried by civilian air services, where available, rather than state aircraft. Regulations of the United States National Military Establishment permit the carriage of passengers by United States Military aircraft under exceptional circumstances, and when such travel is deemed to be in the national interest. However, it is anticipated that any such traffic into or through India would be either nil or negligible. If desired by the Government of India, the Embassy will be pleased to discuss this matter further.

The Hon'ble
Minister for External Affairs
and Commonwealth Relations
New Delhi
[p. 574]

## APPENDIX 2

**Agreement between the Government of the United States of America and the Government of India effected by exchange of notes signed at New Delhi, on July 2 and 4, 1949:** Department of State, United States Treaties and other International Agreements [USTIA], Vol.3, Part I, Washington, D.C., 1952, pp. 575–80

I. *The American Ambassador [Loy Henderson] to the Indian Minister for External Affairs [Jawaharlal Nehru], 2 July 1949*

American Embassy
New Delhi, India, July 2, 1949

Excellency,

I have the honour to refer to this Embassy's note of July 1, 1947, and to note no. D5005-FEA, dated July 5, 1947 of the Government of India in reply embodying the text of an agreement between our Governments with respect to flights across India by military aircraft of the United States of America and to the facilities to be accorded such aircraft while within

Indian territory, and to recent discussions which have taken place during the past several weeks between members of the Department of External Affairs, Government of India, and representatives of the Embassy of the United States of America in New Delhi concerning the renewal of the agreement under reference.

It is my Government's understanding that the Government of India agrees to the operating of the aircraft of the United States National Military Establishment to and across India, subject to the following stipulations:

1. The Government of India has no objection to the temporary stationing of American ground crews at specified airfields on special occasions for the purpose of servicing American military aircraft transiting India in groups or units, provided such crews depart as soon as their task is completed. The stationing of such personnel is not expected to exceed one to two weeks. It also has no objection to the stationing of not more than four liaison personnel for purposes of expediting flights of United States Military aircraft.

2. For these flights transiting India the facilities described in Clause 4 are to be available at Bombay (Santa Cruz), Agra, Palam, and Dum Dum. An aircraft making a stop in India should land for customs and health examination at
 (i) Bombay (Santa Cruz) Airport if it enters India direct from the west without landing at Karachi, or
 (ii) Palam if it has already been cleared at Karachi by the Health authorities,
(iii) Dum Dum if it enters India from the east. Agra can be used for intermediate landings, and any aerodrome can be used in an emergency.

3. In general, forty-eight hours notice is to be given to Air Headquarters (India) of any projected arrivals. If in a special case it should be impossible or impracticable to give such notice, information regarding flight plans and other pertinent data should be furnished at the earliest possible moment, including reason for failure to give notice.

4. Facilities which are available to Indian Air Forces pertaining to servicing, accommodation, refuelling, messing and transport are also to be available to American military aircraft, subject to conditions stated in this paragraph. Since the civil aerodromes at Santa Cruz and Dum Dum lack adequate facilities even for existing civil aircraft, the Government of India under this agreement can provide only refuelling, communications and meteorological facilities at these aerodromes; parking on the aprons will be permitted but no space (except in emergency) or hangar can be made available for repair and maintenance. The United States National Military Establishment is to provide all specialist equipment and specialist personnel required for the maintenance of its aircraft, whereas non-specialised equipment held by the Indian Air Force for servicing Indian Air Force

aircraft is to be available to the United States National Military Establishment on loan where such loan does not conflict with Indian Air Force commitments. The Government of India does not propose to charge landing or housing fees with respect to American military aircraft, and all normal facilities relating to radio, metereology and flying aids will be provided free of charge; but the United States Government agrees to pay for supplies of fuel, lubricants and spares received from the Government of India, as well as for any repairs to or maintenance of American military aircraft which might be performed by the Government of India. Accounts in the foregoing connection are to be rendered to the United States Air Attache stationed in New Delhi, who will also be responsible for working out other administrative arrangements with the appropriate Indian officials. American air crews will also be charged for accommodation and messing.

5. The regulations of the Government of India relating to customs, health and passport examination which are observed by Indian Air Force aircraft and personnel will likewise be applied to American military aircraft and personnel.

6. The facilities accorded to the United States Government under the present agreement are confined to United States military aircraft bearing appropriate service markings and manned by crews in uniform and on duty.

7. The United States Government will on reciprocal basis grant to Indian military aircraft transit and landing rights in continental United States, comparable to those referred to in Clauses 1 to 4, both inclusive, and the use of airfields to be designated on request of the Government of India.

8. The permission and arrangements as described above are to extend for an indefinite period, subject however to termination on six months' notice either by the Government of India or the Government of the United States of America. In the event of either of the signatory governments becoming directly involved in hostilities, each Government reserves the right to terminate this agreement forthwith or to reconsider the extent of its adherence thereto.

I shall be glad to have you inform me whether the above terms of the agreement governing the transit of India by aircraft of the United States National Military Establishment, which meet the approval of the Government of the United States, are also approved by the Government of India. If so, it is suggested that July 5, 1949 be the date on which this agreement comes into force in lieu of the previously existing arrangements. If your Government concurs in this suggestion – the Government of the United States will regard the agreement as becoming effective on that date.

Please accept, Excellency, the assurances of my highest consideration.

Loy W. Henderson

His Excellency
Pandit J. Nehru
Ministry of External Affairs, New Delhi

**II.** *The Indian Foreign Secretary [K P S Menon] to the United States Ambassador [Loy Henderson], New Delhi, 4th July 1949*

Ministry of External Affairs and
Commonwealth Relations
New Delhi, 4th July 1949

Excellency,

I have the honour to acknowledge your note No. 232 of the 2nd July, 1949, which reads as follows:-

'I have the honour . . . . . . . . . as becoming effective on that date.' [exact copy of above note from Ambassador Loy Henderson to Prime Minister Pandit Jawaharlal Nehru]

2. I am pleased to inform you that the Government of India accept the terms of the agreement as communicated in your note quoted above and agree with your suggestion that the agreement should become effective on the 5th July, 1949.

Please accept, Excellency, the assurances of my highest consideration.

K P S Menon
Foreign Secretary

His Excellency the Ambassador of
the United States of America
American Embassy, New Delhi

## APPENDIX 3

United States of America and Pakistan, Mutual Defence Agreement effected by exchange of notes signed at Washington, D.C., November 29 and December 15, 1950; entered into force December 15, 1950. Department of State, USTIA 1950, Vol. I, Washington, D.C., USGPO, 1952, pp. 884–886.

**I.** *The Secretary of State to the Pakistani Ambassador, Washington, D.C. 29 November 1950*

DEPARTMENT OF STATE
WASHINGTON

November 29, 1950

Excellency,

I have the honour to address your Excellency concerning the request of the Government of Pakistan for the transfer of certain items of military supplies and equipment by the Government of the United States of America. There are certain assurances and undertakings by the Government of Pakistan which the Government of the United States of America must obtain before completing any transaction under Section 408 (e) of the Mutual Defence Assistance Act of 1949, (Public Law 329, 81st Congress) as amended by PL621, 81st Congress.

The Department understands the Government of Pakistan is prepared to agree to use such items as may be provided to foster international peace and security within the framework of the Charter of the United Nations through measures which will further the ability of nations dedicated to the principles and purposes of the Charter to participate effectively in arrangements for individual and collective self-defence in support of those purposes and principles; and, moreover, that the items to be provided by the Government of the United States are required by the Government of Pakistan to maintain its internal security, its legitimate self-defence or permit it to participate in the defence of the area of which it is a part; and that it will not undertake any act of aggression against any other state.

The Department understands also that the Government of Pakistan will obtain the consent of the Government of the United States prior to the transfer of title to or possession of any equipment, materials, information, or services furnished, and the Government of Pakistan will take appropriate measures to protect the security of any article, service or information furnished. The Government of Pakistan also understands, the Department is informed, that the Government of the United States necessarily retains the privilege of diverting items of equipment or of not completing services undertaken if such action is dictated by considerations of United States national interest.

Finally; the Department understands that the Government of Pakistan is prepared to accept terms and conditions of payment for the items transferred, to be agreed upon between the Government of Pakistan and the Government of the United States, which accord with the terms of Section 408(e) of the Mutual Defence Assistance Act of 1949, as amended.

A reply by the Government of Pakistan to the effect that these understandings are correct will be considered as constituting an agreement between the Government of the United States and the Government of Pakistan.

Accept, Excellency, the renewed assurances of my highest consideration.

For the Secretary of State:
George C. McGhee

His Excellency
M. A. H. Ispahani;
Ambassador of Pakistan

II. *The Pakistani Ambassador [M.A.H. Ispahani] to the Assistant Secretary of State [George C. McGhee], Washington, D.C., December 15, 1950*

Embassy of Pakistan
Washington, D.C.
Telegraphic Address 'PAREP'
December 15, 1950

Dear Mr. Assistant Secretary,

I have the honour to refer to your letter of November 29, 1950, concerning the request of the Government of Pakistan for the transfer of certain items of military supplies and equipment by the Government of the United States which my government desires to purchase. The assurances and undertakings (as stated by you in your letter under reference) required by the Government of the United States under Section 408 (e) of the Mutual Defense Assistance Act of 1949 (Public Law 329, 81st Congress) as amended by PL 621, 81st Congress, are agreed to by my Government.

The Government of Pakistan is prepared to accept terms and conditions of payment for the items transferred, to be agreed upon between the Government of Pakistan and the Government of the United States which accord with the terms of Section 408 (e) of the Mutual Defense Assistance Act of 1949, as amended.

Accept, Mr Assistant Secretary, the renewed assurances of my highest consideration.

For the Amabassador
M.O.A. Baig

The Honourable George C. McGhee,
Assistant Secretary of State,
Department of State,
Washington, D.C.

## APPENDIX 4

United States of America and India: Exchange of notes constituting an agreement relating to mutual defense assistance. Washington, 7 and 16 March 1951. (Registered by the United States of America on 14 October 1952) United Nations Secretariat, United Nations Treaty Series (UNTS), Vol.141, New York, 1952, pp. 47–53.

No.1904. EXCHANGE OF NOTES CONSTITUTING AN AGREEMENT BETWEEN THE UNITED STATES OF AMERICA AND INDIA RELATING TO MUTUAL DEFENSE ASSISTANCE. WASHINGTON, 7 AND 16 MARCH 1951

**I.** *The Acting Secretary of State to the Ambassador of India*

DEPARTMENT OF STATE
WASHINGTON

Mar. 7, 1951

Excellency,

I have the honour to address Your Excellency concerning the request of the Government of India for the transfer of certain items of military supplies and equipment by the Government of the United States of America. There are certain assurances and undertakings by the Government of India which the Government of the United States of America must obtain before completing any transaction under Section 408 (e) of the Mutual Defense Assistance Act of 1949, (Public Law 329, 81st Congress) as amended by Public Law 621, 81st Congress.

The Government of the United States of America understands the Government of India is prepared to agree to use such items as may be provided to foster international peace and security within the framework of the Charter of the United Nations through measures which will further the ability of nations dedicated to the principles and purposes of the Charter to participate effectively in arrangements for individual and collective self-defense in support of those purposes and principles; and, moreover, that the items to be provided by the Government of the United States of America are required by the Government of India to maintain its internal security, its legitimate self-defense or permit it to participate in the defense of the area of which it is a part, and that it will not undertake any act of aggression against any other state.

The Government of the United States of America understands also that the Government of India will obtain the consent of the Government of the United States of America prior to the transfer of title to or possession of any equipment, materials, information, or services furnished, will take appropriate measures to protect the security of any article, service, or information furnished, and agrees to the Government of the United States of America's retaining the privilege of diverting items of equipment or of not completing services undertaken if such action is dictated by consideration of United States national interest.

Finally, the Government of the United States of America understands that the Government of India is prepared to accept terms and conditions of payment for the items transferred, to be agreed upon between the Government of India, which accord with the terms of Section 408 (e) of the Mutual Defense Assistance Act of 1949, as amended.

A reply to the effect that these understandings are correct will be considered as constituting an agreement between the Government of the United States of America and the Government of India, which shall come into force on the date of the note in reply from the Government of India.

Accept, Excellency, the renewed assurances of my highest consideration.

James E. Webb

Her Excellency Vijaya Lakshmi Pandit
Ambassador of India

**II.** *The Ambassador of India to the Secretary of State*

EMBASSY OF INDIA
WASHINGTON, D.C.

16th March, 1951

Mr. Secretary,

I have the honour to refer to your letter dated 7th March regarding the transfer of certain items of military supplies and equipment by the Government of the United States of America to the Government of India under the terms, assurances and undertakings which are to the effect as follows;

[*See note I* ]

The terms, conditions and assurances affecting such a transfer as quoted above have been carefully considered and I have the honour to inform you that the Government of India are in agreement with the terms, conditions and assurances proposed.

I avail myself of the opportunity to convey to you, Mr. Secretary, the assurances of my highest consideration.

Vijaya Lakshmi Pandit
Ambassador of India

The Honourable The Secretary of State
Washington 25, D.C.

## APPENDIX 5

**Agreement between the Government of India and the Central People's Government of China on trade and cultural relations between India and the Tibet region of China; Peking, 29 April 1954.** Government of India, Foreign Policy of India, Third Edition, Texts of Documents 1947–1964, New Delhi, Loksabha Secretariat, 1966, pp. 198–206

[Extended Preamble followed by statement of five principles of friendship and co-operation – so-called *Panchshil-* with the text of notes exchanged following thereafter]

The Government of the Republic of India and the Central People's Government of the People's Republic of China:

Being desirous of promoting trade and cultural intercourse between the Tibet region of China and India and of facilitating pilgrimage and travel by the people of China and India;

Have resolved to enter into the present agreement based on the following principles:

1) Mutual respect for each other's territorial integrity and sovereignty;
2) Mutual non-aggression;
3) Mutual non-interference in each other's internal affairs;
4) Equality and mutual benefit; and
5) Peaceful co-existence;


**Text of Notes Exchanged**

*I*

Your Excellency,
Mr. Vice-Foreign Minister,

In the course of our discussion regarding the agreement on trade and intercourse between the Tibet region of China and India, which has happily concluded on Thursday (April 29) the delegation of the Government of the Republic of India and the delegation of the Government of the People's Republic of China agreed that certain matters be regulated by an exchange of notes. In pursuance of this understanding, it is hereby agreed between the two Governments as follows:

(1) The Government of India will be pleased to withdraw completely within six months from the date of exchange of the present notes the military escort now stationed at Yatung and Gyantse in the Tibet region of China. The Government of China will render facilities and assistance in such withdrawal.

(2) The Government of India will be pleased to handover to the Government of China at a reasonable price the post, telegraph and public telephone services together with their equipment operated by the Government of India in the Tibet region of China. The concrete measures in this regard will be decided upon through further negotiations between the Indian Embassy in China and the Foreign Ministry of China, which shall start immediately after the exchange of the present notes.

(3) The Government of India will be pleased to handover to the Government of China at a reasonable price the twelve rest houses of the Government of India in the Tibet region of China. The concrete measures in this regard will be decided upon through further negotiations between the

Indian Embassy in China and the Foreign Ministry of China which will start immediately after the exchange of the present notes. The Government of China agree that they shall continue as rest-houses.

(4) The Government of China agree that all buildings within the compound wall of the Trade Agencies of the Government of India at Yatung and Gyantse in the Tibet region of China may be retained by the Government of India; and the Government of India may continue to lease the land within its agency compound wall from the Chinese side. And the Government of India agree that the Trade Agencies of the Government of China at Kalimpong and Calcutta may lease land from the Indian side for the use of the Agencies and construct buildings thereon. The Government of China will render every possible assistance for housing the Indian Trade Agency at Gartok. The Government of India will also render every possible assistance for housing the Chinese Trade Agency at New Delhi.

(5) The Government of India will be pleased to return to the Government of China all land used or occupied by the Government of India other than the lands within its Trade Agency compound wall at Yatung. If there are godowns and buildings of the Government of India on the above-mentioned land used or occupied and to be returned by the Government of India and if Indian traders have stores or godowns or buildings on the above-mentioned land so that there is a need to continue leasing land, the Government of China agree to sign a contract with the Government of India or Indian traders, as the case may be, for leasing to them those parts of the land occupied by the said godowns, buildings or stores and pertaining thereto.

(6) The Trade Agents of both parties may, in accordance with the laws and regulations of the local government, have access to their nationals in civil or criminal cases.

(7) The Trade Agents and traders of both countries may hire employees in the locality.

(8) The hospitals of the Indian Trade Agencies at Gyantse and Yatung will continue to serve personnel of the Indian Trade Agencies.

(9) Each Government shall protect the person and property of the traders and pilgrims of the other country.

(10) The Government of China agree, so far as possible, to construct rest-houses for use of pilgrims along the route from Pulanchung (Taklakot) to Kang Rimpoche (Kailash) and Mavana Tse (Manasarowar), and the Government of India agree to place all possible facilities in India at the disposal of pilgrims.

(11) Traders and pilgrims of both countries shall have the facilities of hiring means of transportation at normal and reasonable rates.

(12) The three Trade Agencies of each party may function throughout the year.

(13) Traders of each country may rent buildings and godowns in accordance with local regulations in places under the jurisdiction of the other party.

(14) Traders of both countries may carry on normal trade in accordance with local regulations at places as provided in Article II of the agreement.

(15) Disputes between traders of both countries over debts and claims shall be handled in accordance with local laws and regulations.

On behalf of the Government of the Republic of India I hereby agree that the present note, along with your reply, shall become an agreement between our two Governments which shall come into force upon the exchange of the present notes.

I avail myself of this opportunity to express to you the assurances of my highest consideration.

N. Raghavan<br>Ambassador Extraordinary & Plenipotentiary of the Republic of India

29 April 1954

*II*

Your Excellency Mr. Ambassador,

I have the honour to receive your note dated April 29, 1954 which reads:
[*See Note I* ]

On behalf of the Central People's Government of the People's Republic of China, I hereby agree to Your Excellency's note, and your note along with the present note in reply shall become an agreement between our two Governments, which shall come into force upon the exchange of the present notes.

I avail myself of this opportunity to express to Your Excellency, Mr. Ambassador, the assurances of my highest consideration.

Chang Han-Fu<br>Vice Minister, Ministry of Foreign Affairs<br>People's Republic of China

29 April 1954

## APPENDIX 6

**Mutual Defence Assistance Agreement between The Government of the United States of America and the Government of Pakistan, Karachi, May 19, 1954.** Department of State, USTIA, Vol.5, Part 1, 1954, Washington, D.C., USGPO, 1955, pp. 854–858

The Government of the United States of America and the Government of Pakistan,

Desiring to foster international peace and security within the framework of the Charter of the United Nations through measures which will further the ability of nations dedicated to the purposes and principles of the Charter to participate effectively in arrangements for individual and collective self-defence in support of those purposes and principles;

Reaffirming their determination to give their full co-operation to the efforts to provide the United Nations with armed forces as contemplated by the Charter and to participate in United Nations collective defence arrangements and measures, and to obtain agreement on universal regulation and reduction of armaments under adequate guarantee against violation or evasion;

Taking into consideration the support which the Government of the United States has brought to these principles by enacting the Mutual Defence Assistance Act of 1949, as amended, and the Mutual Security Act of 1951, as amended;

Desiring to set forth the conditions which will govern the furnishing of such assistance;

Have agreed:

### ARTICLE I

1. The Government of the United States will make available to the Government of Pakistan such equipment, materials, services or other assistance as the Government of the United States may authorize in accordance with such terms and conditions as may be agreed. The furnishing and use of such assistance shall be consistent with the Charter of the United Nations. Such assistance as may be made available by the Government of the United States pursuant to this Agreement will be furnished under the provisions and subject to all the terms, conditions and termination provisions of the Mutual Defence Assistance Act of 1949 and the Mutual Security Act of 1951, acts amendatory or supplementary thereto, appropriation acts thereunder, or any other applicable legislative provisions. The two governments will, from time to time, negotiate detailed arrangements necessary to carry out the provisions of this paragraph.

2. The Government of Pakistan will use this assistance exclusively to maintain its internal security, its legitimate self-defence, or to permit it to participate in the defence of the area, or in United Nations collective security arrangements and measures, and Pakistan will not undertake any act of aggression against any other nation. The Government of Pakistan will not, without the prior agreement of the Government of the United States, devote such assistance to purposes other than those for which it was furnished.

3. Arrangements will be entered into under which equipment and materials furnished pursuant to this Agreement and no longer required or used exclusively for the purposes for which originally made available will be offered for return to the Government of the United States.

4. The Government of Pakistan will not transfer to any person not an officer or agent of that Government, or to any other nation, title to or possession of any equipment, materials, property, information or services received under this Agreement, without the prior consent of the Government of the United States.

5. The Government of Pakistan will take such security measures as may be agreed in each case between the two Governments in order to prevent the disclosure or compromise of classified military articles, services or information furnished pursuant to this Agreement.

6. Each Government will take appropriate measures consistent with security to keep the public informed of operations under this Agreement.

7. The two Governments will establish procedures whereby the Government of Pakistan will so deposit, segregate or assure title to all funds allocated to or derived from any programme of assistance undertaken by the Government of the United States so that such funds shall not, except as may otherwise be mutually agreed, be subject to garnishment, attachment, seizure or other legal process by any person, firm, agency, corporation, organization or government.

## ARTICLE II

The two Governments will, upon request of either of them, negotiate appropriate arrangements between them relating to the exchange of patent rights and technical information for defence which will expedite such exchanges and at the same time protect private interests and maintain necessary security safeguards.

## ARTICLE III

1. The Government of Pakistan will make available to the Government of the United States rupees for the use of the latter Government for its administrative and operating expenditures in connection with carrying out

the purposes of this Agreement. The two Governments will forthwith initiate discussions with a view to determining the amount of such rupees and to agreeing upon arrangements for the furnishing of such funds.

2. The Government of Pakistan will, except as may otherwise be mutually agreed, grant duty-free treatment on importation or exportation and exemption from internal taxation upon products, property, materials or equipment imported into its territory in connection with this Agreement or any similar Agreement between the Government of the United States and the Government of any other country receiving military assistance

3. Tax relief will be accorded to all expenditures in Pakistan by, or on behalf of, the Government of the United States for the common defence effort, including expenditure for any foreign aid programme of the United States. The Government of Pakistan will establish procedures satisfactory to both Governments so that such expenditure will be net of taxes.

## ARTICLE IV

1. The Government of Pakistan will receive personnel of the Government of the United States who will discharge in its territory the responsibilities of the Government of the United States under this Agreement and who will be accorded facilities and authority to observe the progress of the assistance furnished pursuant to this Agreement. Such personnel who are United States nationals, including personnel temporarily assigned, will, in their relations with the Government of Pakistan, operate as part of the Embassy of the United States of America under the direction and control of the Chief of the Diplomatic Mission, and will have the same privileges and immunities as are accorded other personnel with corresponding rank of the Embassy of the United States who are United States nationals. Upon appropriate notification by the Government of the United States the Government of Pakistan will grant full diplomatic status to the senior military member assigned under this Article and the senior Army, Navy and Air Force officers and their respective immediate deputies.

2. The Government of Pakistan will grant exemption from import and export duties on personal property imported for the personal use of such personnel or of their families and will take reasonable administrative measures to facilitate and expedite the importation and exportation of the personal property of such personnel and their families.

## ARTICLE V

1. The Government of Pakistan will:
   (a) join in promoting international understanding and goodwill, and maintaining world peace;

(b) take such action as may be mutually agreed upon to eliminate causes of international tension;

(c) make, consistent with its political and economic stability, the full contribution permitted by its manpower, resources, facilities and general economic condition to the development and maintenance of its own defensive strength and the defensive strength of the free world;

(d) take all reasonable measures which may be needed to develop its defence capacities; and

(e) take appropriate steps to insure the effective utilisation of the economic and military assistance provided by the United States.

2. (a) The Government of Pakistan will, consistent with the Charter of the United Nations, furnish to the Government of the United States, or to such other Governments as the Parties hereto may in each case agree upon, such equipment, materials, services or other assistance as may be agreed upon in order to increase their capacity for individual and collective self-defence and to facilitate their effective participation in the United Nations system for collective security.

(b) In conformity with the principle of mutual aid, the Government of Pakistan will facilitate the production and transfer to the Government of the United States, for such period of time, in such quantities and upon such terms and conditions as may be agreed upon, of raw and semi-processed materials required by the United States as a result of deficiencies or potential deficiencies in its own resources, and which may be available in Pakistan. Arrangements for such transfers shall give due regard to reasonable requirements of Pakistan for domestic use and commercial export.

## ARTICLE VI

In the interest of their mutual security the Government of Pakistan will co-operate with the Government of the United States in taking measures designed to control trade with nations which threaten the maintenance of world peace.

## ARTICLE VII

1. This Agreement shall enter into force on the date of signature and will continue in force until one year after the receipt by either party of written notice of the intention of the other party to terminate it, except that the provisions of Article I, paragraphs 2 and 4, and arrangements entered into under Article I, paragraphs 3, 5 and 7, and under Article II, shall remain in force unless otherwise agreed by the two Governments.

2. The two Governments will, upon the request of either of them, consult regarding any matter relating to the application or amendment of this Agreement.

3. This Agreement shall be registered with the Secretariat of the United Nations.

Done in two copies at Karachi the 19th day of May one thousand nine hundred and fifty four.

<table>
<tr><td>For the Government of the<br>United States of America</td><td>For the Government<br>of Pakistan</td></tr>
<tr><td>JOHN K EMMERSON<br>Charge d'Affaires a.i., of<br>the United States of America<br>[SEAL]</td><td>ZAFRULLA KHAN<br>Minister of Foreign Affairs<br>and Commonwealth Relations<br>[SEAL]</td></tr>
</table>

## APPENDIX 7

**Pakistan-US Mutual Security: Defense Support Assistance. Agreement signed at Karachi, January 11, 1955; entered into force January 11, 1955.** Department of State, USTIA 1955, Vol.6, Part 1, Washington, D.C., USGPO, 1956, pp. 501–506 [TIAS 3183 Jan. 11, 1955]

AGREEMENT BETWEEN THE GOVERNMENT OF PAKISTAN AND THE GOVERNMENT OF THE UNITED STATES OF AMERICA ON UNITED STATES AID UNDER CHAPTER 3-DEFENCE SUPPORT-OF TITLE I IN THE MUTUAL SECURITY ACT OF 1954

The Government of the United States of America and the Government of Pakistan,

In order to contribute further to the development of Pakistan's capacity to maintain its independence and security, in a manner which will assist the people of Pakistan in strengthening the economy of their country as a sound basis for a strong democratic society, and

In order to provide the basis upon which the Government of the United States is prepared to extend defense support assistance to the Government of Pakistan,

Have agreed as follows:

### ARTICLE I

The Government of the United States will, subject to the requirements and conditions of any applicable United States legislation and to the availability of funds for this purpose, furnish to the Government of Pakistan such commodities, services or such other assistance as may be requested by it and authorized by the Government of the United States. The two Governments will, from time to time and as necessary, negotiate detailed arrangements to carry out the provisions of this Agreement.

## ARTICLE II

For the period ending June 30, 1955, the Government of the United States is prepared to allocate about Sixty Million Dollars ($60,000,000) for the furnishing of assistance under this Agreement, provided that the two Governments agree on the content of such a program in time to obligate such funds within the periods during which they will be legally available for this purpose. Future allocations of funds by the United States for assistance requested by Pakistan may be made in accordance with this Agreement and subject to the availability of funds for this purpose; the Government of the United States will notify the Government of Pakistan of any such allocations. The two Governments will cooperate to assure that any procurement under this program will be carried out at reasonable prices and on reasonable terms, and in order to achieve the greatest benefit from the assistance will agree on terms and conditions for the distribution and use within Pakistan of items and services which may be made available under this Agreement.

## ARTICLE III

A. In order to assure maximum benefits to the people of Pakistan from assistance furnished under this Agreement, the Government of Pakistan will continue to use its best endeavours:

1. To assure efficient use of all resources available to it and to promote the economic development of Pakistan on a sound basis;
2. To assure that the commodities and services obtained under this Agreement are used exclusively for the purposes for which furnished;
3. To foster and maintain the stability of its currency and confidence in its economic condition; and
4. To take measures insofar as practicable, and to cooperate with other countries, to reduce barriers to international trade and to prevent, on the part of private or public enterprises, business practices or business arrangements which restrain competition or limit access to markets, whenever such practices hinder domestic or international trade.

B. The Government of Pakistan will:

1. Join in promoting international understanding and good will, and maintaining world peace;

2. Take such action as may be mutually agreed upon to eliminate causes of international tension;
3. Make, consistent with its political and economic stability, the full contribution permitted by its manpower, resources, facilities and general economic condition to the development and maintenance of its own defensive strength and the defensive strength of the free world;
4. Take all reasonable measures which may be needed to develop its defense capacities; and
5. Take appropriate steps to insure the effective utilization of any assistance provided by the United States in furtherance of the purposes of such assistance.

## ARTICLE IV

The provisions of this Article shall apply with respect to assistance which may be furnished by the Government of the United States of America on a grant basis:

1. The Government of Pakistan will establish in its own name a Special Account (referred to below as the "Special Account") in the State Bank of Pakistan. The Government of Pakistan will deposit in this account amounts of local currency at least equivalent to the dollar cost to the Government of the United States of all commodities, services, and other assistance furnished pursuant to this Agreement. It is understood that such deposits by the Government of Pakistan shall be made not later than forty (40) days after notification has been given to the Government of Pakistan by the Government of the United States that there has been disbursement of funds for commodities or services furnished to the Government of Pakistan pursuant to this Agreement, except that with regard to the disbursement of funds for goods not intended for sale the Government of the United States may defer the date of deposit of equivalent local currency beyond the specified forty days.

2. It is understood, further, that in the event that there are any sums accruing to the Government of Pakistan, or to any of the States or Provinces of Pakistan from the sale of any commodities, services, or other assistance supplied under this Agreement, or otherwise accruing to the Government of Pakistan or the States or Provinces of Pakistan as a result of the import of such commodities or services, then the amount deposited in the Special Account shall not be less than the total of any such sales proceeds, provided, however, that computations of and adjustments on such sales proceeds shall be made every six months. Representatives of the two Governments will promptly agree upon necessary reasonable accounting procedures for arriving at aggregate accruals for the purposes of this paragraph. It is understood, further, that the sums accruing from any such

sale shall include import duties imposed and collected by any agency of the Government of Pakistan or any of its constituent states. The Government of Pakistan may at any time make advance deposits into the Special Account.

3. The rate of exchange to be used for the purpose of computing the rupee equivalent to be deposited under paragraph 1 of this Article, shall be the par value at the time of the notification for the Pakistani rupee agreed with the International Monetary Fund, provided that this par value is the single rate then applicable to the purchase of dollars for commercial transactions in Pakistan. If there is no agreed par value or if there are two or more effective rates that are not unlawful for the purchase of dollars for commercial transactions the particular rates used shall be those effective rates (including the amount of any exchange certificate) which, at the time of deposit, are applicable to the purchase of other dollars for similar imports.

4. Drawings upon the Special Account shall be made by mutual consent. Such drawings will be made for programs in furtherance of the objectives of this Agreement, as may be from time to time agreed between the two Governments. The Government of Pakistan will make available to the Government of the United States such amounts [but not to exceed five percent) of the deposits made into the Special Account as may be requested from time to time by the Government of the United States for any of its expenditures in Pakistan, including its administration and operating expenditures in Pakistan in connection with any assistance supplied by the Government of the United States to the Government of Pakistan under this Agreement. Any unencumbered balance of funds which may remain in the Special Account upon termination of assistance under this Agreement shall be disposed of as may be agreed betwen the two Governments.

## ARTICLE V

1. Any assistance furnished under this Agreement on a loan basis shall be made available subject to the terms of separate agreements to be arranged between the Government of Pakistan and the Export-Import Bank of Washington, an agency of the United States.

2. In the period ending June 30, 1955, it is agreed that of the amount referred to in Article II about Twenty Million Dollars ($20,000,000) shall be made available on loan terms for the development of Pakistan's economic strength.

## ARTICLE VI

The Government fo Pakistan will receive persons designated by the Government of the United States to discharge the responsibilities of the latter Government under this Agreement and will permit continuous observation and review by such persons of programs of assistance under this agreement, including the utilization of any such assistance. The Government of Pakistan will cooperate in facilitating the discharge of these responsibilities by such persons, and will provide the United States with full and complete information relating to programs under this Agreement, including statements on the use of assistance received. Upon appropriate notification by the government of the United States, the Government of Pakistan will accord such persons and accompanying members of their families, except as may otherwise be mutually agreed, the privileges and immunities specified in paragraphs 4 and 5 of the 1954 Supplementary Program Agreement for Technical Cooperation and Economic Assistance between the two Governments, signed at Karachi on December 28, 1953.

## ARTICLE VII

The Government of Pakistan will so deposit, segregate or assure title to all funds allocated to or derived from any program of assistance undertaken by the Government of the United States so that such funds shall not, except as may otherwise be mutually agreed, be subject to garnishment, attachment, seizure or other legal process by any person, firm, agency, corporation, organization or government.

The Government of Pakistan will permit and give full publicity to the objectives and progress of the program under this Agreement and will make public each quarter full statements of operations under it, including information as to the use of funds, commodities and services made available under the Agreement.

## ARTICLE VIII

1. This Agreement shall enter into force upon signature and shall remain in force until ninety days after the receipt by either Government of written notice of the intention of the other Government to terminate it, except that arrangements for repayment of loans pursuant to Article V shall remain in force on their own terms.

2. The two Governments will consult at any time at the request of either of them on any matter relating to the application or amendment of this Agreement.

3. This Agreement is complementary to existing agreements between the two Governments and is not intended to supersede or modify them.

Done at Karachi in duplicate in the English language, this 11th day of January, 1955.

FOR THE GOVERNMENT
OF THE UNITED STATES
OF AMERICA
HORACE A HILDRETH
Horace A. Hildreth
*Ambassador of the
United States of
America in Pakistan*
[SEAL]

FOR THE GOVERNMENT
OF PAKISTAN
MOHAMAD ALI
Mohamad Ali
*Minister for Finance
and Economic Affairs*
[SEAL]

## APPENDIX 8

United States of America and Pakistan: Mutual Defence Assistance Agreement effected by signature on a note to the Pakistani Minister of Foreign Affairs and Commonwealth Relations from the United States Ambassador to Pakistan. Karachi, 15 March 1956. Department of State, USTIA 1956, Vol.7, Part 3, Washington, D.C., USGPO, 1957.

MUTUAL DEFENCE ASSISTANCE: DISPOSITION OF EQUIPMENT AND MATERIALS. AGREEMENT IMPLEMENTING ARTICLE I, PARAGRAPH 3, OF THE AGREEMENT OF MAY 19, 1954. SIGNED AT KARACHI MARCH 15 AND MAY 15, 1956; ENTERED INTO FORCE MAY 15, 1956.

AMERICAN EMBASSY
Karachi, March 15, 1956

Dear Mr. Minister:

Members of my staff have discussed with officials of the Pakistani Ministry of Defence a draft setting forth procedural arrangements intended to implement Article I, paragraph 3 of the Mutual Defence Assistance Agreement of May 19, 1954. I am informed that agreement was tentatively reached on the following text:

'The Government of the United States of America and the Government of Pakistan undertake the following arrangements in accordance with Article I, paragraph 3 of the Mutual Defence Assistance Agreement of May 19, 1954 between the two Governments, respecting the disposition of military equipment and materials furnished by the Government of the United States and no longer required or used exclusively for the purposes for which they were made available:

1. The Government of Pakistan will report to the Government of the United States such equipment or materials as are no longer required or used exclusively and effectively for the purposes of and in accordance with

213

Article I, paragraph 2 of the Mutual Defence Assistance Agreement. The Government of the United States may also draw to the attention of the appropriate authorities of the Government of Pakistan any equipment or materials which it considers to fall within the scope of these arrangements. When so notified the Pakistani authorities will consult with the representatives of the United States Government to determine whether such items do in fact fall within such scope. Upon such determination, such items will be disposed of in accordance with the procedures set out in the following paragraphs.

2. The Government of the United States may accept title to such equipment or materials for transfer to a third country or for such other disposition as may be made by the Government of the United States.

3. When title is accepted by the Government of the United States, such equipment or materials will be delivered as it may request free alongside ship at a Pakistani port or free on board inland carrier at a shipping point in Pakistan designated by the Government of the United States, or, in the case of flight-deliverable aircraft, at such airfield in Pakistan as may be designated by the Government of the United States.

4. Such equipment or materials as are not accepted by the United States will be disposed of by the Government of Pakistan as may be agreed between the two Governments.

5. Any salvage or scrap from military equipment or materials furnished by the Government of the United States shall be reported to the Government of the United States and shall be disposed of in accordance with paragraphs 2, 3, and 4 of the present arrangements.'

If the foregoing is satisfactory to you as an implementation of Articl I, para 3, of the Mutual Defence Assistance Agreement of May 19, 1954, I suggest you to signify by indicating your approval in the space provided below on both the original hereof and the enclosed copy and return the original hereof for our files and keep the copy for your files.

Sincerely yours

Horace A. Hildreth
Ambassador

The Honourable Mr Hamidul Huq Chowdhury
Minister of Foreign Affairs and Commonwealth Relations
Government of Pakistan, Karachi

Approved and confirmed this 15th day of May 1956:

Hamidul Huq
Foreign Minister

## APPENDIX 9

United States of America and India: Exchange of notes constituting an agreement for assurances regarding mutual defense assistance. New Delhi, 16 April and 17 December 1958. (Registered by the United States of America on 6 May 1960]. United Nations Secretariat, UNTS., Vol.358, New York, 1959, pp. 77–81.

No. 5125. EXCHANGE OF NOTES CONSTITUTING AN AGREEMENT BETWEEN THE UNITED STATES OF AMERICA AND INDIA FOR ASSURANCES REGARDING MUTUAL DEFENSE ASSISTANCE. NEW DELHI, 16 APRIL AND 17 DECEMBER 1958

I. *The American Charge' d'Affaires ad interim to the Minister for External Affairs of India*

THE FOREIGN SERVICE OF
THE UNITED STATES OF AMERICA
New Delhi, April 16, 1958

Excellency:

I have the honour to refer to the Agreement between our two Governments effected by an exchange of notes signed at Washington on March 7 and 16, 1951. It is the understanding of my Government that Your Excellency's Government considers the assurances contained in that Agreement regarding transactions under the Mutual Defense Assistance Act of 1949, as amended, to be applicable also to equipment, materials, information and services furnished under the Mutual Security Act of 1954, the Act as amended from time to time, and such other applicable United States laws as may come into effect.

I should appreciate it if Your Excellency's Government would confirm the understanding of my Government as stated above.

Accept, Excellency, the renewed assurances of my highest consideration.

Winthrop G. Brown
Charge' d'Affaires ad interim

His Excellency Jawaharlal Nehru
Minister for External Affairs
New Delhi

II. *The Foreign Secretary, Ministry of External Affairs of India, to the American Ambassador*

MINISTRY OF EXTERNAL AFFAIRS
NEW DELHI
Foreign Secretary

No. FS/1402

December 17, 1958

Dear Mr. Ambassador,

Please refer to the following letter to the Prime Minister from Mr Winthrop G. Brown:

[*See note I*]

2. I am directed by the Government of India to confirm that the assurances contained in the Agreement between our two Governments effected by an exchange of notes signed at Washington on March 7 & 16, 1951 are applicable also to supplies and services furnished to the Government of India by the Government of the United States of America under the Mutual Security Act of 1954 as amended from time to time. I am to add that in fact, as is well known, the firm policy of India is to work for international peace and on no account does the Government of India even consider the possibility of aggression against any other State.

Accept, Excellency, the assurances of my highest consideration.

S. Dutt
Foreign Secretary

His Excellency Mr. Ellsworth Bunker
Ambassador of the United States of America
New Delhi

## APPENDIX 10

**United States of America and Pakistan: Cooperation – Agreement signed at Ankara on March 5, 1959; Entered into force, March 5, 1959.** Department of State, USTIA 1959, Washington,D.C., USGPO, 1960, pp. 317–319 [TIAS 4190]

AGREEMENT OF COOPERATION BETWEEN THE GOVERNMENT OF THE UNITED STATES OF AMERICA AND THE GOVERNMENT OF PAKISTAN

The Government of the United States of America and the Government of Pakistan,

Desiring to implement the Declaration in which they associated themselves at London on July 28, 1958;

Considering that under Article I of the Pact of Mutual Cooperation signed at Baghdad on February 24, 1955, the parties signatory thereto agreed to cooperate for their security and defense, and that, similarly, as stated in the above-mentioned Declaration, the Government of the United States of America, in the interest of world peace, agreed to cooperate with the Governments making that Declaration for their security and defense;

Recalling that, in the above-mentioned Declaration, the members of the Pact of Mutual Cooperation making that Declaration affirmed their determination to maintain their collective security and to resist aggression, direct or indirect;

Considering further that the Government of the United States of America is associated with the work of the major committees of the Pact of Mutual Cooperation signed at Baghdad on February 24, 1955;

Desiring to strengthen peace in accordance with the principles of the Charter of the United Nations;

Affirming their right to cooperate for their security and defense in accordance with Article 51 of the Charter of the United Nations;

Considering that the Government of the United States of America regards as vital to its national interest and to world peace the preservation of the independence and integrity of Pakistan;

Recognizing the authorization to furnish appropriate assistance granted to the President of the United States of America by the Congress of the United States of America in Mutual Security Act of 1954, as amended, and in the Joint Resolution to Promote Peace and Stability in the Middle East; and

Considering that similar agreements are being entered into by the Government of the United States of America and the Governments of Iran and Turkey, respectively,

Have agreed as follows:

## ARTICLE I

The Government of Pakistan is determined to resist aggression. In case of aggression against Pakistan, the Government of the United States of America, in accordance with the Constitution of the United States of America, will take such appropriate action, including the use of armed forces, as may be mutually agreed upon and as is envisaged in the Joint Resolution to Promote Peace and Stability in the Middle East, in order to assist the Government of Pakistan at its request.

## ARTICLE II

The Government of the United States of America, in accordance with the Mutual Security Act of 1954, as amended, and related laws of the United States of America, and with applicable agreements heretofore or hereafter entered into between the Government of the United States of America and the Government of Pakistan, reaffirms that it will continue to furnish the Government of Pakistan such military and economic assistance as may be mutually agreed upon between the Government of the United States of America and the Government of Pakistan, in order to assist the Government of Pakistan in the preservation of its national independence and integrity and in the effective promotion of its economic development.

## ARTICLE III

The Government of Pakistan undertakes to utilize such military and economic assistance as may be provided by the Government of the United States of America in a manner consonant with the aims and purposes set forth by the Governments associated in the Declaration signed at London on July 28, 1958, and for the purpose of effectively promoting the economic development of Pakistan and of preserving its national independence and integrity.

## ARTICLE IV

The Government of the United States of America and the Government of Pakistan will cooperate with the other Governments associated in the Declaration signed at London on July 28, 1958, in order to prepare and participate in such defensive arrangements as may be mutually agreed to be desirable, subject to the other applicable provisions of this agreement.

## ARTICLE V

The provisions of the present agreement do not affect the cooperation between the two Governments as envisaged in other international agreements or arrangements.

## ARTICLE VI

This agreement shall enter into force upon the date of its signature and shall continue in force until one year after the receipt by either Government of written notice of the intention of the other Government to terminate the agreement.

Done in duplicate at Ankara, this fifth day of March, 1959.

FOR THE GOVERNMENT
OF THE UNITED STATES
OF AMERICA:

FLETCHER WARREN.

Fletcher Warren
[SEAL]

FOR THE GOVERNMENT
OF PAKISTAN:

SAYID M HASSAN.

Sayid M. Hassan
[SEAL]

## APPENDIX 11

United States and Pakistan: Establishment of a Communications Unit; Agreement effected by exchange of notes; Signed at Karachi on July 18, 1959; Entered into force July 18, 1959. With minute of understanding and exchange of notes. Department of State, USTIA 1959, Vol.10, Part 2, Washington, D.C., USGPO, 1960, pp. 1366–1381 [TIAS 4281]

I. *The Pakistani Minister of Foreign Affairs and Commonwealth Relations to the American Ambassador*

Ministry of External Affairs and
Commonwealth Relations
*Karachi, the 18th July, 1959*

Your Excellency,

I refer to our recent discussion regarding the desire of the United States to station a Communications Unit in Pakistan. I have the honour to inform you that the Government of Pakistan agrees to the stationing of such a Unit on the following basis:

1. The Government of Pakistan will make available to the United States the land areas and rights-of way required for the establishment and operations of the Communications Unit and will provide protection for such Unit. The agreed areas and rights-of-way are set forth in Annex A.

2. The Communications Unit and personnel assigned to it may install and use communications equipment, including antennas; use continuously agreed radio frequencies and agreed wire communications facilities; purchase locally goods and services including construction materials, electrical power and transportation services; make arrangements for the internal security of those small areas, within the agreed areas, designated for the exclusive use of the Communications Unit (only authorized persons may enter these latter areas); carry arms in connection with official duties within the areas designated for the exclusive use of the Communications

Unit and in connection with the courier duties outside the agreed areas; move freely within, into and out of and between the agreed areas; and may engage in such other activities as may be necessary for the effective operation of the Unit and the health and welfare of its personnel.

3. The Communications Unit and personnel assigned to it shall respect the laws of Pakistan and shall abstain from any activity which would adversely affect the interest of the people or the Government of Pakistan. The Government of the United States will take necessary measures to prevent abuse of the privileges granted by the Government of Pakistan under the present Agreement.

4. The Government of Pakistan will, upon request, assist the Communications Unit in the local procurement of goods, materials, supplies and services required for the establishment, operation and support of the Unit. The Unit shall enjoy any preferential rates, charges, or priorities which are available to the Armed Forces of Pakistan for goods or services purchased locally in connection with the operation of the Unit.

5. (a) The personnel of the Communications Unit shall receive exemption from payment of all duties and taxes, including export duties, on their personal and household goods brought into the country for their own use within six months of their arrival

Goods imported under this section will not ordinarily be sold or disposed of in Pakistan by the owner, except to other persons enjoying comparable privileges. In the event of their sale or disposal to a person who does not enjoy comparable privileges, the duty and taxes thereon will be paid.

The Pakistan Customs Department will issue appropriate regulations regarding the provisions of this section.

(b) The temporary presence in Pakistan of a member of the Unit will constitute neither residence nor domicile therein and shall not of itself subject him to taxation in Pakistan, either on his income or on his property, the presence of which in Pakistan is due to his temporary presence there, nor, in the event of his death, shall it subject his estate to a levy of death duties.

6. No tax, duty or other charge will be levied or assessed on activities of the Unit or on material, equipment, supplies or goods brought into or procured in Pakistan by the United States authorities for the use of the Unit, its agencies or personnel assigned to the Unit.

7. The United States Government may construct within the agreed areas the facilities required for support of the Communications Unit under the terms and conditions set forth in Articles II through VII of the Military Defense Construction Agreement signed at Karachi on May 28, 1956.

8. Title to removable materials, equipment or property brought into or acquired in Pakistan by or on behalf of the Communications Unit will

remain in the United States Government. Such material, equipment or property may be brought into or removed tax and duty free at any time from Pakistan by the United States Government. The materials, equipment and property of the Unit and its official papers will be exempt from inspection, search and seizure and may be removed freely by the United States Government at any time.

9. Jurisdiction over personnel of the Unit shall be exercised in accordance with the provisions of Annex B, an integral part hereof.

10. Arrangements required to give effect to this Agreement will be the subject of agreement between the Commanding Officer of the Communications Unit and Senior Military Officer of the Pakistan Forces in the area.

11. In this Agreement the expressions 'personnel assigned to the Unit' include persons who are in Pakistan in connection with the Agreement and who are (a) members of the United States armed forces; (b) civilian personnel employed by, serving with, or accompanying the United States armed forces (except persons who are nationals of Pakistan or ordinarily resident therein); or (c) dependents of the persons defined in (a) and (b) above.

12. This agreement shall remain in force for a period of ten years and for a second period of ten years thereafter unless either party gives written notice to the other at least twelve months before the end of the first ten year period of its desire to terminate this Agreement.

If the foregoing arrangements are acceptable to Your Excellency's Government, I have the honour to propose that this note and Your Excellency's note in reply to that effect shall constitute an Agreement between our two Governments on this matter which shall enter into force on the date of your note in reply.

I avail myself of this opportunity to renew to Your Excellency the assurance of my highest consideration.

MANZUR QADIR
(Manzur Qadir)
*Minister of Foreign Affairs and*
*Commonwealth Relations*

Enclosures:

1. Annex A-Agreed Areas and Rights of Way
2. Annex B-Jurisdiction

His Excellency Mr. James M. Langley,
*The Ambassador of the United States of America*
*in Pakistan,*
*Karachi.*

**II.** *The American Ambassador to the Pakistani Minister of Foreign Affairs and Commonwealth Relations*

EMBASSY OF THE UNITED STATES OF AMERICA
*Karachi, July 18, 1959.*

Excellency,

I have the honour to acknowledge the receipt of your note of today's date, together with Annex A and Annex B attached thereto, the texts of which read as follows:

*[See note I ]*

I have the honour to inform Your Excellency that the Government of the United States of America accepts the arrangements contained in your note, together with Annex A and Annex B attached thereto, and regards your note and this reply as constituting an Agreement between our two Governments, the Agreement to enter into force on this day.

Accept, Excellency, the renewed assurances of my highest consideration.

JAMES M. LANGLEY

His Excellency
MANZUR QADIR,
*Minister of Foreign Affairs*
*and Commonwealth Relations, Karachi*


**III.** *Minute of understanding*

It is agreed that the following conditions shall apply to the privileges extended to the personnel of the Communications Unit in paragraph 5(a) of the Agreement on the United States Communications Unit of July 18, 1959:

1. The exemption applies to direct imports only and not to local purchases or clearances from bond.

2. No Pakistan foreign exchange is involved in such imports.

3. The number of motor cars imported under this section by each person assigned to the Unit shall not exceed one.

JAMES M. LANGLEY
James M. Langley
*United States Ambassador*

MANZUR QADIR
Manzur Qadir
*Minister of Foreign Affairs*
*and Commonwealth Relations*

KARACHI
*July 18, 1959*

**IV** *The American Ambassador to the Pakistani Minister of Foreign Affairs and Commonwealth Relations*

EMBASSY OF THE UNITED STATES OF AMERICA
*Karachi, July 18, 1959.*

Dear Mr. Minister,

Today the Governments of the United States of America and Pakistan exchanged notes formalizing our Agreement on the United States Communications Unit and the status of the members of the Unit who enter Pakistan in connection therewith.

Annex B of that Agreement provides for the exercise of jurisdiction over such members. In this regard, I would be grateful for your confirmation of the following understandings:

1. That no cruel or unusual punishment would be inflicted upon any person over whom the Pakistani authorities might exercise jurisdiction pursuant to Annex B;

2. That should any person over whom the Pakistani authorities exercise such jurisdiction subsequently be confined by those authorities, the United States military authorities would be permitted to visit such person periodically at the place of confinement;

3. That in implementation of the provisions of paragraph 3(c) of Annex B, it shall not be necessary for the United States to make a request for waiver in each particular case, and it shall be taken for granted that Pakistan has waived its primary right to exercise jurisdiction thereunder except where the Government of Pakistan determines in a specific case that it is of particular interest that jurisdiction be exercised therein by the authorities of Pakistan;

4. That with reference to paragraph 5(c) of Annex B, concerning custody of an accused member of the Unit, the United States authorities will give full consideration to the special wishes of the appropriate Pakistan authorities as to the manner in which the custody of an accused member of the Unit shall be carried into effect;

5. That with respect to paragraph 11 of Annex B, concerning civil suits or claims arising out of any act or omission done in the performance of official duty over which the authorities of Pakistan shall not exercise their jurisdiction, meritorious claims thereunder will be settled by the United States military authorities in accordance with procedures which enable them to make expeditious settlement of such claims.

Sincerely yours,

JAMES M. LANGLEY
James M. Langley, *Ambassador*

Mr. MANZUR QADIR,
*Minister of Foreign Affairs
and Commonwealth Relations, Karachi.*

223

## V. *The Pakistani Minister of Foreign Affairs and Commonwealth Relations to the American Ambassador*

MINISTER FOR FOREIGN AFFAIRS
AND COMMONWEALTH RELATIONS, KARACHI.
*July 18th, 1959.*

DEAR MR. AMBASSADOR:

As requested in your letter of July 18th, 1959, I am pleased to confirm our understandings:

1. That no cruel or unusual punishment would be inflicted upon any person over whom the Pakistani authorities might exercise jurisdiction pursuant to Annex B;

2. That should any person over whom the Pakistani authorities exercise such jurisdiction subsequently be confined by those authorities, the United States military authorities would be permitted to visit such person periodically at the place of confinement;

3. That in implementation of the provisions of paragraph 3(c) of Annex B, it shall not be necessary for the United States to make a request for waiver in each particular case, and it shall be taken for granted that Pakistan has waived its primary right to exercise jurisdiction thereunder except where the Government of Pakistan determines in a specific case that it is of particular importance that jurisdiction be exercised therein by the authorities of Pakistan;

4. That with reference to paragraph 5(c) of Annex B, concerning custody of an accused member of the Unit, the United States authorities will give full consideration to the special wishes of the appropriate Pakistani authorities as to the manner in which the custody of an accused member of the Unit shall be carried into effect;

5. That with respect to paragraph 11 of Annex B, concerning civil suits or claims arising out of any act or omission done in the performance of official duty over which the authorities of Pakistan shall not exercise their jurisdiction, meritorious claims thereunder will be settled by the United States military authorities in accordance with procedures which enable them to make expeditious settlement of such claims.

Sincerely yours,

MANZUR QADIR
(Manzur Qadir)
*Minister of Foreign Affairs and Commonwealth Relations*

His Excellency Mr. JAMES M. LANGLEY
*The Amabassador of the United States of America
in Pakistan, Karachi*

## APPENDIX 12

United States and India: Exchange of notes constituting an agreement between the United States of America and India relating to mutual defense assistance. Washington,D.C., 14 November 1962. (Registered by the United States of America on 24 April 1963). United Nations Secretariat, UNTS, Vol.461, New York, 1963, pp. 224–227.

No. 1904. EXCHANGE OF NOTES CONSTITUTING AN AGREEMENT BETWEEN THE UNITED STATES OF AMERICA AND INDIA RELATING TO MUTUAL DEFENSE ASSISTANCE. WASHINGTON, 7 AND 16 MARCH 1951

EXCHANGE OF NOTES CONSTITUTING AN AGREEMENT SUPPLEMENTING THE ABOVE-MENTIONED AGREEMENT, AS AMENDED. WASHINGTON, 14 NOVEMBER 1962

I. *The Secretary of State to the Ambassador of India*

DEPARTMENT OF STATE
WASHINGTON

November 14, 1962

Excellency:

I have the honour to refer to the Agreement between our two Governments effected by an exchange of notes on March 7 and 16, 1951 at Washington, as amended by an Agreement effected by an exchange of notes on April 16 and December 17, 1958, at New Delhi. In response to requests from the Government of India, my Government is prepared to furnish assistance to the Government of India for the purpose of defense against the outright Chinese aggression directed from Peking now facing your country. It is the understanding of my Government that, with regard to defense articles made available to the Government of India under special arrangements to be concluded between representatives of our two Governments, and including defense articles provided between November 3 and November 14, 1962, the Government of India considers the assurances contained in the Agreement effected by the exchange of notes of March 7 and 16, 1951 to be applicable and that the Government of India is prepared:

(1) to offer necessary facilities to representatives of the Government of the United States of America attached to the United States Embassy in India for the purpose of observing and reviewing the use of such articles and to provide them with such information as may be necessary for the purpose; and

(2) to offer for return to the Government of the United States of America such articles furnished by the Government of the United States of America which are no longer needed for the purposes for which originally made available.

A reply to the effect that these understandings are correct will constitute an agreement between the Government of India and the Government of the United States of America, which shall come into force on the date of the note of reply from the Government of India.

Accept, Excellency, the renewed assurances of my highest consideration.

For the Secretary of State:
Phillips Talbot

His Excellency Braj Kumar Nehru
Ambassador of India

## II. *The Ambassador of India to the Secretary of State*

EMBASSY OF INDIA
WASHINGTON, D.C.

November 14, 1962

Mr. Secretary,

I have the honour to refer to your note dated November 14, 1962 reading as follows:

*[See note I]*

I have the honour to confirm that the understandings set forth in the above quoted note are correct. I agree that your note together with this reply shall constitute an agreement between our two Governments which comes into force on the date of this reply.

I avail myself of the opportunity to convey to you, Mr Secretary, the assurances of my highest consideration.

Braj Kumar Nehru
Ambassador of India

The Honourable The Secretary of State
Washington D.C.
[Seal]

# Annexures 1–14

## ANNEXURE 1

The Agreement of the Central People's Government and the Local Government of Tibet on Measures for the Peaceful Liberation of Tibet, 23 May 1951, cited in Union Research Institute, **Tibet, 1950–1967**, Document 6, Hong Kong, 1968, pp. 19–23.

The Tibetan nationality is one of the nationalities with a long history within the boundaries of China and, like many other nationalities, it has done its glorious duty in the course of the creation and development of the great motherland. But over the last hundred years and more, imperialist forces penetrated into China, and in consequence, also penetrated into the Tibetan region and carried out all kinds of deceptions and provocations. Like previous reactionary Governments, the KMT (Guomindang) reactionary government continued to carry out a policy of oppression and sowing dissention among the nationalities, causing division and disunity among the Tibetan people. The Local Government of Tibet did not oppose imperialist deception and provocations, but adopted an unpatriotic attitude towards the great motherland. Under such conditions, the Tibetan nationality and people were plunged into the depths of enslavement and suffcring. In 1949, basic victory was achieved on a nationwide scale in the Chinese people's war of liberation; the common domestic enemy of all nationalities – the KMT reactionary government – was overthrown; and the common foreign enemy of all nationalities – the aggressive imperialist forces – was driven out. On this basis, the founding of the People's Republic of China and of the Central People's Government was announced. In accordance with the Common Programme passed by the Chinese People's Political Consultative Conference, the Central People's Government declared that all nationalities within the boundaries of the People's Republic of China are equal, and that they shall establish unity and mutual aid and oppose imperialism and their own public enemies, so that the People's Republic of China may become one big family of fraternity and co-operation, composed of all its nationalities. Within this big family of nationalities of the People's Republic of China, national regional autonomy is to be exercised in areas where national minorities are concentrated, and all national minorities are to have freedom to develop their spoken and written languages and to preserve or reform their customs, habits and religious beliefs, and the Central People's Government will assist all national minorities to develop their political, economic, cultural and educational construction work. Since then, all nationalities within the country, with the exception of those in the areas of Tibet and Taiwan, have gained liberation. Under the unified leadership of the Central People's Government and the direct leadership of the higher levels of People's Governments, all national minorities have fully enjoyed the right of national equality and have exercised, or are exercising, national regional autonomy. In order that the influences of aggressive imperialist forces in Tibet may be successfully eliminated, the unification of the territory and sovereignty of the People's Republic of China accomplished, and national defence safeguarded; in order that the Tibetan nationality and people may be freed and return to the big family of the People's Republic of China to enjoy the same rights of national equality as all other nationalities in the country and develop their political, economic, cultural, and educational work, the Central People's Government, when it ordered the People's Liberation Army to march into Tibet, notified the local government of Tibet to send delegates to the Central Authorities to hold talks for the conclusion of an agreement on measures for the peaceful liberation of Tibet. At the latter part of April, 1951, the delegates with full powers from the Local Government of Tibet arrived in Peking. The Central People's Government appointed representatives with full powers to conduct talks on a friendly basis with the delegates of the Local Government of Tibet. The result of the talks is that both parties have agreed to establish this agreement and ensure that it be carried into effect.

1. The Tibetan people shall be united and drive out the imperialist aggressive forces from Tibet; that the Tibetan people shall return to the big family of the motherland – the People's Republic of China.

2. The Local Government of Tibet shall actively assist the People's Liberation Army to enter Tibet and consolidate the national defences.

3. In accordance with the policy towards nationalities laid down in the Common Programme of the Chinese People's Political Consultative Conference, the Tibetan people have the right of exercising national regional autonomy under the unified leadership of the Central People's Government.

4. The Central Authorities will not alter the existing political system in Tibet. The Central Authorities also will not alter the established status, functions and powers of the Dalai Lama. Officials of various ranks shall hold office as usual.

5. The established status, functions, and powers of the Panchen Ngoerh-tehni shall be maintained.

6. By the established status, functions and powers of the Dalai Lama and of the Panchen Ngoerhtehni is (sic) meant the status, functions and powers of the 13th Dalai Lama and of the 9th Panchen Ngoerhtehni when they were in friendly and amicable relations with each other.

7. The policy of freedom of religious belief laid down in the Common Programme of the Chinese People's Political Consultative Conference will be protected. The Central Authorities will not effect any change in the income of the monasteries.

8. The Tibetan troops will be reorganised step by step into the People's Liberation Army, and become a part of the national defence forces of the Central People's Government.

9. The spoken and written language and school education of the Tibetan nationality will be developed step by step in accordance with the actual conditions in Tibet.

10. Tibetan agriculture, livestock raising, industry and commerce will be developed step by step, and the people's livelihood shall be improved step by step in accordance with the actual conditions in Tibet.

11. In matters related to various reforms in Tibet, there will be no compulsion on the part of the Central Authorities. The Local Government of Tibet should carry out reforms of its own accord, and when the people raise demands for reform, they must be settled through consultation with the leading personnel of Tibet.

12. In so far as former pro-imperialist and pro-KMT officials resolutely sever relations with imperialism and the KMT and do not engage in sabotage or resistance, they may continue to hold office irrespective of their past.

13. The People's Liberation Army entering Tibet will abide by the above-mentioned policies and will also be fair in all buying and selling and will not arbitrarily take even a needle or a thread from the people.

14. The Central People's Government will handle all external affairs of the area of Tibet; and there will be peaceful co-existence with neighbouring countries and the establishment and development of fair commercial and trading relations with them on the basis of equality, mutual benefit and mutual respect for territory and sovereignty.

15. In order to ensure the implementation of this agreement, the Central People's Government will set up a military area headquarters in Tibet, and apart from the personnel sent there by the Central People's Government it will absorb as many local Tibetan personnel as possible to take part in the work. Local Tibetan personnel taking part in the

military and administrative committee may include patriotic elements from the Local Government of Tibet, various districts and various principal monasteries; the namelist is to be prepared after consultation between the representatives designated by the Central People's Government and various quarters concerned, and is to be submitted to the Central People's Government for approval.

16. Funds needed by the military and administrative committee, the military area headquarters and the People's Liberation Army entering Tibet will be provided by the Central People's Government. The Local Government of Tibet should assist the People's Liberation Army in the purchases and transportation of food, fodder, and other daily necessities.

17. This agreement shall come into force immediately after signatures and seals are affixed to it.

Signed and sealed by delegates of the Central People's Government with full powers:

Chief Delegate : Li Wei-han (Chairman of the Commission of Nationalities Affairs); Delegates: Chang Ching-wu, Chang Kuo-hua, Sun Chih-yuan.

Delegates with full powers of the Local Government of Tibet:

Chief Delegate : Kaloon Ngabou Ngawang Jigme (Ngabo Shape)
Delegates: Dzasak Khemey Sonam Wangdi, Khentrung Thupten Tenthar, Khenchung Thupten Lekmuun Rimshi, Samposey Tenzin Thundup

## ANNEXURE 2

Letter from the US embassy in New Delhi to the Dalai Lama, July 1951, cited in Department of State, **FRUS 1951**, Vol. VII, Part II, Washington, D.C., USGPO, 1984, pp. 1744–1745 (unsigned, undatelined, and undated)

We sent you a letter two months ago about the danger of the Chinese Communists. Some of your advisers presumably think that they understand the Chinese Communists and can make a bargain with them. We do not think they understand Communism or the record of their leaders. Your Holiness is the chief hope of Tibet. If the Chinese Communists seize control of Tibet, you will be of greater help to Tibet outside Tibet where you will be the recognized leader and will symbolize the hopes of the Tibetans for the recovery of Tibet's freedom.

We do not know whether you received our letter about the Chinese Communists. We would like to know.

Since sending the previous letter we have read in the newspapers your delegation to Peiping signed an agreement with the Chinese Communists.

We do not believe they signed it with your permission but were forced to do so. However, the world is begining to think that you do not object to the agreement because you have made no statement about it. We think you should make this statement soon because the Chinese Communists are sending a delegation to Yatung through India. If you make a statement before they reach India, it should make it difficult for the Chinese delegation to come to Tibet. If you do not make such a statement, we think that Tibetan autonomy is gone forever.

The only access we have to Tibet is through the country of India. It is therefore important that Tibet tell India what you now want to do and persuade India to help you or permit other countries to help you. We do not know for sure but we think it possible India will permit help because although India now seems friendly with the Chinese Communists we know many Indians are fearful of the Communists near India.

We are willing to help Tibet now and we will do the following things at this time:

1. After you issue the statement disavowing the agreement which your delegation signed with the Chinese Communists in Peiping, we will issue a public statement of our own supporting your stand.

2. If you decide to send a new appeal to the United Nations, we will support your case in the United Nations.

3. If you leave Tibet, we think you should seek asylum in India, Thailand, or Ceylon in that order of priority because then you will be closer to Tibet and will be able to organize its resistance to the Chinese Communists. Although we have not consulted India, we think it would let you come to India because it said you could come last year. We have not consulted Thailand or Ceylon but we will ask them if you can come if you want us to talk to them. If you are unable to remain in any of these countries, you can come to our country with some of your followers.

4. If you leave Tibet and if you organize resistance to the Chinese Communists, we are prepared to send you light arms through India. We think, however, that you should first ask India for arms and, if they cannot give to you ask India for permission for other countries to send them through India. If you are able to organize resistance within Tibet, we will also give consideration to supplying you with loans of money to keep up the resistance, spirit and morale of the Tibetan people. This is important if Tibet's autonomy is to be maintained or regained in the event that you should feel impelled to seek asylum outside of Tibet. We will discuss plans and programmes of military assistance and loans of money with your representatives when you tell us who your representatives are.

5. We have already told your brother, Taktse Rinpochi (sic), that he can go to our country and we are making arrangements for his departure.

We are willing to do all these things. We have sent you many messages to this effect. We do not know if you have received them. Therefore we ask you to write us when you have this letter. We ask you also to send us a personal representative or write us which Tibetan representatives in India have your confidence.

## ANNEXURE 3

Letter from India's Ambassador B R Sen in Washington, D.C., to Indian Finance Minister Chintaman Deshmukh, letter no. 9-Amb.Washington/52 dated 11 January 1952, following dinner with Congressman Jacob K. Javits of the Foreign Affairs Committee, recorded in **Cabinet Secretariat file no.F.14(1)-ECC/52,** pp. 4–6; Indian National Archives, New Delhi. (relevant extract follows)

'In his (recent State of the Union) speech, Truman said: "Perhaps the most amazing thing about our economic progress is the way we are increasing our basic capacity to produce. For example, we are now in the second year of a three-year programme which will double our output in aluminium, increase our electric power supply by 40 per cent, and increase our steelmaking capacity by 15 per cent. We can then produce 120 million tons of steel a year – as much as the rest of the world put together.' Javits expressed the view that *if war did not come* (sic) by the end of 1953, United States would have developed a basic productive capacity which she could maintain only by taking a larger interest in foreign markets than now. In other words, United States would then face a recession or even a real depression unless she could find an outlet for her high production.

'I am sure you will agree that there is a real point in this argument. Javits emphasised the need on our side to realise this possibility and plan from now on that basis. As you will see, he makes several suggestions . . . .' pp. 4–5

Counsellor W R Natu's addendum in the same file, pp. 7–9:

'(ii) India commands an enormous attraction in the United States because of its ancient past and its geographical position. It is considered to be the only stable country in that part of the region. The United States have a feeling that they have failed in China and they should make up for it by success in India (sic). There is a romantic interest in India among the people of the United States, and this will encourage the flow of investment to India. While this is true, it is equally essential that some kind of a call should come from India and a welcome extended.

'(iii) The first thing that India should do immediately is to announce boldly and calmly her willingness to go ahead with the Five-Year Plan as a whole, including that part of it which depends on foreign assistance . . . .' p. 7.

## ANNEXURE 4

Letter from President Dwight D. Eisenhower to Prime Minister Jawaharlal Nehru, delivered by the US Ambassador in Delhi, on 24 February 1954, cited in the Ministry of External Affairs, **Ministry of External Affairs Report** (MEAR) **1953–1954**, Delhi, Government of India, 1954, pp. 51–52.

My Dear Prime Minister,

I send you this personal message because I want you to know about my decision to extend military aid to Pakistan before it is public knowledge and also because I want you to know directly from me that this step does not in any way affect the friendship we feel for India. Quite the contrary. We will continually strive to strengthen the warm and enduring friendship between our two countries. Our two governments have agreed that our desire for peace are in accord. It has also been understood that if our interpretation of existing circumstances and our belief in how to achieve our goals differ, it is the right and duty of our sovereign nations to make their own decisions. Having studied long and carefully the problem of opposing possible aggression in the Middle East, I believe that consultation between Pakistan and Turkey about security problems will serve the interests not only of Pakistan and Turkey, but also of the whole free world. Improvement in Pakistan's defensive capabilities will also serve these interests and it is for this reason that our aid will be given. The Government's view on this subject are elaborated in a public statement I will release, a copy of which the Ambassador will give you.

What we are proposing to do, and what Pakistan is agreeing to, is not directed in any way against India and I am confirming publicly that if our aid to any country, including Pakistan, is misused and directed against another in aggression, I will undertake immediately, in accordance with my constitutional authority, appropriate action, both within and without the United Nations to thwart such aggression. I believe the Pakistan-Turkey collaboration agreement which is being discussed, is sound evidence of the defensive purposes which both countries have in mind.

I know that you and your Government are keenly aware of the need for economic progress as a prime requisite for stability and strength. This Government has extended assistance to India in recognition of this fact, and I am recommending to Congress a continuation of substantial economic and technical aid for this reason. We also believe it in the interest of the free world that India have strong military defense capability and have admired the effective way your Government has administered your military establishment. If your Government should conclude that circumstances require military aid of a type contemplated by our mutual security legislation, please be assured that your request would receive my most sympathetic consideration.

I regret that there has been such widespread and unfounded speculation on this subject. Now that the facts are known, I hope the real import of our decision will be understood.

I am, my dear Mr Prime Minister,

Sincerely

Dwight D. Eisenhower.

## ANNEXURE 5

Text of a statement by President Dwight D. Eisenhower, Washington, D.C., 25 February 1954, cited in the Ministry of External Affairs, **MEAR 1953–1954**, Delhi, Government of India, 1954, pp. 53–54.

On February 19, Turkey and Pakistan announced their intention to study methods of achieving closer collaboration on various matters including means designated towards strengthening peace and security. This Government welcomed this move and called it a constructive step towards better ensuring the security of the whole area of the Middle East. The Government of Pakistan has now asked the United States for grant of military assistance.

I have said repeatedly that regional groupings to ensure security against aggression constitute the most effective means to assure survival and progress. No nation can stand alone today. My report to the Congress on June 30, 1953, stated that we should strengthen efforts towards regional political, military and economic integration. I, therefore, under the authority granted by the Congress, am glad to comply with Pakistan's request, subject to the negotiation of the required Mutual Defense Assistance Program agreement. This Government has been gravely concerned over the weakness of the defense service capabilities in the Middle East. It was with the purpose of helping to increase the defense potential in this area that Congress in its last session appropriated funds to be used to assist those nations in the area which desired such assistance, which would pledge their willingness to promote international peace and security within the framework of the United Nations, and which would take effective collective measures to prevent and remove threats to peace.

Let me make it clear that we shall be guided by the stated purposes and requirements of the mutual security legislation. These include specifically the provision that equipment, materials, or services provided will be used solely to maintain the recipient country's internal security and for its legitimate self-defense, or to permit it to participate in the defense of the area of which it is a part. Any recipient country also must undertake that it will not engage in any act of aggression against any other nation. These undertakings afford adequate assurance to all nations, regardless of their political orientation and whatever their international policies may be, that the arms the United States provides for the defense of the free world will in no way threaten their own security.

I can say that if our aid to any country, including Pakistan, is misused and directed against another in aggression, I will undertake immediately, in accordance with my constitutional authority, appropriate action both within and without the United Nations to thwart such aggression. I would also consult with the Congress on further steps.

The United States earnestly desires that there be increased stability and strength in the Middle East, as it has desired this same thing in other parts of the free world. It believes that the aspirations of the peoples in this area for maintaining and developing their way of life and for realizing the social advances close to their hearts will be best served by strength to deter aggression and to reduce the fear of aggression. The United States is prepared to help in this endeavour, if its help is wanted.

## ANNEXURE 6

Letter from Prime Minister Jawaharlal Nehru to President Eisenhower delivered with a covering note from Indian ambassador G.L. Mehta in Washington to the US president on 27 May 1955; in Eisenhower Library, Abilene, Kansas, Whitman Files, International Series.

My Dear Mr. President:

I have the honour to convey the following message from my Prime Minister:

Dear Mr. President:

I have received from Krishna Menon, on his return today from Peking his report on his talks with Prime Minister Chou En-lai and others. His visit to Peking was in response to an invitation from the Chinese Prime Minister and he went there on our behalf.

2. While we were *not* speaking on behalf of any country or government, we have at the same time felt that we have contacts with and friendship of the main parties concerned, namely United States and China, and some knowledge of their respective positions. This as well as recent developments in respect of this problem on both sides also encouraged the belief that ways of fruitful negotiations could be found.

3. The decision of the United States Government to remove restrictions on some 58 Chinese students now in the United States, of which Krishna

Menon was informed after his talks with Secretary of States Dulles in March last and the impression that he formed then which reported to me, also encouraged the belief that progress towards peaceful approach and solutions should be attempted.

4. The recent talks in Peking have led me to the belief that steps both to reduce tension and to pave the way for negotiation can be established and the desire to bring about this exists.

5. Progress was made in regard to the main issues integral to the solution of the problem, namely:
   (a) reduction of tensions and definite steps towards this end.
   (b) findings of a basis for negotiation acceptable to both sides.
   (c) progressive steps and procedures for bringing about negotiations.

6. If after discussion the progress made in this direction appears acceptable to the United States, then advance towards solutions will become possible.

7. The Chinese Government have decided to release four of the United States airmen of the Fischer Group (led by Capt. Harold Fischer) 'as a first step' and as a contribution to easing tension. Announcement of this will be made on the evening of the 30th May. Until then this decision is secret and this communication to you is made on that basis. This decision with regard to the four airmen paves the way for the further and final solution of this issue and the return of the United States nationals including the airmen, in a reasonably short period, therefore, appears possible, given goodwill.

8. Progress has been made in regard to the abstention from the use of force pending negotiations and while negotiations continue. This is a distinct gain.

9. The talks have been private and it is the understanding that this character should be maintained. It is my hope that by informal and private talks between you Mr. President and your Secretary of State, we may be able to communicate more fully and to pursue the useful purpose on a friendly basis the progress made in Peking. I hope, therefore, subject to your approval, it will be possible without delay to engage in informal conversations in Washington. I express the hope that as a result of further endeavours in this way progress towards a peaceful settlement will be made.

Mr. President, I assure you of my best wishes and high regard.
Jawaharlal Nehru. Ends.
With my high regards and esteem,

Yours sincerely,

G L Mehta

## ANNEXURE 7

Telegraphic memorandum from Counsellor Frederick P. Bartlett in New Delhi to the Department of State, 7 December 1956, recommending the approach President Eisenhower should take in negotiating with Indian Prime Minister Jawaharlal Nehru during the latter's forthcoming visit to the US. In Department of State, Central Files, 033.9111/12-756.

. . . Nehru, therefore, comes to Washington in a sensitive position of weakness. He and his advisers know that they have fumbled internationally, that UK no longer represents acceptable alternative leadership to US, and that they are in grave economic difficulties. As consequence, we feel opportunities for personal diplomacy are offered President which could start process of our filling vacuum resulting from loss of prestige by USSR and UK, of assisting India in her unquestioned determination to build democratic counterpoise to Red China, and of securing greater Indian sympathy with free world, and especially US political objectives. We feel overall objective of talks should be to lay foundation for anchoring India more firmly to West and of orienting Indian external policy in directions which will, in turn, permit American public opinion and Congress to support India by lines of credit substantial enough to assure Indian capacity and confidence in keeping abreast of China by democratic norms.

In context of his problems and disappointments with USSR and China, we feel Nehru would be more amenable to frank, friendly discussion our problems than he might have been in past. He is perhaps less sure and hence will be more sensitive. We feel his economic problem may perhaps be uppermost in his mind . . . (suggest President raise development issues early with Nehru). If this approach were taken, we feel Nehru would be more tractable on some larger political issues on which we probably cannot agree now and that talks would be cast in framework of a positive policy toward which both countries could work while narrowing their differences. Additionally, we feel there is another crucial factor which should govern President's attitude toward Nehru's sensitivities and biases in areas where he and Nehru must now obviously agree to disagree – China, Pakistan, military bases and pacts, nuclear tests. This factor is that Nehru and present governing team in India is perhaps as able and as Western-oriented, and certainly as committed to democratic norms, as any team India is likely to produce for some years after Nehru's passing.

Despite presence Chou En-lai in India, we have information from Mrs Dutt, wife of FS (Indian Foreign Secretary Subimal Dutt), that India gravely worried about Chinese motivations and moves and suspects that Pakistan and China may in some fashion connive against Indian interests. Nehru, of course, is not convinced that Pakistan is arming against USSR or China. It

237

would be well to repeat Secretary's assurance to Nehru in March that US would come to Indian assistance if attacked by Pakistan. It would be better if Nehru could be convinced that US could prevent attack. Mention might be made that it is better for US to be ally of Pakistan than for some other military power.

Difficulty of justifying American policy to Nehru is that he believes so firmly that Chinese Communists could be 'morally contained' more effectively if moral conscience of world focused on them through membership in UN. President should certainly explain our tedious efforts to obtain no-use-of-force commitment Chi Coms in Formosa Strait. Our case against Red China's use of hostages to further its international policies should be stressed.

Information to be sought from Nehru: 1. Underlying rationale for India's policy of non-alignment: Here, and against context of preparing American opinion and Congress for possibilities of long-term economic assistance, President should, we think, frankly discuss with Nehru the difficulty of providing large-scale assistance to India until and unless American opinion convinced that India and US are somewhat closer together on political problems and objectives.

2. Underlying rationale for Nehru's faith in Panch Shila, so recently disregarded by USSR.

3. Evidences that India is aware of Chinese danger along her northern border and Chinese threat of subverting Nepal and Burma. We believe Nehru highly conscious and worried on these scores and sees parallel between USSR and Yenan and Red China and Nepal and Burma.

Conclusions: We feel strongly that 'moment of history' has arrived which if seized and exploited, can give US much firmer anti-Communist and anti-Red China counterpoise in India. We can, as it were, redress our emphasis in Europe and on the periphery of Asia by more firmly consolidating our position with Indian land power. We think this should be possible without prejudicing our NATO and other pact relationships. If India were convinced of our enduring interest in seeing her through the critical years ahead, India might be expected to ameliorate some of her present objections to American policy, especially as regards Pakistan, SEATO, the Baghdad Pact. Risks are involved but it appears to us that the risks are greater of losing India through failure to exploit the opportunities now presented.

# ANNEXURE 8

Note given by the People's Republic of China Foreign Office to the Indian Counsellor, Beijing, 10 July 1958, Ministry of External Affairs, **Notes, Memoranda, and Letters exchanged and Agreements signed between the Governments of India and China 1954–1959** (NMLAIC), White Paper No.I, New Delhi, Government of India, 1959, pp. 60–62.

The Ministry of Foreign Affairs of the People's Republic of China presents its compliments to the Embassy of the Republic of India in China and has the honour to state as follows regarding the exigency of the stepped up subversive and disruptive activities against China's Tibetan region carried out by the United States and Chiang Kai-shek clique in collusion with fugitive reactionaries from Tibet using India's Kalimpong as a base.

Since the peaceful liberation of the Tibetan region of China, reactionaries who have fled from Tibet to the Kalimpong area have been carrying on subversive and disruptive activities against China's Tibetan region under the instigation and direction of the United States and the Chiang Kai-Shck clique and in collusion with local reactionaries in Kalimpong. On his visit in (sic) India at the end of 1956 Premier Chou En-lai called the attention of the Government of India and His Excellency the Prime Minister Nehru to this question. His Excellency the Prime Minister Nehru indicated at the time that if the Chinese Government could produce evidence in this regard, the Government of India would take action. Later, on 12th January 1958 Premier Chou En-lai referred again to this question in an interview with Ambassador B.K. Nehru. On 22nd January 1958 the Ministry of Foreign Affairs delivered to the Indian Embassy in China samples of a reactionary propaganda leaflet sent to Tibet from Kalimpong which it had collected.

According to reliable material available to the Chinese Government the American-Chiang Kai-shek clique and local special agents and Tibetan reactionaries operating in Kalimpong have recently stepped up their conspiratorial and disruptive activities against the Tibet region of China. Using Kalimpong as a base they are actively inciting and organising a handful of reactionaries hidden in Tibet for an armed revolt there in order to attain the traitorious aim of separating the Tibet region from the People's Republic of China. The Chinese Government would like hereby to convey to the Government of India certain information concerning the activities of the above said special agents and reactionaries in Kalimpong as follows:

(1) Chief among Tibetan reactionary elements who have fled China are Gyalodenju, Shakapa, Losangjanzan, Thubten Nobo, Alohrze and Luka-niona (sic). In collusion with American-Chiang Kai-shek clique and local special agents in Kalimpong they frequently hold meetings in Kalimpong

and other Indian cities to plan disruptive activities against Tibet. Gyalodenju has been to the United States in 1951. At the instance of the United States Thubten Nobo made a special trip from the United States to India in the winter of 1956 to take part in the conspiratorial moves of the other Tibetan reactionaries.

(2) Under the manipulation of Gyalodenju and others, various reactionary organisations have been set up in Kalimpong under such names as 'Tibetan Freedom League', 'Kalimpong Tibetan Welfare Conference', and 'Buddhist Association'. These organisations are used to collect information from Tibet, carrying out reactionary propaganda against Tibet and expanding reactionary forces etc.

(3) There is openly published in Kalimpong the 'Tibetan Mirror' a reactionary newspaper hostile to the Chinese Government and people. The Tibetan reactionaries and the organisations under their control also printed various reactionary leaflets and other propaganda material and smuggled them into Tibet. Such newspapers and propaganda material spread vicious rumours and slanders against the Chinese Government, the Chinese Communist Party and the Chinese People's Liberation Army and fabricated all sorts of lies, moreover attempted to sow discord between the Han and the Tibetan nationalities of China, between the Chinese Central Government and the Tibetan local authorities as well as between Dalai Lama and Panchen Lama. Some of the propaganda material even openly called on the Tibetan people to rise up against the Chinese Government and advocated the separation of Tibet from China. Gyalodenju, Shakapa, Losangjanzan and others wrote to the Lamas of the three big monasteries in Tibet to entice them to participate in their subversive activities.

(4) Taking advantage of the fact that Kalimpong is situated near Tibet and that few formalities are required for travel across the India-China Tibet region border, the Tibetan reactionaries and Americans, Chiang Kai-shek clique and local special agents in Kalimpong have continuously dispatched agents and saboteurs to Tibet to contact the hidden reactionaries there. They smuggle weapons and ammunition into Tibet in preparation for armed revolt.

The Chiang Kai-shek clique has special agents and organisations in Kalimpong. Among the leading agents is one called Yeh Cheng-yung. They also use Kalimpong as a base to collect intelligence from Tibet, smuggle arms and despatch agents into Tibet and incite riots in Tibet. They maintain a close contact with the Tibetan reactionaries in Kalimpong and provide Gyalodenju with important maps of Tibet for military use.

The conspiratorial and disruptive activities against the People's Republic of China, carried out by the above-said Americans, Chiang Kai-shek clique and local special agents and Tibetan reactionaries in Kalimpong cannot but engage the Chinese Government and people and put them on the alert. The

Chinese Government regards the criminal activities of the above-said reactionaries and special agents as a direct threat to China's territorial integrity and sovereignty and yet another malicious scheme of United States imperialists to create tension in Asia and Africa. It cannot be overlooked that in using Indian territory adjacent to China to perpetrate disruptive activities against the People's Republic of China, the American and Chiang Kai-shek clique special agents have also the hideous object of damaging China-India friendship. In order to shatter the underhand schemes of United States imperialists, defend China's territorial integrity and sovereignty and safeguard China-India friendship, the Chinese Government hereby requests the Government of India to repress the subversive and disruptive activities against China's Tibet region carried out in Kalimpong by American and Chiang Kai-shek clique special agents. China and India are co-initiators of the five principles of peaceful co-existence, to uphold and propagate which the Government of India has made unremitting efforts. The Chinese Government is confident that the Government of India, pursuing a consistent policy of defending peace and opposing aggression, will accept its request and take effective measures.

10 July 1958

## ANNEXURE 9

Note sent by the Ministry of External Affairs to the Embassy of China, New Delhi, 2 August 1958, Ministry of External Affairs, **Notes, Memoranda and Letters exchanged and Agreements signed between the Governments of India and China 1954–1959**, White Paper I, New Delhi, Government of India, 1959, pp. 63–65.

The Ministry of External Affairs of the Government of India presents its compliments to the Embassy of the People's Republic of China and, with reference to the Note handed over on July 10, 1958, by His Excellency Lo Kwe Po, Vice-Minister of the People's Republic of China, to Shri K.M. Kannampilly, Charge' d'Affaires of the Embassy of India at Peking, has the honour to state as follows:

2. As the Government of the People's Republic of China are aware, the Government of India attach the highest importance to friendly relations between India and China. This friendship is traditional and was emphatically reaffirmed in the agreement which was entered upon by the two Governments in 1954. This agreement enunciated the famous five principles which the Government of India faithfully follows in the relations with China as with all other countries. The Government of India recognize that the Tibetan region is part of the People's Republic of China.

3. The Government of India were therefore greatly surprised by the note which the Government of the People's Republic of China handed over to the Indian Charge' d'Affaires at Peking on July 10. They regret to say that the statements contained in this note must have been based on a complete misunderstanding of facts. The Government of India have no evidence that the United States Government and the Kuomintang regime are using Kalimpong as a base for disruptive activities against China's Tibetan region. The Government of India will never permit any portion of its territory to be used as a base of activities against any foreign Government, not to speak of the friendly Government of the People's Republic of China.

4. As the Government of the People's Republic of China must be aware, from time immemorial, there has been inter-communication between India and the Tibet region of China through passes on the northern frontier of India. In fact, for centuries the only feasible outlet for that region was through India. Movement of people between India and Tibet was free and easy. Most of the people living in the Tibet region of China (hereafter referred to as Tibetans) who enter India come here either as traders or pilgrims. This fact was recognised in the 1954 agreement between India and the People's Republic of China. Many Tibetans have been settled in north-eastern India for years. The Government of india have made it clear to all Tibetans that they will be permitted to stay in India only if they carry on their vocations peacefully.

5. The Government of the People's Republic of China have mentioned six persons by name in their note as among those who are carrying on anti-China activities on Indian territory. Some of these persons have already been warned that if their activities, political or other, are such as to have adverse effect on the relations between India and China, the Government of India will take the severest action against them. The Government of India have no definite evidence that these persons have been indulging in unfriendly activities. Even so, the Government of India propose to warn them again.

6. In their note, the Government of the People's Republic of China state that various reactionary organisations have been set up in Kalimpong under different names. Enquiries made by the Government of India reveal that no organisations or associations with the names mentioned in the note are functioning in Kalimpong. So far as the Government of India are aware, there are two associations in Kalimpong of people who formerly lived in the Tibet region of China namely, the Tibetan Association and the Indian Tibetan Association. The first named association has been in existence for about twenty five years, the second was formed in september 1954. The aims and objects of both these associations are religious, cultural and social, such as promoting study of Buddhism or rendering medical aid to Tibetans, arranging their funeral rituals etc. The Government of India are not aware

that these two associations have been indulging in any undesirable activities such as those mentioned in the Chinese Government's note.

7. The Government of the People's Republic of China refer to a newspaper named the 'Tibetan Mirror'. There is no daily or weekly newspaper of that name published in Kalimpong. A monthly periodical called the 'Tibetan Mirror' is published there. The editor of this newspaper is not a Chinese but an Indian national. The Government of India have noted with displeasure that some of the articles published in this periodical are objectionable and calculated to affect the friendly relations between India and China. The law in India is, however, such that it is not easy to take executive or legal action against newspapers and periodicals of this character. There are other newspapers in India which severely criticize other friendly Governments. In fact, strong criticisms are voiced by some newspapers against the Government of India themselves. However, the Government of India are most anxious that an unimportant magazine like the 'Tibetan Mirror' should not adversely affect the relations between our two friendly countries and are directing their local officers to administer a severe warning to this periodical. If it continues to create mischief, the Government of India will take whatever other action is feasible.

8. The Government of the People's Republic of China have stated in their note that taking advantage of the liberal travel regulations across the border of India and the Tibet region of China near Kalimpong, weapons and ammunition have been smuggled into Tibet by Tibetan reactionaries, the Americans and followers of the Kuomintang regime. Both the Government of the People's Republic of China and the Government of India have got Customs Posts and Check Posts on this border. Officers of the Posts under the Government of India have got strict instructions to be particularly vigilant regarding the possible smuggling of articles like arms and ammunition which are contraband according to Indian law. No case of such smuggling of arms and ammunition has been detected by these Indian Check Posts in the locality.

9. The Government of the People's Republic of China have, in their note, referred to the photostat copy of a leaflet in Tibetan language handed over by them to the Indian Embassy at Peking. Though this leaflet was handed over on the 22nd January 1958, the date of its publication given at the bottom is 17 December 1956. This was the time when all manner of people from Tibet came to India in connection with the Buddha Jayanti celebrations and the visit of His Holiness the Dalai Lama. At about this time the Prime Minister of India discussed the entire situation in the Tibet region of China and other relevant matters with the Premier Chou En-lai. The Government of India did not, therefore, attach any great importance to the circulation of this particular leaflet in December 1956. It is mentioned at the bottom of this leaflet that it was issued by the 'Tibetan Welfare

Association'. It has already been stated earlier in this note that, according to the Government of India's information, no association with this name is functioning in Kalimpong.

10. The Government of the People's Republic of China have stated that there are special agents of the Kuomintang regime in Kalimpong. Their note, however, mentions only one name, namely, Yeh Cheng-yung. The Government of India have not been able to trace any such individual in Kalimpong and a preliminary examination of their records shows no visa to enter India has been issued to any individual of that name. Even so, the Government of India are pursuing their enquiries and will communicate the results later to the Embassy of the People's Republic of China at New Delhi.

11. The Government of India reiterate their friendship for the people and the Government of the People's Republic of China. They have no doubt that the Chinese Government's note is based on misinformation and express the hope that, in the light of the facts now mentioned, the Government of the People's Republic of China will feel assured that India does not and will not permit any activities on its territory directed against the People's Republic of China and the Government of India are determined to take action under the law of the country against those who indulge in any such illegal activities.

The Ministry of External Affairs of the Government of India takes this opportunity of renewing to the Embassy of the People's Republic of China the assurances of its highest consideration.

2 August 1958

## ANNEXURE 10

Memorandum Prepared in the Central Intelligence Agency, **REVIEW OF TIBETAN OPERATIONS,** Washington, 25 April 1959, Eisenhower Library, Abilene, Kansas, Whitman File, Intelligence Matters (9).

### REVIEW OF TIBETAN OPERATIONS

1. *Background.* The international legal status of Tibet has been a question for decades. China has made sporadic invasions into Tibet and, in recent history, has made constant attempts to affirm her right of suzerainty over Tibet, which she claims to have inherited from the Ching Dynasty.

a. The Chinese Communist attitude towards Tibet is that Tibet is politically a part of China as a result of historic military conquest.

b. Tibet, on the other hand, has sought complete independence, although in 1951 the Tibetans and the Dalai Lama under duress signed an agreement recognizing Chinese Communist suzerainty over Tibet.

c. The British and the United States have long recognized Chinese suzerainty over Tibet but only on the understanding that Tibet was to be regarded as autonomous.

d. Since 1948, the Government of India has appeared to give tacit acceptance to the suzerainty status of Tibet. This was reaffirmed in 1951(sic) through the joint declaration with Peking which announced mutual agreement to the five principles of peaceful coexistence publicised as the 'Panchshila'.

e. The Tibetans, particularly the Khambas, Goloks and other tribes of East Tibet, are a fierce, brave and warlike people. Battle in defense of their religion and the Dalai Lama is looked upon as a means of achieving merit towards their next reincarnation.

f. The greater part of the terrain in Tibet, and especially in the centers of active resistance in the east, is exceedingly rugged, with few established lines of communications. To add to the problems of the Chinese Communists, the area is unable to support a large occupation force and almost all supplies must be brought overland or by air.

[*9 paragraphs (3 pages of source text) not declassified*]

a. In may 1956 the Dalai Lama visited India as a guest of the Indian Government upon the occasion of the 2500th anniversary of the Buddhist religion. During this visit the Dalai Lama appealed to the Indian government for support of the anti-Communist resistance in his country, but this appeal was rejected.

[31 *lines of source text not declassified*]

[10 *paragraphs (5 pages of source text) not declassified*]

8. Later intelligence from [*less than 1 line of source text not declassified*] Tibet – the last message was received today, April 25 – reports that the Tibetan resistance in the South has been heavily engaged and decimated, and is tragically short of food and ammunition.

## ANNEXURE 11

Letter from President John F. Kennedy to President Mohammad Ayub Khan, Washington, 28 October 1962, Department of State, **Central Files, 691.93/10-2862.**

Dear Mr. President:

I was heartened by your response to my message on the Cuban Crisis that was delivered to you by Ambassador McConaughy. In times like these, the support of friends and allies has a personal, as well as a political, significance.

245

We see another instance of Communist aggression almost as close to your borders as Cuba is to ours – the Chinese Communist attack on India. It also concerns me greatly. The Chinese have moved quickly, with large forces to take territory beyond that immediately in dispute; it is no longer a border wrangle. In my judgment, the long-run significance of this move cannot be exaggerated. The Chinese Communists, having established themselves on the near slopes of the Himalayas, will have secured a favorable position for further aggression. Thus they will put themselves in a politically dominant posture vis-a'-vis India. But I think this will be more than counter-balanced if their aggression has the effect of awakening India to the dangerous intentions of the Peiping regime, and turning the attention of the Indian Government and people to their true long-run security interests. These are interests which we all share. Certainly the United States as a leader of the free world must take alarm at any aggressive expansion of Communist power, and you as the leader of the other great nation in the subcontinent will share this alarm.

Unfortunately, press comment in Pakistan has already produced a negative reaction in India. This is particularly distressing at a time when a unique opportunity exists for laying the basis for future solidarity.

We now intend to give the Indians such help as we can for their immediate needs. We will ensure, of course, that whatever help we give will be used only against the Chinese. You, on your part, are in a position to make a move of the greatest importance which only you can make. This is to signal to the Indians in a quiet but effective way that the concerns – which you know I think totally unjustified – that have led them to maintain the greater part of their military power on their borders with you, should be put aside in the present crisis. Perhaps an effective way would be a private message from you to Nehru. You can tell him that he can count on Pakistan's taking no action on the frontiers to alarm India. No possible outside aid can increase the ability of the Indians to withstand the Chinese offensive as much as a shift in their own dispositions.

Knowing the history of Kashmir, I do not make this suggestion lightly, but in the hope and belief that the painful moments which India is now experiencing will teach them how much more important the threat from the North is to the whole of the subcontinent than any regional quarrels within it. Our own recent experience with the response of our Latin American neighbors when they were confronted with the Soviet threat in Cuba gives me ground for this belief. Action taken by you now in the larger interests of the subcontinent will do more in the long run to bring about a sensible resolution of Pakistan-Indian differences than anything else I can think of.

Further, I am sure that the lesson of such a change in Indian dispositions would not be lost on the Peiping regime. Communism has always advanced in the face of disunity in the free world. This crisis is a test of the vision of all of us, our sense of proportion and our sense of the historic destiny of the free nations.

With warmest personal regards,

Sincerely, John F. Kennedy

## ANNEXURE 12

Letter from President Mohammad Ayub Khan to President John F. Kennedy, (Rawalpindi) 5 November 1962 (delivered on 12 November), Department of State, **Central Files, 791.56/11-1362.**

From: Field Marshal Mohammad Ayub Khan, N.Pk., H.J.
5th November, 1962

Dear Mr. President,

I am grateful to you for your kind message of October 28, 1962, which was delivered by your Ambassador.

For the last fifteen years, India has posed a major military threat to Pakistan. She has built up her forces, may I say, mainly with American and British equipment three to four times our strength and has openly declared that Pakistan is her enemy number one.

Eighty per cent or more of her Armed Forces have already been earmarked against us and the bulk of them remain concentrated on our borders on ten days' state of readiness. We have been exposed to these aggressive designs all these years simply because the Indian Prime Minister himself is not prepared to honour his pledge in regard to so many agreements and especially in regard to the solution of Kashmir in which Pakistan is vitally interested for profound economic and security reasons. Therefore, by and large, we have spent these fifteen years in a state of mobilization which has been forced upon us by India. On top of all this, the recent conflict between India and China has led to developments of grave concern to us.

However, our own information, although meagre, leads us to believe that Chinese intention seems to be to occupy the territory which they believe belongs to them and over which there has been a dispute between her and India. Even Mr. Nehru thought it fit in his wisdom to declare in the Indian Parliament in 1954 with reference to the Chinese position in Tibet that 'I am not aware of any time during the last few hundred years when Chinese sovereignty, or if you like suzerainty, was challenged by any outside country. All during this period, whether China was weak or strong,or whatever the Government of China was, China always maintained its claim to sovereignty over Tibet . . . The British Empire in the days of Lord Curzon had expanded into and made several types of arrangements in

247

Tibet. Now it is impossible or improper for us to continue any such arrangements . . . These maps and treaties are all prepared by British Imperialists. These treaties and maps are intended to show that we must act as they did.'

Militarily, however, we do not believe that China can bring to bear against India her major forces through the difficult terrain of the Himalayas to achieve decisive results, and even if she has any such intention the way to do it would be to outflank India through Burma. In our opinion, that would be a simpler way of doing it and in cost it would be cheaper. If the Chinese intentions were more than limited and they were to expand into the territories of Assam, we would have as much cause for concern as India, as our East Pakistan would be directly affected. We are making this appreciation about the actual situation in no light hearted mood.

Why has such a situation developed on this sub-continent and around India? We believe that this is the direct outcome of distorted and fallacious thinking on the part of Mr. Nehru and his associates and a consequence of a baseless foreign policy that he has been following. This foreign policy has been based on the following factors:

(a) bend backwards to appease Communism;

(b) hoist the white flag of Neutralism to appease Communism and get other wavering nations to join him in order to be able to create a world nuisance value for themselves;

(c) intimidate and threaten Pakistan in order to politically isolate it and economically weaken it; and

(d) abuse the West, and especially the U.S.A., in season and out of season.

The events have proved that all that is happening to Mr. Nehru is the direct consequence of this warped thinking. We have been warning and pointing to this all along.

Mr. President, what you now ask of us is to give an assurance to Mr. Nehru of a kind that will enable him to deploy his troops at present concentrated against us elsewhere. I am surprised that such a request is being made to us. After all, what we have been doing is nothing but to contain the threat that was continuously posed by India to us. Is it in conformity with human nature that we should cease to take such steps which are necessary for our self-preservation? Or, will our own people ever accept such a position?

According to our information, India has withdrawn an infantry division and a half away from us but there are definite indications that they are moving forward their reserve armoured formations of one division and one brigade to battle locations against Pakistan. Similarly they now have a corps headquarters to control troops deployed against East Pakistan. The bulk of their Navy, barring a couple of small vessels, have been concentrated in

248

Bombay harbour, ostensibly for refit but in reality to pose a threat to us. Under no stretch of imagination, Mr. President, can these moves be described as indications of peaceful intentions towards us by India. So, how can we, in a situation like this, be expected to show our friendship to them!

No, Mr. President, the answer to this problem lies elsewhere. It lies in creating a situation whereby we are free from the Indian threat, and the Indian are free from any apprehensions about us. This can only be done if there is a settlement of the question of Kashmir. This matter is sometimes stated as very difficult to resolve. I do not agree with that. I believe that if there is a change of heart on the part of India, it should not be difficult to find an equitable and an honourable settlement.

Our object is to have peace, and especially with our neighbours. I am very grateful for the assurance you have given that the arms you are now supplying to India will not be used against us. This is very generous of you, but knowing the sort of people you are dealing with, whose history is a continuous tale of broken pledges, I would not ask a friend like you to place yourself in an embarrassing situation. India's conduct over the question of Junagadh, Mangrol, Hyderabad, Kashmir and Goa should be well-known to you. Our belief is that arms now being obtained by India from you for use against China will undoubtedly be used aganst us at the very first opportunity. However, in the light of the promise that you were good enough to make, namely, that we shall be consulted before you gave any military assistance to India, we did expect to be consulted and also informed as to the types and the quantities of weapons and equipment which are now in the process of being supplied to them. It is regrettable that none of this has been done.

I would also like to draw your attention to the fact that although India today poses as an aggrieved and oppressed party, in reality she has been constantly threatening and intimidating, in varying degrees, small neighbouring countries around her. Let me assure you that in the eyes of many people in free Asia, Indian intentions are suspect and the Indian image as a peace-loving nation has been destroyed.

You have referred, Mr. President, to press comments in Pakistan. While we have endeavoured to restrain expression of extremist views in our newspapers, it is not possible to interfere with the freedom of the press which reflects the real sentiment of the people. It must be realised that public opinion is gravely exercised by the new developments as the result of arms aid to India, more so, as India continues to pose a serious threat to our security. I am afraid it is going to be extremely difficult for my Government to discount public opinion.

With kind regards, Yours sincerely,

Mohammad Ayub Khan

## ANNEXURE 13

Letter From President John F. Kennedy to President Mohammad Ayub Khan, Washington, 22 December 1962, Department of State, **Central Files, 690D.91/12-2262**.

Dear President Ayub:

Thank you for your two letters of December 17. I will answer you separately on the matter of the Tarbela Dam after I have had a chance to hear the views of my advisors on this difficult and complex problem.

I have reviewed your other letter with Prime Minister Macmillan at Nassau. After a full discussion of the problems created by the Chinese Communist aggression against India, we have come to what seems to us a prudent course of action at this time to meet the challenge – a course of action which is in the best interests of the Free World. We agreed on a reasonable and frugal program of military assistance designed solely to enable India to defend itself better should the Chinese Communists renew their attacks at an early date.

To deny India the minimum requirement of defense would only encourage further Chinese Communist aggression, an aggression whch we both see as posing as grave an ultimate threat to Pakistan as to India. Therefore, the supply of arms for this purpose should not be made contingent on a Kashmir settlement. Beyond this stage, however, we will certainly take any one-sided intransigence on Kashmir into account as a factor determining the extent and pace of our assistance.

The Prime Minister and I are fully conscious of the great opportunity that now exists for the settlement of this major issue within the Free World. As you know our primary concern is the long-range defense of the subcontinent within the context of our global strategy. No single step could contribute as much to the security of the subcontinent as the resolution of the Kashmir problem. Despite the probably painful and time consuming process required, we look forward with confidence to real progress in the ministerial discussions which lie ahead.

Ambassador McConaughy, who participated in all the deliberations, will give you a full account of the meetings in Washington and Nassau.

With warm personal regards,

Sincerely, John F. Kennedy

## ANNEXURE 14

Letter From President John F. Kennedy to Prime Minister Jawaharlal Nehru, Washington, 22 December 1962, Department of State, **Central Files, 691.93/12-2262.**

Dear Mr. Prime Minister:

I have thought a great deal about the problems of the defense of the subcontinent since I received your letters of December 8 and 10, 1962. Ambassador Galbraith has been here and we have had several good talks. I discussed these problems with Prime Minister Macmillan at some length in Nassau.

Prime Minister Macmillan and I reviewed the urgent problems caused by the Chinese Communist threat to the subcontinent and what best we could do to strengthen India's defenses. On the particular problem of air defense, we propose to send at an early date a joint UK-US team for full explorations with you and your people.

We also discussed what the subcontinent can do to direct its energies more fully toward its defense. We were both greatly encouraged by the historic decision by India and Pakistan to take up in direct talks the great problems which separate you. Protracted and time consuming as these talks may have to be, we were confident that you and President Ayub will be able to work out solutions. Nothing could contribute more to the security and progress of the subcontinent.

I have asked Ambassador Galbraith to go over these matters with you in some detail.

Sincerely,

John F. Kennedy

# Notes

## Preface

1 The lower house of the Indian parliament.
2 Pandit Jawaharlal Nehru in the Lower House of Parliament, New Delhi, 12 June 1952, cited in the Government of India, **Loksabha Debates**, Vol.II, Part II, Loksabha Secretariat, New Delhi, 1952, Colms. 1668–9. Emphasis added.
3 Vernon Marston Hewitt, **The International Politics of South Asia**, Manchester University Press, Manchester, 1992, p. 66.

## Introduction

1 Bruce Loudon, 'Ganges "Poisoned" by CIA', **The Daily Telegraph**, London, 14 April 1978; Richard Wigg, 'Delhi knew of nuclear device spying on China', **The Times**, London, 18 April 1978; Bruce Loudon, 'Desai Admits India-US plot for Spy Device in Himalayas', **The Daily Telegraph**, London, 18 April 1978; Charles Holley, 'Height of Embarrassment for India', **The Scotsman**, Edinburgh, 21 April 1978.
2 Morarji Desai cited in Bruce Loudon, **The Daily Telegraph**, 18 April, op cit.
3 ''60s Radar Plan in India Cited', **The International Herald Tribune**, New York, 20 April 1978.
4 M L Kotru, 'New twist in Himalay spy saga', **The Sunday Times**, London, 21 May 1978.
5 A number of Latin American states had gained independence over a century before India and Pakistan did, but the latter were the first successor states where post-colonial authority was transferred to native middle classes.
6 The context in which NSC-68 was formulated is described in Henry Kissinger, **Diplomacy**, London, Simon & Schuster, 1994, p. 463.
7 Department of State, **United States Relations with China** [With special reference to the period 1944–1949], Washington, D.C., Office of Public Affairs, 1949, p. 940.
8 Ibid., p. 942.
9 Ibid., p. 945–6.
10 Ibid., p. 946.
11 Ibid., pp. 1050–51.

## Chapter One: The Early Treaties

1 United States of America and India: Agreement on the continued use of Indian air-space and ground facilities by aircraft of the United States National Military Establishment and crew on a Special Mission basis. Department of State, **United States Treaties and other International Agreements** (USTIA) **1951**, Vol.2, Part 2, Washington, D.C., USGPO, 1952, pp. 568–572. [see Appendix 1]

2 Of the Viceroy's Executive Council, effectively pre-independence India's cabinet.

3 There is nothing in this letter to suggest that six weeks prior to Partition, the US ambassador knew anything about Karachi becoming the capital of Pakistan; nor was there any such indication in Nehru's response dated 5 July 1947.

4 USTIA 1951 , Vol.2, Part 2, op cit., pp. 570–572.

5 Nehru's note to Grady, New Delhi, 22 April 1948, paragraph 3; cited in **USTIA 1951**, ibid., pp. 573–574.

6 Office of Strategic Services, a wartime special operations group which became a principal precursor of the CIA.

7 The American Charge' d'Affaires ad interim's note to the Indian Minister for External Affairs and Commonwealth Relations, New Delhi, 3 May 1948; cited in **USTIA**, op cit., p. 574.

8 In his capacity as 'the Indian Minister for External Affairs'.

9 Loy Henderson to Jawaharlal Nehru, New Delhi, 2 July 1949, cited in Department of State, **USTIA**, Vol.3, Part 1, Washington, D.C., USGPO, 1952, pp. 575–576.[See Appendix 2]

10 Ibid.

11 Ibid.

12 The senior-most permanent civil servant/diplomat in the Ministry of External Affairs.

13 John Foster Dulles was the Secretary of State under President Eisenhower; his brother Allen Dulles was the Director, Central Intelligence.

14 Ilia Tolstoy, 'Across Tibet from India to China', **National Geographic Magazine**, 90;2: 1946, pp. 169–222.

15 This concern was reflected in the UK Foreign Office Telegram 371/93002.IOLR L/P&S/12/4229 Ext.731/43, London, 1943, India Office Library.

16 George Merrell to the Secretary of State, New Delhi, 9 December 1946, Main Decimal File (1945–1949), Box 7024, 893.00 **Tibet/12–946**,National Archives, Diplomatic Branch, Washington, D.C. Office of Intelligence Research, Department of State, **Tibet**, No.4731, 19 July 1948, USGPO, Washington, D.C.

17 Donovan cited in Department of State, **Foreign Relations of the United States 1943** (FRUS) – **China**, Washington, D.C., USGPO, 1967, p. 626.

18 George R Merrell, cited in **FRUS 1947**, Vol.VII, (The Far East: China), Washington, D.C., USGPO, 1972, pp. 588–592.

19 Ibid.

20 Ibid.

21 A number of accounts of this period exist. Two of the more useful ones are, A Tom Grunfeld, **The Making of Modern Tibet**, London, Zed Books, London & M E Sharpe, New York, 1987; and a revised edition, 1996; Tsering Wangdu Shakya, **The Dragon in the Land of Snows: A History of Modern Tibet since 1947**, Pimlico, London, 1999.

22 DuPre Jones (Ed.), **China: US Policy Since 1945**, Washington, D.C., Congressional Quarterly Inc., 1980, p. 89.

23 National Security Council (NSC), 'NSC-68: United States Objectives and

Programs for National Security', **FRUS 1950**, Vol.I, Washington, D.C., USGPO, 1976, p. 240.

24 Tsering Shakya, op cit., p. 68, citing Chinese sources.

25 Zhou En-lai quoted in the Summary of World Broadcasts (SWB), the BBC, London, 1950, No.77, pp. 39–40.

26 George C. McGhee for the Secretary of State to the Pakistani Ambassador, Washington, D.C., 29 November 1950, **USTIA 1950**, Vol.1, Department of State, Washington, D.C., USGPO, 1952, pp. 884–885. [See Appendix 3]

27 Ibid.

28 Ibid.

29 Ibid.

30 The Pakistani Ambassador to the Assistant Secretary of State, Washington, D.C., 15 Decmber 1950, **USTIA 1950**, op cit., pp. 885–6 [See Appendix 3]

31 Jawaharlal Nehru quoted in Foreign Office telegraph FO 371-84457, cited in Shakya 1999, op cit., p. 23.

32 B N Mullik, **My Years with Nehru: The Chinese Betrayal**, New Delhi, Allied Publishers, 1971, p. 64.

33 Excerpted from the Government of India's protest note to the Central People's Government of China, **The Times**, London, 3 November 1950. The Times reports that this note was sent on 26 October. However, the then Director of the Indian Intelligence Bureau, B N Mullik, op cit., is more likely to have been correct about the dates.

34 Mullik, ibid., pp. 64–65.

35 The Central People's Government of the People's Republic of China to the Government of India, Beijing, 30 October 1950, **The Times**, London, 3 November 1950, and also, Mullik, ibid.

36 Ibid. Also see **The Manchester Guardian**, Manchester, 3 November 1950.

37 Report in the **Yorkshire Post**, cited in Grunfeld, 1987, op cit., p. 101.

38 'Peking's fear of Intrigue', **The Daily Telegraph**, London, 31 October 1950.

39 Sardar Patel to Nehru, New Delhi, 7 December 1950, cited in Premen Addy, 'British and Indian Strategic Perceptions of Tibet', in Robert Barnett and Shirin Akiner (Eds.), **Resistance and Reform in Tibet**, London, C Hurst and Co., 1994, pp. 41–42; also see Mullik, op cit., pp. 115–122.

40 Mullik, ibid., pp. 122–124.

41 Ibid., pp. 80–81.

42 Government of India to the Central People's Government of the People's Republic of China, New Delhi, 31 October 1950. **The Times**, London, 3 November 1950.

43 Nehru in the Loksabha, New Delhi, 7 December 1950, Government of India, **Parliament of India – Official Report**, Vol.VI, Part II, New Delhi, Loksabha Secretariat, nd, colms.1376–7.

44 United States and India: Exchange of Notes Constituting an Agreement relating to Mutual Defence Assistance, Washington, D.C., 7 and 16 March 1951. (Registered with the United Nations by the United States of America on 14 October 1952), **United Nations Treaty Series** (UNTS), Vol.141, New York, 1952,pp. 47–53. [See Appendix 4]

45 Acting Secretary of State James E. Webb to Ambassador Vijaya Lakshmi Pandit, Washington, D.C., 7 March 1951, in ibid.

46 Ambassador Pandit's reply dated 16 March 1951, in ibid.

47 Mullik, op cit., p. 71.

## Chapter Two: Histrionics in the High Himalayas

1 The Foreign Bureau of the Government of Tibet, Lhasa, to Mao Ze-dong, Chairman of the Chinese Communist Party, Beijing, November 1949, cited in Michael C. van Walt van Praag, **The Status of Tibet: History, Rights and Prospects in International Law,** Boulder, Colorado, Westview Press, 1987, pp. 89–90.

2 Much of this correspondence is recorded in the Department of State, **Foreign Relations of the United States** (FRUS) **1950,** Vols. VI and VII, Washington, D.C., 1976

3 Shakabpa Wangchuk Deden, **A Political History of Tibet,** Kalimpong, (privately published), 1976, p. 420; cited in Tsering W Shakya, 'The Genesis of the Sino-Tibetan Seventeen Point Agreement of 1951', unpublished monograph, London, 1997, p. 3.

4 Many accounts of the campaign, Tibetan, Chinese and Western, exist. The figures are from van Praag, op cit., p. 142. Also see Shakya, 1999, op cit., pp. 43–45.

5 Tsipon Shakabpa in Reuters interview in October 1950, cited in telegraph from British mission in Calcutta to the Foreign Office in London, in file FO 371–84469, Public Record Office (PRO), Kew.

6 Editorial in the **People's Daily,** 17 November 1950, Beijing, cited in Shakya, op cit., p. 4.

7 van Praag, op cit., p. 145.

8 Department of State, Washington, D.C., to British Embassy, Washington, D.C., Aide-Memoire, 30 December 1950; FRUS 1950, Vol.VI, op cit., p. 613.

9 The negotiations and their juridical implications are described in van Praag, op cit., pp. 147–155.

10 Preamble to the Agreement of the Central People's Government and the Local Government on Tibet on Measures for the Peaceful Liberation of Tibet, cited in Union Research Institute, **Tibet, 1950–1967,** Document 6, Hong Kong, 1968, pp. 19–23. [See Annexure 1]

11 See the US Consul-General's cables from Calcutta to the Department of State, no. 793B.00/7-152 dated 1 July 1952, and no.793B.11/9-1052 dated 10 September 1952. In Department of State, **FRUS 1952–1954,** Vol.XIV, Part I, Washington, D.C., USGPO, 1985, pp. 73, 96.

12 Dean Acheson to the US mission in New Delhi, 2 June 1951, in **FRUS 1951,** Vol.VII, Part II, Washington, D.C., USGPO, 1984, pp. 1694–1695.

13 Unsigned letter from the US mission in India to the Dalai Lama, quoted in full in **FRUS 1951,** ibid., pp. 1744–1745 [See Annexure 2].

14 Jamyang Norbu, 'The Tibetan Resistance Movement', in Robert Barnett and Shirin Akiner (Eds.), **Resistance and Reform in Tibet,** London, C. Hurst & Co., 1994, op cit., p. 190.

15 Ibid., pp. 191–192.

16 NSC Staff study on US Objectives, Policies and Courses of Action in Asia, Annexure 2 to NSC 48/5, Washington, D.C., 17 May 1951, in Department of State, **FRUS 1951,** Vol.VI, Part I, Washington, D.C., USGPO, 1977, pp. 61–62.

17 Ibid., p. 61.

18 Ibid., p. 62.

19 Conversation between Foreign Secretary Bajpai and Counsellor Steer quoted in **FRUS 1951,** Vol.VII, Part II, Washington, D.C., USGPO, 1984, p. 1692.

20 Department of State, **FRUS 1952–1954,** Vol.XIV, Part 1, Washington, D.C., USGPO, 1985, p. 8–9.

21 Ibid., p. 10.

22 General Hoyt S. Vandenberg, JCS, to Secretary of Defence, Washington D.C., 4 March 1952, in **FRUS 1952–1954**, Ibid., p. 18.
23 Chester Bowles to Department of State, telegram-793.00/4-952, Delhi, 9 April 1952, in **FRUS 1952–1954**, ibid., pp. 29–31.
24 Acheson to Bowles, telegram DEPTEL-2399, no.611.93/4-1152 Washington, D.C., 25 April 1952, in ibid., p. 47.
25 The US Charge' in Delhi to the Department of State, telegram no.691.93/6-1252, 12 June 1952, in **FRUS 1952–1954**, ibid., pp. 63–66.
26 Chester Bowles to State, Telegram-793.00/7-752, Delhi, 7 July 1952, in ibid., pp. 73–76.
27 Tsering Wangdu Shakya, **The Dragon in the Land of Snows: A History of Modern Tibet since 1947**, London, Pimlico, 1999, pp. 102–103.
28 Department of State memorandum no.611.93B/5-1452, Washington, D.C., 14 May 1952, in **FRUS 1952–1954**, op cit., pp. 51–52.
29 Ibid.
30 US Consul-General, Calcutta, to State, telegram no.793B.00/7-152, 1 July 1952; in **FRUS 1952–1954**, ibid, p. 73. In his message, the Dalai Lama said what the review in Washington had reported, ie, that dissent was widespread, the Tibetans were optimistic about their eventual success against the PLA, that the food situation in Lhasa was very bad, and that 90 per cent of the 10,000 Chinese soldiers in Lhasa were poorly fed and badly clothed conscripts. The Consul had sent letters to the Dalai Lama in July 1951 and August 1951. See the Consul-General's Despatch 21, Calcutta, to State, 16 July 1951, in **FRUS 1951**, Vol.VII, Part II, p. 1753; and Consul-General's telegram 121, Calcutta, to State, 16 August 1951, in **FRUS 1951**, ibid., p. 1791.
31 US Consul-General, Calcutta, to State, telegram no. 793B.11/9-1052, 10 September 1952, in **FRUS 1952–1954**, op cit., p. 96.
32 Department of State, memorandum no.611.93/3-1953, Washington, D.C., 19 March 1953, ibid., pp. 159–160.
33 H.P. Jones, Taipei, to Department of State, telegram no.611.90/6-1853, 18 June 1953, ibid., p. 206.
34 Ibid.
35 Department of State memorandum no. 611.93/7-2453, 1 July 1953, in **FRUS 1952–1954**, ibid, pp. 223–224.
36 Chester Bowles to State, telegram 293.1111/8-252, 2 August 1952, in **FRUS 1952–1954**, Vol.XIV, Part I, 1985, op cit., p. 76.
37 Secretary of State, Washington, D.C., telegram 293.1111/11-752, to US Embassy, Delhi, 7 November 1952, in **FRUS 1952–1954**, ibid., pp. 114–115.
38 'Statement of Policy by the NSC', NSC 166/1, 6 November 1953, S/S-NSC Files, lot 63D351, NSC 166 Series, in ibid., pp. 278–306.
39 Ibid., p. 282.
40 Ibid., pp. 301–302.
41 Ibid., p. 305.
42 'United States Objectives and Courses of Action with Respect to Formosa and the Chinese National Government', NSC 146/2, 6 November 1953, S/S-NSC Files, lot 63D351, NSC 146 Series, in **FRUS 1952–1954**, op cit., pp. 307–330.
43 Ibid., p. 308.
44 Ibid., p. 329.
45 'Memorandum of Discussion at the 177th Meeting of the National Security Council', Washington, D.C., 23 December 1953, drafted by S Everett Gleason, Eisenhower Library, Abilene, Kansas, Eisenhower Papers, Whitman File; also in **FRUS 1952–1954**, op cit., pp. 345–349.

## Chapter Three: The Kashmir Fallout

1 The most 'traditional' separatist group, the Jammu & Kashmir Liberation Front (JKLF), has proclaimed itself as a 'secular' political organisation seeking independence of the state. Other, more 'Islamic' groups such as the Hizbul Mujahedeen (army of religious warriors/crusaders) seek the establishment of an Islamic order in Kashmir in close association with if not integration into Pakistan. Thirteen disparate organisations are joined in an umbrella organisation called the All-Party Hurriyat Conference (APHC) which has emerged as the representative body of the insurrectionists, although the degree of APHC's influence with component militias varies widely.

2 Alastair Lamb in Michael Diamond, **History Today: Kashmir**, a radio documentary for the BBC World Service, London, 14 August 1995.

3 The name Pakistan was coined to represent Punjab, Afghana (Frontier Pathans), Kashmir, Sind and Baluchistan. Eastern Bengal elected to join much later.

4 Two works explaining the background are both by Alastair Lamb, **Kashmir: A Disputed Legacy**, Hertingfordbury, Herts., Roxford Books, 1991; and **Birth of a Tragedy: Kashmir 1947**, Hertingfordbury, Herts., Roxford Books, 1994. The Pakistani arguments are mustered in the Government of Pakistan, **White Paper on the Jammu & Kashmir Dispute**, Islamabad, Ministry of Foreign Affairs, 1977. Indian authors have published numerous books on the dispute. Perhaps the most enlightening and yet intriguing of these is Durga Das (Ed.), **Sardar Patel's Correspondence 1945–1950**, Vol.I, **New Light on Kashmir**, Ahmedabad, Navajiban Publishing House, 1971. Also see, S Mahmud Ali, 'South Asia: The Perils of Covert Coercion', in Lawrence Freedman (Ed.), **Strategic Coercion: Concepts and Cases**, Oxford, Oxford University Press, 1998, ch.10.

5 See, for instance, Department of State, **United States Treaties and Other International Agreements** (USTIA) **1950**, Vol.I, Washington, D.C., USGPO, 1952, pp. 383–389, 630–637; and **USTIA 1951**, Vol.II, Part I, USGPO, 1952, pp. 425–429, 875–879

6 Ambassador B.R. Sen, Washington, D.C., to Finance Minister Chintaman Deshmukh, Delhi, letter no. 9-Amb.Washington/52 dated 11 January 1952, recorded in **Cabinet Secretariat file no.F.14(1)-ECC/52**, pp. 4–6, Indian National Archives, New Delhi. (See Annexure 3)

7 Ibid.

8 Ibid.

9 W.R. Natu in an appendix to Ambassador B.R. Sen's letter to the Finance Minister, ibid., p. 7.

10 To underscore this point, Nehru wrote to Mohammad Ali in early November 1953, 'I had suggested that the plebiscite should be for the State as a whole and the detailed result of the plebiscite would then be the major factor for the decision to be taken. That detailed result will give us a fairly clear indication of the wishes of the people not only in the State as a whole but in different areas. Obviously, one cannot go by that completely, because some absurd result might follow. Any boundary,which is to be an international frontier,must take into consideration a number of other factors. It must be geographical, clear and suitable from a number of other important points of view.' Jawaharlal Nehru, in Government of India, **Kashmir: Meetings and Correspondence between the Prime Ministers of India and Pakistan**, White Paper, New Delhi, Ministry of External Affairs, not dated, p. 40.

11 Jawaharlal Nehru to Mohammad Ali, Delhi, letter dated 9 December 1953, in

Kashmir: Meetings and Correspondence between the Prime Ministers of India and Pakistan, ibid., pp. 44–46.

12 Nehru to Ali, Delhi, letter dated 18 January 1954, in A Appadorai, **Select Documents on India's Foreign Policy and Relations 1947–1972**, Vol.II, Delhi, Oxford University Press, 1985, pp. 256–257.

13 Eisenhower to Nehru, 24 February 1954, in Ministry of External Affairs, **Ministry of External Affairs Report** (MEAR) – **1953–1954**, New Delhi, Government of India, 1955, pp. 51–52. (See Annexure 4)

14 Ibid., p. 52.

15 'Text of a Statement by President Eisenhower', 25 February 1954, in Ministry of External Affairs, **MEAR 1953–1954**, ibid., pp. 53–54. (See Annexure 5)

16 Nehru to Eisenhower, 28 February 1954, in A Appadorai, **Select Documents on India's Foreign Policy and Relations 1947–1972**, Vol.I, New Delhi, Oxford University Press, 1985, p. 264.

17 Nehru in the lower house of parliament on 1 March 1954, cited in Appadorai, ibid., p. 267.

18 Nehru to Mohammad Ali, 5 March 1954, **Kashmir: Meetings and Correspondence between the Prime Ministers of India and Pakistan**, op cit., pp. 70–72.

19 Nehru in a speech in New Delhi on 14 April 1956, cited in **The Hindu**, Madras, 15 April 1956.

20 Preamble to the 'Agreement between the Government of India and the Central People's Government of China on Trade and Cultural Relations between India and the Tibet Region of China', Beijing, 29 April 1954, in the Government of India, **Foreign Policy of India-Texts of Documents 1947–1964**, Third Edition, New Delhi, Loksabha Secretariat, 1966, pp. 198–206 (See Appendix 5)

21 Ibid., pp. 204–205.

22 Jawaharlal Nehru in parliament, 15 May 1954, cited in the Government of India, **Loksabha Debates**, Vol.V, Part II, New Delhi, Loksabha Secretariat, 1955, colms. 7495–7496.

23 Ibid., colms.7496–7497.

24 Nehru in New Delhi, 26 June 1954, quoted in the Government of India, **India's Foreign Policy: Selected Speeches September 1946-April 1961, Jawaharlal Nehru**, New Delhi, 1961, Ministry of Information and Broadcasting, pp. 306–7.

25 Mutual Defence Assistance Agreement between the Government of the United States of America and the Government of Pakistan, Karachi, 19 May 1954., in Department of State, **United States Treaties and other International Agreements** (USTIA), Vol.5, Part 1, 1954, Washington, D.C., USGPO, 1955, pp. 854–858. (See Appendix 6)

26 Nehru cited in Ambassador George Allen to State, telegram 790.00/7-1754, Delhi, 17 July 1954, in Department of State, **FRUS 1952–1954**, Vol.XIV, Part I, Washington D.C., 1985, USGPO, pp. 498–499.

27 Radhakrishnan cited in ibid., pp. 499–500.

28 In his memorandum 793.5/3-2054-WDS of 27 August 1954, to the Assistant Secretary of State for Far Eastern Affairs, the Assistant Secretary of State for Near-Eastern, South Asian and African Affairs wrote about Indian unhappiness with US collective security efforts tying Pakistan, SEATO and Taiwan. The latter felt if the US went on to sign a defence agreement with Formosa, 'Indians friendly to the United States might lose power.' **FRUS 1952–1954**, ibid., p. 551.

29 CIA, National Intelligence Estimate NIE-43-54 dated 14 September 1954, INR-NIE files, cited in ibid., p. 639.

30 Secretary of State's report, NSC-PPS files, lot 65 D 101 "China", Washington, D.C., 28 October 1954, in ibid., p. 810.

31 Memorandum by the Joint Strategic Survey Committee to the Joint Chiefs of Staff, 611.93/10-2954, Washington, D.C., 29 October 1954; para 4, NSC 166/1 of same date, in **FRUS 1952–1954**, ibid, pp. 819–820,836.
32 National Security Council memorandum NSC-5429/2, 29 October 1954, in ibid., p. 835.
33 National Security Council policy proposal NSC 5429/4, Washington, D.C., 10 December 1954, S/S-NSC files, lot 63 D 351, NSC 5429 series, in ibid., p. 1011.
34 National Security Council policy proposal NSC 5441, Washington, D.C., 28 December 1954, S/S-NSC files, lot 63 D 351, NSC 5441 series, in ibid., pp. 1052–1053.
35 B.N. Mullik, **My Years with Nehru: The Chinese Betrayal**, New Delhi, Allied Publishers, 1971, pp. 178–180. Mullik was the first Indian to head the Indian Intelligence Bureau to be appointed by the post-1947 government. A close confidante of Nehru, his revelations scandalised the Delhi establishment.
36 Nehru cited in Mullik, ibid., pp. 180–181.
37 Ibid., p. 183.
38 Ibid., pp. 183–184.
39 Department of State memorandum 611.95 A 241/12-354, New York, 3 December 1954, in **FRUS 1952–1954**, op cit., pp. 985–987; also see US Charge' d'Affaires' telegram to State, 611.95 A 241/12-1354, Delhi, 13 December 1954, in ibid., pp. 1027–1028.

## Chapter Four: Covert Collaboration in Diplomacy and War

1 Pakistan-US Mutual Security: Defence Support Assistance. Agreement signed at Karachi, 11 January 1955, Department of State, **United States Treaties and other International Agreements** (USTIA) **1955, Vol.6, Part I, Washington, D.C., USGPO, 1956, pp. 501–506.** (See Appendix 7)
2 National Security Council, United States Policy toward Formosa and the Government of the Republic of China, NSC 5503, Department of State, S/S-NSC files: Lot 63 D 351, NSC 5503 Series, Washington, D.C., 15 January 1955, in **Foreign Relations of the United States (FRUS) 1955–1957, Vol.II, USGPO, 1986, pp. 30–34.** Among the courses of action specified by the NSC was 'Continue covert operations'.
3 Winthrop W. Aldrich to State, London, 3 February 1955, Department of State, Central Files, 793.5/2-355, in **FRUS 1955–1957**, ibid., pp. 200–201.
4 Jawaharlal Nehru cited in ibid., p. 202.
5 John Sherman Cooper to State, New Delhi, 1 May 1955, Department of State, Central Files, 793.00/5-155, in **FRUS 1955–1957**, ibid., pp. 536–538.
6 **The New York Times**, New York, 1 May 1955.
7 Cooper to State, New Delhi, 30 May 1955, Department of State, Central Files, 791.13/5-3055, in **FRUS 1955–1957**, Vol.II, ibid., p. 590.
8 Hugh S. Cumming to Department of State, Telegram 2044, 'Djakarta', 26 April 1955; a similar message was repeated by the US ambassador in Karachi in Karachi telegram no.1771 to State, after Ali's return from Bandung; in **FRUS**, ibid, p. 534.
9 Secretary of State J.F. Dulles to the Embassy in Pakistan, Washington, D.C., 30 April 1955, Department of State, Central Files, 793.00/4-2655, in ibid., pp. 534–535. Perhaps the most prominent supporter of US policies among Pakistan's civilian politicians, Ali lost Prime Ministership in August 1955.
10 Nehru to Eisenhower, in G.L. Mehta to President Eisenhower, Washington, D.C., 27 May 1955, in the Eisenhower Library, Abilene, Kansas, Whitman Files,

International Series; also, Department of State, Central Files, 611.93/5-2755, in **FRUS**, ibid., pp. 574–575. (See Annexure 6).

11 Department of State to Embassy in Delhi, Telegram-1901, Washington, D.C., 27 May 1955, Department of State, Central Files, 611.95A241/5-2755; also **FRUS**, ibid., p. 578.

12 John Foster Dulles to Jawaharlal Nehru, Washington, D.C., 29 May 1955, Department of State, Lot 66 D 204, Eisenhower/Dulles Correspondence with Prime Minister Nehru; also in **FRUS**, ibid., p. 580.

13 William J. Sebald to John Foster Dulles, Washington, D.C., 10 June 1955, Department of State, Central Files, 033.9111/6-1055, in ibid., pp. 589–591.

14 Memorandum of a conversation, Washington, D.C., 14 June 1955, Department of State, Central Files, 611.91/6-1455, in ibid., pp. 594–595.

15 Memorandum of a conversation, Washington, D.C., 14 June 1955, Department of State, Central Files, 793.00/6-1455, in ibid., pp. 595–602.

16 General memorandum of Conversation, New York, 15 June 1955, Eisenhower Library, Abilene, Kansas, Dulles Papers, Personal and Private; also ibid., pp. 603–604.

17 Memorandum of a conversation between the President and the Secretary of State, San Francisco, 19 June 1955, drafted on 20 June 1955, Eisenhower Library, Abilene, Kansas, Dulles Papers, 'Meetings with the President', Personal and Private; also in ibid., p. 605.

18 Memorandum of a conversation between the Secretary of State and the British Foreign Secretary, San Francisco, 20 June 1955, in **FRUS 1955–1957**, Vol.II, ibid., pp. 605–606.

19 Memorandum of a conversation, Washington, D.C., 1 July 1955, Department of State, Central Files, 790.00/7-155, in ibid., pp. 622–626.

20 Memorandum of a conversation, Washington, D.C., 6 July 1955, Department of State, Central Files, 790.00/7-655, in ibid., pp. 631–637.

21 Entry in President Eisenhower's diary, Washington, D.C., 6 July 1955, in the Eisenhower Library, Abilene, Kansas; also in **FRUS**, ibid., p. 637.

22 Eisenhower to Nehru, Washington, D.C., 7 July 1955, Department of State, Central Files, 711.11-E1/7-755, in **FRUS**, ibid., pp. 637–639.

23 Nehru to Eisenhower, Cairo, 11 July 1955, Department of State, Central Files, 611.93/7-1155, in ibid., pp. 644–645.

24 Eisenhower to Nehru, Washington, D.C., 12 July 1955, Department of State, Central Files, 611.93/7-1255, in ibid., p. 647.

25 **FRUS 1955–1957**, Vol.II, ibid., p. 678.

26 Michel Peissel, **Cavaliers of Kham: The Secret War in Tibet**, London, William Heinemann Ltd., 1972, pp. 54–55.

27 **The New York Times**, New York, 28 August 1954.

28 **The Manchester Guardian**, Manchester, 2 September 1954; **The New York Times**, 19 September 1954.

29 **The New York Times,** 21 October 1954

30 Peissel, op cit., pp. 60–61.

31 Gompo Tashi Andrugtsang, **Four Rivers, Six Ranges: Reminiscences of the Resistance Movement in Tibet**, Dharamsala, Information and Publicity Office of H.H. The Dalai Lama, 1973, pp. 74–75; also see Jamyang Norbu, 'The Tibetan Resistance Movement and the Role of the C.I.A.' in Robert Barnett and Shirin Akiner (Eds.), **Resistance and Reform in Tibet**, London, C Hurst & Co., 1994, p. 194.

32 A Tom Grunfeld, **The Making of Modern Tibet**, London, Zed Books, 1987, pp. 128–129.

33 Ibid.
34 See Appendices 1 and 2.
35 Christopher Robbins, **The Invisible Airforce: The Story of the CIA's Secret Airlines**, London, Macmillan, 1979, p. 81.
36 Ibid., pp. 84, 94.
37 Ibid., p. 96.
38 Jawaharlal Nehru, **India's Foreign Policy: Selected Speeches September 1946-April 1961**, New Delhi, Publications Division, Ministry of Information & Broadcasting, Government of India, 1961, p. 102.
39 Operations Co-ordination Board's Progress Report, 30 March 1956, Department of State, S/S-NSC Files: Lot 63 D 351, NSC-5409, Washington, D.C., in **Foreign Relations of the United States** (FRUS) **1955–1957**, Vol.VIII, USGPO, 1987, pp. 1–13.
40 Ibid., pp. 4–5.
41 Herbert Hoover to John Foster Dulles, New Delhi, 9 March 1956, Department of State, Conference Files: Lot 62 D 181, CF 679, in ibid., pp. 460.
42 Ibid., pp. 5–6.
43 Ibid., p. 13.
44 United States of America and Pakistan: Mutual Defence Assistance Agreement effected by signature on a note to the Pakistani Minister of Foreign Affairs and Commonwealth Relations from the United States Ambassador to Pakistan. Karachi, 15 March 1956; in **United States Treaties and other International Agreements** (USTIA) **1956**, Vol.7, Part 3, Department of State, Washington D.C., USGPO, 1957. (See Appendix 8)
45 Ibid.
46 Counsellor Arthur Z. Gardiner's memorandum of a conversation, Karachi, 9 July 1956, Department of State, Karachi Embassy Files: Lot 64 F 16, 361.1
47 Ibid.
48 **FRUS 1955–1957**, Vol.VIII, op cit., pp. 20–21.
49 Eisenhower quoted in ibid., pp. 25–26.
50 Ibid., pp. 26–27.
51 Krishna Menon cited in US mission at the UN, telegram to Department of State, Central Files, 690 D.91/1-1057, New York, 10 January 1957, **FRUS 1955–1957**, ibid., pp. 107–110.
52 Menon cited in telegram from Lodge to State, New York, 11 January 1957, Department of State, Central Files, 690 D.91/1-1157, in ibid., pp. 110–111.
53 Ibid., p. 111.
54 Ibid.
55 Frederik P. Bartlett to State, New Delhi, 7 December 1956, Department of State, Central Files, 033.9111/12-756, in **FRUS 1955–1957**, Vol.VIII, ibid., pp. 320–325. (See Annexure 7)
56 Ibid., p. 325.
57 Jawaharlal Nehru, **India's Foreign Policy: Selected Speeches September 1946-April 1961**, New Delhi, 1961, op cit., pp. 597–599.
58 NSC-5701, Washington, D.C., 10 January 1957, in **FRUS 1955–1957**, Vol.VIII, op cit., pp. 29–43.
59 Michael C. van Walt van Praag, **The Status of Tibet: History, Rights and Prospects in International Law**, Boulder, Colorado, Westview Press, 1987, p. 162.
60 Mao Tse-tung, 'On the Correct Handling of Contradictions Among the People', speech delivered in Beijing, 27 February 1957, cited in Department of State memorandum, Central Files, 793.11/6-2057, Washington, D.C., 20 June 1957; in **FRUS 1955–1957**, Vol.III, USGPO, 1986, pp. 549–552.

61 Allen Dulles cited in the Minutes of the 327th meeting of the National Security Council, Washington, D.C., 20 June 1957, in NSC Records, Whitman Files (drafted on 21 June 1957), at the Eisenhower Library, Abilene, Kansas.
62 Operations Coordination Board (OCB) Report, Washington, D.C., 3 July 1957, Department of State, OCB Files: Lot 62 D 430-India, in **FRUS 1955–1957**, Vol.VIII, op cit., pp. 353–354.
63 Christian Herter to State, Seoul, 16 September 1957, Department of State, Central Files, 110.12-HE/9-1657,
64 National Intelligence Estimate, NIE 13-2-57, Washington D.C., 3 December 1957, Department of State, INR-NIE Files, in **FRUS 1955–1957**, Vol.III, op cit., pp. 649–653, especially p. 652.
65 Robert McClintock, **Policy Review**, Department of State, PPS Files: Lot 67 D 548, China, Washington, D.C., 31 December 1957.

## Chapter Five: War Clouds Gather

1 Delhi based its claims on the McMahon Line which ran along the Himalayan crest-line broadly on the watershed principle, agreed on by British and Tibetan delegates in March 1914 and confirmed by the Shimla Convention, initialled on 3 July 1914 by British, Tibetan and Chinese representatives, but never signed or ratified by the Chinese authorities. A map showing this delineation is appended to Ministry of External Affairs (MEA), **Notes, Memoranda, and Letters Exchanged Between the Governments of India and China** (NMLAIC), **September-November 1959**, White Paper No.II, New Delhi, Government of India, 1959. The Chinese, on the other hand, based their claims on the very much older Chien Lung Line which showed the Kalimpong-Darjeeling region of Sikkim and the Tawang Tract in Assam as part of Tibetan, and hence, in Beijing's view, Chinese, territory. It was not until the PLA's occupation of Tibet that Delhi moved its own civil and paramilitary administration into these regions. See Memorandum of Conversation between George K.C. Yeh, Ambassador of the Republic of China, Walter Robertson, Assistant Secretary of State for Far Eastern Affairs, and LaRue R. Lutkins, Director for Chinese Affairs, in Washington, D.C., on 23 April 1959, Department of State, Central Files, 793B.00/4-2359, cited in Department of State, **Foreign Relations of the United States** (FRUS), **1958–1960**, Vol.XIX, Washington, D.C., USGPO, 1992, pp. 756–757.
2 Note from the American *Charge' d'Affaires ad interim* to the Minister for External Affairs of India, New Delhi, 16 April 1958, in 'United States of America and India: Exchange of Notes Constituting an Agreement for Assurances regarding Mutual Defense Assistance', in the United Nations, **United Nations Treaty Series** (UNTS), Vol.358, New York, 1959, pp. 77–81. (See Appendix 9)
3 Note Verbale handed by the MEA to the Chinese Counsellor in India, New Delhi, 2 July 1958, cited in MEA, **Notes, Memoranda, and Letters exchanged and Agreements Signed between the Governments of India and China 1954–1959** (NMLAIC), White Paper No.I, New Delhi, Government of India, 1959, p. 22.
4 Note Verbale handed by the Chinese Counsellor in India to the MEA, New Delhi, 2 August 1958, in NMLAIC, ibid., p. 23.
5 MEA note to the Chinese embassy in India, New Delhi, 8 August 1958, in ibid., pp. 24–25.
6 Note given by the People's Republic of China Foreign Office to the Indian Counsellor, Beijing, 10 July 1958, in ibid., pp. 60–62. (See Annexure 8)

7 Ibid., p. 62.

8 Ibid.

9 Note sent by the Ministry of External Affairs to the Embassy of China, New Delhi, 2 August 1958, cited in NMLAIC, op cit., pp. 63–65. (See Annexure 9)

10 Ibid.

11 Ibid., p. 65.

12 Statement made by the Chinese Amabassador to the Indian Foreign Secretary, New Delhi, 3 August 1958, in NMLAIC, ibid., p. 66.

13 Note given by the Ministry of External Affairs to the Counsellor of China in India, New Delhi, 21 August 1958, in NMLAIC, ibid., p. 46.

14 Memorandum given by the Foreign Office of China to the Counsellor of India in Beijing, 3 November 1958, in ibid., pp. 28,47.

15 Note from the Indian Ambassador in Beijing to the Vice-Minister of Foreign Affairs, China, Beijing, 8 November 1958, in ibid., p. 29.

16 Note handed to the Chinese Counsellor in Delhi by the Ministry of External Affairs, New Delhi, 10 December 1958, in NMLAIC, ibid., pp. 30–32.

17 Prime Minister Jawaharlal Nehru to Premier Zhou En-lai, 14 December 1958, New Delhi, in NMLAIC, ibid., pp. 48–51.

18 The Foreign Secretary, Ministry of External Affairs of India (S. Dutt), to the American Ambassador (Ellsworth Bunker), New Delhi, 17 December 1958, in 'United States of America and India: Exchange of notes constituting an agreement for assurances regarding mutual defense assistance', New Delhi, 16 April and 17 December 1958, **UNTS**, Vol.358, op cit., pp. 77–81. (See Appendix 9)

19 Letter from the Prime Minister of China to the Prime Minister of India, 23 January 1958, Beijing, in NMLAIC, op cit., pp. 52–54.

20 United States of America and Pakistan: Cooperation-Agreement signed at Ankara on March 5, 1959; Entered into force, March 5, 1959, in Department of State, **United States Treaties and other International Agreements** (USTIA) **1959**, Washington, D.C., USGPO, 1960, pp. 317–319. (See Appendix 10)

21 Ibid., Article I.

22 A collection of several regional and local militias under the command of their own warlords, the NVDA had by the summer of 1958 coalesced into a better-organised, trained and armed band with the CIA's assistance and partly under some supervision of Indian Intelligence. Gompo Tashi Andrugtsang, the guerrilla leader who emerged as perhaps the best known among his peers and the commander of the largest group, writes of a meeting of the *Chushi Gangdruk* on 16 June 1958 at which the various factions were united under the banner of the Volunteer Freedom Fighters, the VFF; see Andrugtsang, **Four Rivers, Six Ranges: Reminiscences of the Resistance Movement in Tibet**, Dharamsala, Information & Publicity Office of H.H. The Dalai Lama, 1973, p. 62. However, the more formal name used by the Resistance's supporters in Delhi and Washington was the National Volunteer Defence Army, the NVDA.

23 Ibid., pp. 72–74.

24 B.N. Mullik, **My Years with Nehru: The Chinese Betrayal**, New Delhi, Allied Publishers, 1971,p. 214. However, Andrugtsang says that 'the existence of our freedom fighters base in Trigu Thang had become widely known and for reasons of security, we deemed it prudent to disperse our forces and divide them into three groups. Our new headquarters were set up in Tsona.' Op cit., p. 68. The strength of the Tibetan resistance in the autumn of 1958 is cited in Michael C van Walt van Praag, **The Status of Tibet: History, Rights and Prospects in International Law**, London, Wisdom Publications, 1987, p. 162

25 Mullik, ibid., p. 216.

26 A Tom Grunfeld, **The Making of Modern Tibet**, London, Zed Books, 1987, p. 152.

27 Andugtsang, op cit., p. 96.

28 David Howarth (Ed.), **My Land and My People: The Autobiography of HIS HOLINESS THE DALAI LAMA**, London, Panther Books, 1964; and Tenzin Gyatso, the Fourteenth Dalai Lama of Tibet, **Freedom in Exile**, London, Hodder & Stoughton, 1990.

29 The CIA's Tibetan operations were considered so sensitive that even in the mid-1990s, the Agency refused to release any documentation connected to these. Citing exemptions to the Freedom of Information Act designed to protect 'information concerning intelligence sources and methods', the CIA rejected requests to transfer copies of 'records that would reveal a covert connection between the CIA and the subject'. Cited from J. Wright's letter F94-1312 dated 19 July 1994 on behalf of the CIA to the author.

30 Gyatso, op cit., p. 144 (in the Sphere Books edition, 1991)

31 Ibid., p. 149. A brief account of the CIA's air-support to the NVDA using C-130 sorties out of Thailand, East Pakistan and India appears in Christopher Robbins, **The Invisible Air Force: The Story of the CIA's Secret Airlines**, London, Macmillan, 1979, pp. 94–101.

32 Ibid.,p. 154. Also see T. Allman, 'Cold wind of Change', **The Guardian**, London and Manchester, 19 December 1973.

33 Gyatso, Ibid., pp. 155–156.

34 Jawaharlal Nehru to the Dalai Lama, New Delhi, n.d.,1959, cited in ibid., p. 158.

35 Jawaharlal Nehru to Zhou En-lai, New Delhi, 22 March 1959, **NMLAIC**, op cit., pp. 55–57.

36 Ibid., pp. 56–57.

37 Jawaharlal Nehru in the *Loksabha*, 30 March 1959, Loksabha Secretariat, **Loksabha Debates**, Second Series, Vol.XXVIII, Government of India, New Delhi, 1960, cols.8514-8521. Emphasis added.

38 Statement by the Foreign Secretary to the Chinese Ambassador, New Delhi, 26 April 1959, **NMLAIC**, op cit., pp. 68–69.

39 Jawaharlal Nehru in the *Loksabha*, 27 April 1959, **Loksabha Debates**, op cit., Second Series, Vol.XXX, cols.13493–13503.

40 Ibid.

41 Statement made by the Chinese Ambassador to the Foreign Secretary, New Delhi, 16 May 1959, in **NMLAIC**, op cit., pp. 73–76.

42 Ibid., p. 76.

43 Minutes of a Meeting in Washington, D.C., cited in the Department of State, **Foreign Relations of the United States** (FRUS), **1958–1960**, Vol.XIX, Washington, D.C., USGPO, 1992, p. 756.

44 Chris Mullin, 'How the CIA went to war in Tibet', **The Guardian**, London, 19 January 1976.

45 Memorandum of Conversation, Washington, 23 April 1959, Department of State, **Central Files, 793B.00/4-2359**.

46 Memorandum Prepared in the Central Intelligence Agency, **Review of Tibetan Operations**, Washington,nd (however, concluding paragraph of text dates the review on 25 April 1959), filed with a covering memorandum dated 27 April 1959 from CIA Executive Officer J.S. Earman and retained in the Eisenhower Library, Abilene, Kansas, Whitman File, Intelligence Matters (9). (See Annexure 10)

47 Gyatso, op cit., pp. 210–211.

48 Memorandum of Conversation, Washington, 29 April 1959, Department of State, **Central Files, 793B.00/4-2959.**

49 Marion W. Boggs, **Minutes of the 404th Meeting of the National Security Council,** Washington, D.C., 30 April 1959, the Eisenhower Library, Abilene, Kansas, Whitman File, NSC Records; also see **FRUS 1958–1960,** Vol.XIX, op cit., p. 762.

50 Ibid.

51 Acting Secretary of State Douglas Dillon to President Eisenhower, **Message from the Dalai Lama,** Washington, 30 April 1959, Eisenhower Library, Abilene, Kansas, Whitman File, International File. A handwritten notation by the President's aide and son John Eisenhower on the source text reads 'Briefed to President 2 May 59. JSDE.'

52 Allen W. Dulles, Memorandum from Director of Central Intelligence to President Eisenhower, **Dalai Lama's Request for Supplies for the Tibetan Resistance,** Washington, 7 May 1959, Central Intelligence Agency, DCI (Dulles) Files: Job 80 M 01009 A, Box 9, Folder 11, Dulles Correspondence with White House, Jan-June 1959. The initials "DE" on the source text indicate the President's approval. Gordon Gray was President Eisenhower's Special Assistant on National Security.

53 Department of State, Memorandum on the Substance of Discussion at a Department of State-Joint Chiefs of Staff Meeting, Washington, 8 May 1959, **State-JCS Meetings: Lot 61 D 417, Vol.VII.**

54 Ibid.

55 S. Everett Gleason, **Memorandum of Discussion at the 409th Meeting of the National Security Council,** Washington, 4 June 1959, the Eisenhower Library, Abilene, Kansas, Whitman File, NSC Records.

56 Department of Defense, **Memorandum from the Chairman, Collateral Activities Coordinating Group to the Secretary of Defense,** Washington, 15 June 1959, Washington National Records Center, RG 330, OSD Files: FRC 63 A 1574, Tibet 1959.

57 Department of State, **Memorandum From Acting Secretary of State Dillon to President Eisenhower,** Washington, 16 June 1959, Eisenhower Library, Abilene, Kansas, Whitman File, International File.

58 The end of British authority in 1947 saw the 'partition' of the empire into the states of India and Pakistan erected on the bases of mutually exclusive founding principles. Pakistan's *raison d'etre* was the claim that religion, in this instance, Islam, was the source of national identity, and the basis of statehood; that of the Indian Union, on the other hand, was that religion had nothing whatever to do with either national identity or statehood – what mattered were cultural unity, shared historical experience and a sense of belonging together shaped over the centuries. Founded on such contradictory bases, each successor state challenged the validity of the other's legitimacy and were thus born into a philosophical duel to the death. The claim of each to existence was premised on the subversion if not destruction of the other. Amity while pre-partition memories lived on in the collective psyche was an unrealistic goal. Washington, and indeed members of the local elites, did not appear to grasp this. See S Mahmud Ali, **Nation-building and the Nature of Conflict in South Asia: A Search for Patterns in the Use of Force as a Political Instrument,** unpublished Ph.D. thesis, University of London, 1992, pp. 77–81.

59 CIA, **National Intelligence Estimate: The Outlook for Pakistan,** Washington, 5 May 1959, NIE 52–59, paragraph 50.

60 Douglas Dillion, **Memorandum of Conversation,** Washington, 5 May 1959, Department of State, Central Files,791.5-MSP/5-559 (marked 'off the record').

61 National Security Council, **Planning Paper NSC 5701 Series**, Washington, 26 May 1959, Department of State, S/S-NSC Files: Lot 63D 351, paragraph 8.
62 US Ambassador to the Department of State, Telegram 2485, Karachi, 5 May 1959, Department of State, Central Files,790D.5622/5–559.
63 William Rountree, **Memorandum of Conversation**, Washington, 8 May 1959, Department of State, Central Files,790D.5622/5-859, drafted on 12 May 1959.
64 The Pakistani Minister of Foreign Affairs and Commonwealth Relations to the American Ambassador, Karachi, 18 July 1959, in **United States and Pakistan: Establishment of a Communications Unit effected by the exchange of notes; Signed at Karachi on July 18, 1959; Entered into force July 18, 1959. With minute of understanding and exchange of notes**, in Department of State, **USTIA 1959**, Vol.10, Part 2, Washington, D.C., USGPO, 1960, pp. 1366–1381 (See Appendix 11).
65 Douglas Dillon, **Memorandum of Conversation**, Washington, 31 July 1959, Department of State, Central Files,790D.5-MSP/7-3159.
66 Michel Peissel, **Cavaliers of Kham: The Secret War in Tibet**, London, William Heinemann Ltd., 1972, p. 170.
67 Parsons and Walmsley, **Memorandum from the Assistant Secretary of State for Far Eastern Affairs and the Acting Assistant Secretary for International Organization Affairs to Secretary of State Herter**, Washington, 5 August 1959, Department of State, Central Files, 793B.00/8-559.
68 Ibid., citing US Embassy telegram 161, New Delhi, 20 July 1959, Department of State, Central Files, 793B.00/7-1659.
69 National Security Council, **NSC-5909/1**, Washington, 21 August 1959, Department of State, S/S-NSC Files: Lot 63D 351, paragraph 1.
70 Ibid., paragraph 29.
71 Ibid., paragraphs 15, 32.
72 Ibid., paragraph 35.
73 Ibid., paragraphs 49–52.
74 Jawaharlal Nehru in the *Loksabha*, New Delhi, 28 July 1959, Loksabha Secretariat, **Loksabha Debates**, 2nd Series, Vol.XXXIII, 1960, Cols.4793–4800.
75 Ibid.
76 Jawaharlal Nehru in the *Rajyasabha*, New Delhi, 31 August 1959, Government of India, **Rajyasabha Official Records**, Vol.XXVI, 1960, Cols.2281–2287.
77 President Eisenhower to Prime Minister Nehru, Paris, 2 September 1959, Department of State, **Central Files, 711.11-E1/9-259**.
78 Prime Minister of the People's Republic of China to the Prime Minister of India, Beijing, 8 September 1959, NMLAIC, Vol.II, pp. 27–33.
79 Ibid.
80 Prime Minister Jawaharlal Nehru to Premier Zhou En-lai, New Delhi, 26 September 1959, NMLAIC, Vol.II, ibid., pp. 34–52.
81 See, for instance, Telegram From the Embassy in India to the Department of State, New Delhi, 4 September 1959, Department of State, **Central Files,793B.00/9-459**; Telegram From the Embassy in India to the Department of State, New Delhi, 5 September 1959, Department of State, **Central Files,793B.00/9-559**; Memorandum of Conversation, Washington, 5 September 1959, Department of State, **Central Files,793B.00/9-559**; Telegram From the Department of State to the Embassy in India, Washington, 9 September 1959, Department of State, **Central Files,793B.00/9-459**; Telegram From the Delegation to the U.N. General Assembly to the Department of State, New York, 18 September 1959, Department of State, **Central Files,793B.00-1859**; Telegram From the Delegation to the U.N. General Assembly to the Department of State,

New York, 19 September 1959, Department of State, **Central Files, 793B.00/9-1959**; Telegram From the Delegation to the U.N. General Assembly to the Department of State, New York, 28 September 1959, Department of State, **Central Files,793B.00/9-2859**; Telegram From the Department of State to the Embassy in India, Washington, 6 October 1959, Department of State, **Central Files,793B.00/10-659**; and Telegram From the Delegation to the U.N. General Assembly to the Department of State, New York, 8 October 1959, Department of State, **Central Files, 793B.00/10-859**.

82 The text of the resolution appears in the Department of State, **American Foreign Policy: Current Documents**, Washington, 1959, USGPO, p. 1187.

83 See, for instance, Memorandum From the Assistant Secretary of State for Far Eastern Affairs (Parsons) to Secretary of State Herter, Washington, 14 October 1959, Department of State, **FE/EA Files: Lot 66 D 225**.

84 Memorandum of Conversation, Washington, 29 October 1959, Department of State, **Central Files,793B.00/10-2959**.

85 B.N. Mullik, 1971, op cit., pp. 240–246.

86 Telegram From the Embassy in India to the Department of State, New Delhi, 23 November 1959, Department of State, **Central Files,711.11-E1/11-2359**.

87 Telegram From the Department of State to the Embassy in India, Washington, 25 November 1959, Department of State, **Central Files,793B.00/11-2559**.

88 Telegram From the President to the Department of State, Paris, 14 December 1959, Department of State, **Central Files,690D.91/12-1459**.

89 Ibid. Eisenhower had seen the Tibetan events as a possible trigger for transforming Indo-Pakistani relations. At the 404th meeting of the NSC on 30 April 1959, 'The President said that the present situation should promote a better understanding between Pakistan and India . . . The President thought that in this situation the United States should work quite actively toward promoting a better understanding between India and Pakistan.' in Memorandum of Discussion, Washington, 30 April 1959, Eisenhower Library, Abilene, Kansas, Whitman File, NSC Records. At another meeting on 4 May, the President felt 'that in the present situation, particularly the deterioration in India-Communist China relations as a result of the Tibetan revolt, the United States should make special efforts to promote better understanding between Pakistan and India.' Department of State, **S/S-NSC (Miscellaneous) Files: Lot 66 D 95, NSC Action no.2073-B**, Washington, 4 May 1959. During his Delhi visit, Eisenhower was determined to give practical shape to his conviction.

90 Telegram From the Ambassador of the United States in Pakistan to the Department of State, Karachi, 23 December 1959, Department of State, **Central Files,690D.91/ 12-2359**.

91 Memorandum for the Record by the President's Special Assistant for National Security (Gray), Washington, 4 February 1960, Eisenhower Library, Abilene, Kansas, **White House Office Files, Project Clean Up**.

92 Tenzin Gyatso, 1990, op cit., p. 210.

93 Nehru cited in Mullik, op cit., p. 264.

94 Tsering Wangdu Shakya, **The Dragon in the Land of Snows: A History of Modern Tibet since 1947**, London, Pimlico, 1999, p. 281.

95 Jawaharlal Nehru, **Selected Speeches September 1946 – April 1961**, New Delhi, Ministry of Information & Broadcasting, Government of India, 1961, pp. 97–98.

96 Letter from Secretary of State Herter to the Dalai Lama, Washington, 20 February 1960, Department of State, **Central Files,793B.00/2-2060**.

97 Letter From Secretary of State Herter to the Dalai Lama, Washington, 11 October 1960, Department of State, **Central Files,795B.00/9-1660**.

98 Memorandum of Conversation, Washington, 27 October 1960, Department of State, **Central Files,793B.00/10-2760**

99 Mullik, op cit., pp. 284–285.

100 Telegram from the Embassy in India to the Department of State, New Delhi, 26 November 1960, Department of State, **Central Files,691.93/11-2660**.

## Chapter Six: The Denouement

1 Prime Minister Nehru said this to US Under-Secretary of State Chester Bowles on 8 August 1961 in New Delhi. See fn.2.

2 Memorandum of Conversation, Prime Minister Jawaharlal Nehru and Under-Secretary of State Chester Bowles, New Delhi, 8 and 9 August 1961, Department of State, **Central Files, 611.91/8-961**. Emphasis added.

3 Memorandum of Conversation, President Kennedy and Krishna Menon, Washington, 21 November 1961, Kennedy Library, Boston, **National Security Files, Countries Series, India, General, 11/21/61-11/31/61.**

4 Department of State telegram to Embassy in Pakistan, with copy to Embassy in India, Washington, 27 September 1961, Department of State, **Central Files, 790D.11/9-2762.**

5 Ibid.

6 Letter From Prime Minister Jawaharlal Nehru to President John F. Kennedy, New Delhi, 29 December 1961, Kennedy Library, Boston, **National Security Files, Countries Series, India, Nehru Correspondence, 11/1/61-1/14/62.**

7 Letter From President Ayub Khan to President John F. Kennedy, Rawalpindi, 2 January 1962, Department of State, **Central Files, 690D.91/1-262.**

8 Letter From President John F. Kennedy to Prime Minister Jawaharlal Nehru, Washington, 18 January 1962, Kennedy Library, Boston, **National Security Files, Countries Series, India, Nehru Correspondence, 1/15/62-3/31/62.**

9 Letter From President Ayub Khan to President John F. Kennedy, Sibi, 18 January 1962, Department of State, **Central Files, 690D.91/1-862.**

10 Letter From President Ayub Khan to President John F. Kennedy, Rawalpindi, 20 April 1962, Department of State, **Central Files, 690D.91/4-3062.**

11 The Embassy in India to Department of State, New Delhi, 8 May 1962, Department of State, **Central Files, 791.5622/5-862.**

12 The Embassy in India to the Department of State, New Delhi, 13 May 1962, Department of State, **Central Files, 791.5622/5-1362.**

13 Letter From President John F. Kennedy to President Mohammad Ayub Khan, Washington, 19 May 1962, Department of State, **Central Files, 711.11-KE/5-1962.**

14 Telegram From the Embassy in India to the Department of State, telegram-4165, New Delhi, 24 June 1962, Department of State, **Central Files, 690D.91/6-2462.**

15 Telegram From Ambassador Galbraith to Department of State, Calcutta, 1 July 1962, Department of State, **Central Files, 690D.91/7-162.**

16 Telegram From the Department of State to Ambassador Galbraith, Washington, 2 July 1962, Department of State, **Central Files, 690D.91/7-162.**

17 Special Assistant to the President for National Security Affairs to the Ambassador in India, Washington, 3 July 1962, Kennedy Library, Boston, **National Security Files, Countries Series, India, General, 7/1/62-7/10/62.**

18 Letter From Prime Minister Jawaharlal Nehru to President John F. Kennedy, New Delhi, 5 August 1962, Kennedy Library, Boston, **National Security Files, Countries Series, India, Nehru Correspondence, 4/1/62-8/31-62.**

19 Memorandum From the Department of State Executive Secretary (Brubeck) to the President's Special Assistant for National Security (Bundy), Washington,

15 October 1962, Kennedy Library, Boston, **National Security Files, Countries Series, India, General, 10/15/62-10/20/62.**

20 Ibid.

21 Ibid.

22 Telegram From the Embassy in India to the Department of State, New Delhi, 15 October 1962, Department of State, **Central Files, 691.93/10-1562.**

23 Telegram From the Department of State to the Embassy in Pakistan, Washington, 16 October 1962, Department of State, **Central Files, 790D.11/ 10-1662.**

24 Ibid.

25 Telegram From the Embassy in India to the Department of State, New Delhi, 18 October 1962, Department of State, **Central Files, 691.93/10-1862.**

26 Ibid.

27 Ibid.

28 See, for instance, Telegram From the Department of State to the Embassy in Afghanistan, Washington, 22 October 1962, Department of State, **Central Files, 689.90D/10-762.**

29 Telegram From the Department of State to the Embassy in Pakistan, telegram-660, Washington, 21 October 1962, Department of State, **Central Files, 691.93/ 10-2162.**

30 Telegram From the Embassy in Pakistan to the Department of State, telegram-748, Karachi, 22 October 1962, Department of State, **Central Files, 691.93/10-2262.**

31 Telegram From the Department of State to the Embassy in Pakistan, telegram-664, Washington, 22 October 1962, Department of State, **Central Files, 691.93/ 10-2262.**

32 Ibid.

33 Telegram from the Embassy in India to the Department of State, with copy to Secretary of Defense Robert McNamara and Special Assistant to the President for National Security Affairs McGeorge Bundy, New Delhi, 25 October 1962, Department of State, **Central Files, 791.56/10-2562.**

34 Ibid.

35 Ambassador Galbraith to President Kennedy, New Delhi, 25 October 1962 (date handwritten; hence uncertainty), Kennedy Library, Boston, **National Security Files, Countries Series, India, General, 9/27/62-10/5/62.**

36 Memorandum From the President's Deputy Special Assistant for National Security Affairs to President Kennedy, Washington, 26 October 1962, Kennedy Library, Boston, **National Security Files, Countries Series, India, General, 10/26/ 62-10/27/62.**

37 Ibid.

38 Telegram From the Department of State to the Embassy in India, telegram-1663, Washington, 26 October 1962, Department of State, **Central Files, 691.93/10-2562.**

39 Letter From Prime Minister Jawaharlal Nehru to President John F. Kennedy, New Delhi, 26 October 1962, Kennedy Library, Boston, **National Security Files, Countries Series, India, Nehru Correspondence, 10/1/62-11/10/62.**

40 Memorandum of Conversation, Washington, 26 October 1962, Kennedy Library, Boston, **National Security Files, Countries Series, India, General, 10/ 26/62-10/27/62.**

41 Telegram From the Department of State to the Embassy in India, telegram-1677, Washington, 27 October 1962, Department of State, **Central Files, 691.93/10-2762.**

42 Letter From President Mohammad Ayub Khan to President John F. Kennedy, Rawalpindi, 27 October 1962, Department of State, **Central Files, 611.3722/10-2762.**

43 Telegram From the Embassy in Pakistan to the Department of State, telegram-764, Karachi, 27 October 1962, Department of State, **Central Files, 691.93/10-2762.**

44 Ibid.

45 Telegram From the Embassy in Pakistan to the Department of State, telegram-765, Karachi, 27 October 1962, Department of State, **Central Files, 691.93/10-2762.**

46 Telegram From the Department of State to the Embassy in Pakistan, telegram-680, Washington, 27 October 1962, Department of State, **Central Files, 691.93/10-2762.**

47 Ibid.

48 Telegram From the White House to the Embassy in India, Washington, 27 October 1962, Kennedy Library, Boston, **National Security Files, Countries Series, India, Ambassador Galbraith, Special File, Miscellaneous Messages, 10/62-12/62.**

49 Letter From President John F. Kennedy to President Mohammad Ayub Khan, Washington, 28 October 1962, Department of State, **Central Files, 691.93/10-2862.** (See Annexure 11)

50 Ibid.

51 Ibid.

52 Letter From President John F. Kennedy to Prime Minister Jawaharlal Nehru, Washington, 28 October 1962, Department of State, **Central Files, 691.93/10-2862.**

53 Telegram From the Department of State to the Embassy in India, telegram-1686, Washington, 28 October 1962, Department of State, **Central Files, 690D.91/10-2862.**

54 Telegram From the Embassy in India to the Department of State, telegram-1443, New Delhi, 29 October 1962, Department of State, **Central Files, 791.5/10-2962.** Also see **Telegram-1448** from New Delhi, 29 October 1962, in ibid.

55 Telegram From the Embassy in India to the Department of State, telegram-1525, New Delhi, 1 November 1962, Department of State, **Central Files, 791.5/11-162.**

56 Telegram from the Department of State and Department of Defense to the Embassy in India, telegram-1904, Washington, 6 November 1962, Department of State, **Central Files, 791.5/11-462.**

57 Memorandum From the President's Deputy Special Assistant for National Security Affairs (Kaysen) to President Kennedy, Washington, 3 November 1962, Kennedy Library, Boston, **National Security Files, Countries Series, India, General, 11/3/62-11/4/62.**

58 Memorandum From the Department of State Executive Secretary (Brubeck) to the President's Special Assistant for National Security Affairs (Bundy), Washington, 3 November 1962, Kennedy Library, Boston, attachment to ibid.

59 Ibid.

60 Ibid.

61 Ibid. A more detailed assessment of the war and its implications was prepared by the CIA. 'Short-Term Outlook and Implications for the Sino-Indian Conflict', SNIE 13/31-62, Central Intelligence Agency, Langley,Va., Job 79 R 01012A, ODDI Registry of NIE and SNIE Files, Box 210.

62 Telegram From the Embassy in Pakistan to the Department of State, telegram-820, Karachi, 5 November 1962, Department of State, **Central Files, 691.93/11-562.**

63 Airgram A-883 From the Embassy in Pakistan to the Department of State, Karachi, 23 February 1963, Washington National Records Center, **RG84, Karachi Embassy Files: FRC 67 F 74, 320 Pak/US Assurances.**

64 Department of State, **Bulletin,** Washington, 3 December 1962, pp. 837–838.

65 Memorandum from the President's Deputy Special Assistant for National Security Affairs (Kaysen) to President Kennedy, Washington, 9 November 1962, Kennedy Library, Boston, **President's Office Files, Countries Series, Pakistan, Security, 1962.**

66 Memorandum From Robert W. Komer of the National Security Council Staff to President Kennedy, Washington, 12 November 1962, Kennedy Library, Boston, **National Security Files, Countries Series, Pakistan, General, 11/62.**

67 Telegram From the Embassy in India to the Department of State, telegram-1665, New Delhi, 7 November 1962, Department of State, **Central Files, 791.13/11-762.** Also see Letter From the Ambassador to India to President Kennedy, New Delhi, 13 November 1962, Kennedy Library, Boston, **National Security Files, Countries Series, India, General, 11/11/62-11/13/62.**

68 Letter From President Mohammad Ayub Khan to President Kennedy, (Rawalpindi) 5 November 1962, Department of State, **Central Files, 791.56/11-1362.** (See Annexure 12)

69 Ibid.

70 Letter From the Ambassador to India to President Kennedy, New Delhi, 13 November 1962, op cit.

71 Ibid.

72 Ibid.

73 Ibid.

74 An Exchange of Notes Constituting a Mutual Defense Assistance Agreement between the Government of the United States of America and the Government of India, Washington, 14 November 1962, Department of State, **Bulletin,** 3 December 1962, p. 838 (see Appendix 12)

75 Memorandum From the President's Deputy Special Assistant for National Security Affairs (Kaysen) to President Kennedy, Washington, 16 November 1962, Kennedy Library, Boston, **National Security Files, Countries Series, India, General, 11/16/62.**

76 Ibid.

77 Telegram From the Embassy in India to the Department of State, telegram-1853, New Delhi, 17 November 1962, Department of State, **Central Files, 791.56/11-1762.**

78 Ibid.

79 Ibid.

80 Telegram From the Department of State to the Embassy in India, telegram-2140, Washington, 18 November 1962, Department of State, **Central Files, 791.56/11-1762.**

81 Telegram From the Department of State to the Embassy in Pakistan, telegram-782, Washington, 18 November 1962, Department of State, **Central Files, 791.56/11-1862.**

82 Ibid.

83 Memorandum for the Record, Washington, 19 November 1962, Kennedy Library, Boston, **National Security Files, Countries Series, India, General, 11/26/62-11/27/62.**

84 A copy of the first letter was given to Ambassador Galbraith who sent a copy to Washington immediately. See Telegram From the Embassy in India to the Department of State, telegram-1891, New Delhi, 19 November 1962, Department of State, **Central Files, 691.93/11-1962**. The second arrived at the White House in the evening and the Department of State wired a copy of it to Galbraith. See Telegram From the Department of State to the Embassy in India, telegram-2167, Washington, 19 November 1962, Department of State, **Central Files, 691.93/11-1962**

85 Ibid.

86 Telegram From the Department of State to the Embassy in India, telegram-2170, Washington, 19 November 1962, Department of State, **Central Files, 791.5/11-1962.**

87 Ibid.

88 Telegram From the Department of State to the Embassy in India, telegram-2172, Washington, 20 November 1962, Department of State, **Central Files, 691.93/11-2062.**

89 Ibid.

90 Ibid.

91 Telegram From the Embassy in Pakistan to the Department of State, telegram-913, Karachi, 20 November 1962, Department of State, **Central Files, 791.56/11-2062.**

92 **The New York Times**, New York, 21 November 1962.

93 Letter From President John F. Kennedy to Prime Minister Jawaharlal Nehru, Washington, 20 November 1962, Department of State, **Central Files, 691.93/11-2062.**

94 Letter From Prime Minister Jawaharlal Nehru to President John F. Kennedy, New Delhi, 21 November 1962, in Telegram From the Embassy in India to the Department of State, telegram-1973, New Delhi, 21 November 1962, Department of State, **Central Files, 691.93/11-2162.**

95 Telegram From the Department of State to the Embassy in India, telegram-2274, Washington, 23 November 1962, Department of State, **Central Files, 691.93/11-2362.**

96 Telegram From the Embassy in India to the Department of State, telegram-2032, New Delhi, 24 November 1962, Department of State, **Central Files, 691.93/11-2462.**

97 Telegram From the Embassy in India to the Department of State, telegram-2178, New Delhi, 30 November 1962, Department of State, **Central Files, 120.1591/11-3062**

98 Telegram From the Department of State to the Embassy in India, telegram-2329, Washington, 25 November 1962, Department of State, **Central Files, 691.93/11-2562.**

99 Ibid.

100 Memorandum of conversation, Rawalpindi, 28 November 1962, Department of State, **Central Files, 690D.91/11-2862.**

101 Ibid.

102 Memorandum of Conversation, Rawalpindi, 29 November 1962, Department of State, **Central Files, 690D.91/11-2962.**

103 Ibid.

104 Harriman's report was filed in Department of State, **S/S Files: Lot 70 D 265, NSC Subcommittee on South Asia.** Also see, Summary of Conclusions of Harriman Mission to India, Circular Telegram From the Department of State to Certain Diplomatic Posts, telegram-1066, Washington, 8 December 1962, Department of State, **Central Files, 120.1591/12-862.**

105 Memorandum of Meeting of the Executive Committee of the National Security Council, Washington, 3 December 1962, Central Intelligence Agency, **McCone Files, Job 80 B 01285A, Box 6, DCI Meetings with the President, 1 July 1962–3 December 1962.**

106 Letter From President John F. Kennedy to Prime Minister Harold Macmillan, Washington, 5 December 1962, Department of State, **S/S Files: Lot 66 D 204, Kennedy Correspondence with Macmillan, 1962–63.**

107 Ibid.

108 Letter From President John F. Kennedy to President Mohammad Ayub Khan, Washington, 5 December 1962, Department of State, **Central Files, 790D.11/12-562.**

109 Letter From President John F. Kennedy to Prime Minister Jawaharlal Nehru, Washington, 6 December 1962, Department of State, **Central Files, 690D.91/12-662.**

110 Telegram From the Embassy in Pakistan to the Department of State, telegram-1026, Karachi, 9 December 1962, Department of State, **Central Files, 791.56/12-962.**

111 Telegram From the Embassy in India to the Department of State, telegram-2305, New Delhi, 10 December 1962, Department of State, **Central Files, 690D.91/12-1062.**

112 Telegram From the Department of State to the Embassies in India and Pakistan, telegram-2599, Washington, 8 December 1962, Department of State, **Central Files, 690D.91/12-862.**

113 Ibid.

114 Ibid.

115 Ibid.

116 Telegram From the Department of State to the Embassy in India, telegram-2601, Washington, 8 December 1962, Department of State, **Central Files, 791.56/12-862.**

117 National Security Action Memorandum No.209, Washington, 10 December 1962, Kennedy Library, Boston, **National Security Files, Meetings and Memoranda Series, Memoranda, NSAM 209.**

118 Letter From Prime Minister Jawaharlal Nehru to President John F. Kennedy, New Delhi, 8 December 1962, Kennedy Library, Boston, **National Security Files, Countries Series, India, Nehru Correspondence, 11/20/62-12/14/62.**

119 Letter From Prime Minister Harold Macmillan to President John F. Kennedy, London, 13 December 1962, Department of State, **S/S Files: Lot 66 D 204, Macmillan Correspondence with Kennedy, 1962.**

120 Ibid.

121 Ibid.

122 Memorandum from the Joint Chiefs of Staff to Secretary of Defense Robert McNamara, JCSM-996-62, Washington, 14 December 1962, Department of State, **S/S Files: Lot 70 D 265, NSC Subcommittee on South Asia.**

123 Memorandum From Robert W. Komer of the National Security Council Staff to President Kennedy, Washington, 16 December 1962, Kennedy Library, Boston, **National Security Files, Countries Series, India, General, 12/16/62.**

124 Memorandum of Conversation, Washington, 17 December 1962, Department of State, **NEA/INC Files: Lot 66 D415, Kashmir, May-December 1962 (Miscellaneous Papers).**

125 Letter From President Mohammad Ayub Khan to President John F. Kennedy, Karachi, 17 December 1962, Department of State, **Central Files, 690D.91/12-2262.**

126 Ibid.
127 Memorandum of Conversation, Nassau, 20 December 1962, Department of State, **Central Files, 691.93/12-2062.**
128 Ibid.
129 Ibid.
130 Final Agreed Text: Sequence of Action With Respect to India and Pakistan, Nassau, 21 December 1962, Kennedy Library, Boston, **National Security Files, Countries Series, India, General, 12/19/62-12/29/62.**
131 Letter From President John F. Kennedy to President Mohammad Ayub Khan, Washington, 22 December 1962, Department of State, **Central Files, 690D.91/12-2262.** (See Annexure 13)
132 Ibid.
133 Letter From President John F. Kennedy to Prime Minister Jawaharlal Nehru, Washington, 22 December 1962, Department of State, **Central Files, 691.93/12-2262.** (See Annexure 14)
134 Ibid.
135 Telegram From the Embassy in India to the Department of State, telegram-2522, New Delhi, 27 December 1962, Department of State, **Central Files, 791.56/12-2762.**
136 Telegram from the Embassy in Pakistan to the Department of State, Murree, 27 December 1962, Department of State, **Central Files, 791.56/12-2762.**
137 Ibid.
138 Telegram From the Embassy in Pakistan to the Department of State, telegram-19, Murree, 28 December 1962, Department of State, **Central Files, 690D.91/12-2862;** and telegram-1165, Karachi, 29 December 1962, ibid., **Central Files, 690D. 91/12-2962.**

## Chapter Seven: Epilogue

1 **The New York Times,** New York, 27 December 1962, and 29 December 1962.
2 Telegram From the Department of State to the Embassy in India, telegram-2775, Washington, 4 January 1963, Department of State, **Central Files, 690D.91/1-463.**
3 Ibid.
4 Letter From Prime Minister Jawaharlal Nehru to President John F. Kennedy, New Delhi, 29 December 1962, Kennedy Library, Boston, **National Security Files, Countries Series, India, Nehru Correspondence, 12/15/62–2/10/63.**
5 Letter From President John F. Kennedy to Prime Minister Harold Macmillan, Washington, 9 January 1963, Department of State, **Central Files, 791.5/1-1163.**
6 Letter From Prime Minister Harold Macmillan to President John F. Kennedy, London, 13 January 1963, Department of State, **S/S Files: Lot 66 D 204, Macmillan Correspondence with Kennedy, 1963.**
7 Letter From President Mohammad Ayub Khan to President John F. Kennedy, Rawalpindi, 2 January 1963, Kennedy Library, Boston, **National Security Files, Countries Series, India, General, 1/11/63–1/15/63.**
8 Memorandum for the Executive Committee of the National Security Council, Washington, 7 January 1963, Kennedy Library, Boston, **National Security Files, Countries Series, India, General, 1/11/63–1/15/63.**
9 Ibid.
10 It was this line of activity which led to the proposal, eventually aborted, to establish a large radar network along India's Himalayan borders, and the decision to install a nuclear-powered monitoring device on the Nanda Devi peak (See Introduction)

11  Telegram From the Department of State to the Embassy in India, telegram-2871, Washington, 15 January 1963, Department of State,**Central Files, 690D.91/1-1563**.

12  Letter From President John F. Kennedy to Prime Minister Harold Macmillan, Washington, 21 January 1963, Department of State, **Central Files, 791.5/1-2163**.

13  Letter From Minister for External Affairs Mohammad Ali to Secretary of State Dean Rusk, Karachi, 21 January 1963, Department of State, **Central Files, 791.56/ 1-2263**. ('Unessential words omitted' by US Embassy before transmission)

14  Notes by Director of Central Intelligence John McCone before the National Security Council, Washington, 22 January 1963, Central Intelligence Agency, **Job 80 B 01285A, Box 6, McCone Files, DCI Meetings with the President, 1 January–31 March 1963**.

15  Memorandum for the Record, Presidential Meeting on India, Washington, 25 April 1963, National Security Council records, Department of State, **Foreign Relations of the United States 1961–1963**, Vol.XIX, South Asia, USGPO, 1996, pp. 561–565.

16  Ibid., p. 562.

17  Ibid., p. 563.

18  Ibid., p. 564.

19  Ibid.

20  Subir Bhaumik, **Insurgent Crossfire: North-East India**, New Delhi, Lancer Publishers, 1996, pp. 11,27–31.

21  Ibid., pp. 31–43; also see S Mahmud Ali, **The Fearful State: Power,People and Internal War in South Asia**, London, Zed Books, 1993, pp. 32–37.

22  Bhaumik, op cit., pp. 33–40.

23  Ali, op cit., pp. 37–43.

24  Ibid., pp. 44–45.

25  Literally, refugees; those who had immigrated from India to Pakistan at and since the Partition in 1947; largely Urdu-speaking professionals and skilled and semi-skilled workers from Uttar Pradesh, Bihar and the former Bombay Presidency to be eventually concentrated in and around Karachi, Pakistan's largest city.

26  The present author was a member of the Bangladeshi delegation which negotiated this outcome with the new government in Delhi in April–May 1977.

27  See, for instance, S Mahmud Ali, **Civil-Military Relations in the Soft State: The Case of Bangladesh**, Bath, University of Bath, 1994, p. 34; also see Bhaumik, op cit., pp. 272–287.

28  For a background to these developments, see Ali, 1993, op cit., pp. 204–246.

29  *Xinhua* (New China News Agency), **Communique on Recent Events in Lhasa** (in English), Beijing, 28 March 1959.

30  Ibid.

31  Ibid. Also see *Xinhua*, **Facts on the 'Khamba Rebellion'** (in English), Beijing, 26 April 1959.

32  *Xinhua*, **Communique**, ibid.

33  Lobsang Choekyi Gyaltsen, **A report on the sufferings of the masses in Tibet and other Tibetan regions and suggestions for future work to the central authorities through the respected Premier Zhou Enlai**, Beijing, May 1962, cited in full in Chinese and English languages in **A Poisoned Arrow: The Secret Report of the 10th Panchen Lama**, London, Tibet Information Network, 1997, pp. 1–124 (p. 116 missing).

34  Ibid.pp. 11,13.
35  Ibid.p. 15,23.
36  Ibid.p. 24.
37  Ibid.pp.  29,112–113.
38  Ibid.pp. 52,57.
39  For a more historiographical explanation of the beginning of the Indo-Pakistani dispute over Kashmir, see Alastair Lamb, **Incomplete Partition: The Genesis of the Kashmir Dispute 1947–1948**, Hertingfordbury, Roxford Books, 1997.

# Bibliography

S. Mahmud Ali, *Nation-building and the Nature of Conflict in South Asia: A Search for Patterns in the Use of Force*, unpublished phd dissertation, University of London, London, 1992;
—— *The Fearful State: Power, People and Internal War in South Asia*, Zed Books, London, 1993;
Gompo Tashi Andrugtsang, *Four Rivers, Six Ranges: Reminiscences of the Resistance Movement in Tibet*, Information and Publicity Office of His Holiness the Dalai Lama, Dharamsala, 1973;
A. Appadorai, *Select Documents on India's Foreign Policy and Relations, 1947–1972*, Vols.I and II, Oxford University Press, New Delhi, 1985;
Robert Barnett and Shirin Akiner (Eds.), *Resistance and Reform in Tibet*, C. Hurst and Co., London, 1994;
Subir Bhaumik, *Insurgent Crossfire: North-East India*, Lancer Publishers, New Delhi, 1996;
King C. Chen (Ed.), *China and the Three Worlds*, Macmillan Press Ltd., London, 1979;
The Government of China, *Tibet – Its Ownership And Human Rights Situation*, Information Office of the State Council of The People's Republic of China, Beijing, 1992;
Durga Das (Ed.), *Sardar Patel's Correspondence 1945–1950*, Vol.I, *New Light on Kashmir*, Navajiban Publishing House, Ahmedabad, 1971;
Shakabpa Wangchuk Deden, *A Political History of Tibet*, (privately published), Kalimpong, 1976;
Lawrence Freedman (Ed.), *Strategic Coercion: Concepts and Cases*, Oxford University Press, Oxford, 1998;
A. Tom Grunfeld, *The Making of Modern Tibet*, Zed Books, London, 1987; and revised edition, M.E. Sharpe, New York, 1996;
Lobsang Choekyi Gyaltsen (the 10th Panchen Lama), *A Report on the Sufferings of the Masses in Tibet and other Tibetan Regions and Suggestions for Future Work to the Central Authorities through the Respected Premier Zhou Enlai*, Beijing, 1962, cited in full in Chinese and English in *A Poisoned Arrow: The Secret Report of the 10th Panchen Lama*, Tibet Information Network, London, 1997;
Tenzin Gyatso, the Fourteenth Dalai Lama of Tibet, *Freedom in Exile*, Hodder and Stoughton, London, 1990;
Vernon Marston Hewitt, *The International Politics of South Asia*, Manchester University Press, Manchester, 1992;
David Howarth (Ed.), *My Land and My People: The Autography of His Holiness of the Dalai Lama*, Panther Books, London, 1964;

277

The Government of India, *Loksabha Debates,* Vol.II, Part II, Loksabha Secretariat, New Delhi, 1952;

—— *Parliament of India: Official Report*, Vol.VI, Part II, Loksabha Secretariat, New Delhi, not dated;

—— *Kashmir: Meetings and Correspondence between the Prime Ministers of India and Pakistan* (White Paper), Ministry of External Affairs, New Delhi, not dated;

—— *Ministry of External Affairs Report 1953–1954*, Ministry of External Affairs, New Delhi, 1955;

—— *Loksabha Debates*, Vol.V,Part II, Loksabha Secretariat, New Delhi, 1955;

—— *Notes, Memoranda, and Letters Exchanged between the Governments of India and China, September-November 1959* (White Papers no.I and II), Ministry of External Affairs, New Delhi, 1959;

—— *Rajyasabha Official Records*, Vol.XXVI, Loksabha Secretariat, New Delhi, 1960;

—— *Foreign Policy of India: Texts of Documents 1947–1964*, 3rd Edition, Loksabha Secretariat, New Delhi, 1966;

—— *Loksabha Debates*, 2nd series, Vols.XXVIII, XXX, and XXXIII, Loksabha Secretariat, New Delhi, 1969;

Union Research Institute, *Tibet, 1950–1967*, Document 6, URI Publications, Hong Kong, 1968;

DuPre Jones (Ed.), *China: US Policy since 1945*, Congressional Quarterly Inc., Washington, D.C., 1980;

Henry Kissinger, *Diplomacy*, Simon and Schuster, London, 1994;

Alastair Lamb, *Kashmir: A Disputed Legacy*, Roxford Books, Hertingfordbury, Herts., 1991;

—— *Birth of a Tragedy: Kashmir 1947*, Roxford Books, Hertingfordbury, Herts., 1994;

—— *Incomplete Partition: The Genesis of the Kashmir Dispute 1947–1948*, Roxford Books, Hertingfordbury, Herts., 1997;

B. N. Mullik, *My Years with Nehru: The Chinese Betrayal*, Allied Publishers, New Delhi, 1971;

Jawaharlal Nehru, *India's Foreign Policy: Selected Speeches, September 1946–April 1961*, Publications Division, Ministry of Information and Broadcasting, New Delhi, 1961;

Government of Pakistan, *White Paper on Jammu & Kashmir Dispute*, Ministry of Foreign Affairs, Islamabad, 1977;

Michael C. van Walt van Praag, *The Status of Tibet: History, Rights and the Prospects in International Law*, Westview Press, Boulder, Colorado, 1987;

Michel Peissel, *Cavaliers of Kham: The Secret War in Tibet*, William Heinemann Ltd., London, 1972;

Hugh E. Richardson, *Tibet and its History*, 2nd edition, Shambala Publications Ltd., Boulder, Colorado, 1984;

Christopher Robbins, *The Invisible Air Force: The Story of the CIA's Secret Airlines,* Macmillan, London, 1974;

Tsering W. Shakya, *The Dragon in the Land of Snows: A History of Modern Tibet since 1947*, Pimlico, London, 1999;

Department of State, *United States Relations with China (1944–1949)*, Office of Public Affairs, Washington, D.C., 1949;

—— *United States Treaties and other International Agreements* (USTIA) *1950*, Vol.1, United States Government Printing Office (USGPO), Washington, D.C., 1952;

—— *USTIA 1951*, Vol.2, Parts I and II, USGPO, Washington, D.C., 1952;

—— *USTIA 1951*, Vol.3, Part I, USGPO, Washington, D.C., 1952;

—— *USTIA 1954*, Vol.5, Part I, USGPO, Washington, D.C., 1955;

—— *USTIA 1955*, Vol.6, Part I, USGPO, Washington, D.C., 1955;

—— *USTIA 1956*, Vol.7, Part III, USGPO, Washington, D.C, 1957;

—— *American Foreign Policy: Current Documents*, USGPO, Washington, D.C., 1959;

—— *USTIA 1959*, Vol.10, Part II, USGPO, Washington, D.C., 1960;

—— *Foreign Relations of the United States* (FRUS) *1943 – China*, USGPO, Washington, D.C., 1967;

—— *FRUS 1947*, Vol.VII, USGPO, Washington, D.C., 1972;

—— *FRUS 1950*, Vols.I,VI and VII, USGPO,Washington, D.C.,1976;

—— *FRUS 1951*, Vol.VI, Part I, USGPO, Washington, D.C., 1977;

—— *FRUS 1951*, Vol.VII, Part II, USGPO,Washington, D.C., 1984;

—— *FRUS 1952–4*, Vol.XIV, Part I, USGPO,Washington, D,C.,1985;

—— *FRUS 1955–7*, Vols.II and III, USGPO, Washington, D.C., 1986;

—— *FRUS 1955–7*, Vol.VIII, USGPO, Washington, D.C., 1987;

—— *FRUS 1958–60*, Vol.XIX, USGPO, Washington, D.C., 1992;

—— *FRUS 1961–3*, Vol.XIX, USGPO, Washington, D.C., 1996;

United Nations, *United Nations Treaty Series* (UNTS), Vol.141, UN Secretariat, New York, 1952;

—— *UNTS*, Vol.358, UN Secretariat, New York, 1959;

—— *UNTS*, Vol.461, UN Secretariat, New York, 1963;

Chris Mullin and Phuntsog Wangyal, *The Tibetans: Two Perspectives on Tibetan-Chinese Relations*, Minority Rights Group, London, 1983;

Dick Wilson, *China, The Big Tiger: A Nation Awakes*, Little, Brown and Company, London, 1996.

# Index